THE BEDFORD SERIES IN HISTORY AND CULTURE

The Souls of Black Folk
by W. E. B. Du Bois

Related Titles in
THE BEDFORD SERIES IN HISTORY AND CULTURE
Advisory Editors: Natalie Zemon Davis, Princeton University
Ernest R. May, Harvard University

THE BEDFORD SERIES IN HISTORY AND CULTURE

The Souls of Black Folk
by W. E. B. Du Bois

Edited with an Introduction by

David W. Blight
Amherst College

and

Robert Gooding-Williams
Amherst College

BEDFORD BOOKS   Boston   New York

For Bedford Books

President and Publisher: Charles H. Christensen
General Manager and Associate Publisher: Joan E. Feinberg
History Editor: Katherine E. Kurzman
Developmental Editor: Joan E. Feinberg
Editorial Assistant: Charisse Kiino
Managing Editor: Elizabeth M. Schaaf
Production Editor: John Amburg
Copyeditor: Barbara G. Flanagan
Indexer: Steve Csipke
Text Design: Claire Seng-Niemoeller
Cover Design: Richard Emery Design, Inc.
Cover Art: Photograph of W. E. B. Du Bois (detail). Special Collections and Archives, W. E. B. Du Bois Library, University of Massachusetts Amherst. Photograph of original manuscript page from *The Souls of Black Folk* (detail). Special Collections and Archives, W. E. B. Du Bois Library, University of Massachusetts Amherst.

Library of Congress Catalog Card Number: 96-86763

Manufactured in the United States of America.

1   0   9   8   7
f   e   d   c   b   a

For information, write: Bedford Books, 75 Arlington Street, Boston, MA 02116
(617-426-7440)

ISBN: 0-312-09114-1 (paperback)
ISBN: 0-312-12806-1 (hardcover)

Foreword

The Bedford Series in History and Culture is designed so that readers can study the past as historians do.

The historian's first task is finding the evidence. Documents, letters, memoirs, interviews, pictures, movies, novels, or poems can provide facts and clues. Then the historian questions and compares the sources. There is more to do than in a courtroom, for hearsay evidence is welcome, and the historian is usually looking for answers beyond act and motive. Different views of an event may be as important as a single verdict. How a story is told may yield as much information as what it says.

Along the way the historian seeks help from other historians and perhaps from specialists in other disciplines. Finally, it is time to write, to decide on an interpretation and how to arrange the evidence for readers.

Each book in this series contains an important historical document or group of documents, each document a witness from the past and open to interpretation in different ways. The documents are combined with some element of historical narrative—an introduction or a biographical essay, for example—that provides students with an analysis of the primary source material and important background information about the world in which it was produced.

Each book in the series focuses on a specific topic within a specific historical period. Each provides a basis for lively thought and discussion about several aspects of the topic and the historian's role. Each is short enough (and inexpensive enough) to be a reasonable one-week assignment in a college course. Whether as classroom or personal reading, each book in the series provides firsthand experience of the challenge—and fun—of discovering, recreating, and interpreting the past.

Natalie Zemon Davis
Ernest R. May

Preface

Published originally in 1903, *The Souls of Black Folk* is W. E. B. Du Bois's classic collection of thirteen essays and one short story. Assembled from pieces the young Du Bois wrote between 1897 and 1903 (age twenty-nine to thirty-five), the book as a whole is a moving evocation of black American folk culture and a critical response to the racism and economic subjugation afflicting black Americans at the end of the nineteenth century. In this edition of *Souls,* we have attempted to set Du Bois's book in various social and historical contexts and, as best we can, to help readers understand the turn-of-the-century America in which it was written. In particular, we have emphasized Du Bois's distinctive conception of black racial identity, his interpretation of the postemancipation history of the American South, and his tragic portrait of the African American struggle for social recognition and cultural integrity.

To identify some key elements in Du Bois's philosophical thought, we have reprinted in this volume "The Conservation of Races" (1897), an essay in which Du Bois begins to articulate the understanding of race that later informs *Souls.* To highlight the sociological motifs in *Souls,* we have also reprinted "The Development of a People" (1904), a little-noticed but remarkable article in which Du Bois continues to refine his book's insistently historical perspective on the social circumstances shaping African American life. In addition, we have included a short piece Du Bois wrote in 1904, a review of his own book that offers an uneasy, but intriguing, explanation of its contents. To begin to illuminate the range of responses *Souls* has elicited since it was published, we have gathered a small selection of the correspondence that the book prompted between Du Bois and his readers. Finally, as teaching tools, we have provided a series of photographs of Du Bois, a chronology of his life, and an extensive list of questions for classroom consideration.

A NOTE ON THE TEXT

The text of *Souls* published here is a copy of the original 1903 edition.
Nine of *Souls'* fourteen chapters had been previously published when Du
Bois revised them, to differing degrees, for inclusion in his book. Chapter 1, "Of Our Spiritual Strivings," was a revision of "Strivings of the
Negro People," *Atlantic Monthly,* August 1897, 194–98; chapter 2, "Of the
Dawn of Freedom," was a revision of "The Freedman's Bureau," *Atlantic
Monthly,* March 1901, 354–65; chapter 3, "Of Mr. Booker T. Washington
and Others," was a revision of "The Evolution of Negro Leadership," *Dial,*
July 16, 1901, 53–55; chapter 4, "Of the Meaning of Progress," was a revision of "A Negro Schoolmaster in the New South," *Atlantic Monthly,* January 1899, 99–104; chapter 6, "Of the Training of Black Men," was a revision of an essay with the same title appearing in *Atlantic Monthly,*
September 1902, 289–97; chapters 7 and 8, "Of the Black Belt" and "Of
the Quest of the Golden Fleece," were revisions of "The Negro As He
Really Is," *World's Work,* June 1901, 848–66; chapter 9, "Of the Sons of
Master and Man," was a revision of "The Relation of the Negroes to the
Whites in the South," *Annals of the American Academy of Political and
Social Science,* July–December 1901, 121–40; and chapter 10, "Of the
Faith of the Fathers," was a revision of "The Religion of the American
Negro," *The New World: A Quarterly Review of Religious Ethics and Theology,* December 1900, 614–25.

This edition of *Souls* is the most fully annotated yet published. In our
introductory essay and in the notes on the text, we have combined the
sensibilities of a historian and a philosopher—which Du Bois himself
combined in writing *Souls*—to enhance students' and scholars' appreciation of this singular American classic.

ACKNOWLEDGMENTS

We have accumulated many debts in editing this volume and writing the
introductory essay. From the beginning, the editors at Bedford Books
have supported the idea of a new edition of *The Souls of Black Folk.*
Chuck Christensen, Sabra Scribner, and Niels Aaboe shepherded the initial stage of the project. Richard Keaveny expertly guided the review
process and gave us a valuable reading. Joan Feinberg, Katherine Kurzman, John Amburg, and Charisse Kiino patiently ushered the book to
completion. We are most grateful to Thomas Bender, Bernard Boxill,
David Levering Lewis, and John David Smith for their careful readings
of our introduction and their many useful criticisms. Gerald Early and

Werner Sollors also gave us timely readings and support. Many colleagues and friends provided insightful reactions to the manuscript or helpful conversations about Du Bois. At Amherst College they include Rowland Abiodun, Robert Doran, Tom Dumm, Jeffrey Ferguson, Dale Peterson, Caryl Phillips, Kim Townsend, and David Wills. Elsewhere, they include John Bracey, Nahum Chandler, Clark Dougan, Anita Goldman, James Horton, Amy Kaplan, Lawrence Levine, Lorenzo Simpson, William Strickland, Clarence Walker, and Michael Wolff. We are deeply indebted to Linda Seidman, at the Du Bois Papers at the University of Massachusetts Amherst, for her customary expertise and graciousness with documents, photographs, and Du Bois scholarship. We have benefited greatly from the help of three research assistants: Charlton Copeland, Kim Gittens, and Chip Turner. We could not have completed the annotations without the help of Amherst College librarians Michael Casper and Margaret Groesbeck. Without the skills and perseverance of Nancy Board in preparing the final manuscript, we would have been hard-pressed to complete this project. We owe much to the commitment Nancy brings to her work. We both have learned and grown intellectually from our first effort at collaborative writing. Finally, as always, David wishes to thank Karin Beckett, patient friend, supporter, translator, and critic. Bob wishes to thank Sara for encouragement and careful criticism, and Talia for humor and inspiration.

David W. Blight
Robert Gooding-Williams

Contents

THE BEDFORD SERIES IN HISTORY AND CULTURE

The Souls of Black Folk

by W. E. B. Du Bois

INTRODUCTION
THE STRANGE MEANING OF BEING BLACK:
DU BOIS'S AMERICAN TRAGEDY

"What, then, is a race?"
—W. E. B. Du Bois, *"The Conservation of Races,"* 1897

"If we are to judge intelligently or clearly of the development of a people, we must allow ourselves neither to be dazzled by figures nor misled by inapt comparisons, but we must seek to know what human advancement historically considered has meant and what it means today."
—W. E. B. Du Bois, *"The Development of a People,"* 1904

"I knew . . . that practically my sole chance of earning a living combined with study was to teach, and after my work . . . in United States history, I conceived the idea of applying philosophy to an historical interpretation of race relations."
—W. E. B. Du Bois, *The Autobiography of W. E. B. Du Bois,* 1968

The Souls of Black Folk is a complex, tragic, and deeply compelling vision of the fate of black folk in America. Published originally by A. C. McClurg and Company in April 1903, it is W. E. B. Du Bois's poignant but often biting dissent from the racist and nationalist ideologies animating post-Reconstruction political culture. Insisting that "the problem of the Twentieth Century is the problem of the color-line," Du Bois wrote *Souls* to explore the "strange meaning of being black" in a society that viewed blacks with contempt. To that end, he detailed a sweeping tableau of African American social and spiritual life, emphasizing the struggle for civil rights, the economic and social legacies of slavery, and the contributions of blacks to America's identity as a nation. By expounding on a small family of concepts that characterized the plight and passion of the slaves and their descendants—including, for example, the notions of "double-consciousness" and "spiritual striving"—Du Bois brilliantly described African American efforts to cope with a society riven by racial prejudice. Writing as a philosopher, a historian, and a social critic, he aspired to unsettle that prejudice, hoping fervently to create a society in which it no longer held sway.[1]

Souls is a diverse collection of essays and stories that defies any single category or genre. Still, it can be conveniently divided into three parts: chapters 1–3 have a distinctively historical character; chapters 4–9 display a sociological perspective in style and argument; and chapters 10–14 demonstrate Du Bois's attempt to capture the religious-spiritual meanings in the culture and experience of African Americans. Useful as they are, however, these groupings mask as much as they reveal of the complexity of the book. Du Bois worried that the fourteen pieces he had written over a seven-year period did not cohere, either as a whole or as parts of a whole. Indeed, in an extraordinary apologia (see p. 254) written just over a year after *Souls* was published, he showed his uneasiness about the collection, calling it "bits of history and biography, some descriptions of scenes and persons, something of controversy and criticism, some statistics and a bit of story-telling." Uncharacteristically self-effacing and perhaps stung by some reviewers, Du Bois noted the book's "sense of incompleteness." Yet he affirmed *Souls'* "personal and intimate tone of self-revelation," arguing that whatever had been "lost in authority" had been "gained in vividness."[2]

An enduring contribution to American letters, *Souls,* in fact, is remarkable for its vividness *and* its authority. Punctuated throughout by the rhythms of human passion and intellectual insight, the text rewards an attentive, chapter-by-chapter perusal. By placing *Souls* in historical context and sketching a biographical portrait of Du Bois through the years surrounding the publication of the book, this introduction lays a basis for careful readings of his masterpiece. *Souls* is an extended meditation on racial prejudice, political leadership, the economic oppression of black laborers, and the development of African American culture both before and after emancipation. Most significantly, it is an original, philosophically informed, and tragic vision of American history, a gripping revelation of the triumphs, betrayals, and legacies that, in the wake of emancipation, shaped the souls of black folk through the first years of the twentieth century. Finally, *Souls* can be usefully illuminated by examining the wide range of responses that, over time, it has inspired in its readers.

SOULS IN THE AGE OF JIM CROW

During an era ruled by a seemingly permanent white consensus on segregation and disfranchisement, Du Bois's book offered black readers a unique burst of hope. For many blacks, writes biographer David Levering Lewis, *Souls* was "like fireworks going off in a cemetery . . . sound and light enlivening the inert and the despairing. It was an electrifying manifesto, mobilizing a people for bitter, prolonged struggle to win a place in history." Reacting to turn-of-the-century white supremacist thought that had been buttressed in the popular mind by widely circulated "scientific" views of "the Negro" as inferior, beastlike, and uncivilized, *Souls* came as a profound refutation of prevailing racist dogma.[3]

Souls should be read as a testament against the American system of racial apartheid that developed from approximately 1890 to 1910. That system consisted of many elements. "Jim Crow" laws emerged in every southern state, restricting black suffrage and segregating the races in schools, housing, transportation, and the use of public facilities. Historians fashioned a vision of American history that saw emancipation and the establishment of black civil and political rights during Reconstruction (1865–1877) as a tragic mistake. And segregation stiffened a form of economic subjugation by which white landowners and industrialists controlled southern black laborers. The United States Supreme Court sanctioned this system of apartheid when, in *Plessy v. Ferguson* (1896), it affirmed the power of a state to separate the races on railroads, thus declaring the "separate but equal" doctrine the law of the land.[4]

When Du Bois's *Souls* was published, thousands of signs were visible across the South indicating the "colored" sections of railway cars, waiting rooms, theaters, and parks. In countless southern counties, there were no "colored" sections at the voting polls. In the course of daily human contact, the Jim Crow system was an assault on the dignity and humanity of black people. African Americans continued, however, to build their own schools, churches, and community life. Approximately 20 percent of southern blacks owned their own property by 1900 and could thus sustain a degree of independence from the larger political structure that denied them their citizenship rights. Still, the vast majority of southern blacks were sharecroppers, bound to the land as tenants by a cycle of debt, giving half of their cotton crop to a landowner or a furnishing merchant, and eking out a difficult living with the other half. Blacks who challenged this system of political and economic oppression frequently met with terrorist violence, the brutality of "lynch mobs" that did their deadly work to a frightful and largely unpunished extent during the years around 1903.[5]

In fact, 1903 was an especially bad year in the downward spiral of American race relations. In several southern states "whitecapping"—a practice in which bands of white tenant farmers drove black landowners from their rightful lands—resumed. Accusations and revelations of "peonage" were prevalent in the press in 1903, especially emanating from the remote turpentine districts of Alabama. (Peonage was a practice in which black debtors could be forced to sign labor contracts, held in stockades, and hunted if they escaped. Federal investigations and trials led to only a handful of convictions for this new form of slavery.) Also in that year, a new breed of southern politician—the racist demagogue advocating strict enforcement of segregation, curtailment of black education, and even lynching—came to prominence when James K. Vardaman was elected governor of Mississippi.

The Supreme Court upheld disfranchisement laws in 1903 (in *Giles v. Harris*), thereby encouraging more states to pass them. And in popular culture, from cartooning to song, film, and children's stories, blacks had become the objects of jokes and widespread denigration. For example, *The Leopard's Spots,* a play by the virulently racist Thomas Dixon, became one of the most popular productions on Broadway in 1903, while two years later Dixon published *The Clansman,* a best-selling, melodramatic novel that sang the praises of the Ku Klux Klan and argued that sectional reconciliation after the Civil War had redeemed the blunder of emancipating the slaves. (*The Clansman* became the basis for D. W. Griffith's famous epic film about the Civil War and Reconstruction, *The Birth of a Nation,* released to wide acclaim and protest in 1915.)[6] In the context of these events, and in order to counter the racism that pervaded turn-of-the-century America, Du Bois wrote the essays he compiled in his book of 1903.

BIRTHPLACE AND "BIRTH-TIME"

William Edward Burghardt Du Bois was born in Great Barrington, a small town nestled in the Berkshire hills of southwestern Massachusetts, on February 23, 1868. He grew up during Reconstruction and came of age as a young intellectual in the era of Jim Crow. Heir to a rich and complicated ancestry, he wrote proudly yet deceptively of his forebears in his autobiographical writings. Du Bois's paternal grandfather, Alexander Du Bois, was descended from French Huguenots who immigrated to New York State in the eighteenth century and then to the Bahamas to become slaveholding planters after the American Revolution. Born in Haiti, Alexander was the son of James, the planter, and one of his mulatto slave women. Du Bois's father, Alfred Du Bois, was born in Haiti in 1825 and moved to the United States sometime in the 1850s. After briefly serving in the Union army during the Civil War, Alfred Du Bois moved to Great Barrington in 1867. It is not likely that William Du Bois ever saw his father after infancy, because Alfred abandoned the family before his son was two years old.

William was raised by his mother, Mary Silvina Burghardt, who was born in 1831 of African and Dutch ancestry and worked much of her life as a domestic. Mary Burghardt's great-grandfather Tom Burghardt was born in the early 1730s. He was enslaved in West Africa and brought to western Massachusetts, where he labored as the property of the Burghardts, one of the rich Dutch landowning families of the Hudson River valley. Through service in a company of Continental soldiers in the American Revolution, Tom received his freedom and settled on a farm near Great Barrington. Tom's grandson Othello Burghardt still owned that farm in 1868 when William was born in the town of some four thousand inhabitants, about fifty of whom formed a small black community.[7] When Du Bois probed the complexity of African American identity formation, he understood fully that he was the fifth-generation descendant of a West African slave and the fourth-generation descendant of a West Indian slaveholder. His roots were African, Caribbean, and North American; they were also African American, Dutch, French, and, not least of all, New England.

"My birthplace was less important than my birth-time," Du Bois wrote in 1940. He was born in the year the Fourteenth Amendment was ratified, Andrew Johnson impeached, Ulysses S. Grant elected president of the United States, and blacks first voted in large numbers and helped draft the new radical state constitutions in the Reconstruction South. During Du Bois's childhood, Frederick Douglass was still at the zenith of his leadership of black America, Booker T. Washington was getting an education and learning hygiene at Hampton Institute, and Mark Twain was writing *Huckleberry Finn*. Du Bois lived a long life — to the age of ninety-five — dying in Ghana, West Africa, in 1963, a day before a grandson of slaves (Martin Luther King Jr.) delivered his "I Have a Dream" speech and only a few months before John F. Kennedy was assassinated.

Growing up in the wake of emancipation, Du Bois also survived to see the modern civil rights movement. When writing of the Reconstruction era, he contemplated the history in which he came of age. Du Bois lived ten years beyond the publication of a fiftieth-anniversary edition of *Souls;* he thus observed the consequences of two world wars and fell victim to America's vicious anti-radical politics during the Cold War. Having witnessed firsthand the cultural heritage of the generation of the freedpeople, he lived long enough to deliver speeches to the generation of the 1960s. Born three years after the Civil War, he endured to write critically of the centennial of that event.[8]

The wellsprings of great intellect and ambition are not easy to fathom in a life of such scope and humble beginnings. Du Bois's mother was poor and struggled mightily to provide for him until her death in 1885, but she somehow raised a boy of lonely determination, extraordinary intellectual gifts, and fierce educational ambition. A year after graduating from high school in Great Barrington, the only black in a class of thirteen, the seventeen-year-old Du Bois enrolled at Fisk University, a black college founded during Reconstruction in Nashville, Tennessee. Supported by Great Barrington ministers and teachers who raised money for his first scholarship, he studied for three years at Fisk, spending two of his summers as a rural schoolteacher among poor black folk in a village in eastern Tennessee.

Du Bois powerfully evokes the experience of these summers in the beautifully written and persistently ironic fourth chapter of *Souls,* "Of the Meaning of Progress." One of the most gripping essays in the book, this anthropological portrait of a folk culture is the sad story of Josie, of her community, and of what Du Bois called the "unconscious moral heroism" of a peasantry that hoped against and hated its fate. Du Bois grew to love these folk, he wrote, "for their honest efforts to be decent and comfortable, and for their knowledge of their own ignorance. There was with them no affectation."[9]

Du Bois earned a bachelor's degree at Fisk in 1888 and was admitted to Harvard College as a junior in the autumn of that year. As a Harvard undergraduate, he received an extraordinary education, studying philosophy with William James and George Santayana, history with Albert Bushnell Hart, English rhetoric with Barrett Wendell, and the emerging social sciences, such as economics, with Frank Taussig. Still, he felt frustrated while attending Harvard by his frequent encounters with racial segregation.

Largely avoiding the social life of Harvard, Du Bois did become active as a lecturer in the black community of Cambridge and Boston. "I was in Harvard, but not of it," Du Bois would later write, capturing his insatiable embrace of the classical education the place offered him as well as his cunning negotiation of the color line that would become the multidisciplinary subject of his life's work. His contemptuous silence in response to the question with which he begins chapter 1 of *Souls*—"How does it feel to be a problem?"—expressed an attitude, even a way of life, conditioned into his bones, in great part during his Harvard years. "Being a problem is a strange experience," he wrote in *Souls,* "even for one who has never been anything else, save perhaps in babyhood and in Europe."[10]

After graduating with a bachelor of arts degree from Harvard in 1890, Du Bois entered Harvard's graduate school, first enrolling in political science. By 1892, after two years of applications, he received a scholarship from the Slater Fund for the Education of Negroes to study abroad at the Friedrich Wilhelm University in Berlin. Du Bois spent two resplendent and intellectually stimulating years enjoying Berlin and traveling across Europe as a young gentleman–scholar. Cultivating his love of opera and admiring the great capitals of the colonial empires, he also fell in love with a young German woman. Just a day after hearing a performance of Schubert's Unfinished Symphony, Du Bois celebrated his twenty-fifth birthday in Berlin. Reflecting on the brief program he prepared for his private fete, he wrote passionately of Europe's "great inspiring air of world culture." Echoing the Bible's Esther, he dedicated his life to his people: "to make a name in science, to make a name in literature and thus to raise my race . . . I will go unto the king—which is not according to the law and if I perish—I perish."[11]

In 1894 Du Bois returned from Germany a changed but still young man whose soul, he later recalled, had been permeated by "the beauty and elegance of life." Expressing a temperament shared by many Americans, he declared that he "had been, above all, in a hurry. I wanted a world, smooth, and swift, and had no time for rounded corners and ornament, for unhurried thought and slow contemplation. . . . I saw in arch and stone and steeple the history and striving of men and also their taste and expression. Form, color, and worlds took new combinations and meanings."[12]

In 1895 Du Bois became the first African American to receive a Ph.D. from Harvard, completing a dissertation in history that was published a year later as *The Suppression of the African Slave Trade to the United States of America, 1638–1870.* Upon leaving Harvard, he took his first teaching position, at Wilberforce College in Xenia, Ohio, remaining only two years at an institution that he found intellectually stunting and religiously too conservative. In 1896, with a fellowship from the University of Pennsylvania, Du Bois returned east to conduct a door-to-door study of Philadelphia's black population that resulted in his second book, a landmark in the sociological study of urban America, *The Philadelphia Negro* (1899). The following year he took a position in history and economics at Atlanta University, where he remained until 1910, teaching, sponsoring conferences, and producing sixteen detailed reports *(The Atlanta University Studies)* on various aspects of African American economic, social, cultural, and educational life. While living in segregated Atlanta between 1897 and 1903, Du Bois completed the essays that became *The Souls of Black Folk.*

WHAT THEN IS A RACE?

In March 1897, in the busy months before moving to Atlanta, Du Bois laid the basis for the argument of *Souls* with a paper he delivered in Washington, D.C. to the inaugural meeting of the American Negro Academy. Founded by Du Bois, Alexander Crummell, and several other African American intellectuals, the American Negro Academy was the first national black learned society; its purpose was to promote the cultivation of a specifically Negro contribution to American culture and world civilization. Members of the academy shared a belief that it was the duty of intellectual elites to lead the masses by diffusing knowledge among them, to uplift the ordinary people in their midst. Until its demise in 1928, the Academy and its small, all-male membership published twenty-two "occasional papers" on subjects ranging from civil and political rights, history, and religion to the place of black institutions in American life. Their aim was almost always the cultural assimilation of African Americans, although they also valued the distinctive elements of African American culture.[13]

Titled "The Conservation of Races" (see p. 228), Du Bois's paper before the American Negro Academy was a philosophically significant critique of the racial theories dominant in his day. As Du Bois well knew, nineteenth-century racial thought was largely committed to the now discredited view that an individual's racial identity is fixed by his or her racial type, a kind of biological racial essence. In general, advocates of this position held that two or more individuals belonged to the same race if, and only if, they embodied the same physical racial type.[14]

By assuming that physical racial types exist, racial theorists could claim to account for the supposed fact that members of different races display different psychological and social tendencies. They maintained that the characteristic psychological and social traits (habits and abilities) of distinct racial groups were effects of the distinct racial types defining those groups. Nineteenth-century racial theorists thus embraced a form of biological determinism, often called "scientific racism," that invoked physical racial differences to explain the perceived psychological and social differences among the races.[15]

In his paper "The Conservation of Races," Du Bois challenges this biological determinism, explicitly rejecting the belief that physical differences (such as in color, blood, and size of the skull) between the races account for psychological or "spiritual" differences. Instead he looks to social and historical factors for an explanation. "While race differences have followed mainly physical race lines," he proclaims, "no mere physical distinctions would really define or explain the deeper differences . . . the deeper differences are spiritual, psychical differences." According to Du Bois, one needs to invoke the "subtle forces" of history, law, habits of thought, the ends of human striving, and religion to account for the distinctive spiritual lives of racial groups. In other words, explaining the unique spiritual message of a race is a matter for the human sciences (history and sociology), not the natural sciences (biology and chemistry). For Du Bois, studying the social history of a racial group is essential to making sense of its spiritual identity. Experience and condition, he asserts, forge the habits of head and heart separating one people from another.[16]

Du Bois's turn from the natural to the human sciences was closely related to his attempt to modify the concept of race. In addition to explaining spiritual differences between races in sociohistorical terms, he defines a race as a group whose identity is partly fixed by sociohistorical characteristics. A race, Du Bois writes, is "a vast family of human beings, generally of common blood and language, always of common history, traditions and impulses, who are both voluntarily and involuntarily striving together for the accomplishment of certain more or less vividly conceived ideals of life." With this formulation, Du Bois analyzes the concept of race by citing both biological (common blood) *and* sociohistorical (common language and common history) attributes. Although his references to some of these attributes may puzzle the reader, there can be little doubt that, in stressing sociohistorical conditions, he aims to deny the thesis that physical type alone constitutes racial identity. Invoking the perspective of the human sciences, Du Bois rejects biological determinism and insists that racial identity per se has a nonphysical, sociohistorical dimension.[17]

In *Souls,* Du Bois explicitly draws on his belief that the spiritual life of a race can be best explained in historical and sociological terms. To be sure, the book contains some passages that appear to tie Negro temperament to Negro biology. For example, Du Bois seems to embrace some sort of biological determinism when, in chapter 10, he describes "the Negro" as a "religious animal," with a "native appreciation of the beautiful," whose emotional nature "turns instinctively toward the super-natural." Still, the dominant thrust of *Souls* is Du Bois's attempt to put the spiritual world of blacks in historical and social perspective. Du Bois writes that "Negro blood has a message for the world," yet his interpretations of the "soul-life" and striving which express that message allude never to blood but always to social and historical circumstance. As Du Bois depicts it, African American spirituality derives its character from the distinctive drama that is African American history. Indeed, it is this multifaceted drama, with its richly textured vignettes of slavery, emancipation, emerging leadership, and the psychological striving of a people, that *Souls* portrays as the complicated and nonbiological substance of a black identity in America.[18]

TRAGEDY AND TWONESS

Because Du Bois never intended *Souls* to be a straightforward history of race in America, his book may disorient readers who do not go slowly and read deeply in a text that is in part a poet's history—an attempt to take the pulse and capture the pathos of an historical era. The product of a nineteenth-century tradition that made history into *literature, Souls* is a group of essays intended more to inspire the historical imagination than to amass scholarly knowledge or recount facts and figures.

Du Bois began early in life to appreciate history as literature. As a fourteen-year-old high school sophomore in Great Barrington, he purchased the five-volume *History of England* by Thomas Babington Macaulay, apparently devouring Macaulay's famous narrative of the English nation with great relish. Du Bois would later recoil from the arguments in that book, for they virtually sang in the service of imperialism. But as biographer David Levering Lewis writes, Macaulay's "matchless narrative powers" may have never ceased to ring in Du Bois's "inner ear." Writing in 1828, Macaulay declared that "the perfect historian is he in whose work the character and spirit of an age is exhibited in miniature. He relates no fact, he attributes no expression to his characters, which is not authenticated by sufficient testimony. But by judicious selection, rejection, and arrangement, he gives to truth those attractions which have been usurped by fiction."[19] In *Souls,* Du Bois avoids the kind of nationalism that drove Macaulay's narrative of English progress and glory. But he does search for the spirit of the Age of Emancipation, for the searing ironies in America's promise, and for the troubled uncertainties of the post-freedom generations of black people.

Du Bois's history in *Souls* is by no means a narrow picture of the black experience alone. It is history that assumes that broad generalization is the ultimate aim of historical understanding, that nations have discernible stories with central themes and living responsibilities. Ultimately, this is history that seeks to understand the *legacies* of epochal events, to face honestly the "heritage of slavery," to know how emancipation came as cosmic deliverance, but how Reconstruction, an extraordinary experiment in "social regeneration," was "in large part foredoomed to failure." The "attractions" in *Souls* as history, to borrow from Macaulay, are in Du Bois's ability to help the reader see and feel an American tragedy, the "great republic's" failure at its most "concrete test."[20]

Souls sings like a prayerful wail from the shipwreck of black freedom as it lists on the shoals of segregation. Yet it appeals because it is an original and lyrical expression of the ways African Americans have forged an old, beautiful, and sustaining culture, a musical, religious, and growing intellectual heritage that offered many "gifts" to a nation that might yet redeem itself. *Souls* is social and cultural history that pleads for recognition of both the suffering and the art in the souls of black folk. Together, the essays form the tale of peasants surviving on a faith that makes them strive for a better day and of an emerging leadership class readying itself to think and to organize in a modern age. Its historical and sociological essays (roughly the first two-thirds of the book) lead the reader to Du Bois's meditations on the religious lives of African Americans and to his compelling rendition of their most enduring creations, their plaintive expressions of profound trust in a higher, ethical order—the sorrow songs at the end of the book.

As poetic history, *Souls* contains probing descriptions of the spirituality, or "soul-life," which Du Bois attributes to the African American experience. For example, Du Bois uses the metaphors of "double-consciousness" and "the veil" to depict a two-dimensional pattern of estrangement that shaped the lives of black Americans in the age of Jim Crow. For Du Bois, the refusal of whites to recognize black Americans' humanity and culture has resulted, first, in whites seeing blacks as strangers and, second, in the tendency of blacks to see themselves as strangers. "It is a peculiar sensation," he remarks, "this double-consciousness, this sense of always looking at oneself through the eyes of others, of measuring one's soul by the tape of a world that looks on in amused contempt and pity." Seeing himself from the white world's perspective, Du Bois's American Negro views himself in a dark and false light, as if "born with a veil." Knowing no "true self-consciousness," he knows himself always as others know him, and so always as *other.* Ever feeling his "twoness," he succumbs to a conflict between two opposed selves: the one seeing and the other seen; the one contemptuous and the other remote; the one American and the other Negro. The essence of the Negro's soul-life, Du Bois says, is a perpetual and difficult struggle to overcome this conflict and self-estrangement; it is a "history . . . of strife . . . [of] longing to attain self-conscious manhood, to merge his double self into a better and truer self."[21]

"Tragedy" is Du Bois's name for the suffering wrought by the two-dimensional pattern of estrangement burdening blacks' lives. In merging his double self, Du Bois's Negro wishes "neither of the older selves to be lost . . . to be both a Negro and an American, without being cursed and spit upon by his fellows." White Americans, however, by deriding the Negro and refusing to see him as a co-worker in the nation's culture, persist in disavowing their ties to black folk. By so behaving, they thwart the Negro's effort to form a complex identity that admits and integrates duality. The tragedy resulting from such behavior is apparent, Du Bois claims, in the lives of blacks and whites alike. It was evident, for example, in the life of Alexander Crummell, the black theologian and missionary whose life Du Bois praises in chapter 12. Crummell, Du Bois suggests, worked in estranged isolation, "with . . . little human sympathy," epitomizing "the tragedy" of an age in which "men know so little of men."[22]

Du Bois's America is a tragic land, for although America would not be America "without her Negro people," and thus without her Negroes' gifts of "story and song . . . sweat and brawn . . . and spirit," white Americans still repudiate the Negro and so alienate themselves from a group whose presence has shaped *their* identities *as Americans.* In *Souls'* only piece of fiction, "Of the Coming of John" (chapter 13), Du Bois again explores the tragic effects of this sort of estrangement in a harrowing tale of two young men whose deeply connected lives neither blacks nor whites see as connected. In Du Bois's words, "the black folk thought of one John, and he was black, and the white folk thought of another John, and he was white. And neither world thought the other world's thought, save with a vague unrest."[23]

As historian Joel Williamson has observed, Du Bois's interpretation of the Negro's historical striving owes a debt to the nineteenth-century German philosopher Georg Friedrich Hegel. Characterizing the Negro as a "seventh son," Du Bois, in chapter 1, depicts him as a latecomer to the stage of the world's history. Appearing in the aftermath of the six peoples who, in Hegel's scheme, have already realized their spiritual destinies (the Chinese, Indians, Persians, Greeks, Romans, and Germans), Du Bois's Negro struggles relentlessly for a recognition and a self-realization that would heal the wound of America's double-edged tragedy.[24]

Du Bois revises Hegel's philosophy of history by portraying black Americans as agents in the drama of the world's historical development (Hegel had relegated blacks to the "threshhold" of history. Africa, he said, "is no historical part of the world."). Speaking of the "history of the American Negro," he refers neither to individuals nor to aggregates of individuals but to the Negro race as a spiritual force with a developing and unique world-historical destiny.[25] Consistent with his argument in "The Conservation of Races" (see p. 228), Du Bois uses the idea of a racially shared and distinctive spiritual identity (born of a people's collective experience) to frame his more specific accounts of emancipation, the Civil War, and Reconstruction.

TRAGEDY AND AMERICAN HISTORY

Du Bois's approach to the legacies of emancipation is most immediately evident in chapter 1, where, after analyzing the notion of "double-consciousness," he offers up what David Levering Lewis calls his "signature"—the compression of huge pieces of history into single paragraphs, images, or metaphors. Beginning with an allusion to "the days of bondage" and ending two paragraphs later with an image of education as the "mountain path to Canaan," Du Bois sweeps his reader through the forty years since emancipation. There are no details here to aid the reader nor to block the feelings of unrestrained joy at the moment of freedom and unfathomable pain in the aftermath of freedom's prolonged denials. Instead, the reader feels the legacy of emancipation as though it were a haunting, murky, even frightful cloud hanging over the body politic. "Forty years of national life" brought great change, Du Bois says, "and yet the swarthy spectre sits in its accustomed seat at the Nation's feast. In vain do we cry to this our vastest social problem:— 'Take any shape but that, and my firm nerves / shall never tremble!' " Comparing the Negro to Banquo's ghost, come to terrify the tyrant (Macbeth) who has had Banquo murdered, Du Bois suggests that black folk and their history will forever torment post-emancipation America. Drawing on the complex and ambiguous imagery of Shakespearean tragedy, he compels his reader to hear what he would later call his "cry at midnight thick within the veil, when none rightly knew the coming day." *Souls* should not be the only thing one reads about emancipation and its aftermath. But it provides an evocative and moving chorus for more standard, equally valuable histories.[26]

Throughout *Souls,* Du Bois attempts to revise history, to dislodge the dominant, white supremacist historical memory of the nation in favor of a more inclusive, if tragic vision of America's past. In chapter 2, "Of the Dawn of Freedom," for example, he presents a logical case for viewing the Freedmen's Bureau (the federal agency created to facilitate the transition from slavery to freedom) as a positive force rather than as an arch villain of the alleged debacle of Reconstruction. Far ahead of his time with such an interpretation, and as a prologue to his later, more scholarly works (such as "The Benefits of Reconstruction" in 1909 and his classic *Black Reconstruction* in 1935), Du Bois offers a sympathetic portrayal of the Bureau's all too short life.[27] He ignores neither the flaws and failings of the Bureau nor those of its agents. But in a combination of descriptive history and theatrical pageantry, he creates a new framework in which the plight of the freedmen might be better understood.

In another attempt to revise historical memory, Du Bois speaks in the voice of a prophet. Urging the reader to cast his or her vision to the rear of the grim parade of history, he identifies three images in the procession of Sherman's march across Georgia at the end of the Civil War: "the Conqueror, the Conquered, and the Negro. Some see all significance in the grim front of the destroyer," writes Du Bois, "and some in the bitter sufferers of the Lost Cause. But to me neither soldier nor fugitive speaks with so deep a meaning as that dark human cloud that clung like remorse on the rear of those swift columns. . . . In vain were they ordered back . . . ; on they trudged and writhed and surged, until they rolled into Savannah, a starved and naked horde of tens of thousands."[28] Here are the nameless freedpeople, inexorably liberated and self-liberated in a terrible war, given equal billing in this historical theater with the tragic southern planters and the awesome symbol of Yankee destruction and victory, William Tecumseh Sherman.

Finally, in a stunning metaphor about passion in the New South, Du Bois characterizes "two figures" that typified the Reconstruction era and the power of its legacy: "the one, a gray-haired gentleman, whose fathers had quit themselves like men, whose sons lay in nameless graves . . . ; — and the other, a form hovering dark and mother-like, her awful face black with the mists of centuries." Past and present meet in this imagery with frightful intensity; the picture Du Bois paints is nothing less than an alternative vision of the meaning of the Civil War, one that most white Americans did their best not to see in the late nineteenth century. "These were the saddest sights of that woful day," Du Bois writes, "and no man clasped the hands of these two passing figures of the present-past; but, hating, they went to their long home, and, hating, their children's children live to-day."[29] Here are not the customary forms of old soldiers who had met in battle and could now clasp hands in mutual respect, images one could find by the 1890s all over American culture, on town greens, and at Blue-Gray reunions. Rather, Du Bois's "two figures" are *veterans* of an even deeper conflict and, perhaps, of a violence equal to that of the war itself. Here are the images of an old male slaveholder, the broken symbol of wealth, power, and sexual domination, and an old black woman, representing "Mammy," mother and survivor. The heritage of slavery lives on in these "two passing figures of the present-past," demonstrating that racial reconciliation, unlike sectional reconciliation, demands a serious confrontation with the hostility rooted in rape, lynching, and racism. Deep memories in the South, in Du Bois's vision, make bridging this chasm of race and gender all but impossible.

Readers will hear many echoes of chapters 1–3 later in the book: duality as the burdensome yet strengthening fate of being black in America; the celebration of education for its own sake; the significance of black suffrage as the bedrock of the freedpeople's liberty; the complex interplay between "success" and "failure" in the story of Reconstruction; the role of leadership for a people and a nation undergoing rebirth; and the crucial question of civic responsibility for the freedpeople's destiny, of what governments owe their people, and of what people must accomplish by themselves. Indeed, the book can be read as an extended reflection on the stakes of the Civil War and emancipation for American society.

Du Bois uses Reconstruction as a symbolic measure of the losses and gains in the politics of race and as a means of formulating his ironic conception of "progress." As literary scholar Eric Sundquist has written, Du Bois's "Of the Dawn of Freedom" becomes a "false dawn." The bleak, brooding ending of chapter 2 argues that in order for America to find its soul, it had to free the slaves. The American emancipation, compelled by history, ideology, and necessity, seemed nevertheless to require betrayal; the ex-slaves were reborn from bondage, many only to die in a wasteland of debt peonage. "Thus Negro suffrage ended a civil war by beginning a race feud," Du Bois writes. "And some felt gratitude toward the race thus sacrificed in its swaddling clothes on the altar of national integrity; and some felt and feel only indifference and contempt."[30] It is significant that Du Bois's tragic vision of history and the haunting images of strife he laces throughout "Of the Dawn of Freedom" are placed between two chapters that end with ringing appeals to the first principles of the Declaration of Independence. In *Souls,* history is a prophetic demand upon the creeds of a forgetful country.

THE WIZARD OF TUSKEGEE AND THE EGYPT OF THE CONFEDERACY

Du Bois's stingingly, if respectfully, critical treatment of Booker T. Washington in chapter 3 is a good introduction to the developing debate between the Du Bois and Washington camps of black leadership in the early twentieth century. Washington, who was born a slave in western Virginia in 1856 and had been educated at Hampton Institute, a freedmen's school, was the founder and principal of Tuskegee Institute in Alabama. By the time Du Bois began to challenge him in *Souls* and other writings, Washington had established himself as an educational statesman, the primary spokesman of black America, and the leader of a large network of disciples—the "Tuskegee Machine"—who edited newspapers, owned businesses, and directed schools modeled on Tuskegee.

Washington's doctrine of accommodationism—according to which blacks would acquiesce in legal segregation and disfranchisement while engaging in self-reliant economic development within their own communities—gained a wide following among blacks and admiration among whites. Although he never held elective office, Washington was an adroit power broker; he exercised his clout by some occasionally ruthless methods. Rival black newspaper editors or aspiring young educators and intellectuals risked unemployment and other forms of intimidation if they embraced political activism rather than Washington's accommodationist social policy. Known as the "Wizard of Tuskegee," Washington became an informal adviser to American presidents and wielded great influence among wealthy white philanthropists. Du Bois's statement that Washington's "ascendancy" was "easily the most striking thing in the history of the American Negro since 1876" was not hyperbole in 1903.[31]

Du Bois and other largely northern-born and -educated black leaders increasingly objected to Washington's willingness to exchange political and social equality for industrial education and economic self-determination. Du Bois led an effort to counter Washington's authority by turning the attention of black and white Americans alike to demands for full citizenship rights, full economic opportunity, and access to classical as well as industrial education. By 1903, a debate over educational and leadership strategies had become an all-out political struggle over the distribution of power and resources in black America. Careers, ideas, and human rights were at stake in the battles between the Tuskegee Machine and the cultured and classically educated black elite that Du Bois called the "Talented Tenth."[32]

In *Souls,* Du Bois places Washington's rise to prominence in a broad historical context; his program of "adjustment and submission" and his "gospel of Work and Money" found fertile ground in "the time when war memories and ideals were rapidly passing." Du Bois sees Washington's leadership as the direct product of sectional reconciliation; the Wizard of Tuskegee became a kind of grand master of ceremonies, emerging from the ashes of wartime and Reconstruction bitterness. Fair or not, Du Bois claims that Washington had become "the leader not of one race but of two, — a compromiser between the South, the North, and the Negro." Thus does Du Bois bitterly contest the memory of the Civil War, as well as Washington's leadership during the emerging age of Jim Crow. If the American reconciliation would mean "industrial slavery and civic death … with permanent legislation [putting blacks] into a position of inferiority," then Booker Washington must be resisted. Otherwise, Du Bois, the historian/social critic, predicts a "harvest of disaster" for blacks and whites.[33]

It has never been adequate to describe Du Bois exclusively as an "elitist" while portraying Washington as a practical builder of institutions and livelihoods. It is equally inadequate to say that Washington and Du Bois had the same ultimate goals for their people, because their educational aims and social and political strategies were very different. An understanding of this famous dispute in African American history may be better served by oppositions such as "work and thought," "craft and culture," "livelihood and the meaning of life." But even these dichotomies flatten out the complexity of the ideological conflict that Du Bois explores in chapter 3 of *Souls.* Such dichotomies, moreover, fail to do justice to Du Bois's proud demands for black higher education in chapters 5 and 6, "Of the Wings of Atalanta" and "Of the Training of Black Men." Du Bois's "training" at Fisk, Harvard, and Berlin informs every page of those chapters. Only his superior education, rare for a black man in turn-of-the-century America, could account for the audacity and the confidence of the famous passage at the end of chapter 6: "I sit with Shakespeare and he winces not. Across the color line I move arm in arm with Balzac and Dumas, where smiling men and welcoming women glide in gilded halls. … I summon Aristotle and Aurelius and what soul I will, and they come all graciously with no scorn nor condescension. So, wed with Truth, I dwell above the Veil."[34]

Du Bois's eloquent praise of higher learning and his personal challenges to national black leadership give way in chapters 7–9 to the observations of a historical sociologist. Written like a historical travelogue depicting the "Egypt of the Confederacy," chapter 7 provides some of the most moving and plaintive images of the South in the book. This essay may have been Du Bois's self-styled answer to the multitude of articles that had appeared in *Harper's* and other popular magazines for at least two decades.[35] Typically inviting northern readers to journey into America's romantic past, these articles described an exotic South surviving in stock characters — old planters, new entrepreneurs, and especially the old-time plantation "darkies." In Du Bois's Black Belt, however, there are no happy darkies and no myth of a harmonious South left to its own devices. Combining the beauty and power of nature, the sweep of history in epic proportions, and the painful ruck of sharecroppers' daily lives, Du Bois forges indelible memories that counter the romance of the Lost Cause and national reunion. His landscape and the people on it seem to inhabit another time, trapped in a past they cannot escape.

In chapter 8 Du Bois the sociologist engages in his own brand of muckraking journalism, writing in the spirit and purpose of a Progressive reformer. Du Bois's descriptive journey through Dougherty County, his exposure of the living conditions and despair of this black peasantry, is a rural southern equivalent to northern muckrakers' exposure of urban political corruption and the tenement housing conditions of America's laboring class. Du Bois does not idealize his peasants; he gives them no false agency. Some are simply "lewd" or "vicious"; others are "intelligent and responsible persons" and are likely to end up landowners. On the whole, however, Du Bois's journalism shames the nation by confronting it with a world of impoverished sharecroppers, doomed to live out their lives in a "hopeless serfdom."[36]

Finally, in chapter 9, Du Bois shifts from the psyche of the black peasantry to one of his great themes — the meaning of segregation itself. With remarkable sympathy for the whole South and for the essential irony in its history, Du Bois writes of a place full of "tragedies and comedies . . . a swaying and lifting and sinking of human hearts which have made this land a land of mingled sorrow and joy, of change and excitement and unrest." Du Bois's South is certainly no undifferentiated seat of evil. We tend too often perhaps to see the Jim Crow world as a system of laws, divided institutions and politics, even of separate economies. So it was. But in this chapter Du Bois reaches for the psychological meanings and historical roots of segregation, for the moral consequences and sheer loss of human knowledge and potential in a "world" that flows by him "in two great streams" that rarely touch. Whites and blacks are "strangers," says Du Bois, with a mutual fate.[37]

Souls is historical literature that breathed a heavy sigh of tragedy into America's optimistic sense of itself. In Du Bois's own time, many perceptive readers wondered about the book's somber tones. In 1906, William James wrote to Du Bois congratulating him on the power of *Souls,* but questioning the despair of the book. "You must not think I am personally wedded to the minor key," Du Bois answered his mentor. "On the contrary I am tuned to the most aggressive and unquenchable hopefulness. I wanted in this case simply to reveal fully the other side to the world"[38] (see p. 262). The endless tension between pain and beauty, between the full range of suffering and the persistence of possibility in American history, is what Du Bois sought to capture by bringing the black experience to the center of the story.

THE POLITICAL BIBLE OF THE NEGRO RACE

In 1956, Langston Hughes penned a letter (see p. 267) to the eighty-eight-year-old Du Bois, declaring that he had just read *Souls* "for perhaps the tenth time — the first time having been some forty years ago." "Its beauty and passion and power," wrote Hughes, "are as moving and as meaningful as ever." Hughes had just sat rapturously with the fiftieth-anniversary edition and, by that time, twenty-sixth printing of Du Bois's classic work. *Souls* had fallen out of print for ten years (throughout the 1940s) before Du Bois himself bought the plates from McClurg and Company for $100 in 1949.[39]

By the early 1950s, Du Bois was among a growing number of American academics, writers, and artists who were attacked, and sometimes ruined, by McCarthyism. The anti-Communist crusade led by Wisconsin Senator Joseph McCarthy suppressed the works of left-leaning American intellectuals in many schools and in mainstream publishing. Through the concerted efforts of friends such as Howard Fast and Herbert Aptheker, who themselves became victims of censorship, the Blue Heron Press brought out the 1953 commemorative edition in which Du Bois made a small number of significant changes that we cite in our notes.

During the first five years of publication, the original edition of *Souls* sold 9,595 copies. As Aptheker has demonstrated, the book influenced a wide variety of readers and received a remarkable range of reviews. Although much of the African American press controlled by Booker T. Washington's political machine ignored the book, numerous independent black journals and individual voices rejoiced. Bostonian John Daniels spoke for many black leaders in seeing beyond the emerging Du

Bois–Washington conflict, urging his readers to judge *Souls* "not as an argument, as an anti-Washington protest, but as a poem, a spiritual, not intellectual offering, an appeal not to the head but to the heart." The book deserved the "highest place," said Daniels, "not that of a polemic, a transient thing, but that of a poem, a thing permanent."[40] Du Bois's prose poem was, indeed, to become a permanent fixture and a renewable literary resource in the fight against racism.

Souls also elicited a wide range of personal responses, especially of pride and gratitude among blacks. As a student at Cornell University, the eighteen-year-old Jessie Fauset wrote to Du Bois, thanking him "as though it had been a personal favor, for your book 'The Souls of Black Folk.' " Fauset was an ecstatic and perceptive reader and would later emerge as a literary figure of the Harlem Renaissance. "I am glad, glad you wrote it," she said, "we have needed someone to voice the intricacies of the blind maze of thought and action along which the modern, educated colored man and woman struggles. It hurt you to write that book, didn't it?" For so young a person to see, and even share in, what she called the author's "exquisite suffering" was to grasp the heart of Du Bois's sense of tragedy.[41] Part 2 of this book reprints a variety of such correspondence to and from Du Bois, demonstrating the range of responses that *Souls* stimulated in its readers.

White southern newspapers reviewed *Souls* more than one might suppose, although many found only disfavor with Du Bois's alternatives to Washington's accommodationism and industrial training. Some southern papers declared the book "dangerous for the Negro to read" and one paper urged Du Bois's indictment for "inciting rape." In at least one instance, a white southern intellectual tried, if falteringly, to meet Du Bois across the chasm separating what both would consider the "best" of the two races. In the *South Atlantic Quarterly,* John Spencer Bassett, a southern historian with a keen, if paternalistic, interest in black life and history, wrote a careful review of *Souls.* With a remarkable combination of respect and racist condescension, Bassett admired Washington yet praised Du Bois's embrace of "ethical culture," his representation of how "the soul is more than the body." Despite his commitment to racial segregation, Bassett understood Du Bois the intellectual. "He makes us feel what an awful thing it is to be in America a Negro," wrote Bassett, "and at the same time be a man of culture." Ordinary blacks experienced race prejudice in "frowns" and "Jim Crow cars." But to the "man of culture," prejudice was a "locked door in his face." While Washington would have blacks accept the "Veil," said Bassett, "Du Bois would chafe and fret and tear his heart out."[42]

Northern reviews of *Souls* were remarkably sympathetic, although many found only the chapter on Washington worth noting, while some were especially concerned with Du Bois's anger. Typical of such responses was a review published in the *Annals of the American Academy of Political and Social Science* that protested Du Bois's "tendency to snarl against social customs, as evidence of mental bitterness." The reviewer, Carl Kelsey of the University of Pennsylvania, admired Du Bois's discussion of the "psychical evolution of the Negro," but, speaking perhaps for many fellow American academics, he simply could not abide the author's chronicling of "the failures, the injustices and the wrongs." "Of the Coming of John" (chapter 13) was a "good story," said Kelsey, "but it ends in tragedy."[43]

Other favorable notices for *Souls* celebrated the very presence of such a book. A Chicago journal, *The Public,* said it was "drawn irresistibly . . . into full sympathy" by Du Bois's style and argument. Sounding much like the reactions of white abolitionist readers to the great slave narratives of Frederick Douglass and others in the 1840s, *The Public* declared that "never before has the Negro asked with so much emphasis and such power of thought and persuasiveness of diction, 'Am I not a man and a brother?' as in this book." For white radicals, *Souls* came as political inspiration. The socialist Horace L. Traubel, writing in the *Conservator* of Philadelphia, announced that Du Bois's "fiery appeals encourage our faith against the despair of democracy." Using Du Bois to speak about African Americans as the abolitionist John Brown might have a half century earlier, Traubel declared that the black man "must not humiliate himself to any cry of the hounds . . . he has every right to liberty in all its clauses. If he has no right to that liberty . . . then no man has that right now or hereafter."[44]

Souls inspired enormous national and international acclaim (a British edition was published in 1905, it was warmly reviewed in Germany and New Zealand, and it was widely read by African leaders throughout the twentieth century), which suggests that its politics involved much more than opposition to Washington and the Tuskegee Machine. In 1913 the black scholar William Ferris named *Souls* "the political Bible of the Negro race." Ferris also remembered the "thrill and pleasure" with which he first read *Souls:* "It was an eventful day in my life. It affected me just like Carlyle's 'Heroes and Hero Worship' . . . , Emerson's 'Nature and Other Addresses.' . . . *Souls* came to me as a bolt from the blue. It was the rebellion of a fearless soul, the protest of a noble nature against the blighting American caste prejudice. It proclaimed in thunder tones and in words of magic beauty the worth and sacredness of human personality even when clothed in a black skin." In 1933 the writer and diplomat James Weldon Johnson observed that *Souls'* impact was "greater upon and within the Negro race than any other single book published in this country since *Uncle Tom's Cabin."* And in 1961 the literary historian J. Saunders Redding described the book as "more history-making than historical." Thus we can begin to see how a literary classic evolves through time, how, as contemporary critic Henry Louis Gates Jr. has written, *Souls* became a "cultural initiation rite" for black writers, as well as for their legion of readers.[45] At the end of the twentieth century, it remains an influential text. However, the book should be read not only for its literary value, but as a work of history, sociology, and philosophical analysis about race in America.

SORROW AND HOPE

Du Bois was fully aware that *Souls* affected his readers aesthetically as well as intellectually. He wanted to unveil for them the mournful dramas of American history, to help them see history itself as something evolving slowly over time, with whole peoples laboring, heroically and rudely, against their fate. He wanted to take readers on journeys they had not imagined and, as in all great travels, bring them home changed. With similar aims in mind, in 1904 Du Bois wrote an essay for the *International Journal of Ethics,* "The Development of a People" (see p. 238). Most of *Souls'* major themes—the irony of progress, the complexity of human identity, the nature of cultural development, and, above all, the thought that all questions must be examined *historically*—are evident in this essay, which reads as though Du Bois intended to provide a succinct reprise of *Souls.* In the South Du Bois revisits in "The Development of a People," "the awful incubus of the past broods like a writhing sorrow, and when we turn our faces from that past, we turn it not to forget but to remember."[46] "The Development of a People" appears in this book as a postscript to *Souls;* written after Du Bois had no doubt read most of his reviews, it offers a brief restatement of his case.

The joy in reading *Souls* often comes from the power of its late Victorian prose style, its masterly use of the essay form, and its tragic vision translated into story and analysis. In short, *Souls* gives pleasure in its *eloquence.* As literary historian Arnold Rampersad has shown, Du Bois the artist–historian was always aware of the classical forms of rhetoric in which he was trained at Fisk and Harvard. He was the scientific researcher and the self-conscious craftsman, the historian, writes Rampersad, who applied "moral standards and mythopoeic imagination to accumulated data."[47]

Souls is an example of style that is not mere decoration in the place of argument. Images become explanation in many chapters, whether they represent real places in Dougherty County or at Atlanta University; half-mythic sites like Josie's grave or the visage of the unnamed Abraham Lincoln (the "long-headed man with the care-chiselled face"); or the fully mythic individual portrayed by the "figure veiled and bowed," sitting by the "King's Highway" at the end of chapter 2. "The very idea of style is infected with a central ambiguity," writes historian Peter Gay, "it must give information as well as pleasure. It opens windows on both truth and beauty — a bewildering double vista." *Souls* should be read with this ambiguity in mind; its author saw the mutual infection of narration and analysis as a good thing. As Eric Sundquist has put it, *Souls* should be read as a "narrative experiment with dramatic form" and as a "musical book."[48]

Of the many personal responses to *Souls* that Du Bois received, none were more poignant than the one written by a Russian Jewish immigrant living on New York City's Lower East Side (see p. 260). Having discovered a copy of *Souls* on Delancey Street, D. Tabak read it with an unforgettable combination of anguish, guilt, and exhilaration and declared himself "overpowered by a peculiar pain that was so much akin to bliss." Tabak's words aptly capture the spirit of Du Bois's celebration of the sorrow songs in the final chapter. Borrowing from numerous interpreters before him, Du Bois gives a meaning to these songs that has withstood the test of time. "Through all the sorrow of the Sorrow Songs there breathes a hope," he writes, "a faith in the ultimate justice of things. The minor cadences of despair change often to triumph and calm confidence . . . that sometime, somewhere, men will judge men by their souls and not by their skins." Du Bois's statement comes coupled with his bold insistence on the originality of black folk music, "blending," he says, with many European forms to produce "the most beautiful expression of human experience born this side the seas." Ultimately, Du Bois returns his celebration of the spirituals to one of the book's primary themes — the centrality of the black experience in American history. The final pages of *Souls* ring with questions of a sort that voluntary immigrants have also asked: "Your country? How came it yours? . . . Would America have been America without her Negro people?"[49]

Du Bois's famous epigraphs, consisting of bars of music from the Negro spirituals, balanced in every chapter but one with poetic verse from the Western literary tradition, provide the extraordinary framework for

Souls. With these bars and verses Du Bois reaches for a harmoniously integrated cultural identity, the "true self-consciousness" which this book so movingly seeks. In Du Bois's epigraphs, and in his final chapter, the unnamed American slaves and world-famous poets speak from the same text of life and sing in the same church. Friedrich Schiller sits with Josie singing "My Way's Cloudy," waiting for the Lord to "send them angels down," and James Russell Lowell sits with all the freedpeople singing "My Lord What a Mourning." At the end of the book, Du Bois waxes somber and passionate all at once; he himself becomes the prayerful singer, naming sorrows and breathing hope. He sees a vision and hears the sounds of freedom through his office window in Atlanta; the children below are "singing to the sunshine" a song of weariness and cheer.[50]

NOTES

[1]Du Bois first used the statement "The problem of the Twentieth Century is the problem of the color-line" in an address to the first Pan-African conference, in London in July 1900. See *Souls,* 34. "Spiritual striving," though a theme in many sections of *Souls,* is the subject of chapter 1. The idea of "double-consciousness," though a leitmotif of the entire book, is introduced in a familiar passage in chapter 1.

[2]"The Souls of Black Folk," *Independent,* November 17, 1904. The three-part categorization of the chapters in *Souls* follows Arnold Rampersad's interpretation in *The Art and Imagination of W. E. B. Du Bois* (Cambridge: Harvard University Press, 1976), 70–71.

[3]David Levering Lewis, *W. E. B. Du Bois: Biography of a Race, 1869–1919* (New York: Holt, 1993), 277.

[4]On the Jim Crow system, see C. Vann Woodward, *The Strange Career of Jim Crow* (New York: Oxford University Press, 1955), chaps. 1–4. On *Plessy v. Ferguson,* see Otto H. Olsen, *The Thin Disguise: Plessy v. Ferguson, a Documentary Presentation* (New York: Humanities Press, 1967).

[5]On sharecropping, see Roger Ransom and Richard Sutch, *One Kind of Freedom: The Economic Consequences of Emancipation* (Cambridge: Cambridge University Press, 1977), 81–105. On violence and lynching, see Fitzhugh Brundage, *Lynching in the New South: Georgia and Virginia, 1880–1930* (Urbana: University of Illinois Press, 1993), and Joel Williamson, *The Crucible of Race: Black-White Relations in the American South since Emancipation* (New York: Oxford University Press, 1984), 180–223.

[6]James M. McPherson, *The Abolitionist Legacy: From Reconstruction to the NAACP* (Princeton: Princeton University Press, 1975), 368–71. On peonage, see Pete Daniel, *The Shadow of Slavery: Peonage in the South, 1901–1969* (Urbana: University of Illinois Press, 1972). On Dixon, see Williamson, *Crucible of Race,* 140–76.

[7]On Du Bois's family history and growing up in Great Barrington, see Lewis, *Du Bois,* 11–25. Lewis is especially effective in ferreting out some of the deceptive elements in Du Bois's autobiographical writings. Du Bois wrote about himself and his family, says Lewis, in the "language of saga" and "chords of destiny" (19).

[8]W. E. B. Du Bois, *Dusk of Dawn: An Essay toward an Autobiography of a Race Concept* (1940), reprinted in *W. E. B. Du Bois: Writings* (New York: Library of America, 1986), 559. In *Dusk of Dawn,* Du Bois's third formal work of autobiography (at age seventy-two), he writes of his life in terms of these broad epochs and contexts, as in the opening lines of chapter 1: "From 1868 to 1940 stretch seventy-two mighty years, which are incidentally the years of my own life but more especially years of cosmic significance, when one remembers that they rush from the American Civil War to the reign of the second Roosevelt; from Victoria to the Sixth George; from the Franco-Prussian to the two World Wars. . . . Into the folds of this European civilization I was born and shall die, imprisoned, conditioned, depressed, exalted and inspired" (555). On Du Bois's struggles against anti-Communist repression, see Manning Marable, *W. E. B. Du Bois: Black Radical Democrat* (Boston: Twayne, 1986), 190–217, and Gerald Horne, *Black and Red: W. E. B. Du Bois and the Afro-American Response to the Cold War, 1944–1963* (Albany: State University of New York Press, 1986).

[9]*Souls,* 74. Du Bois's "little world," as he calls it in chapter 4, is Alexandria, Tennessee. On his teaching sojourn into eastern Tennessee for two summers, see Lewis, *Du Bois,* 67–71. Chapter 4 touches on many interesting themes, not the least of which is Du Bois's discussion of the tensions dividing the freedom and post-freedom generations of southern black folk in a poor, rural community.

[10]W. E. B. Du Bois, *The Autobiography of W. E. B. Du Bois: A Soliloquy on Viewing My Life from the Last Decade of Its First Century* (New York: International Publishers, 1968), 136; *Souls,* 37. See also Kim Townsend, " 'Manhood' at Harvard: W. E. B. Du Bois," *Raritan* 15 (Spring 1996): 70–82.

[11]For Du Bois's celebration of his twenty-fifth birthday, see Herbert Aptheker, ed., *Against Racism: Unpublished Essays, Papers, Addresses, 1887–1961* (Amherst: University of Massachusetts Press, 1985), 26–29. Also see Esther 4:16.

[12]Du Bois, *Dusk of Dawn,* 586–87.

[13]On the American Negro Academy, see Alfred A. Moss Jr., *The American Negro Academy: Voice of the Talented Tenth* (Baton Rouge: Louisiana State University Press, 1981).

[14]For a detailed discussion of nineteenth-century typological theories of race, see Michael Banton, *Racial Theories* (Cambridge: Cambridge University Press, 1987), chap. 2. See also Ernst Mayr, "Typological versus Population Thinking," in *Evolution and the Diversity of Life* (Cambridge: Harvard University Press, 1975), 26–29. For a clear and accessible account of the "population genetics" notion of race, which in the twentieth century has tended to displace the typological notion, see Richard Goldsby, *Race and Races* (New York: Macmillan, 1971).

[15]See Robert Miles, *Racism* (New York: Routledge, 1989), 32. For a general discussion of biological determinism, see Stephen Jay Gould, *The Mismeasure of Man* (New York: Penguin, 1981), especially the Introduction, and Richard C. Lewontin, Steven Rose, and Leon J. Kamin, eds., *Not in Our Genes* (New York: Pantheon, 1981).

[16]W. E. B. Du Bois, "The Conservation of Races," in *The Oxford W. E. B. Du Bois Reader,* ed. Eric J. Sundquist (New York: Oxford University Press, 1996), 41. On Du Bois's delivery of his paper at the first official meeting, on March 5, 1897, see Moss, *American Negro Academy,* 45, 54–61, 94–96, and Wilson Jeremiah Moses, *Alexander Crummell: A Study of Civilization and Its Discontents* (New York: Oxford University Press, 1990), 258–75. For a more detailed development of the point that, for Du Bois, history rather than biology explains the spiritual and cultural identity of a race, see Robert Gooding-Williams, "Outlaw, Appiah, and Du Bois's 'The Conservation of Races,' " in *W. E. B. Du Bois on Race and Culture: Philosophy, Politics and Poetics,* ed. Bernard Bell, Emily Grosholz, and James Stewart (New York: Routledge, 1996), forthcoming. For a similar approach to the explanation of African American culture by an important contemporary of Du Bois, see Franz Boas, "Race Problems in the United States," *Atlanta University Studies,* no. 20, "Select Discussions of Race Problems" 97–108, May 24, 1915, copy in W. E. B. Du Bois Papers, University of Massachusetts-Amherst (hereafter cited as Du Bois Papers). For further discus-

sion of Du Bois's "The Conservation of Races," see K. Anthony Appiah, "The Uncompleted Argument: Du Bois and the Illusion of Race," *Critical Inquiry* 12 (Autumn 1985): 21–37; Wilson J. Moses, "W. E. B. Du Bois's 'The Conservation of Races' and Its Context: Idealism, Conservatism, and Hero Worship," *Massachusetts Review* 34 (Summer 1993): 275–94; Eric J. Sundquist, *To Wake the Nations: Race in the Making of American Literature* (Cambridge: Harvard University Press, 1993), 462–63; Bernard R. Boxill, *Blacks and Social Justice* (Totowa, N.J.: Rowman and Allanheld, 1984), 173–85; and Anita Haya Goldman, "Negotiating Claims of Race and Rights: Du Bois, Emerson, and the Critique of Liberal Nationalism," *Massachusetts Review* 35 (Spring–Summer 1994): 169–201.

[17]Du Bois, "Conservation of Races," 40. For an important discussion of the tension between the biological and sociohistorical elements in Du Bois's definition of race, see Kwame Anthony Appiah, *In My Father's House* (New York: Oxford University Press, 1992), chap. 2. For an alternative interpretation and a critique of Appiah's view, see Gooding-Williams, "Outlaw, Appiah, and Du Bois's 'The Conservation of Races.' " In *Dusk of Dawn,* in 1940, Du Bois retrospectively notes the shift in his education and thinking in the 1890s from a biological concept of racial identity that emphasized "brain capacity" and the "cephalic index" (a formula for the ratio of the length to the width of the head) to a sociohistorical concept of racial identity as "a matter of culture and cultural history" (625–26).

[18]*Souls,* 153–54, 39. Adolph Reed mentions the passages cited from chapter 10 in his provocative interpretation of the early Du Bois as a neo-Lamarkian social scientist. See Reed, "Du Bois's 'Double Consciousness': Race and Gender in Progressive Era American Thought," *Studies in American Political Development* 6 (Spring 1992): 132–37, esp. 135. Also see Thomas Holt, "The Political Uses of Alienation: W. E. B. Du Bois on Politics, Race, and Culture, 1893–1940," *American Quarterly* 42 (June 1990): 304.

[19]Lewis, *Du Bois,* 37–38; Thomas Babington Macaulay, "History," in *The Varieties of History: From Voltaire to the Present,* ed. Fritz Stern (New York: Vintage, 1956), 86. On the influence of Macaulay on Du Bois, see Rampersad, *Art and Imagination,* 33. Lewis and Rampersad have also argued persuasively that the historian and essayist Thomas Carlyle influenced Du Bois's understanding of history. See Lewis, *Du Bois,* 74–75, and Rampersad, *Art and Imagination,* 66–67.

[20]*Souls,* 54, 43–44.

[21]Ibid., 38–39. For a careful and succinct discussion of the sources on which Du Bois may have drawn in using the term "double consciousness," see Dickson D. Bruce Jr., "W. E. B. Du Bois and the Idea of Double Consciousness," *American Literature* 64 (June 1992): 299–309. For some recent responses to Du Bois's use of the term, see Gerald Early, ed., *Lure and Loathing: Essays on Race, Identity, and the Ambivalence of Assimilation* (New York: Allen Lane, 1993). Other significant discussions of Du Bois's idea of a divided consciousness include Wernor Sollors, *Beyond Ethnicity: Consent and Descent in American Culture* (New York: Oxford University Press, 1986), 249; Rampersad, *Art and Imagination,* 73–74; Sundquist, *To Wake the Nations,* 571–72; Reed, "Du Bois's 'Double Consciousness' "; and Lewis, *W. E. B. Du Bois,* 96. See also Sandra Adell, *Double Consciousness/Double Bind* (Urbana: University of Illinois Press, 1994), 11–19, and Shamoon Zamir, *Dark Voices: W. E. B. Du Bois and American Thought, 1888–1903* (Chicago: University of Chicago Press, 1995), 113–68. On the theme of alienation in Du Bois's thought, see Holt, "The Political Uses of Alienation," and Rampersad, *Art and Imagination,* 89.

[22]*Souls,* 39, 170–71.

[23]Ibid., 192–193, 174. For a recent discussion of Shakespearean tragedy that, echoing Du Bois, emphasizes the connection between tragedy and the refusal of human beings to acknowledge the ties that bind them, see Stanley Cavell, *Disowning Knowledge in Six Plays of Shakespeare* (Cambridge: Cambridge University Press, 1984). For a more general discussion of tragedy in Western culture, see Richard B. Sewell, *The Vision of Tragedy* (New Haven: Yale University Press, 1980). On Crummell, see Moses, *Alexander Crummell,* and Wilson Jeremiah Moses, ed., *Destiny and Race: Selected Writings, 1840–1898, Alexander Crummell* (Amherst: University of Massachusetts Press, 1992). For a more detailed dis-

cussion of Crummell as a tragic figure, see Robert Gooding-Williams, "Du Bois's Counter-Sublime," *Massachusetts Review* 35 (Spring–Summer 1994): 202–24.

[24]Du Bois adheres almost exactly to Hegel's scheme. Like Hegel, Du Bois mentions Greeks, Romans, and Indians. Du Bois's "Teuton" corresponds to Hegel's Germanic peoples. His "Mongolian" corresponds to Hegel's Chinese peoples (with whom Hegel explicitly associates the Mongols). Du Bois mentions Egyptians but not Persians. For Hegel, however, Egyptian spirit marked the last stage in the development of Persian civilization. For Williamson's discussion of the Hegelian echoes at work in Du Bois's philosophy of history, see Williamson, *Crucible of Race,* 401–11. On this point, see also Robert Gooding-Williams, "Evading Narrative Myth, Evading Prophetic Pragmatism: Cornel West's *The American Evasion of Philosophy,*" *Massachusetts Review* 32 (Winter 1991–92): 521–28. On Du Bois's indebtedness to Hegel's *Phenomenology of Spirit* (which was no less important to his thinking than Hegel's philosophy of history per se), see Robert Gooding-Williams, "Philosophy of History and Social Critique in *The Souls of Black Folk,*" *Social Science Information* 26 (1987): 99–114; Adell, *Double Consciousness/Double Bind;* and, especially, Zamir, *Dark Voices.* For a brief discussion of the folk roots of the figure of the seventh son, see page 197 n. 5.

[25]For Hegel's remarks on Africa, see G. W. F. Hegel, *The Philosophy of History,* trans. J. Sibree (New York: Dover, 1956), 91–99. For a striking and ironic treatment of these remarks that contrasts sharply with Du Bois's revision of Hegel, see James A. Snead, "Repetition as a Figure of Black Culture," in *Black Literature and Literary Theory,* ed. Henry Louis Gates Jr. (New York: Methuen, 1984); *Souls,* 59–79.

[26]Lewis, *Du Bois,* 280; *Souls,* 40–41; Shakespeare, *Macbeth,* 3.4.102–3; Du Bois, *Dusk of Dawn,* 551. Standard scholarly histories of Reconstruction with which a reading of *Souls* might be combined include John Hope Franklin, *Reconstruction after the Civil War* (Chicago: University of Chicago Press, 1960); Leon F. Litwack, *Been in the Storm So Long: The Aftermath of Slavery* (New York: Knopf, 1979); and Eric Foner, *Reconstruction: America's Unfinished Revolution, 1863–1877* (New York: Harper and Row, 1988). Du Bois later wrote a monumental history of Reconstruction, a book that is also written in a poetic mode and driven by his desire to bring class analysis, as well as a more favorable interpretation, to the role of Reconstruction in American history. That book, published in 1935, eventually inspired a modern revision of the interpretation of Reconstruction. See W. E. B. Du Bois, *Black Reconstruction in America, 1860–1880* (New York: Atheneum, 1935).

[27]W. E. B. Du Bois, "Reconstruction and Its Benefits," *American Historical Review* 15 (1909–10): 781–99. On Du Bois and American historical memory, see David W. Blight, "W. E. B. Du Bois and the Struggle for American Historical Memory," in *History and Memory in African-American Culture,* ed. Genevieve Fabre and Robert O'Meally (New York: Oxford University Press, 1994), 45–71. On Du Bois as historian, see Charles H. Wesley, "W. E. B. Du Bois, Historian," *Freedomways* 5 (Winter 1965): 59–72; Jessie P. Guzman, "W. E. B. Du Bois—The Historian," *Journal of Negro Education* 30 (Fall 1961): 27–46; August Meier and Elliot Rudwick, *Black History and the Historical Profession, 1915–1980* (Urbana: University of Illinois Press, 1986), 5–6, 70–71, 279–80; and Clarence E. Walker, "Black Reconstruction in America: W. E. B. Du Bois's Challenge to the Dark and Bloody Ground of Reconstruction Historiography," manuscript copy provided by the author. An analysis rooted in literary and cultural theory is Keith E. Byerman, *Seizing the Word: History, Art, and Self in the Work of W. E. B. Du Bois* (Athens: University of Georgia Press, 1994). An important discussion of Du Bois's use of the rhetoric of the Jeremiad is David Howard-Pitney, *The Afro-American Jeremiad: Appeals for Justice in America* (Philadelphia: Temple University Press, 1990), chaps. 4–5.

[28]*Souls,* 48.

[29]*Souls,* 54–55. The phrase "clasping hands across the bloody chasm" became a shibboleth, a common bonding slogan in the gradual development of a culture of reconciliation in the decades after the Civil War. Du Bois's use of language such as "no man clasped the hands of these passing figures of the present-past" is probably an allusion to this

much-used phrase. He gives it a decidedly different cast and meaning. On the role of the romantic in the culture of reconciliation, see Nina Silber, *The Romance of Reunion: Northerners and the South, 1865–1900* (Chapel Hill: University of North Carolina Press, 1993), esp. chaps. 2–4.

[30]Sundquist, *To Wake the Nations,* 498; *Souls,* 60.

[31]*Souls,* 62. On the rise of Booker T. Washington and the Tuskegee Machine, see Louis R. Harlan, *Booker T. Washington: The Making of a Black Leader, 1856–1901* (New York: Oxford University Press, 1972), and *Booker T. Washington: The Wizard of Tuskegee, 1901–1915* (New York: Oxford University Press, 1984), chaps. 2–3; August Meier, *Negro Thought in America, 1880–1915: Racial Ideologies in the Age of Booker T. Washington* (Ann Arbor: University of Michigan Press, 1963), esp. 100–18; and Hugh Hawkins, ed., *Booker T. Washington and His Critics* (Lexington, Mass.: Lexington Books, 1974).

[32]See W. E. B. Du Bois, "The Talented Tenth," in *Negro Social and Political Thought, 1850–1920, Representative Texts,* ed. Howard Brotz (New York: Basic Books, 1966), 518–33.

[33]*Souls,* 67, 62, 70.

[34]Ibid., 102.

[35]Ibid., 111. Thirty-seven articles or series of articles on the South from *Harper's* are reprinted in *The South: A Collection from* Harper's *Magazine* (New York: Gallery Books, 1990). Thomas Nelson Page, Rebecca Harding Davis, John Esten Cooke, and others made the South into an object of nostalgia and exoticism, an image which dominated the content of popular magazines in the late nineteenth and early twentieth centuries. The articles were often travelogues and accounts of tourists' adventures. The opening lines of Davis's "Here and There in the South" series aptly represent the genre Du Bois sought to appropriate and critique in *Souls:* "The train that rushed out of the wide winding suburbs of Washington down into Virginia, in the dawn of a cold February morning, was filled with Northerners going to New Orleans. They had, oddly enough, the alert, expectant air of explorers into an unknown country. The men looked out on the sleepy streets of Alexandria with as critical eyes as if it had been its namesake in Egypt, and the women buttoned their tight ulsters more closely, and slung their alligator satchels to their sides in readiness for any emergency. . . . This three-cornered segment of their country, which had a climate, history, and character of its own, was foreign to them as Arabia Felix" (*The South,* 485). Du Bois's use of a journey motif in *Souls* and in other writings is both part of and subversive of this popular travel genre.

[36]*Souls,* 121, 131, 132.

[37]Ibid., 143–45.

[38]Du Bois to William James, June 12, 1906, Du Bois Papers, reel 2. On the dialectic between pain and beauty in *Souls,* also see John Edgar Wideman, introduction to *The Souls of Black Folk,* by W. E. B. Du Bois (New York: Vintage, Library of America, 1990), xi, xv–xvi.

[39]Langston Hughes to Du Bois, May 22, 1956, Du Bois Papers, reel 71. On the number of editions, see Paul Partington to A. C. McClurg & Co., May 23, 1961, and R. W. Barber of McClurg to Partington, June 1, 1961, Du Bois Papers, box 360. On plates, see Du Bois to Herbert Aptheker, January 7, 1949, and A. C. McClurg to Du Bois, January 18, 1949, Du Bois Papers, box 359. At least as early as 1926, Du Bois urged McClurg to publish a more "popular edition" of *Souls,* or at least to allow him to purchase the plates. At that time McClurg responded that the book was still selling approximately five hundred copies per year and that it would not sell the plates. See Du Bois to A. C. McClurg, March 4, 1926, and A. C. McClurg & Co. to Du Bois, March 9, 1926, Du Bois Papers, reel 19. On the various editions until the late 1980s, especially the Blue Heron Press edition, see Herbert Aptheker, *The Literary Legacy of W. E. B. Du Bois* (White Plains, N.Y.: Kraus International, 1989), 75–86. On the effort to produce the fiftieth-anniversary edition by a private group, see memorandum by Kyrle Elkin, New York, December 21, 1951, Du Bois Papers, reel 66.

[40]John Daniels, review of *Souls, Alexander's Magazine,* September 15, 1905, 10–11, reprinted in *Critical Essays on W. E. B. Du Bois,* ed. William L. Andrews (Boston: G. K. Hall,

1985), 37–38. On the pride demonstrated in a variety of black reviews and for a thorough survey of the reviews generally, see Aptheker, *Literary Legacy*, 51–69.

[41]Jessie Fauset to Du Bois, December 16, 1903, in *The Correspondence of W. E. B. Du Bois, Selections, 1877–1934*, ed. Herbert Aptheker (Amherst: University of Massachusetts Press, 1973), 1:66.

[42]*Nashville American*, September 26, 1903; *Houston Chronicle*, August 15, 1903. John Spencer Bassett, "Two Negro Leaders," *South Atlantic Quarterly* 2 (July 1903): 267–72. *Souls*, 141. The Bassett review of *Souls* has not been noted by other scholars. This is ironic, since later in 1903 Bassett created a storm of protest over an article he wrote condemning lynching, declaring Washington the greatest southerner since Robert E. Lee, and suggesting that blacks might one day rise and demand their equality. Some members of the board of trustees of Trinity College (later Duke University), where Bassett taught, as well as much of the white press in North Carolina, sought Bassett's ouster. The professor narrowly retained his job, but not before denouncing social equality between the races and aligning himself securely with the "conservative" tradition of southern racial thought. Bassett in fact had a low regard for black capacities generally, and he believed in permanent segregation. But he had allowed himself to admire the style and content of Du Bois's book, and reading *Souls* probably helped inspire the controversial piece that nearly got him fired. See John Spencer Bassett, "Stirring Up the Fires of Race Antipathy," *South Atlantic Quarterly* 2 (October 1903): 297–305. Bassett was trained in the detached, "scientific" historical method by Herbert Baxter Adams at Johns Hopkins University in the 1890s, at the same time Du Bois was trained by Albert Bushnell Hart in similar methods at Harvard. Bassett wrote two books on slavery in North Carolina; more than any other white southern scholar of his time, he treated the black experience, especially slave religion, seriously. On Bassett as a scholar, see John David Smith, *An Old Creed for the New South: Proslavery Ideology and Historiography, 1865–1918* (1985; reprint, Athens: University of Georgia Press, 1991), 144–47. On the Bassett case in North Carolina and the ways he fits the tradition of southern "conservatism" on race in that era, see Williamson, *Crucible of Race*, 261–71. This strange encounter across the color line remained literary; so far as can be determined, Du Bois and Bassett may never have met. Du Bois had a similar, and more direct, encounter over *Souls* in correspondence. See p. 264 in this book.

[43]*The Annals of the American Academy of Political and Social Science* 22 (July–December 1903): 230–31.

[44]*The Public*, April 18, 1903; *Conservator*, May, 1903, 43.

[45]William H. Ferris, *The African Abroad* (New Haven: Tuttle, Morehouse, and Taylor, 1913), quoted in Andrews, *Critical Essays*, 127, 125. James Weldon Johnson, *Along This Way: The Autobiography of James Weldon Johnson* (New York: Viking, 1933), 203. Johnson's reaction comes in the context of remembering his first meeting with Du Bois in 1904: "I had been deeply moved and influenced by the book, and was anxious to meet the author. I met a quiet, handsome and unpedantic young man. . . . Indeed, it was at first slightly difficult to reconcile the brooding but intransigent spirit of *The Souls of Black Folk* with this apparently so light-hearted man, this man so abundantly endowed with the gift of laughter. I noted then what, through many years of close association, I have since learned well, and what the world knows not at all: that Du Bois in battle is a stern, bitter, relentless fighter, who, when he has put aside his sword, is among his particular friends the most jovial and fun-loving of men." J. Saunders Redding, introduction to *The Souls of Black Folk*, by W. E. B. Du Bois (Greenwich, Conn.: Faucet, 1961), ix; Henry Louis Gates Jr., ed., introduction, "Darkly as Through a Veil," *The Souls of Black Folk*, by W. E. B. Du Bois (New York: Bantam, 1989), xvii. One of the most probing, critical essays on *Souls* is Robert B. Stepto, "The Quest of the Weary Traveler: W. E. B. Du Bois's *The Souls of Black Folk*," in *From behind the Veil: A Study of Afro-American Narrative* (Urbana: University of Illinois Press, 1979), 52–91. Other important literary treatments of *Souls* can be found in Andrews, ed., *Critical Essays*. Also see Arnold Rampersad, "Slavery and the Literary Imagination: Du Bois's *The Souls of Black*

Folk," in *Slavery and the Literary Imagination: Selected Papers from the English Institute, 1987,* ed. Deborah E. McDowell and Arnold Rampersad (Baltimore: Johns Hopkins University Press, 1989), 104–24.

[46]W. E. B. Du Bois, "The Development of a People," *International Journal of Ethics* 14 (April 1904): 292–311, reprinted in *Writings of W. E. B. Du Bois in Periodicals Edited by Others,* vol. 1, *1891–1909,* ed. Herbert Aptheker (Millwood, N.Y.: Kraus-Thompson, 1982), 203–15.

[47]Rampersad, *Art and Imagination,* 229, 73–80.

[48]Peter Gay, *Style in History: Gibbon, Ranke, Macaulay, Burghardt* (New York: Oxford University Press, 1974), 6; Sundquist, *To Wake the Nations,* 530, 539. For more on *Souls* as a "musical book," see Houston A. Baker, *Modernism and the Harlem Renaissance* (Chicago: University of Chicago Press, 1987), 53–69.

[49]D. Tabak to Du Bois, undated, Du Bois Papers, reel 3 (see p. 260 in this book); *Souls,* 192, 189, 186, 192–93.

[50]*Souls,* 193. On the epigraphs, and for the most thorough discussion of Du Bois's study of and sources for understanding the spirituals, see Sundquist, *To Wake the Nations,* 467–539. Also see Shamoon Zamir, "The Sorrow Songs / 'Song of Myself': Du Bois, the Crisis of Leadership, and Prophetic Imagination," in *The Black Columbiad: Defining Moments in African-American Literature and Culture,* ed. Wernor Sollors and Maria Diedrich (Cambridge: Harvard University Press, 1994), 145–66.

PART ONE

The Document

The Souls of Black Folk

Herein Is Written

The Forethought

Herein lie buried many things which if read with patience may show the strange meaning of being black here in the dawning of the Twentieth Century. This meaning is not without interest to you, Gentle Reader; for the problem of the Twentieth Century is the problem of the color-line.[1]

I pray you, then, receive my little book in all charity, studying my words with me, forgiving mistake and foible for sake of the faith and passion that is in me, and seeking the grain of truth hidden there.

I have sought here to sketch, in vague, uncertain outline, the spiritual world in which ten thousand thousand Americans live and strive. First, in two chapters I have tried to show what Emancipation meant to them, and what was its aftermath. In a third chapter I have pointed out the slow rise of personal leadership, and criticised candidly the leader[2] who bears the chief burden of his race to-day. Then, in two other chapters I have sketched in swift outline the two worlds within and without the Veil,[3] and thus have come to the central problem of training men for life. Venturing now into deeper detail, I have in two chapters studied the struggles of the massed millions of the black peasantry, and in another have sought to make clear the present relations of the sons of master and man.

Leaving, then, the world of the white man, I have stepped within the Veil, raising it that you may view faintly its deeper recesses, — the meaning of its religion, the passion of its human sorrow, and the struggle of its greater souls. All this I have ended with a tale twice told but seldom written.[4]

Some of these thoughts of mine have seen the light before in other guise. For kindly consenting to their republication here, in altered and extended form, I must thank the publishers of *The Atlantic Monthly, The World's Work, The Dial, The New World,* and the *Annals of the American Academy of Political and Social Science.*

Before each chapter, as now printed, stands a bar of the Sorrow

Songs,—some echo of haunting melody from the only American music which welled up from black souls in the dark past. And, finally, need I add that I who speak here am bone of the bone and flesh of the flesh of them that live within the Veil?

W. E. B. Du B.

ATLANTA, GA., Feb. 1, 1903.

I

Of Our Spiritual Strivings

O water, voice of my heart, crying in the sand,
   All night long crying with a mournful cry,
As I lie and listen, and cannot understand
     The voice of my heart in my side or the voice of the sea,
O water, crying for rest, is it I, is it I?
   All night long the water is crying to me.

Unresting water, there shall never be rest
   Till the last moon droop and the last tide fail,
And the fire of the end begin to burn in the west;
     And the heart shall be weary and wonder and cry like the sea,
All life long crying without avail,
   As the water all night long is crying to me.

ARTHUR SYMONS.

Between me and the other world there is ever an unasked question: unasked by some through feelings of delicacy; by others through the difficulty of rightly framing it. All, nevertheless, flutter round it. They approach me in a half-hesitant sort of way, eye me curiously or compassionately, and then, instead of saying directly, How does it feel to be a problem? they say, I know an excellent colored man in my town; or, I fought at Mechanicsville;[2] or, Do not these Southern outrages make your blood boil? At these I smile, or am interested, or reduce the boiling to a simmer, as the occasion may require. To the real question, How does it feel to be a problem? I answer seldom a word.

And yet, being a problem is a strange experience,—peculiar even for one who has never been anything else, save perhaps in babyhood and in Europe. It is in the early days of rollicking boyhood that the revelation first bursts upon one, all in a day, as it were. I remember well when the shadow swept across me. I was a little thing, away up in the hills of New England, where the dark Housatonic[3] winds between Hoosac and Taghkanic to the sea. In a wee wooden schoolhouse, something put it into the boys' and girls' heads to buy gorgeous visiting-cards—ten cents a package—and exchange. The exchange was merry, till one girl, a tall newcomer, refused my card,—refused it peremptorily, with a glance. Then it dawned upon me with a certain suddenness that I was different from the others; or like, mayhap, in heart and life and longing, but shut out from their world by a vast veil. I had thereafter no desire to tear down that veil, to creep through; I held all beyond it in common contempt, and lived above it in a region of blue sky and great wandering shadows. That sky was bluest when I could beat my mates at examination-time, or beat them at a foot-race, or even beat their stringy heads. Alas, with the years all this fine contempt began to fade; for the worlds I longed for, and all their dazzling opportunities, were theirs, not mine. But they should not keep these prizes, I said; some, all, I would wrest from them. Just how I would do it I could never decide: by reading law, by healing the sick, by telling the wonderful tales that swam in my head,—some way. With other black boys the strife was not so fiercely sunny: their youth shrunk into tasteless sycophancy, or into silent hatred of the pale world about them and mocking distrust of everything white; or wasted itself in a bitter cry, Why did God make me an outcast and a stranger in mine own house? The shades of the prison-house closed round about us all: walls strait and stubborn to the whitest, but relentlessly narrow, tall, and unscalable to sons of night who must plod darkly on in resignation, or beat unavailing palms against the stone, or steadily, half hopelessly, watch the streak of blue above.[4]

After the Egyptian and Indian, the Greek and Roman, the Teuton and Mongolian, the Negro is a sort of seventh son,[5] born with a veil,[6] and gifted with second-sight in this American world,—a world which yields him no true self-consciousness, but only lets him see himself through the revelation of the other world. It is a peculiar sensation, this double-consciousness,[7] this sense of always looking at one's self through the eyes of others, of measuring one's soul by the tape of a world that looks on in amused contempt and pity. One ever feels his two-ness,—an American, a Negro; two souls, two thoughts, two unreconciled strivings; two warring ideals in one dark body, whose dogged strength alone keeps it from being torn asunder.

The history of the American Negro is the history of this strife, — this longing to attain self-conscious manhood, to merge his double self into a better and truer self. In this merging he wishes neither of the older selves to be lost. He would not Africanize America, for America has too much to teach the world and Africa. He would not bleach his Negro soul in a flood of white Americanism, for he knows that Negro blood has a message for the world. He simply wishes to make it possible for a man to be both a Negro and an American, without being cursed and spit upon by his fellows, without having the doors of Opportunity closed roughly in his face.[8]

This, then, is the end of his striving: to be a co-worker in the kingdom of culture, to escape both death and isolation, to husband and use his best powers and his latent genius. These powers of body and mind have in the past been strangely wasted, dispersed, or forgotten. The shadow of a mighty Negro past flits through the tale of Ethiopia the Shadowy and of Egypt the Sphinx. Throughout history, the powers of single black men flash here and there like falling stars, and die sometimes before the world has rightly gauged their brightness. Here in America, in the few days since Emancipation, the black man's turning hither and thither in hesitant and doubtful striving has often made his very strength to lose effectiveness, to seem like absence of power, like weakness. And yet it is not weakness, — it is the contradiction of double aims. The double-aimed struggle of the black artisan — on the one hand to escape white contempt for a nation of mere hewers of wood and drawers of water, and on the other hand to plough and nail and dig for a poverty-stricken horde — could only result in making him a poor craftsman, for he had but half a heart in either cause. By the poverty and ignorance of his people, the Negro minister or doctor was tempted toward quackery and demagogy; and by the criticism of the other world, toward ideals that made him ashamed of his lowly tasks. The would-be black *savant* was confronted by the paradox that the knowledge his people needed was a twice-told tale to his white neighbors, while the knowledge which would teach the white world was Greek to his own flesh and blood. The innate love of harmony and beauty that set the ruder souls of his people a-dancing and a-singing raised but confusion and doubt in the soul of the black artist; for the beauty revealed to him was the soul-beauty of a race which his larger audience despised, and he could not articulate the message of another people. This waste of double aims, this seeking to satisfy two unreconciled ideals, has wrought sad havoc with the courage and faith and deeds of ten thousand thousand people,—has sent them often wooing false gods and invoking false means of salvation, and at times has even seemed about to make them ashamed of themselves.

Away back in the days of bondage they thought to see in one divine event the end of all doubt and disappointment; few men ever worshipped Freedom with half such unquestioning faith as did the American Negro for two centuries. To him, so far as he thought and dreamed, slavery was indeed the sum of all villainies, the cause of all sorrow, the root of all prejudice; Emancipation was the key to a promised land of sweeter beauty than ever stretched before the eyes of wearied Israelites.[9] In song and exhortation swelled one refrain—Liberty; in his tears and curses the God he implored had Freedom in his right hand. At last it came,—suddenly, fearfully, like a dream. With one wild carnival of blood and passion came the message in his own plaintive cadences:—

> "Shout, O children!
> Shout, you're free!
> For God has bought your liberty!"[10]

Years have passed away since then,—ten, twenty, forty; forty years of national life, forty years of renewal and development, and yet the swarthy spectre sits in its accustomed seat at the Nation's feast. In vain do we cry to this our vastest social problem:—

> "Take any shape but that, and my firm nerves
> Shall never tremble!"[11]

The Nation has not yet found peace from its sins; the freedman has not yet found in freedom his promised land. Whatever of good may have come in these years of change, the shadow of a deep disappointment rests upon the Negro people,—a disappointment all the more bitter because the unattained ideal was unbounded save by the simple ignorance of a lowly people.

The first decade was merely a prolongation of the vain search for freedom, the boon that seemed ever barely to elude their grasp,—like a tantalizing will-o'-the-wisp, maddening and misleading the headless host. The holocaust of war, the terrors of the Ku-Klux Klan,[12] the lies of carpetbaggers,[13] the disorganization of industry, and the contradictory advice of friends and foes, left the bewildered serf with no new watchword beyond the old cry for freedom. As the time flew, however, he began to grasp a new idea. The ideal of liberty demanded for its attainment powerful means, and these the Fifteenth Amendment gave him.[14] The ballot, which before he had looked upon as a visible sign of freedom, he now regarded as the chief means of gaining and perfecting the liberty with which war had partially endowed him. And why not? Had not votes made war and emancipated millions? Had not votes enfranchised the freedmen? Was anything impossible to a power that had done all this? A million black men started with renewed zeal to vote themselves into the kingdom. So the decade flew away, the revolution of 1876 came,[15] and left the half-free serf weary, wondering, but still inspired. Slowly but steadily, in the following years, a new vision began gradually to replace the dream of political power,— a powerful movement, the rise of another ideal to guide the unguided, another pillar of fire by night after a clouded day. It was the ideal of "book-learning"; the curiosity, born of compulsory ignorance, to know and test the power of the cabalistic letters of the white man, the longing to know. Here at last seemed to have been discovered the mountain path to Canaan; longer than the highway of Emancipation and law, steep and rugged, but straight, leading to heights high enough to overlook life.

Up the new path the advance guard toiled, slowly, heavily, doggedly; only those who have watched and guided the faltering feet, the misty minds, the dull understandings, of the dark pupils of these schools know how faithfully, how piteously, this people strove to learn. It was weary work. The cold statistician wrote down the inches of progress here and there, noted also where here and there a foot had slipped or some one had fallen. To the tired climbers, the horizon was ever dark, the mists were often cold, the Canaan was always dim and far away. If, however, the vistas disclosed as yet no goal, no resting-place, little but flattery and criticism, the journey at least gave leisure for reflection and self-examination; it changed the child of Emancipation to the youth with dawning self-consciousness, self-realization, self-respect. In those sombre forests of his striving his own soul rose before him, and he saw himself,— darkly as through a veil;[16] and yet he saw in himself some faint revelation of his power, of his mission. He began to have a dim feeling that, to attain his place in the world, he must be himself, and not another. For the first time he sought to analyze the burden he bore upon his back, that dead-weight of social degradation partially masked behind a half-named Negro problem. He felt his poverty; without a cent, without a home, without land, tools, or savings, he had entered into competition with rich, landed, skilled neighbors. To be a poor man is hard, but to be a poor race in a land of dollars is the very bottom of hardships. He felt the weight of his ignorance,—not simply of letters, but of life, of business, of the humanities; the accumulated sloth and shirking and awkwardness of decades and centuries shackled his hands and feet. Nor was his burden all poverty and ignorance. The red stain of bastardy, which two centuries of systematic legal defilement of Negro women had stamped upon his race, meant not only the loss of ancient African chastity, but also the hereditary weight of a mass of corruption from white adulterers, threatening almost the obliteration of the Negro home.

A people thus handicapped ought not to be asked to race with the world, but rather allowed to give all its time and thought to its own social problems. But alas! while sociologists gleefully count his bastards and his prostitutes, the very soul of the toiling, sweating black man is darkened by the shadow of a vast despair. Men call the shadow prejudice, and learnedly explain it as the natural defence of culture against barbarism, learning against ignorance, purity against crime, the "higher" against the "lower" races.[17] To which the Negro cries Amen! and swears that to so much of this strange prejudice as is founded on just homage to civilization, culture, righteousness, and progress, he humbly bows and meekly does obeisance. But before that nameless prejudice that leaps beyond all this he stands helpless, dismayed, and well-nigh speechless; before that personal disrespect and mockery, the ridicule and systematic humiliation, the distortion of fact and wanton license of fancy, the cynical ignoring of the better and the boisterous welcoming of the worse, the all-pervading desire to inculcate disdain for everything black, from Toussaint[18] to the devil,—before this there rises a sickening despair that would disarm and discourage any nation save that black host to whom "discouragement" is an unwritten word.

But the facing of so vast a prejudice could not but bring the inevitable self-questioning, self-disparagement, and lowering of ideals which ever accompany repression and breed in an atmosphere of contempt and hate. Whisperings and portents came borne upon the four winds: Lo! we are diseased and dying, cried the dark hosts; we cannot write, our voting is vain; what need of education, since we must always cook and serve? And the Nation echoed and enforced this self-criticism, saying: Be content to be servants, and nothing more; what need of higher culture for half-men? Away with the black man's ballot, by force or fraud,—and behold the suicide of a race! Nevertheless, out of the evil came something of good,— the more careful adjustment of education to real life, the clearer perception of the Negroes' social responsibilities, and the sobering realization of the meaning of progress.

So dawned the time of *Sturm und Drang:*[19] storm and stress to-day rocks our little boat on the mad waters of the world-sea; there is within and without the sound of conflict, the burning of body and rending of soul; inspiration strives with doubt, and faith with vain questionings. The bright ideals of the past,—physical freedom, political power, the training of brains and the training of hands,—all these in turn have waxed and waned, until even the last grows dim and overcast. Are they all wrong,—all false? No, not that, but each alone was over-simple and incomplete,—the dreams of a credulous race-childhood, or the fond imaginings of the other world which does not know and does not want to know our power. To be really true, all these ideals must be melted and welded into one. The training of the schools we need to-day more than ever,—the training of deft hands, quick eyes and ears, and above all the broader, deeper, higher culture of gifted minds and pure hearts. The power of the ballot we need in sheer self-defence,[20]—else what shall save us from a second slavery? Freedom, too, the long-sought, we still seek,—the freedom of life and limb, the freedom to work and think, the freedom to love and aspire. Work, culture, liberty,—all these we need, not singly but together, not successively but together, each growing and aiding each, and all striving toward that vaster ideal that swims before the Negro people, the ideal of human brotherhood, gained through the unifying ideal of Race; the ideal of fostering and developing the traits and talents of the Negro, not in opposition to or contempt for other races, but rather in large conformity to the greater ideals of the American Republic, in order that some day on American soil two world-races may give each to each those characteristics both so sadly lack. We the darker ones come even now not altogether empty-handed: there are to-day no truer exponents of the pure human spirit of the Declaration of Independence than the American Negroes; there is no true American music but the wild sweet melodies of the Negro slave; the American fairy tales and folk-lore are Indian and African; and, all in all, we black men seem the sole oasis of simple faith and reverence in a dusty desert of dollars and smartness. Will America be poorer if she replace her brutal dyspeptic blundering with light-hearted but determined Negro humility?[21] or her coarse and cruel wit with loving jovial good-humor? or her vulgar music with the soul of the Sorrow Songs?

Merely a concrete test of the underlying principles of the great republic is the Negro Problem, and the spiritual striving of the freedmen's sons is the travail of souls whose burden is almost beyond the measure of their strength, but who bear it in the name of an historic race, in the name of this the land of their fathers' fathers, and in the name of human opportunity.

And now what I have briefly sketched in large outline let me on coming pages tell again in many ways, with loving emphasis and deeper detail, that men may listen to the striving in the souls of black folk.

II

Of the Dawn of Freedom

Careless seems the great Avenger;
  History's lessons but record
One death-grapple in the darkness
  'Twixt old systems and the Word;
Truth forever on the scaffold,
  Wrong forever on the throne;
Yet that scaffold sways the future,
  And behind the dim unknown
Standeth God within the shadow
  Keeping watch above His own.

LOWELL.

The problem of the twentieth century is the problem of the color-line,
—the relation of the darker to the lighter races of men in Asia and Africa,
in America and the islands of the sea. It was a phase of this problem that
caused the Civil War; and however much they who marched South and
North in 1861 may have fixed on the technical points of union and local
autonomy as a shibboleth, all nevertheless knew, as we know, that the
question of Negro slavery was the real cause of the conflict. Curious it
was, too, how this deeper question ever forced itself to the surface despite
effort and disclaimer. No sooner had Northern armies touched Southern
soil than this old question, newly guised, sprang from the earth,—What
shall be done with Negroes? Peremptory military commands, this way
and that, could not answer the query; the Emancipation Proclamation
seemed but to broaden and intensify the difficulties; and the War Amendments[2] made the Negro problems of to-day.

It is the aim of this essay to study the period of history from 1861 to 1872 so far as it relates to the American Negro. In effect, this tale of the dawn of Freedom is an account of that government of men called the Freedmen's Bureau,[3]—one of the most singular and interesting of the attempts made by a great nation to grapple with vast problems of race and social condition.

The war has naught to do with slaves, cried Congress, the President, and the Nation; and yet no sooner had the armies, East and West, penetrated Virginia and Tennessee than fugitive slaves appeared within their lines. They came at night, when the flickering camp-fires shone like vast unsteady stars along the black horizon: old men and thin, with gray and tufted hair; women, with frightened eyes, dragging whimpering hungry children; men and girls, stalwart and gaunt,—a horde of starving vagabonds, homeless, helpless, and pitiable, in their dark distress. Two methods of treating these newcomers seemed equally logical to opposite sorts of minds. Ben Butler, in Virginia, quickly declared slave property contraband of war, and put the fugitives to work; while Fremont, in Missouri, declared the slaves free under martial law.[4] Butler's action was approved, but Fremont's was hastily countermanded, and his successor, Halleck,[5] saw things differently. "Hereafter," he commanded, "no slaves should be allowed to come into your lines at all; if any come without your knowledge, when owners call for them deliver them." Such a policy was difficult to enforce; some of the black refugees declared themselves freemen, others showed that their masters had deserted them, and still others were captured with forts and plantations. Evidently, too, slaves were a source of strength to the Confederacy, and were being used as laborers and producers. "They constitute a military resource," wrote Secretary Cameron,[6] late in 1861; "and being such, that they should not be turned over to the enemy is too plain to discuss." So gradually the tone of the army chiefs changed; Congress forbade the rendition of fugitives, and Butler's "contrabands" were welcomed as military laborers. This complicated rather than solved the problem, for now the scattering fugitives became a steady stream, which flowed faster as the armies marched.

Then the long-headed man with care-chiselled face who sat in the White House saw the inevitable, and emancipated the slaves of rebels on New Year's, 1863.[7] A month later Congress called earnestly for the Negro soldiers whom the act of July, 1862, had half grudgingly allowed to enlist.[8] Thus the barriers were levelled and the deed was done. The stream of fugitives swelled to a flood, and anxious army officers kept inquiring: "What must be done with slaves, arriving almost daily? Are we to find food and shelter for women and children?"

It was a Pierce of Boston who pointed out the way, and thus became in a sense the founder of the Freedmen's Bureau. He was a firm friend of Secretary Chase; and when, in 1861, the care of slaves and abandoned lands devolved upon the Treasury officials, Pierce was specially detailed from the ranks to study the conditions. First, he cared for the refugees at Fortress Monroe; and then, after Sherman had captured Hilton Head, Pierce was sent there to found his Port Royal experiment of making free workingmen out of slaves.[9] Before his experiment was barely started, however, the problem of the fugitives had assumed such proportions that it was taken from the hands of the over-burdened Treasury Department and given to the army officials. Already centres of massed freedmen were forming at Fortress Monroe, Washington, New Orleans, Vicksburg and Corinth, Columbus, Ky., and Cairo, Ill., as well as at Port Royal.[10] Army chaplains found here new and fruitful fields; "superintendents of contrabands" multiplied, and some attempt at systematic work was made by enlisting the able-bodied men and giving work to the others.

Then came the Freedmen's Aid societies,[11] born of the touching appeals from Pierce and from these other centres of distress. There was the American Missionary Association, sprung from the *Amistad*,[12] and now full-grown for work; the various church organizations, the National Freedmen's Relief Association, the American Freedmen's Union, the Western Freedmen's Aid Commission, — in all fifty or more active organizations, which sent clothes, money, school-books, and teachers southward. All they did was needed, for the destitution of the freedmen was often reported as "too appalling for belief," and the situation was daily growing worse rather than better.

And daily, too, it seemed more plain that this was no ordinary matter of temporary relief, but a national crisis; for here loomed a labor problem of vast dimensions. Masses of Negroes stood idle, or, if they worked spasmodically, were never sure of pay; and if perchance they received pay, squandered the new thing thoughtlessly. In these and other ways were camp-life and the new liberty demoralizing the freedmen. The broader economic organization thus clearly demanded sprang up here and there as accident and local conditions determined. Here it was that Pierce's Port Royal plan of leased plantations and guided workmen pointed out the rough way. In Washington the military governor, at the urgent appeal of the superintendent, opened confiscated estates to the cultivation of the fugitives, and there in the shadow of the dome gathered black farm villages. General Dix gave over estates to the freedmen of Fortress Monroe, and so on, South and West. The government and benevolent societies furnished the means of cultivation, and the Negro turned again slowly to work. The systems of control, thus started, rapidly grew, here and there, into strange little governments, like that of General Banks in Louisiana, with its ninety thousand black subjects, its fifty thousand guided laborers, and its annual budget of one hundred thousand dollars and more. It made out four thousand pay-rolls a year, registered all freedmen, inquired into grievances and redressed them, laid and collected taxes, and established a system of public schools. So, too, Colonel Eaton, the superintendent of Tennessee and Arkansas, ruled over one hundred thousand freedmen, leased and cultivated seven thousand acres of cotton land, and fed ten thousand paupers a year. In South Carolina was General Saxton, with his deep interest in black folk.[13] He succeeded Pierce and the Treasury officials, and sold forfeited estates, leased abandoned plantations, encouraged schools, and received from Sherman, after that terribly picturesque march to the sea, thousands of the wretched camp followers.

Three characteristic things one might have seen in Sherman's raid through Georgia, which threw the new situation in shadowy relief: the Conqueror,[14] the Conquered, and the Negro. Some see all significance in the grim front of the destroyer, and some in the bitter sufferers of the Lost Cause.[15] But to me neither soldier nor fugitive speaks with so deep a meaning as that dark human cloud that clung like remorse on the rear of those swift columns, swelling at times to half their size, almost engulfing and choking them. In vain were they ordered back, in vain were bridges hewn from beneath their feet; on they trudged and writhed and surged, until they rolled into Savannah, a starved and naked horde of tens of thousands. There too came the characteristic military remedy: "The islands from Charleston south, the abandoned rice-fields along the rivers for thirty miles back from the sea, and the country bordering the St. John's River, Florida, are reserved and set apart for the settlement of Negroes now made free by act of war." So read the celebrated "Fieldorder Number Fifteen."[16]

All these experiments, orders, and systems were bound to attract and perplex the government and the nation. Directly after the Emancipation Proclamation, Representative Eliot had introduced a bill creating a Bureau of Emancipation; but it was never reported. The following June a committee of inquiry, appointed by the Secretary of War, reported in favor of a temporary bureau for the "improvement, protection, and employment of refugee freedmen," on much the same lines as were afterwards followed. Petitions came in to President Lincoln from distinguished citizens and organizations, strongly urging a comprehensive and unified plan of dealing with the freedmen, under a bureau which should be "charged with the study of plans and execution of measures for easily guiding, and in every way judiciously and humanely aiding, the passage of our emancipated and yet to be emancipated blacks from the old condition of forced labor to their new state of voluntary industry."

Some half-hearted steps were taken to accomplish this, in part, by putting the whole matter again in charge of the special Treasury agents. Laws of 1863 and 1864 directed them to take charge of and lease abandoned lands for periods not exceeding twelve months, and to "provide in such leases, or otherwise, for the employment and general welfare" of the freedmen. Most of the army officers greeted this as a welcome relief from perplexing "Negro affairs," and Secretary Fessenden, July 29, 1864, issued an excellent system of regulations, which were afterward closely followed by General Howard.[17] Under Treasury agents, large quantities of land were leased in the Mississippi Valley, and many Negroes were employed; but in August, 1864, the new regulations were suspended for reasons of "public policy," and the army was again in control.

Meanwhile Congress had turned its attention to the subject; and in March the House passed a bill by a majority of two establishing a Bureau for Freedmen in the War Department. Charles Sumner,[18] who had charge of the bill in the Senate, argued that freedmen and abandoned lands ought to be under the same department, and reported a substitute for the House bill attaching the Bureau to the Treasury Department. This bill passed, but too late for action by the House. The debates wandered over the whole policy of the administration and the general question of slavery, without touching very closely the specific merits of the measure in hand. Then the national election took place; and the administration, with a vote of renewed confidence from the country, addressed itself to the matter more seriously. A conference between the two branches of Congress agreed upon a carefully drawn measure which contained the chief provisions of Sumner's bill, but made the proposed organization a department independent of both the War and the Treasury officials. The bill was conservative, giving the new department "general superintendence of all freedmen." Its purpose was to "establish regulations" for them, protect them, lease them lands, adjust their wages, and appear in civil and military courts as their "next friend." There were many limitations attached to the powers thus granted, and the organization was made permanent. Nevertheless, the

Senate defeated the bill, and a new conference committee was appointed. This committee reported a new bill, February 28, which was whirled through just as the session closed, and became the act of 1865 establishing in the War Department a "Bureau of Refugees, Freedmen, and Abandoned Lands."[19]

This last compromise was a hasty bit of legislation, vague and uncertain in outline. A Bureau was created, "to continue during the present War of Rebellion, and for one year thereafter," to which was given "the supervision and management of all abandoned lands and the control of all subjects relating to refugees and freedmen," under "such rules and regulations as may be presented by the head of the Bureau and approved by the President." A Commissioner, appointed by the President and Senate, was to control the Bureau, with an office force not exceeding ten clerks. The President might also appoint assistant commissioners in the seceded States, and to all these offices military officials might be detailed at regular pay. The Secretary of War could issue rations, clothing, and fuel to the destitute, and all abandoned property was placed in the hands of the Bureau for eventual lease and sale to ex-slaves in forty-acre parcels.[20]

Thus did the United States government definitely assume charge of the emancipated Negro as the ward of the nation. It was a tremendous undertaking. Here at a stroke of the pen was erected a government of millions of men, — and not ordinary men either, but black men emasculated by a peculiarly complete system of slavery, centuries old; and now, suddenly, violently, they come into a new birthright, at a time of war and passion, in the midst of the stricken and embittered population of their former masters. Any man might well have hesitated to assume charge of such a work, with vast responsibilities, indefinite powers, and limited resources. Probably no one but a soldier would have answered such a call promptly; and, indeed, no one but a soldier could be called, for Congress had appropriated no money for salaries and expenses.

Less than a month after the weary Emancipator passed to his rest, his successor assigned Major-Gen. Oliver O. Howard to duty as Commissioner of the new Bureau. He was a Maine man, then only thirty-five years of age. He had marched with Sherman to the sea, had fought well at Gettysburg, and but the year before had been assigned to the command of the Department of Tennessee. An honest man, with too much faith in human nature, little aptitude for business and intricate detail, he had had large opportunity of becoming acquainted at first hand with much of the work before him. And of that work it has been truly said that "no approximately correct history of civilization can ever be written which does not throw out in bold relief, as one of the great landmarks of political and social progress, the organization and administration of the Freedmen's Bureau."

On May 12, 1865, Howard was appointed; and he assumed the duties of his office promptly on the 15th, and began examining the field of work. A curious mess he looked upon: little despotisms, communistic experiments, slavery, peonage, business speculations, organized charity, unorganized alms-giving, — all reeling on under the guise of helping the freedmen, and all enshrined in the smoke and blood of war and the cursing and silence of angry men. On May 19 the new government— for a government it really was—issued its constitution; commissioners were to be appointed in each of the seceded States, who were to take charge of "all subjects relating to refugees and freedmen," and all relief and rations were to be given by their consent alone. The Bureau invited continued cooperation with benevolent societies, and declared: "It will be the object of all commissioners to introduce practicable systems of compensated labor," and to establish schools. Forthwith nine assistant commissioners were appointed. They were to hasten to their fields of work; seek gradually to close relief establishments, and make the destitute self-supporting; act as courts of law where there were no courts, or where Negroes were not recognized in them as free; establish the institution of marriage among ex-slaves, and keep records; see that freedmen were free to choose their employers, and help in making fair contracts for them; and finally, the circular said: "Simple good faith, for which we hope on all hands for those concerned in the passing away of slavery, will especially relieve the assistant commissioners in the discharge of their duties toward the freedmen, as well as promote the general welfare."

No sooner was the work thus started, and the general system and local organization in some measure begun, than two grave difficulties appeared which changed largely the theory and outcome of Bureau work. First, there were the abandoned lands of the South. It had long been the more or less definitely expressed theory of the North that all the chief problems of Emancipation might be settled by establishing the slaves on the forfeited lands of their masters, — a sort of poetic justice, said some. But this poetry done into solemn prose meant either wholesale confiscation of private property in the South, or vast appropriations. Now Congress had not appropriated a cent, and no sooner did the proclamations of general amnesty appear than the eight hundred thousand acres of abandoned lands in the hands of the Freedmen's Bureau melted quickly away. The second difficulty lay in perfecting the local organization of the Bureau throughout the wide field of work. Making a new machine and sending out officials of duly ascertained fitness for a great work of social reform is no child's task; but this task was even harder, for a new central organization had to be fitted on a heterogeneous and confused but already existing system of relief and control of ex-slaves; and the agents available for this work must be sought for in an army still busy with war operations, — men in the very nature of the case ill fitted for delicate social work, — or among the questionable camp followers of an invading host. Thus, after a year's work, vigorously as it was pushed, the problem looked even more difficult to grasp and solve than at the beginning. Nevertheless, three things that year's work did, well worth the doing: it relieved a vast amount of physical suffering; it transported seven thousand fugitives from congested centres back to the farm; and, best of all, it inaugurated the crusade of the New England school-ma'am.

The annals of this Ninth Crusade are yet to be written, — the tale of a mission that seemed to our age far more quixotic than the quest of St. Louis seemed to his.[21] Behind the mists of ruin and rapine waved the calico dresses of women who dared, and after the hoarse mouthings of the field guns rang the rhythm of the alphabet. Rich and poor they were, serious and curious. Bereaved now of a father, now of a brother, now of more than these, they came seeking a life work in planting New England schoolhouses among the white and black of the South. They did their work well. In that first year they taught one hundred thousand souls, and more.[22]

Evidently, Congress must soon legislate again on the hastily organized Bureau, which had so quickly grown into wide significance and vast possibilities. An institution such as that was well-nigh as difficult to end as to begin. Early in 1866 Congress took up the matter, when Senator Trumbull, of Illinois, introduced a bill to extend the Bureau and enlarge its powers.[23] This measure received, at the hands of Congress, far more thorough discussion and attention than its predecessor. The war cloud had thinned enough to allow a clearer conception of the work of Emancipation. The champions of the bill argued that the strengthening of the Freedmen's Bureau was still a military necessity; that it was needed for the proper carrying out of the Thirteenth Amendment, and was a work of sheer justice to the ex-slave, at a trifling cost to the government. The opponents of the measure declared that the war was over, and the necessity for war measures past; that the Bureau, by reason of its extraordinary powers, was clearly unconstitutional in time of peace, and was destined to irritate the South and pauperize the freedmen, at a final cost of possibly hundreds of millions. These two arguments were unanswered, and indeed unanswerable: the one that the extraordinary powers of the Bureau threatened the civil rights of all citizens; and the other that the government must have power to do what manifestly must be done, and that present abandonment of the freedmen meant their practical re-enslavement. The bill which finally passed enlarged and made permanent the Freedmen's Bureau. It was promptly vetoed by President Johnson as "unconstitutional," "unnecessary," and "extrajudicial," and failed of passage over the veto. Meantime, however, the breach between Congress and the President began to broaden, and a modified form of the lost bill was finally passed over the President's second veto, July 16.[24]

The act of 1866 gave the Freedmen's Bureau its final form, — the form by which it will be known to posterity and judged of men. It extended the existence of the Bureau to July, 1868; it authorized additional assistant commissioners, the retention of army officers mustered out of regular service, the sale of certain forfeited lands to freedmen on nominal terms, the sale of Confederate public property for Negro schools, and a wider field of judicial interpretation and cognizance. The government of the unreconstructed South was thus put very largely in the hands of the Freedmen's Bureau, especially as in many cases the departmental military commander was now made also assistant commissioner. It was thus that the Freedmen's Bureau became a full-fledged government of men.[25] It made laws, executed them and interpreted them; it laid and collected taxes, defined and punished crime, maintained and used military force, and dictated such measures as it thought necessary and proper for the accomplishment of its varied ends. Naturally, all these powers were not exercised continuously nor to their fullest extent; and yet, as General Howard has said, "scarcely any subject that has to be legislated upon in civil society failed, at one time or another, to demand the action of this singular Bureau."

To understand and criticise intelligently so vast a work, one must not forget an instant the drift of things in the later sixties. Lee had surrendered, Lincoln was dead, and Johnson and Congress were at loggerheads; the Thirteenth Amendment was adopted, the Fourteenth pending, and the Fifteenth declared in force in 1870. Guerrilla raiding, the ever-present flickering after-flame of war, was spending its force against the Negroes, and all the Southern land was awakening as from some wild dream to poverty and social revolution. In a time of perfect calm, amid willing neighbors and streaming wealth, the social uplifting of four million slaves to an assured and self-sustaining place in the body politic and economic would have been a herculean task; but when to the inherent difficulties of so delicate and nice a social operation were added the spite and hate of conflict, the hell of war; when suspicion and cruelty were rife, and gaunt Hunger wept beside Bereavement,—in such a case, the work of any instrument of social regeneration was in large part foredoomed to failure.[26] The very name of the Bureau stood for a thing in the South which for two centuries and better men had refused even to argue,—that life amid free Negroes was simply unthinkable, the maddest of experiments.

The agents that the Bureau could command varied all the way from unselfish philanthropists to narrow-minded busybodies and thieves; and even though it be true that the average was far better than the worst, it was the occasional fly that helped spoil the ointment.

Then amid all crouched the freed slave, bewildered between friend and foe. He had emerged from slavery,—not the worst slavery in the world, not a slavery that made all life unbearable, rather a slavery that had here and there something of kindliness, fidelity, and happiness,—but withal slavery, which, so far as human aspiration and desert were concerned, classed the black man and the ox together. And the Negro knew full well that, whatever their deeper convictions may have been, Southern men had fought with desperate energy to perpetuate this slavery under which the black masses, with half-articulate thought, had writhed and shivered. They welcomed freedom with a cry. They shrank from the master who still strove for their chains; they fled to the friends that had freed them, even though those friends stood ready to use them as a club for driving the recalcitrant South back into loyalty. So the cleft between the white and black South grew. Idle to say it never should have been; it was as inevitable as its results were pitiable. Curiously incongruous elements were left arrayed against each other,—the North, the government, the carpet-bagger, and the slave, here; and there, all the South that was white, whether gentleman or vagabond, honest man or rascal, lawless murderer or martyr to duty.

Thus it is doubly difficult to write of this period calmly, so intense was the feeling, so mighty the human passions that swayed and blinded men. Amid it all, two figures ever stand to typify that day to coming ages,— the one, a gray-haired gentleman, whose fathers had quit themselves like men, whose sons lay in nameless graves; who bowed to the evil of slavery because its abolition threatened untold ill to all; who stood at last, in the evening of life, a blighted, ruined form, with hate in his eyes;—and the other, a form hovering dark and mother-like, her awful face black with the mists of centuries, had aforetime quailed at that white master's command, had bent in love over the cradles of his sons and daughters, and closed in death the sunken eyes of his wife,—aye, too, at his behest had laid herself low to his lust, and borne a tawny man-child to the world, only to see her dark boy's limbs scattered to the winds by midnight marauders riding after "cursed Niggers." These were the saddest sights of that woful day; and no man clasped the hands of these two passing figures of the present-past;[27] but, hating, they went to their long home, and, hating, their children's children live to-day.

Here, then, was the field of work for the Freedmen's Bureau; and since, with some hesitation, it was continued by the act of 1868 until 1869, let us look upon four years of its work as a whole. There were, in 1868, nine hundred Bureau officials scattered from Washington to Texas, ruling, directly and indirectly, many millions of men. The deeds of these rulers fall mainly under seven heads: the relief of physical suffering, the overseeing of the beginnings of free labor, the buying and selling of land, the establishment of schools, the paying of bounties, the administration of justice, and the financiering of all these activities.

Up to June, 1869, over half a million patients had been treated by Bureau physicians and surgeons, and sixty hospitals and asylums had been in operation. In fifty months twenty-one million free rations were distributed at a cost of over four million dollars. Next came the difficult question of labor. First, thirty thousand black men were transported from the refuges and relief stations back to the farms, back to the critical trial of a new way of working. Plain instructions went out from Washington: the laborers must be free to choose their employers, no fixed rate of wages was prescribed, and there was to be no peonage or forced labor. So far, so good; but where local agents differed *toto coelo*[28] in capacity and character, where the *personnel* was continually changing, the outcome was necessarily varied. The largest element of success lay in the fact that the majority of the freedmen were willing, even eager, to work. So labor contracts were written,—fifty thousand in a single State,—laborers advised, wages guaranteed, and employers supplied. In truth, the organization became a vast labor bureau,—not perfect, indeed, notably defective here and there, but on the whole successful beyond the dreams of thoughtful men. The two great obstacles which confronted the officials were the tyrant and the idler,—the slaveholder who was determined to perpetuate slavery under another name; and the freedman who regarded freedom as perpetual rest, — the Devil and the Deep Sea.

In the work of establishing the Negroes as peasant proprietors, the Bureau was from the first handicapped and at last absolutely checked. Something was done, and larger things were planned; abandoned lands were leased so long as they remained in the hands of the Bureau, and a total revenue of nearly half a million dollars derived from black tenants. Some other lands to which the nation had gained title were sold on easy terms, and public lands were opened for settlement to the very few freedmen who had tools and capital. But the vision of "forty acres and a mule"[29]—the righteous and reasonable ambition to become a landholder, which the nation had all but categorically promised the freedmen—was destined in most cases to bitter disappointment. And those men of marvellous hindsight who are today seeking to preach the Negro back to the present peonage of the soil know well, or ought to know, that the opportunity of binding the Negro peasant willingly to the soil was lost on that day when the Commissioner of the Freedmen's Bureau had to go to South Carolina and tell the weeping freedmen, after their years of toil, that their land was not theirs, that there was a mistake — somewhere. If by 1874 the Georgia Negro alone owned three hundred and fifty thousand acres of land, it was by grace of his thrift rather than by bounty of the government.

The greatest success of the Freedmen's Bureau lay in the planting of the free school among Negroes, and the idea of free elementary education among all classes in the South. It not only called the schoolmistresses through the benevolent agencies and built them schoolhouses, but it helped discover and support such apostles of human culture as Edmund Ware, Samuel Armstrong, and Erastus Cravath.[30] The opposition to Negro education in the South was at first bitter, and showed itself in ashes, insult, and blood; for the South believed an educated Negro to be a dangerous Negro. And the South was not wholly wrong; for education among all kinds of men always has had, and always will have, an element of danger and revolution, of dissatisfaction and discontent. Nevertheless, men strive to know. Perhaps some inkling of this paradox, even in the unquiet days of the Bureau, helped the bayonets allay an opposition to human training which still to-day lies smouldering in the South, but not flaming. Fisk, Atlanta, Howard, and Hampton were founded in these days, and six million dollars were expended for educational work, seven hundred and fifty thousand dollars of which the freedmen themselves gave of their poverty.

Such contributions, together with the buying of land and various other enterprises, showed that the ex-slave was handling some free capital already. The chief initial source of this was labor in the army, and his pay and bounty as a soldier. Payments to Negro soldiers were at first complicated by the ignorance of the recipients, and the fact that the quotas of colored regiments from Northern States were largely filled by recruits from the South, unknown to their fellow soldiers. Consequently, payments were accompanied by such frauds that Congress, by joint resolution in 1867, put the whole matter in the hands of the Freedmen's Bureau. In two years six million dollars was thus distributed to five thousand claimants, and in the end the sum exceeded eight million dollars. Even in this system fraud was frequent; but still the work put needed capital in the hands of practical paupers, and some, at least, was well spent.

The most perplexing and least successful part of the Bureau's work lay in the exercise of its judicial functions. The regular Bureau court consisted of one representative of the employer, one of the Negro, and one of the Bureau. If the Bureau could have maintained a perfectly judicial attitude, this arrangement would have been ideal, and must in time have gained confidence; but the nature of its other activities and the character of its *personnel* prejudiced the Bureau in favor of the black litigants, and led without doubt to much injustice and annoyance. On the other hand, to leave the Negro in the hands of Southern courts was impossible. In a distracted land where slavery had hardly fallen, to keep the strong from wanton abuse of the weak, and the weak from gloating insolently over the half-shorn strength of the strong, was a thankless, hopeless task. The former masters of the land were peremptorily ordered about, seized, and imprisoned, and punished over and again, with scant courtesy from army officers. The former slaves were intimidated, beaten, raped, and butchered by angry and revengeful men. Bureau courts tended to become centres simply for punishing whites, while the regular civil courts tended to become solely institutions for perpetuating the slavery of blacks. Almost every law and method ingenuity could devise was employed by the legislatures to reduce the Negroes to serfdom, — to make them the slaves of the State, if not of individual owners;[31] while the Bureau officials too often were found striving to put the "bottom rail on top," and give the freedmen a power and independence which they could not yet use. It is all well enough for us of another generation to wax wise with advice to those who bore the burden in the heat of the day. It is full easy now to see that the man who lost home, fortune, and family at a stroke, and saw his land ruled by "mules and niggers," was really benefited by the passing of slavery. It is not difficult now to say to the young freedman, cheated and cuffed about, who has seen his father's head beaten to a jelly and his own mother namelessly assaulted, that the meek shall inherit the earth. Above all, nothing is more convenient than to heap on the Freedmen's Bureau all the evils of that evil day, and damn it utterly for every mistake and blunder that was made.

All this is easy, but it is neither sensible nor just. Some one had blundered, but that was long before Oliver Howard was born; there was criminal aggression and heedless neglect, but without some system of control there would have been far more than there was. Had that control been from within, the Negro would have been re-enslaved, to all intents and purposes. Coming as the control did from without, perfect men and methods would have bettered all things; and even with imperfect agents and questionable methods, the work accomplished was not undeserving of commendation.

Such was the dawn of Freedom; such was the work of the Freedmen's Bureau, which, summed up in brief, may be epitomized thus: For some fifteen million dollars, beside the sums spent before 1865, and the dole of benevolent societies, this Bureau set going a system of free labor, established a beginning of peasant proprietorship, secured the recognition of black freedmen before courts of law, and founded the free common school in the South. On the other hand, it failed to begin the establishment of goodwill between ex-masters and freedmen, to guard its work wholly from paternalistic methods which discouraged self-reliance, and to carry out to any considerable extent its implied promises to furnish the freedmen with land. Its successes were the result of hard work, supplemented by the aid of philanthropists and the eager striving of black men. Its failures were the result of bad local agents, the inherent difficulties of the work, and national neglect.

Such an institution, from its wide powers, great responsibilities, large control of moneys, and generally conspicuous position, was naturally open to repeated and bitter attack. It sustained a searching Congressional investigation at the instance of Fernando Wood in 1870. Its archives and few remaining functions were with blunt discourtesy transferred from Howard's control, in his absence, to the supervision of Secretary of War Belknap[32] in 1872, on the Secretary's recommendation. Finally, in consequence of grave intimations of wrong-doing made by the Secretary and his subordinates, General Howard was court-martialed in 1874. In both of these trials the Commissioner of the Freedmen's Bureau was officially exonerated from any wilful misdoing, and his work commended. Nevertheless, many unpleasant things were brought to light, — the methods of transacting the business of the Bureau were faulty; several cases of defalcation were proved, and other frauds strongly suspected; there were some business transactions which savored of dangerous speculation, if not dishonesty; and around it all lay the smirch of the Freedmen's Bank.[33]

Morally and practically, the Freedmen's Bank was part of the Freedmen's Bureau, although it had no legal connection with it. With the prestige of the government back of it, and a directing board of unusual respectability and national reputation, this banking institution had made a remarkable start in the development of that thrift among black folk which slavery had kept them from knowing. Then in one sad day came the crash, — all the hard-earned dollars of the freedmen disappeared; but that was the least of the loss, — all the faith in saving went too, and much of the faith in men; and that was a loss that a Nation which to-day sneers at Negro shiftlessness has never yet made good. Not even ten additional years of slavery could have done so much to throttle the thrift of the freedmen as the mismanagement and bankruptcy of the series of savings banks chartered by the Nation for their especial aid. Where all the blame should rest, it is hard to say; whether the Bureau and the Bank died chiefly by reason of the blows of its selfish friends or the dark machinations of its foes, perhaps even time will never reveal, for here lies unwritten history.

Of the foes without the Bureau, the bitterest were those who attacked not so much its conduct or policy under the law as the necessity for any such institution at all. Such attacks came primarily from the Border States and the South; and they were summed up by Senator Davis, of Kentucky,[34] when he moved to entitle the act of 1866 a bill "to promote strife and conflict between the white and black races . . . by a grant of unconstitutional power." The argument gathered tremendous strength South and North; but its very strength was its weakness. For, argued the plain commonsense of the nation, if it is unconstitutional, unpractical, and futile for the nation to stand guardian over its helpless wards, then there is left but one alternative, — to make those wards their own guardians by arming them with the ballot. Moreover, the path of the practical politician pointed the same way; for, argued this opportunist, if we cannot peacefully reconstruct the South with white votes, we certainly can with black votes. So justice and force joined hands.

The alternative thus offered the nation was not between full and restricted Negro suffrage; else every sensible man, black and white, would easily have chosen the latter. It was rather a choice between suffrage and slavery, after endless blood and gold had flowed to sweep human bondage away. Not a single Southern legislature stood ready to admit a Negro, under any conditions, to the polls; not a single Southern legislature believed free Negro labor was possible without a system of restrictions that took all its freedom away; there was scarcely a white man in the South who did not honestly regard Emancipation as a crime, and its practical nullification as a duty. In such a situation, the granting of the ballot to the black man was a necessity, the very least a guilty nation could grant a wronged race, and the only method of compelling the South to accept the results of the war. Thus Negro suffrage ended a civil war by beginning a race feud. And some felt gratitude toward the race thus sacrificed in its swaddling clothes on the altar of national integrity; and some felt and feel only indifference and contempt.

Had political exigencies been less pressing, the opposition to government guardianship of Negroes less bitter, and the attachment to the slave system less strong, the social seer can well imagine a far better policy, — a permanent Freedmen's Bureau, with a national system of Negro schools; a carefully supervised employment and labor office; a system of impartial protection before the regular courts; and such institutions for social betterment as savings-banks, land and building associations, and social settlements. All this vast expenditure of money and brains might have formed a great school of prospective citizenship, and solved in a way we have not yet solved the most perplexing and persistent of the Negro problems.

That such an institution was unthinkable in 1870 was due in part to certain acts of the Freedmen's Bureau itself. It came to regard its work as merely temporary, and Negro suffrage as a final answer to all present perplexities. The political ambition of many of its agents and *protégés* led it far afield into questionable activities, until the South, nursing its own deep prejudices, came easily to ignore all the good deeds of the Bureau and hate its very name with perfect hatred. So the Freedmen's Bureau died, and its child was the Fifteenth Amendment.

The passing of a great human institution before its work is done, like the untimely passing of a single soul, but leaves a legacy of striving for other men. The legacy of the Freedmen's Bureau is the heavy heritage of this generation. To-day, when new and vaster problems are destined to strain every fibre of the national mind and soul, would it not be well to count this legacy honestly and carefully? For this much all men know: despite compromise, war, and struggle, the Negro is not free. In the backwoods of the Gulf States, for miles and miles, he may not leave the plantation of his birth; in well-nigh the whole rural South the black farmers are peons, bound by law and custom to an economic slavery, from which the only escape is death or the penitentiary. In the most cultured sections and cities of the South the Negroes are a segregated servile caste, with restricted rights and privileges. Before the courts, both in law and custom, they stand on a different and peculiar basis. Taxation without representation is the rule of their political life. And the result of all this is, and in nature must have been, lawlessness and crime. That is the large legacy of the Freedmen's Bureau, the work it did not do because it could not.[35]

I have seen a land right merry with the sun, where children sing, and rolling hills lie like passioned women wanton with harvest. And there in the King's Highway[36] sat and sits a figure veiled and bowed, by which the traveller's footsteps hasten as they go. On the tainted air broods fear. Three centuries' thought has been the raising and unveiling of that bowed human heart, and now behold a century new for the duty and the deed. The problem of the Twentieth Century is the problem of the color-line.

III

Of Mr. Booker T. Washington and Others

From birth till death enslaved; in word, in deed, unmanned!

· · · · · · · ·

Hereditary bondsmen! Know ye not
Who would be free themselves must strike the blow?

BYRON.

Easily the most striking thing in the history of the American Negro since 1876 is the ascendancy of Mr. Booker T. Washington. It began at the time when war memories and ideals were rapidly passing; a day of astonishing commercial development was dawning; a sense of doubt and hesitation overtook the freedmen's sons,—then it was that his leading began. Mr. Washington came, with a simple definite programme, at the psychological moment when the nation was a little ashamed of having bestowed so much sentiment on Negroes, and was concentrating its energies on Dollars.[2] His programme of industrial education, conciliation of the South, and submission and silence as to civil and political rights, was not wholly original; the Free Negroes from 1830 up to wartime had striven to build industrial schools,[3] and the American Missionary Association had from the first taught various trades; and Price[4] and others had sought a way of honorable alliance with the best of the Southerners. But Mr. Washington first indissolubly linked these things; he put enthusiasm, unlimited energy, and perfect faith into this programme, and changed it from a by-path into a veritable Way of Life. And the tale of the methods by which he did this is a fascinating study of human life.

It startled the nation to hear a Negro advocating such a programme after many decades of bitter complaint; it startled and won the applause of the South, it interested and won the admiration of the North; and after a confused murmur of protest, it silenced if it did not convert the Negroes themselves.

To gain the sympathy and cooperation of the various elements comprising the white South was Mr. Washington's first task; and this, at the time Tuskegee[5] was founded, seemed, for a black man, well-nigh impossible. And yet ten years later it was done in the word spoken at Atlanta: "In all things purely social we can be as separate as the five fingers, and yet one as the hand in all things essential to mutual progress." This "Atlanta Compromise"[6] is by all odds the most notable thing in Mr. Washington's career. The South interpreted it in different ways: the radicals received it as a complete surrender of the demand for civil and political equality; the conservatives, as a generously conceived working basis for mutual understanding. So both approved it, and to-day its author is certainly the most distinguished Southerner since Jefferson Davis,[7] and the one with the largest personal following.

Next to this achievement comes Mr. Washington's work in gaining place and consideration in the North. Others less shrewd and tactful had formerly essayed to sit on these two stools and had fallen between them; but as Mr. Washington knew the heart of the South from birth and training, so by singular insight he intuitively grasped the spirit of the age which was dominating the North. And so thoroughly did he learn the speech and thought of triumphant commercialism, and the ideals of material prosperity, that the picture of a lone black boy poring over a French grammar amid the weeds and dirt of a neglected home soon seemed to him the acme of absurdities. One wonders what Socrates and St. Francis of Assisi[8] would say to this.

And yet this very singleness of vision and thorough oneness with his age is a mark of the successful man. It is as though Nature must needs make men narrow in order to give them force. So Mr. Washington's cult has gained unquestioning followers, his work has wonderfully prospered, his friends are legion, and his enemies are confounded. To-day he stands as the one recognized spokesman of his ten million fellows, and one of the most notable figures in a nation of seventy millions. One hesitates, therefore, to criticise a life which, beginning with so little, has done so much. And yet the time is come when one may speak in all sincerity and utter courtesy of the mistakes and shortcomings of Mr. Washington's career, as well as of his triumphs, without being thought captious or envious, and without forgetting that it is easier to do ill than well in the world.

The criticism that has hitherto met Mr. Washington has not always been of this broad character. In the South especially has he had to walk warily to avoid the harshest judgments, — and naturally so, for he is dealing with the one subject of deepest sensitiveness to that section. Twice — once when at the Chicago celebration of the Spanish-American War he alluded to the color-prejudice that is "eating away the vitals of the South," and once when he dined with President Roosevelt[9]—has the resulting Southern criticism been violent enough to threaten seriously his popularity. In the North the feeling has several times forced itself into words, that Mr. Washington's counsels of submission overlooked certain elements of true manhood, and that his educational programme was unnecessarily narrow. Usually, however, such criticism has not found open expression, although, too, the spiritual sons of the Abolitionists have not been prepared to acknowledge that the schools founded before Tuskegee, by men of broad ideals and self-sacrificing spirit, were wholly failures or worthy of ridicule. While, then, criticism has not failed to follow Mr. Washington, yet the prevailing public opinion of the land has been but too willing to deliver the solution of a wearisome problem into his hands, and say, "If that is all you and your race ask, take it."

Among his own people, however, Mr. Washington has encountered the strongest and most lasting opposition, amounting at times to bitterness, and even to-day continuing strong and insistent even though largely silenced in outward expression by the public opinion of the nation. Some of this opposition is, of course, mere envy; the disappointment of displaced demagogues and the spite of narrow minds. But aside from this, there is among educated and thoughtful colored men in all parts of the land a feeling of deep regret, sorrow, and apprehension at the wide currency and ascendancy which some of Mr. Washington's theories have gained. These same men admire his sincerity of purpose, and are willing to forgive much to honest endeavor which is doing something worth the doing. They cooperate with Mr. Washington as far as they conscientiously can; and, indeed, it is no ordinary tribute to this man's tact and power that, steering as he must between so many diverse interests and opinions, he so largely retains the respect of all.

But the hushing of the criticism of honest opponents is a dangerous thing.[10] It leads some of the best of the critics to unfortunate silence and paralysis of effort, and others to burst into speech so passionately and intemperately as to lose listeners. Honest and earnest criticism from those whose interests are most nearly touched, — criticism of writers by readers, of government by those governed, of leaders by those led, — this is the soul of democracy and the safeguard of modern society. If the best of the American Negroes receive by outer pressure a leader whom they had not recognized before, manifestly there is here a certain palpable gain. Yet there is also irreparable loss, — a loss of that peculiarly valuable education which a group receives when by search and criticism it finds and commissions its own leaders. The way in which this is done is at once the most elementary and the nicest problem of social growth. History is but the record of such group-leadership; and yet how infinitely change-ful is its type and character! And of all types and kinds, what can be more instructive than the leadership of a group within a group?—that curious double movement where real progress may be negative and actual advance be relative retrogression. All this is the social student's inspiration and despair.

Now in the past the American Negro has had instructive experience in the choosing of group leaders, founding thus a peculiar dynasty which in the light of present conditions is worth while studying. When sticks and stones and beasts form the sole environment of a people, their attitude is largely one of determined opposition to and conquest of natural forces. But when to earth and brute is added an environment of men and ideas, then the attitude of the imprisoned group may take three main forms, — a feeling of revolt and revenge; an attempt to adjust all thought and action to the will of the greater group; or, finally, a determined effort at self-realization and self-development despite environing opinion. The influence of all of these attitudes at various times can be traced in the history of the American Negro, and in the evolution of his successive leaders.

Before 1750, while the fire of African freedom still burned in the veins of the slaves, there was in all leadership or attempted leadership but the one motive of revolt and revenge, — typified in the terrible Maroons, the Danish blacks, and Cato of Stono, and veiling all the Americas in fear of insurrection.[11] The liberalizing tendencies of the latter half of the eighteenth century brought, along with kindlier relations between black and white, thoughts of ultimate adjustment and assimilation. Such aspiration was especially voiced in the earnest songs of Phyllis, in the martyrdom of Attucks, the fighting of Salem and Poor, the intellectual accomplishments of Banneker and Derham, and the political demands of the Cuffes.[12]

Stern financial and social stress after the war cooled much of the previous humanitarian ardor. The disappointment and impatience of the Negroes at the persistence of slavery and serfdom voiced itself in two movements. The slaves in the South, aroused undoubtedly by vague rumors of the Haytian revolt, made three fierce attempts at insurrection, — in 1800 under Gabriel in Virginia, in 1822 under Vesey in Carolina, and in 1831 again in Virginia under the terrible Nat Turner.[13] In the Free States, on the other hand, a new and curious attempt at self-development was made. In Philadelphia and New York color-prescription led to a withdrawal of Negro communicants from white churches and the formation of a peculiar socio-religious institution among the Negroes known as the African Church,[14]—an organization still living and controlling in its various branches over a million of men.

Walker's wild appeal[15] against the trend of the times showed how the world was changing after the coming of the cotton-gin. By 1830 slavery seemed hopelessly fastened on the South, and the slaves thoroughly cowed into submission. The free Negroes of the North, inspired by the mulatto immigrants from the West Indies, began to change the basis of their demands; they recognized the slavery of slaves, but insisted that they themselves were freemen, and sought assimilation and amalgamation with the nation on the same terms with other men. Thus, Forten and Purvis of Philadelphia, Shad of Wilmington, Du Bois of New Haven, Barbadoes of Boston, and others, strove singly and together as men, they said, not as slaves; as "people of color," not as "Negroes."[16] The trend of the times, however, refused them recognition save in individual and exceptional cases, considered them as one with all the despised blacks, and they soon found themselves striving to keep even the rights they formerly had of voting and working and moving as freemen. Schemes of migration and colonization arose among them; but these they refused to entertain, and they eventually turned to the Abolition movement as a final refuge.

Here, led by Remond, Nell, Wells-Brown, and Douglass,[17] a new period of self-assertion and self-development dawned. To be sure, ultimate freedom and assimilation was the ideal before the leaders, but the assertion of the manhood rights of the Negro by himself was the main reliance, and John Brown's raid was the extreme of its logic.[18] After the war and emancipation, the great form of Frederick Douglass, the greatest of American Negro leaders, still led the host. Self-assertion, especially in political lines, was the main programme, and behind Douglass came Elliot, Bruce, and Langston, and the Reconstruction politicians, and, less conspicuous but of greater social significance, Alexander Crummell and Bishop Daniel Payne.[19]

Then came the Revolution of 1876,[20] the suppression of the Negro votes, the changing and shifting of ideals, and the seeking of new lights in the great night. Douglass, in his old age, still bravely stood for the ideals of his early manhood, — ultimate assimilation *through* self-assertion, and on no other terms. For a time Price arose as a new leader, destined, it seemed, not to give up, but to re-state the old ideals in a form less repugnant to the white South. But he passed away in his prime. Then came the new leader. Nearly all the former ones had become leaders by the silent suffrage of their fellows,[21] had sought to lead their own people alone, and were usually, save Douglass, little known outside their race. But Booker T. Washington arose as essentially the leader not of one race but of two,—a compromiser between the South, the North, and the Negro. Naturally the Negroes resented, at first bitterly, signs of compromise which surrendered their civil and political rights, even though this was to be exchanged for larger chances of economic development. The rich and dominating North, however, was not only weary of the race problem, but was investing largely in Southern enterprises, and welcomed any method of peaceful cooperation. Thus, by national opinion, the Negroes began to recognize Mr. Washington's leadership; and the voice of criticism was hushed.

Mr. Washington represents in Negro thought the old attitude of adjustment and submission; but adjustment at such a peculiar time as to make his programme unique. This is an age of unusual economic development, and Mr. Washington's programme naturally takes an economic cast, becoming a gospel of Work and Money[22] to such an extent as apparently almost completely to overshadow the higher aims of life. Moreover, this is an age when the more advanced races are coming in closer contact with the less developed races, and the race-feeling is therefore intensified; and Mr. Washington's programme practically accepts the alleged inferiority of the Negro races. Again, in our own land, the reaction from the sentiment of war time has given impetus to race-prejudice against Negroes, and Mr. Washington withdraws many of the high demands of Negroes as men and American citizens. In other periods of intensified prejudice all the Negro's tendency to self-assertion has been called forth; at this period a policy of submission is advocated. In the history of nearly all other races and peoples the doctrine preached at such crises has been that manly self-respect is worth more than lands and houses, and that a people who voluntarily surrender such respect, or cease striving for it, are not worth civilizing.

In answer to this, it has been claimed that the Negro can survive only through submission. Mr. Washington distinctly asks that black people give up, at least for the present, three things,—

First, political power,

Second, insistence on civil rights,

Third, higher education of Negro youth,—and concentrate all their energies on industrial education, the accumulation of wealth, and the conciliation of the South. This policy has been courageously and insistently advocated for over fifteen years, and has been triumphant for perhaps ten years. As a result of this tender of the palm-branch, what has been the return? In these years there have occurred:

1. The disfranchisement of the Negro.
2. The legal creation of a distinct status of civil inferiority for the Negro.
3. The steady withdrawal of aid from institutions for the higher training of the Negro.

These movements are not, to be sure, direct results of Mr. Washington's teachings; but his propaganda has, without a shadow of doubt, helped their speedier accomplishment. The question then comes: Is it possible, and probable, that nine millions of men can make effective progress in economic lines if they are deprived of political rights, made a servile caste, and allowed only the most meagre chance for developing their exceptional men? If history and reason give any distinct answer to these questions, it is an emphatic *No*. And Mr. Washington thus faces the triple paradox of his career:

1. He is striving nobly to make Negro artisans business men and property-owners; but it is utterly impossible, under modern competitive methods, for workingmen and property-owners to defend their rights and exist without the right of suffrage.

2. He insists on thrift and self-respect, but at the same time counsels a silent submission to civic inferiority such as is bound to sap the manhood of any race in the long run.

3. He advocates common-school and industrial training, and depreciates institutions of higher learning; but neither the Negro common-schools, nor Tuskegee itself, could remain open a day were it not for teachers trained in Negro colleges, or trained by their graduates.

This triple paradox in Mr. Washington's position is the object of criticism by two classes of colored Americans. One class is spiritually descended from Toussaint the Savior, through Gabriel, Vesey, and Turner, and they represent the attitude of revolt and revenge; they hate the white South blindly and distrust the white race generally, and so far as they agree on definite action, think that the Negro's only hope lies in emigration beyond the borders of the United States. And yet, by the irony of fate, nothing has more effectually made this programme seem hopeless than the recent course of the United States toward weaker and darker peoples in the West Indies, Hawaii, and the Philippines,—for where in the world may we go and be safe from lying and brute force?[23]

The other class of Negroes who cannot agree with Mr. Washington has hitherto said little aloud. They deprecate the sight of scattered counsels, of internal disagreement; and especially they dislike making their just criticism of a useful and earnest man an excuse for a general discharge of venom from small-minded opponents. Nevertheless, the questions involved are so fundamental and serious that it is difficult to see how men like the Grimkes, Kelly Miller, J. W. E. Bowen,[24] and other representatives of this group, can much longer be silent. Such men feel in conscience bound to ask of this nation three things:

1. The right to vote.
2. Civic equality.
3. The education of youth according to ability.

They acknowledge Mr. Washington's invaluable service in counselling patience and courtesy in such demands; they do not ask that ignorant black men vote when ignorant whites are debarred, or that any reasonable restrictions in the suffrage should not be applied; they know that the low social level of the mass of the race is responsible for much discrimination against it, but they also know, and the nation knows, that relentless color-prejudice is more often a cause than a result of the Negro's degradation; they seek the abatement of this relic of barbarism, and not its systematic encouragement and pampering by all agencies of social power from the Associated Press to the Church of Christ. They advocate, with Mr. Washington, a broad system of Negro common schools supplemented by thorough industrial training; but they are surprised that a man of Mr. Washington's insight cannot see that no such educational system ever has rested or can rest on any other basis than that of the well-equipped college and university, and they insist that there is a demand for a few such institutions throughout the south to train the best of the Negro youth as teachers, professional men, and leaders.

This group of men honor Mr. Washington for his attitude of conciliation toward the white South; they accept the "Atlanta Compromise" in its broadest interpretation; they recognize, with him, many signs of promise, many men of high purpose and fair judgment, in this section; they know that no easy task has been laid upon a region already tottering under heavy burdens. But, nevertheless, they insist that the way to truth and right lies in straightforward honesty, not in indiscriminate flattery; in praising those of the South who do well and criticising uncompromisingly those who do ill; in taking advantage of the opportunities at hand and urging their fellows to do the same, but at the same time in remembering that only a firm adherence to their higher ideals and aspirations will ever keep those ideals within the realm of possibility. They do not expect that the free right to vote, to enjoy civic rights, and to be educated, will come in a moment; they do not expect to see the bias and prejudices of years disappear at the blast of a trumpet; but they are absolutely certain that the way for a people to gain their reasonable rights is not by voluntarily throwing them away and insisting that they do not want them; that the way for a people to gain respect is not by continually belittling and ridiculing themselves; that, on the contrary, Negroes must insist continually, in season and out of season, that voting is necessary to modern manhood, that color discrimination is barbarism, and that black boys need education as well as white boys.[25]

In failing thus to state plainly and unequivocally the legitimate demands of their people, even at the cost of opposing an honored leader, the thinking classes of American Negroes would shirk a heavy responsibility,[26]—a responsibility to themselves, a responsibility to the struggling masses, a responsibility to the darker races of men whose future depends so largely on this American experiment, but especially a responsibility to this nation,—this common Fatherland. It is wrong to encourage a man or a people in evil-doing; it is wrong to aid and abet a national crime simply because it is unpopular not to do so. The growing spirit of kindliness and reconciliation between the North and South after the frightful differences of a generation ago ought to be a source of deep congratulation to all, and especially to those whose mistreatment caused the war; but if that reconciliation is to be marked by the industrial slavery and civic death of those same black men, with permanent legislation into a position of inferiority, then those black men, if they are really men, are called upon by every consideration of patriotism and loyalty to oppose such a course by all civilized methods, even though such opposition involves disagreement with Mr. Booker T. Washington. We have no right to sit silently by while the inevitable seeds are sown for a harvest of disaster to our children, black and white.[27]

First, it is the duty of black men to judge the South discriminatingly. The present generation of Southerners are not responsible for the past, and they should not be blindly hated or blamed for it. Furthermore, to no class is the indiscriminate endorsement of the recent course of the South toward Negroes more nauseating than to the best thought of the South. The South is not "solid"; it is a land in the ferment of social change, wherein forces of all kinds are fighting for supremacy; and to praise the ill the South is to-day perpetrating is just as wrong as to condemn the good. Discriminating and broad-minded criticism is what the South needs,—needs it for the sake of her own white sons and daughters, and for the insurance of robust, healthy mental and moral development.[28]

To-day even the attitude of the Southern whites toward the blacks is not, as so many assume, in all cases the same; the ignorant Southerner hates the Negro, the workingmen fear his competition, the money-makers wish to use him as a laborer, some of the educated see a menace in his upward development, while others—usually the sons of the masters—wish to help him to rise. National opinion has enabled this last class to maintain the Negro common schools, and to protect the Negro partially in property, life, and limb. Through the pressure of the money-makers, the Negro is in danger of being reduced to semi-slavery, especially in the country districts; the workingmen, and those of the educated who fear the Negro, have united to disfranchise him, and some have urged his deportation; while the passions of the ignorant are easily aroused to lynch and abuse any black man. To praise this intricate whirl of thought and prejudice is nonsense; to inveigh indiscriminately against "the South" is unjust; but to use the same breath in praising Governor Aycock, exposing Senator Morgan, arguing with Mr. Thomas Nelson Page, and denouncing Senator Ben Tillman, is not only sane, but the imperative duty of thinking black men.[29]

It would be unjust to Mr. Washington not to acknowledge that in several instances he has opposed movements in the South which were unjust to the Negro; he sent memorials to the Louisiana and Alabama constitutional conventions, he has spoken against lynching, and in other ways has openly or silently set his influence against sinister schemes and unfortunate happenings. Notwithstanding this, it is equally true to assert that on the whole the distinct impression left by Mr. Washington's propaganda is, first, that the South is justified in its present attitude toward the Negro because of the Negro's degradation; secondly, that the prime cause of the Negro's failure to rise more quickly is his wrong education in the past; and, thirdly, that his future rise depends primarily on his own efforts. Each of these propositions is a dangerous half-truth. The supplementary truths must never be lost sight of: first, slavery and race-prejudice are potent if not sufficient causes of the Negro's position; second, industrial and common-school training were necessarily slow in planting because they had to await the black teachers trained by higher institutions,—it being extremely doubtful if any essentially different development was possible, and certainly a Tuskegee was unthinkable before 1880; and, third, while it is a great truth to say that the Negro must strive and strive mightily to help himself, it is equally true that unless his striving be not simply seconded, but rather aroused and encouraged, by the initiative of the richer and wiser environing group, he cannot hope for great success.

In his failure to realize and impress this last point, Mr. Washington is especially to be criticised. His doctrine has tended to make the whites, North and South, shift the burden of the Negro problem to the Negro's shoulders and stand aside as critical and rather pessimistic spectators; when in fact the burden belongs to the nation, and the hands of none of us are clean if we bend not our energies to righting these great wrongs.

The South ought to be led, by candid and honest criticism, to assert her better self and do her full duty to the race she has cruelly wronged and is still wronging. The North—her co-partner in guilt—cannot salve her conscience by plastering it with gold. We cannot settle this problem by diplomacy and suaveness, by "policy" alone. If worse come to worst, can the moral fibre of this country survive the slow throttling and murder of nine millions of men?

The black men of America have a duty to perform, a duty stern and delicate,—a forward movement to oppose a part of the work of their greatest leader. So far as Mr. Washington preaches Thrift, Patience, and Industrial Training for the masses, we must hold up his hands and strive with him, rejoicing in his honors and glorying in the strength of this Joshua[30] called of God and of man to lead the headless host. But so far as Mr. Washington apologizes for injustice, North or South, does not rightly value the privilege and duty of voting, belittles the emasculating effects of caste distinctions, and opposes the higher training and ambition of our brighter minds,—so far as he, the South, or the Nation, does this,—we must unceasingly and firmly oppose them. By every civilized and peaceful method we must strive for the rights which the world accords to men, clinging unwaveringly to those great words which the sons of the Fathers would fain forget: "We hold these truths to be self-evident: That all men are created equal; that they are endowed by their Creator with certain unalienable rights; that among these are life, liberty, and the pursuit of happiness."[31]

IV

Of the Meaning of Progress

Willst Du Deine Macht verkünden,
Wähle sie die frei von Sünden,
Steh'n in Deinem ew'gen Haus!
Deine Geister sende aus!
Die Unsterblichen, die Reinen,
Die nicht fühlen, die nicht weinen!
Nicht die zarte Jungfrau wähle,
Nicht der Hirtin weiche Seele!

SCHILLER.

Once upon a time I taught school in the hills of Tennessee, where the broad dark vale of the Mississippi begins to roll and crumple to greet the Alleghanies. I was a Fisk student then, and all Fisk men thought that Tennessee—beyond the Veil—was theirs alone, and in vacation time they sallied forth in lusty bands to meet the county school-commissioners. Young and happy, I too went, and I shall not soon forget that summer, seventeen years ago.[2]

First, there was a Teachers' Institute at the county-seat; and there distinguished guests of the superintendent taught the teachers fractions and spelling and other mysteries,—white teachers in the morning, Negroes at night. A picnic now and then, and a supper, and the rough world was softened by laughter and song. I remember how—But I wander.

There came a day when all the teachers left the Institute and began the hunt for schools. I learn from hearsay (for my mother was mortally afraid of fire-arms) that the hunting of ducks and bears and men is wonderfully interesting, but I am sure that the man who has never hunted a country school has something to learn of the pleasures of the chase. I see now the white, hot roads lazily rise and fall and wind before me under the burning July sun; I feel the deep weariness of heart and limb as ten, eight, six miles stretch relentlessly ahead; I feel my heart sink heavily as I hear again and again, "Got a teacher? Yes." So I walked on and on — horses were too expensive — until I had wandered beyond railways, beyond stage lines, to a land of "varmints" and rattlesnakes, where the coming of a stranger was an event, and men lived and died in the shadow of one blue hill.

Sprinkled over hill and dale lay cabins and farmhouses, shut out from the world by the forests and the rolling hills toward the east. There I found at last a little school. Josie told me of it; she was a thin, homely girl of twenty, with a dark-brown face and thick, hard hair. I had crossed the stream at Watertown, and rested under the great willows; then I had gone to the little cabin in the lot where Josie was resting on her way to town. The gaunt farmer made me welcome, and Josie, hearing my errand, told me anxiously that they wanted a school over the hill; that but once since the war had a teacher been there; that she herself longed to learn, — and thus she ran on, talking fast and loud, with much earnestness and energy.

Next morning I crossed the tall round hill, lingered to look at the blue and yellow mountains stretching toward the Carolinas, then plunged into the wood, and came out at Josie's home. It was a dull frame cottage with four rooms, perched just below the brow of the hill, amid peach-trees. The father was a quiet, simple soul, calmly ignorant, with no touch of vulgarity. The mother was different, — strong, bustling, and energetic, with a quick, restless tongue, and an ambition to live "like folks." There was a crowd of children. Two boys had gone away. There remained two growing girls; a shy midget of eight; John, tall, awkward, and eighteen; Jim, younger, quicker, and better looking; and two babies of indefinite age. Then there was Josie herself. She seemed to be the centre of the family: always busy at service, or at home, or berry-picking; a little nervous and inclined to scold, like her mother, yet faithful, too, like her father. She had about her a certain fineness, the shadow of an unconscious moral heroism that would willingly give all of life to make life broader, deeper, and fuller for her and hers. I saw much of this family afterwards, and grew to love them for their honest efforts to be decent and comfortable, and for their knowledge of their own ignorance. There was with them no affectation. The mother would scold the father for being so "easy"; Josie would roundly berate the boys for carelessness; and all knew that it was a hard thing to dig a living out of a rocky side-hill.

I secured the school. I remember the day I rode horseback out to the commissioner's house with a pleasant young white fellow who wanted the white school. The road ran down the bed of a stream; the sun laughed and the water jingled, and we rode on. "Come in," said the commissioner,—"come in. Have a seat. Yes, that certificate will do. Stay to dinner. What do you want a month?" "Oh," thought I, "this is lucky"; but even then fell the awful shadow of the Veil, for they ate first, then I—alone.

The schoolhouse was a log hut, where Colonel Wheeler used to shelter his corn. It sat in a lot behind a rail fence and thorn bushes, near the sweetest of springs. There was an entrance where a door once was, and within, a massive rickety fireplace; great chinks between the logs served as windows. Furniture was scarce. A pale blackboard crouched in the corner. My desk was made of three boards, reinforced at critical points, and my chair, borrowed from the landlady, had to be returned every night. Seats for the children—these puzzled me much. I was haunted by a New England vision of neat little desks and chairs, but, alas! the reality was rough plank benches without backs, and at times without legs. They had the one virtue of making naps dangerous,—possibly fatal, for the floor was not to be trusted.[3]

It was a hot morning late in July when the school opened. I trembled when I heard the patter of little feet down the dusty road, and saw the growing row of dark solemn faces and bright eager eyes facing me. First came Josie and her brothers and sisters. The longing to know, to be a student in the great school at Nashville, hovered like a star above this child-woman amid her work and worry, and she studied doggedly. There were the Dowells from their farm over toward Alexandria,—Fanny, with her smooth black face and wondering eyes; Martha, brown and dull; the pretty girl-wife of a brother, and the younger brood.

There were the Burkes,—two brown and yellow lads, and a tiny haughty-eyed girl. Fat Reuben's little chubby girl came, with golden face and old-gold hair, faithful and solemn. 'Thenie was on hand early,—a jolly, ugly, good-hearted girl, who slyly dipped snuff and looked after her little bow-legged brother. When her mother could spare her, 'Tildy came,—a midnight beauty, with starry eyes and tapering limbs; and her brother, correspondingly homely. And then the big boys,—the hulking Lawrences; the lazy Neills, unfathered sons of mother and daughter; Hickman, with a stoop in his shoulders; and the rest.

There they sat, nearly thirty of them, on the rough benches, their faces

shading from a pale cream to a deep brown, the little feet bare and swinging, the eyes full of expectation, with here and there a twinkle of mischief,
and the hands grasping Webster's blue-back spelling-book. I loved my
school, and the fine faith the children had in the wisdom of their teacher
was truly marvellous. We read and spelled together, wrote a little, picked
flowers, sang, and listened to stories of the world beyond the hill. At times
the school would dwindle away, and I would start out. I would visit Mun
Eddings, who lived in two very dirty rooms, and ask why little Lugene,
whose flaming face seemed ever ablaze with the dark-red hair uncombed,
was absent all last week, or why I missed so often the inimitable rags of
Mack and Ed. Then the father, who worked Colonel Wheeler's farm on
shares,[4] would tell me how the crops needed the boys; and the thin,
slovenly mother, whose face was pretty when washed, assured me that
Lugene must mind the baby. "But we'll start them again next week."
When the Lawrences stopped, I knew that the doubts of the old folks
about book-learning had conquered again, and so, toiling up the hill, and
getting as far into the cabin as possible, I put Cicero "pro Archia Poeta"[5]
into the simplest English with local applications, and usually convinced
them—for a week or so.

On Friday nights I often went home with some of the children,—
sometimes to Doc Burke's farm. He was a great, loud, thin Black, ever
working, and trying to buy the seventy-five acres of hill and dale where
he lived; but people said that he would surely fail, and the "white folks
would get it all." His wife was a magnificent Amazon, with saffron face
and shining hair, uncorseted and barefooted, and the children were
strong and beautiful. They lived in a one-and-a-half-room cabin in the hollow of the farm, near the spring. The front room was full of great fat white
beds, scrupulously neat; and there were bad chromos on the walls, and
a tired centre-table. In the tiny back kitchen I was often invited to "take
out and help" myself to fried chicken and wheat biscuit, "meat" and corn
pone, string-beans and berries. At first I used to be a little alarmed at the
approach of bedtime in the one lone bedroom, but embarrassment was
very deftly avoided. First, all the children nodded and slept, and were
stowed away in one great pile of goose feathers; next, the mother and the
father discreetly slipped away to the kitchen while I went to bed; then,
blowing out the dim light, they retired in the dark. In the morning all were
up and away before I thought of awaking. Across the road, where fat
Reuben lived, they all went outdoors while the teacher retired, because
they did not boast the luxury of a kitchen.

I liked to stay with the Dowells, for they had four rooms and plenty
of good country fare. Uncle Bird had a small, rough farm, all woods and

hills, miles from the big road; but he was full of tales,—he preached now and then,—and with his children, berries, horses, and wheat he was happy and prosperous. Often, to keep the peace, I must go where life was less lovely; for instance, 'Tildy's mother was incorrigibly dirty, Reuben's larder was limited seriously, and herds of untamed insects wandered over the Eddingses' beds. Best of all I loved to go to Josie's, and sit on the porch, eating peaches, while the mother bustled and talked: how Josie had bought the sewing-machine; how Josie worked at service in winter, but that four dollars a month was "mighty little" wages; how Josie longed to go away to school, but that it "looked like" they never could get far enough ahead to let her; how the crops failed and the well was yet unfinished; and, finally, how "mean" some of the white folks were.[6]

For two summers I lived in this little world; it was dull and humdrum. The girls looked at the hill in wistful longing, and the boys fretted and haunted Alexandria. Alexandria was "town,"—a straggling, lazy village of houses, churches, and shops, and an aristocracy of Toms, Dicks, and Captains. Cuddled on the hill to the north was the village of the colored folks, who lived in three- or four-room unpainted cottages, some neat and homelike, and some dirty. The dwellings were scattered rather aimlessly, but they centred about the twin temples of the hamlet, the Methodist, and the Hard-Shell Baptist churches. These, in turn, leaned gingerly on a sad-colored schoolhouse. Hither my little world wended its crooked way on Sunday to meet other worlds, and gossip, and wonder, and make the weekly sacrifice with frenzied priest at the altar of the "old-time religion." Then the soft melody and mighty cadences of Negro song fluttered and thundered.

I have called my tiny community a world, and so its isolation made it; and yet there was among us but a half-awakened common consciousness, sprung from common joy and grief, at burial, birth, or wedding; from a common hardship in poverty, poor land, and low wages; and, above all, from the sight of the Veil that hung between us and Opportunity. All this caused us to think some thoughts together; but these, when ripe for speech, were spoken in various languages. Those whose eyes twenty-five and more years before had seen "the glory of the coming of the Lord," saw in every present hindrance or help a dark fatalism bound to bring all things right in His own good time. The mass of those to whom slavery was a dim recollection of childhood found the world a puzzling thing: it asked little of them, and they answered with little, and yet it ridiculed their offering. Such a paradox they could not understand, and therefore sank into listless indifference, or shiftlessness, or reckless bravado. There were, however, some—such as Josie, Jim, and Ben—to whom War, Hell, and Slavery were but childhood tales, whose young appetites had been whetted to an edge by school and story and half-awakened thought. Ill could they be content, born without and beyond the World. And their weak wings beat against their barriers,—barriers of caste, of youth, of life; at last, in dangerous moments, against everything that opposed even a whim.

The ten years that follow youth, the years when first the realization comes that life is leading somewhere,—these were the years that passed after I left my little school. When they were past, I came by chance once more to the walls of Fisk University, to the halls of the chapel of melody. As I lingered there in the joy and pain of meeting old school-friends, there swept over me a sudden longing to pass again beyond the blue hill, and to see the homes and the school of other days, and to learn how life had gone with my school-children; and I went.

Josie was dead, and the gray-haired mother said simply, "We've had a heap of trouble since you've been away." I had feared for Jim. With a cultured parentage and a social caste to uphold him, he might have made a venturesome merchant or a West Point cadet. But here he was, angry with life and reckless; and when Farmer Durham charged him with stealing wheat, the old man had to ride fast to escape the stones which the furious fool hurled after him. They told Jim to run away; but he would not run, and the constable came that afternoon. It grieved Josie, and great awkward John walked nine miles every day to see his little brother through the bars of Lebanon jail. At last the two came back together in the dark night. The mother cooked supper, and Josie emptied her purse, and the boys stole away. Josie grew thin and silent, yet worked the more. The hill became steep for the quiet old father, and with the boys away there was little to do in the valley. Josie helped them to sell the old farm, and they moved nearer town. Brother Dennis, the carpenter, built a new house with six rooms; Josie toiled a year in Nashville, and brought back ninety dollars to furnish the house and change it to a home.

When the spring came, and the birds twittered, and the stream ran proud and full, little sister Lizzie, bold and thoughtless, flushed with the passion of youth, bestowed herself on the tempter, and brought home a nameless child. Josie shivered and worked on, with the vision of school-days all fled, with a face wan and tired,—worked until, on a summer's day, some one married another; then Josie crept to her mother like a hurt child, and slept—and sleeps.

I paused to scent the breeze as I entered the valley. The Lawrences have gone,—father and son forever,—and the other son lazily digs in the earth to live. A new young widow rents out their cabin to fat Reuben. Reuben is a Baptist preacher now, but I fear as lazy as ever, though his cabin has three rooms; and little Ella has grown into a bouncing woman, and is ploughing corn on the hot hillside. There are babies a-plenty, and one half-witted girl. Across the valley is a house I did not know before, and there I found, rocking one baby and expecting another, one of my schoolgirls, a daughter of Uncle Bird Dowell. She looked somewhat worried with her new duties, but soon bristled into pride over her neat cabin and the tale of her thrifty husband, the horse and cow, and the farm they were planning to buy.

My log schoolhouse was gone. In its place stood Progress; and Progress, I understand, is necessarily ugly. The crazy foundation stones still marked the former site of my poor little cabin, and not far away, on six weary boulders, perched a jaunty board house, perhaps twenty by thirty feet, with three windows and a door that locked. Some of the window-glass was broken, and part of an old iron stove lay mournfully under the house. I peeped through the window half reverently, and found things that were more familiar. The blackboard had grown by about two feet, and the seats were still without backs. The county owns the lot now, I hear, and every year there is a session of school. As I sat by the spring and looked on the Old and the New I felt glad, very glad, and yet—

After two long drinks I started on. There was the great double log-house on the corner. I remembered the broken, blighted family that used to live there. The strong, hard face of the mother, with its wilderness of hair, rose before me. She had driven her husband away, and while I taught school a strange man lived there, big and jovial, and people talked. I felt sure that Ben and 'Tildy would come to naught from such a home. But this is an odd world; for Ben is a busy farmer in Smith County, "doing well, too," they say, and he had cared for little 'Tildy until last spring, when a lover married her. A hard life the lad had led, toiling for meat, and laughed at because he was homely and crooked. There was Sam Carlon, an impudent old skinflint, who had definite notions about "niggers," and hired Ben a summer and would not pay him. Then the hungry boy gathered his sacks together, and in broad daylight went into Carlon's corn; and when the hard-fisted farmer set upon him, the angry boy flew at him like a beast. Doc Burke saved a murder and a lynching that day.

The story reminded me again of the Burkes, and an impatience seized me to know who won in the battle, Doc or the seventy-five acres. For it is a hard thing to make a farm out of nothing, even in fifteen years. So I hurried on, thinking of the Burkes. They used to have a certain magnificent barbarism about them that I liked. They were never vulgar, never immoral, but rather rough and primitive, with an unconventionality that spent itself in loud guffaws, slaps on the back, and naps in the corner. I hurried by the cottage of the misborn Neill boys. It was empty, and they were grown into fat, lazy farm-hands. I saw the home of the Hickmans, but Albert, with his stooping shoulders, had passed from the world. Then I came to the Burkes' gate and peered through; the inclosure looked rough and untrimmed, and yet there were the same fences around the old farm save to the left, where lay twenty-five other acres. And lo! the cabin in the hollow had climbed the hill and swollen to a half-finished six-room cottage.

The Burkes held a hundred acres, but they were still in debt. Indeed, the gaunt father who toiled night and day would scarcely be happy out of debt, being so used to it. Some day he must stop, for his massive frame is showing decline. The mother wore shoes, but the lion-like physique of other days was broken. The children had grown up. Rob, the image of his father, was loud and rough with laughter. Birdie, my school baby of six, had grown to a picture of maiden beauty, tall and tawny. "Edgar is gone," said the mother, with head half bowed,—"gone to work in Nashville; he and his father couldn't agree."

Little Doc, the boy born since the time of my school, took me horseback down the creek next morning toward Farmer Dowell's. The road and the stream were battling for mastery, and the stream had the better of it. We splashed and waded, and the merry boy, perched behind me, chattered and laughed. He showed me where Simon Thompson had bought a bit of ground and a home; but his daughter Lana, a plump, brown, slow girl, was not there. She had married a man and a farm twenty miles away. We wound on down the stream till we came to a gate that I did not recognize, but the boy insisted that it was "Uncle Bird's." The farm was fat with the growing crop. In that little valley was a strange stillness as I rode up; for death and marriage had stolen youth and left age and childhood there. We sat and talked that night after the chores were done. Uncle Bird was grayer, and his eyes did not see so well, but he was still jovial. We talked of the acres bought,—one hundred and twenty-five,—of the new guest-chamber added, of Martha's marrying. Then we talked of death: Fanny and Fred were gone; a shadow hung over the other daughter, and when it lifted she was to go to Nashville to school. At last we spoke of the neighbors, and as night fell, Uncle Bird told me how, on a night like that, 'Thenie came wandering back to her home over yonder, to escape the blows of her husband. And next morning she died in the home that her little bow-legged brother, working and saving, had bought for their widowed mother.

My journey was done, and behind me lay hill and dale, and Life and Death. How shall man measure Progress there where the dark-faced Josie lies? How many heartfuls of sorrow shall balance a bushel of wheat? How hard a thing is life to the lowly, and yet how human and real! And all this life and love and strife and failure, — is it the twilight of nightfall or the flush of some faint-dawning day?

Thus sadly musing, I rode to Nashville in the Jim Crow car.[7]

V

Of the Wings of Atalanta

O black boy of Atlanta!
  But half was spoken;
The slave's chains and the master's
  Alike are broken;
The one curse of the races
  Held both in tether;
They are rising—all are rising—
  The black and white together.
WHITTIER.

South of the North, yet north of the South, lies the City of a Hundred Hills, peering out from the shadows of the past into the promise of the future. I have seen her in the morning, when the first flush of day had half-roused her; she lay gray and still on the crimson soil of Georgia; then the blue smoke began to curl from her chimneys, the tinkle of bell and scream of whistle broke the silence, the rattle and roar of busy life slowly gathered and swelled, until the seething whirl of the city seemed a strange thing in a sleepy land.

Once, they say, even Atlanta[2] slept dull and drowsy at the foot-hills of the Alleghanies, until the iron baptism of war awakened her with its sullen waters, aroused and maddened her, and left her listening to the sea. And the sea cried to the hills and the hills answered the sea, till the city rose like a widow and cast away her weeds, and toiled for her daily bread; toiled steadily, toiled cunningly,—perhaps with some bitterness, with a touch of *réclame,*[3]—and yet with real earnestness, and real sweat.

It is a hard thing to live haunted by the ghost of an untrue dream; to see the wide vision of empire fade into real ashes and dirt; to feel the pang of the conquered, and yet know that with all the Bad that fell on one black

82

day, something was vanquished that deserved to live, something killed that in justice had not dared to die; to know that with the Right that triumphed, triumphed something of Wrong, something sordid and mean, something less than the broadest and best. All this is bitter hard; and many a man and city and people have found in it excuse for sulking, and brooding, and listless waiting.[4]

Such are not men of the sturdier make; they of Atlanta turned resolutely toward the future; and that future held aloft vistas of purple and gold:—Atlanta, Queen of the cotton kingdom; Atlanta, Gateway to the Land of the Sun; Atlanta, the new Lachesis,[5] spinner of web and woof for the world. So the city crowned her hundred hills with factories, and stored her shops with cunning handiwork, and stretched long iron ways to greet the busy Mercury[6] in his coming. And the Nation talked of her striving.

Perhaps Atlanta was not christened for the winged maiden of dull Bœotia;[7] you know the tale,—how swarthy Atalanta, tall and wild, would marry only him who outraced her; and how the wily Hippomenes laid three apples of gold in the way.[8] She fled like a shadow, paused, startled over the first apple, but even as he stretched his hand, fled again; hovered over the second, then, slipping from his hot grasp, flew over river, vale, and hill; but as she lingered over the third, his arms fell round her, and looking on each other, the blazing passion of their love profaned the sanctuary of Love, and they were cursed. If Atlanta be not named for Atalanta, she ought to have been.

Atalanta is not the first or the last maiden whom greed of gold has led to defile the temple of Love; and not maids alone, but men in the race of life, sink from the high and generous ideals of youth to the gambler's code of the Bourse;[9] and in all our Nation's striving is not the Gospel of Work befouled by the Gospel of Pay? So common is this that one-half think it normal; so unquestioned, that we almost fear to question if the end of racing is not gold, if the aim of man is not rightly to be rich. And if this is the fault of America, how dire a danger lies before a new land and a new city, lest Atlanta, stooping for mere gold, shall find that gold accursed!

It was no maiden's idle whim that started this hard racing; a fearful wilderness lay about the feet of that city after the War,—feudalism, poverty, the rise of the Third Estate,[10] serfdom, the re-birth of Law and Order, and above and between all, the Veil of Race. How heavy a journey for weary feet! what wings must Atalanta have to flit over all this hollow and hill, through sour wood and sullen water, and by the red waste of sun-baked clay! How fleet must Atalanta be if she will not be tempted by gold to profane the Sanctuary!

The Sanctuary of our fathers has, to be sure, few Gods,—some sneer, "all too few." There is the thrifty Mercury of New England, Pluto[11] of the North, and Ceres[12] of the West; and there, too, is the half-forgotten Apollo[13] of the South, under whose ægis the maiden ran,—and as she ran she forgot him, even as there in Bœotia Venus[14] was forgot. She forgot the old ideal of the Southern gentleman,—that new-world heir of the grace and courtliness of patrician, knight, and noble; forgot his honor with his foibles, his kindliness with his carelessness, and stooped to apples of gold,—to men busier and sharper, thriftier and more unscrupulous. Golden apples are beautiful—I remember the lawless days of boyhood, when orchards in crimson and gold tempted me over fence and field— and, too, the merchant who has dethroned the planter is no despicable *parvenu*.[15] Work and wealth are the mighty levers to lift this old new land; thrift and toil and saving are the highways to new hopes and new possibilities; and yet the warning is needed lest the wily Hippomenes tempt Atalanta to thinking that golden apples are the goal of racing, and not mere incidents by the way.

Atlanta must not lead the South to dream of material prosperity as the touchstone of all success; already the fatal might of this idea is beginning to spread; it is replacing the finer type of Southerner with vulgar money-getters; it is burying the sweeter beauties of Southern life beneath pretence and ostentation. For every social ill the panacea of Wealth has been urged,—wealth to overthrow the remains of the slave feudalism; wealth to raise the "cracker"[16] Third Estate; wealth to employ the black serfs, and the prospect of wealth to keep them working; wealth as the end and aim of politics, and as the legal tender for law and order; and, finally, instead of Truth, Beauty, and Goodness, wealth as the ideal of the Public School.

Not only is this true in the world which Atlanta typifies, but it is threatening to be true of a world beneath and beyond that world,—the Black World beyond the Veil. To-day it makes little difference to Atlanta, to the South, what the Negro thinks or dreams or wills. In the soul-life of the land he is to-day, and naturally will long remain, unthought of, half forgotten; and yet when he does come to think and will and do for himself,— and let no man dream that day will never come,—then the part he plays will not be one of sudden learning, but words and thoughts he has been taught to lisp in his race-childhood. To-day the ferment of his striving toward self-realization is to the strife of the white world like a wheel within a wheel: beyond the Veil are smaller but like problems of ideals, of leaders and the led, of serfdom, of poverty, of order and subordination, and, through all, the Veil of Race. Few know of these problems, few who know notice them; and yet there they are, awaiting student, artist, and seer, — a field for somebody sometime to discover. Hither has the temptation of Hippomenes penetrated; already in this smaller world, which now indirectly and anon directly must influence the larger for good or ill, the habit is forming of interpreting the world in dollars. The old leaders of Negro opinion, in the little groups where there is a Negro social consciousness, are being replaced by new; neither the black preacher nor the black teacher leads as he did two decades ago. Into their places are pushing the farmers and gardeners, the well-paid porters and artisans, the businessmen, — all those with property and money. And with all this change, so curiously parallel to that of the Other-world, goes too the same inevitable change in ideals. The South laments to-day the slow, steady disappearance of a certain type of Negro, — the faithful, courteous slave of other days, with his incorruptible honesty and dignified humility. He is passing away just as surely as the old type of Southern gentleman is passing, and from not dissimilar causes, — the sudden transformation of a fair far-off ideal of Freedom into the hard reality of bread-winning and the consequent deification of Bread.

In the Black World, the Preacher and Teacher embodied once the ideals of this people, — the strife for another and a juster world, the vague dream of righteousness, the mystery of knowing; but to-day the danger is that these ideals, with their simple beauty and weird inspiration, will suddenly sink to a question of cash and a lust for gold. Here stands this black young Atalanta, girding herself for the race that must be run; and if her eyes be still toward the hills and sky as in the days of old, then we may look for noble running; but what if some ruthless or wily or even thoughtless Hippomenes lay golden apples before her? What if the Negro people be wooed from a strife for righteousness, from a love of knowing, to regard dollars as the be-all and end-all of life? What if to the Mammonism of America be added the rising Mammonism of the re-born South, and the Mammonism of this South be reinforced by the budding Mammonism of its half-awakened black millions?[17] Whither, then, is the new-world quest of Goodness and Beauty and Truth gone glimmering? Must this, and that fair flower of Freedom which, despite the jeers of latter-day striplings, sprung from our fathers' blood, must that too degenerate into a dusty quest of gold, — into lawless lust with Hippomenes?

The hundred hills of Atlanta are not all crowned with factories. On one, toward the west, the setting sun throws three buildings in bold relief against the sky. The beauty of the group lies in its simple unity: — a broad lawn of green rising from the red street with mingled roses and peaches; north and south, two plain and stately halls; and in the midst, half hidden in ivy, a larger building, boldly graceful, sparingly decorated, and with one low spire. It is a restful group,—one never looks for more; it is all here, all intelligible. There I live, and there I hear from day to day the low hum of restful life. In winter's twilight, when the red sun glows, I can see the dark figures pass between the halls to the music of the night-bell. In the morning, when the sun is golden, the clang of the day-bell brings the hurry and laughter of three hundred young hearts from hall and street, and from the busy city below,—children all dark and heavy-haired,—to join their clear young voices in the music of the morning sacrifice. In a half-dozen class-rooms they gather then,—here to follow the Love-song of Dido, here to listen to the tale of Troy divine;[18] there to wander among the stars, there to wander among men and nations,—and elsewhere other well-worn ways of knowing this queer world. Nothing new, no time-saving devices,— simply old time-glorified methods of delving for Truth, and searching out the hidden beauties of life, and learning the good of living. The riddle of existence is the college curriculum that was laid before the Pharaohs, that was taught in the groves by Plato, that formed the *trivium* and *quadrivium,* and is to-day laid before the freedmen's sons by Atlanta University.[19] And this course of study will not change; its methods will grow more deft and effectual, its content richer by toil of scholar and sight of seer; but the true college will ever have one goal,—not to earn meat, but to know the end and aim of that life which meat nourishes.

The vision of life that rises before these dark eyes has in it nothing mean or selfish. Not at Oxford or at Leipsic, not at Yale or Columbia,[20] is there an air of higher resolve or more unfettered striving; the determination to realize for men, both black and white, the broadest possibilities of life, to seek the better and the best, to spread with their own hands the Gospel of Sacrifice,—all this is the burden of their talk and dream. Here, amid a wide desert of caste and proscription, amid the heart-hurting slights and jars and vagaries of a deep race-dislike, lies this green oasis, where hot anger cools, and the bitterness of disappointment is sweetened by the springs and breezes of Parnassus;[21] and here men may lie and listen, and learn of a future fuller than the past, and hear the voice of Time:

"Entbehren sollst du, sollst entbehren."[22]

They made their mistakes, those who planted Fisk and Howard and Atlanta before the smoke of battle had lifted; they made their mistakes, but those mistakes were not the things at which we lately laughed somewhat uproariously. They were right when they sought to found a new educational system upon the University: where, forsooth, shall we ground knowledge save on the broadest and deepest knowledge? The roots of the tree, rather than the leaves, are the sources of its life; and from the dawn of history, from Academus to Cambridge,[23] the culture of the University has been the broad foundation-stone on which is built the kindergarten's A B C.

But these builders did make a mistake in minimizing the gravity of the problem before them; in thinking it a matter of years and decades; in therefore building quickly and laying their foundation carelessly, and lowering the standard of knowing, until they had scattered haphazard through the South some dozen poorly equipped high schools and miscalled them universities. They forgot, too, just as their successors are forgetting, the rule of inequality:—that of the million black youth, some were fitted to know and some to dig; that some had the talent and capacity of university men, and some the talent and capacity of blacksmiths; and that true training meant neither that all should be college men nor all artisans, but that the one should be made a missionary of culture to an untaught people, and the other a free workman among serfs. And to seek to make the blacksmith a scholar is almost as silly as the more modern scheme of making the scholar a blacksmith; almost, but not quite.

The function of the university is not simply to teach bread-winning, or to furnish teachers for the public schools, or to be a centre of polite society; it is, above all, to be the organ of that fine adjustment between real life and the growing knowledge of life, an adjustment which forms the secret of civilization. Such an institution the South of to-day sorely needs. She has religion, earnest, bigoted:—religion that on both sides the Veil often omits the sixth, seventh, and eighth commandments,[24] but substitutes a dozen supplementary ones. She has, as Atlanta shows, growing thrift and love of toil; but she lacks that broad knowledge of what the world knows and knew of human living and doing, which she may apply to the thousand problems of real life to-day confronting her. The need of the South is knowledge and culture,—not in dainty limited quantity, as before the war, but in broad busy abundance in the world of work; and until she has this, not all the Apples of Hesperides, be they golden and bejewelled, can save her from the curse of the Bœotian lovers.[25]

The Wings of Atalanta are the coming universities of the South. They alone can bear the maiden past the temptation of golden fruit. They will not guide her flying feet away from the cotton and gold; for—ah, thoughtful Hippomenes!—do not the apples lie in the very Way of Life? But they will guide her over and beyond them, and leave her kneeling in the Sanctuary of Truth and Freedom and broad Humanity, virgin and undefiled. Sadly did the Old South err in human education, despising the education of the masses, and niggardly in the support of colleges. Her ancient university foundations dwindled and withered under the foul breath of slavery; and even since the war they have fought a failing fight for life in the tainted air of social unrest and commercial selfishness, stunted by the death of criticism, and starving for lack of broadly cultured men. And if this is the white South's need and danger, how much heavier the danger and need of the freedmen's sons! how pressing here the need of broad ideals and true culture, the conservation of soul from sordid aims and petty passions! Let us build the Southern university—William and Mary, Trinity, Georgia, Texas, Tulane, Vanderbilt,[26] and the others—fit to live; let us build, too, the Negro universities:—Fisk, whose foundation was ever broad; Howard, at the heart of the Nation; Atlanta at Atlanta, whose ideal of scholarship has been held above the temptation of numbers. Why not here, and perhaps elsewhere, plant deeply and for all time centres of learning and living, colleges that yearly would send into the life of the South a few white men and a few black men of broad culture, catholic tolerance, and trained ability, joining their hands to other hands, and giving to this squabble of the Races a decent and dignified peace?

Patience, Humility, Manners, and Taste, common schools and kindergartens, industrial and technical schools, literature and tolerance,—all these spring from knowledge and culture, the children of the university. So must men and nations build, not otherwise, not upside down.

Teach workers to work,—a wise saying; wise when applied to German boys and American girls; wiser when said of Negro boys, for they have less knowledge of working and none to teach them. Teach thinkers to think,—a needed knowledge in a day of loose and careless logic; and they whose lot is gravest must have the carefulest training to think aright. If these things are so, how foolish to ask what is the best education for one or seven or sixty million souls! shall we teach them trades, or train them in liberal arts? Neither and both: teach the workers to work and the thinkers to think; make carpenters of carpenters, and philosophers of philosophers, and fops of fools. Nor can we pause here. We are training not isolated men but a living group of men,—nay, a group within a group. And the final product of our training must be neither a psychologist nor a brickmason, but a man. And to make men, we must have ideals, broad, pure, and inspiring ends of living,—not sordid money-getting, not apples of gold. The worker must work for the glory of his handiwork, not simply for pay; the thinker must think for truth, not for fame. And all this is gained only by human strife and longing; by ceaseless training and education; by founding Right on righteousness and Truth on the unhampered search for Truth; by founding the common school on the university, and the industrial school on the common school; and weaving thus a system, not a distortion, and bringing a birth, not an abortion.

When night falls on the City of a Hundred Hills, a wind gathers itself from the seas and comes murmuring westward. And at its bidding, the smoke of the drowsy factories sweeps down upon the mighty city and covers it like a pall, while yonder at the University the stars twinkle above Stone Hall. And they say that yon gray mist is the tunic of Atalanta pausing over her golden apples. Fly, my maiden, fly, for yonder comes Hippomenes!

VI

Of the Training of Black Men

Why, if the Soul can fling the Dust aside,
And naked on the Air of Heaven ride,
    Were't not a Shame—were't not a Shame for him
In this clay carcase crippled to abide?

OMAR KHAYYÁM (FITZGERALD)

From the shimmering swirl of waters where many, many thoughts ago the slave ship first saw the square tower of Jamestown,[2] have flowed down to our day three streams of thinking: one swollen from the larger world here and overseas, saying, the multiplying of human wants in culture-lands calls for the world-wide cooperation of men in satisfying them. Hence arises a new human unity, pulling the ends of earth nearer, and all men, black, yellow, and white. The larger humanity strives to feel in this contact of living Nations and sleeping hordes a thrill of new life in the world, crying, "If the contact of Life and Sleep be Death, shame on such Life." To be sure, behind this thought lurks the afterthought of force and dominion,—the making of brown men to delve when the temptation of beads and red calico cloys.

The second thought streaming from the death-ship and the curving river is the thought of the older South,—the sincere and passionate belief that somewhere between men and cattle, God created a *tertium quid*,[3] and called it a Negro,—a clownish, simple creature, at times even lovable within its limitations, but straitly foreordained to walk within the Veil. To be sure, behind the thought lurks the afterthought,—some of them with favoring chance might become men, but in sheer self-defence we dare not let them, and we build about them walls so high, and hang between them and the light a veil so thick, that they shall not even think of breaking through.

And last of all there trickles down that third and darker thought, — the thought of the things themselves, the confused, half-conscious mutter of men who are black and whitened, crying "Liberty, Freedom, Opportunity—vouchsafe to us, O boastful World, the chance of living men!" To be sure, behind the thought lurks the afterthought, — suppose, after all, the World is right and we are less than men? Suppose this mad impulse within is all wrong, some mock mirage from the untrue?

So here we stand among thoughts of human unity, even through conquest and slavery; the inferiority of black men, even if forced by fraud; a shriek in the night for the freedom of men who themselves are not yet sure of their right to demand it. This is the tangle of thought and afterthought wherein we are called to solve the problem of training men for life.

Behind all its curiousness, so attractive alike to sage and *dilettante*,[4] lie its dim dangers, throwing across us shadows at once grotesque and awful. Plain it is to us that what the world seeks through desert and wild we have within our threshold, — a stalwart laboring force, suited to the semi-tropics; if, deaf to the voice of the Zeitgeist,[5] we refuse to use and develop these men, we risk poverty and loss. If, on the other hand, seized by the brutal afterthought, we debauch the race thus caught in our talons, selfishly sucking their blood and brains in the future as in the past, what shall save us from national decadence? Only that saner selfishness, which Education teaches men, can find the rights of all in the whirl of work.

Again, we may decry the color-prejudice of the South, yet it remains a heavy fact. Such curious kinks of the human mind exist and must be reckoned with soberly. They cannot be laughed away, nor always successfully stormed at, nor easily abolished by act of legislature. And yet they must not be encouraged by being let alone. They must be recognized as facts, but unpleasant facts; things that stand in the way of civilization and religion and common decency. They can be met in but one way, — by the breadth and broadening of human reason, by catholicity of taste and culture. And so, too, the native ambition and aspiration of men, even though they be black, backward, and ungraceful, must not lightly be dealt with. To stimulate wildly weak and untrained minds is to play with mighty fires; to flout their striving idly is to welcome a harvest of brutish crime and shameless lethargy in our very laps. The guiding of thought and the deft coordination of deed is at once the path of honor and humanity.

And so, in this great question of reconciling three vast and partially contradictory streams of thought, the one panacea of Education leaps to the lips of all: — such human training as will best use the labor of all men without enslaving or brutalizing; such training as will give us poise to encourage the prejudices that bulwark society, and to stamp out those that in sheer barbarity deafen us to the wail of prisoned souls within the Veil, and the mounting fury of shackled men.

But when we have vaguely said that Education will set this tangle straight, what have we uttered but a truism? Training for life teaches living; but what training for the profitable living together of black men and white? A hundred and fifty years ago our task would have seemed easier. Then Dr. Johnson[6] blandly assured us that education was needful solely for the embellishments of life, and was useless for ordinary vermin. To-day we have climbed to heights where we would open at least the outer courts of knowledge to all, display its treasures to many, and select the few to whom its mystery of Truth is revealed, not wholly by birth or the accidents of the stock market, but at least in part according to deftness and aim, talent and character. This programme, however, we are sorely puzzled in carrying out through that part of the land where the blight of slavery fell hardest, and where we are dealing with two backward peoples. To make here in human education that ever necessary combination of the permanent and the contingent — of the ideal and the practical in workable equilibrium — has been there, as it ever must be in every age and place, a matter of infinite experiment and frequent mistakes.

In rough approximation we may point out four varying decades of work in Southern education since the Civil War. From the close of the war until 1876, was the period of uncertain groping and temporary relief. There were army schools, mission schools, and schools of the Freedman's Bureau in chaotic disarrangement seeking system and cooperation. Then followed ten years of constructive definite effort toward the building of complete school systems in the South. Normal schools and colleges were founded for the freedmen, and teachers trained there to man the public schools. There was the inevitable tendency of war to under-estimate the prejudices of the master and the ignorance of the slave, and all seemed clear sailing out of the wreckage of the storm. Meantime, starting in this decade yet especially developing from 1885 to 1895, began the industrial revolution of the South. The land saw glimpses of a new destiny and the stirring of new ideals. The educational system striving to complete itself saw new obstacles and a field of work ever broader and deeper. The Negro colleges, hurriedly founded, were inadequately equipped, illogically distributed, and of varying efficiency and grade; the normal and high schools were doing little more than common-school work, and the common schools were training but a third of the children who ought to be in them, and training these too often poorly. At the same time the white South, by reason of its sudden conversion from the slavery ideal, by so much the more became set and strengthened in its racial prejudice, and crystallized it into harsh law and harsher custom; while the marvellous pushing forward of the poor white daily threatened to take even bread and butter from the mouths of the heavily handicapped sons of the freedmen. In the midst, then, of the larger problem of Negro education sprang up the more practical question of work, the inevitable economic quandary that faces a people in the transition from slavery to freedom, and especially those who make that change amid hate and prejudice, lawlessness and ruthless competition.

The industrial school springing to notice in this decade, but coming to full recognition in the decade beginning with 1895, was the proffered answer to this combined educational and economic crisis, and an answer of singular wisdom and timeliness. From the very first in nearly all the schools some attention had been given to training in handiwork, but now was this training first raised to a dignity that brought it in direct touch with the South's magnificent industrial development, and given an emphasis which reminded black folk that before the Temple of Knowledge swing the Gates of Toil.

Yet after all they are but gates, and when turning our eyes from the temporary and the contingent in the Negro problem to the broader question of the permanent uplifting and civilization of black men in America, we have a right to inquire, as this enthusiasm for material advancement mounts to its height, if after all the industrial school is the final and sufficient answer in the training of the Negro race; and to ask gently, but in all sincerity, the ever-recurring query of the ages, Is not life more than meat, and the body more than raiment? And men ask this to-day all the more eagerly because of sinister signs in recent educational movements. The tendency is here, born of slavery and quickened to renewed life by the crazy imperialism of the day, to regard human beings as among the material resources of a land to be trained with an eye single to future dividends. Race-prejudices, which keep brown and black men in their "places," we are coming to regard as useful allies with such a theory, no matter how much they may dull the ambition and sicken the hearts of struggling human beings. And above all, we daily hear that an education that encourages aspiration, that sets the loftiest of ideals and seeks as an end culture and character rather than bread-winning, is the privilege of white men and the danger and delusion of black.

Especially has criticism been directed against the former educational efforts to aid the Negro. In the four periods I have mentioned, we find first, boundless, planless enthusiasm and sacrifice; then the preparation of teachers for a vast public-school system; then the launching and expansion of that school system amid increasing difficulties; and finally the training of workmen for the new and growing industries. This development has been sharply ridiculed as a logical anomaly and flat reversal of nature. Soothly we have been told that first industrial and manual training should have taught the Negro to work, then simple schools should have taught him to read and write, and finally, after years, high and normal schools could have completed the system, as intelligence and wealth demanded.

That a system logically so complete was historically impossible, it needs but a little thought to prove. Progress in human affairs is more often a pull than a push, surging forward of the exceptional man, and the lifting of his duller brethren slowly and painfully to his vantage-ground. Thus it was no accident that gave birth to universities centuries before the common schools, that made fair Harvard[7] the first flower of our wilderness. So in the South: the mass of the freedmen at the end of the war lacked the intelligence so necessary to modern workingmen. They must first have the common school to teach them to read, write, and cipher; and they must have higher schools to teach teachers for the common schools. The white teachers who flocked South went to establish such a common-school system. Few held the idea of founding colleges; most of them at first would have laughed at the idea. But they faced, as all men since them have faced, that central paradox of the South,—the social separation of the races. At that time it was the sudden volcanic rupture of nearly all relations between black and white, in work and government and family life. Since then a new adjustment of relations in economic and political affairs has grown up,—an adjustment subtle and difficult to grasp, yet singularly ingenious, which leaves still that frightful chasm at the color-line across which men pass at their peril. Thus, then and now, there stand in the South two separate worlds; and separate not simply in the higher realms of social intercourse, but also in church and school, on railway and street-car, in hotels and theatres, in streets and city sections, in books and newspapers, in asylums and jails, in hospitals and graveyards. There is still enough of contact for large economic and group cooperation, but the separation is so thorough and deep that it absolutely precludes for the present between the races anything like that sympathetic and effective group-training and leadership of the one by the other, such as the American Negro and all backward peoples must have for effectual progress.

This the missionaries of '68 soon saw;[8] and if effective industrial and trade schools were impracticable before the establishment of a common-school system, just as certainly no adequate common schools could be founded until there were teachers to teach them. Southern whites would not teach them; Northern whites in sufficient numbers could not be had. If the Negro was to learn, he must teach himself, and the most effective help that could be given him was the establishment of schools to train Negro teachers. This conclusion was slowly but surely reached by every student of the situation until simultaneously, in widely separated regions, without consultation or systematic plan, there arose a series of institutions designed to furnish teachers for the untaught. Above the sneers of critics at the obvious defects of this procedure must ever stand its one crushing rejoinder: in a single generation they put thirty thousand black teachers in the South; they wiped out the illiteracy of the majority of the black people of the land, and they made Tuskegee[9] possible.

Such higher training-schools tended naturally to deepen broader development: at first they were common and grammar schools, then some became high schools. And finally, by 1900, some thirty-four had one year or more of studies of college grade. This development was reached with different degrees of speed in different institutions: Hampton is still a high school, while Fisk University started her college in 1871, and Spelman Seminary about 1896.[10] In all cases the aim was identical, — to maintain the standards of the lower training by giving teachers and leaders the best practicable training; and above all, to furnish the black world with adequate standards of human culture and lofty ideals of life. It was not enough that the teachers of teachers should be trained in technical normal methods; they must also, so far as possible, be broad-minded, cultured men and women, to scatter civilization among a people whose ignorance was not simply of letters, but of life itself.

It can thus be seen that the work of education in the South began with higher institutions of training, which threw off as their foliage common schools, and later industrial schools, and at the same time strove to shoot their roots ever deeper toward college and university training. That this was an inevitable and necessary development, sooner or later, goes without saying; but there has been, and still is, a question in many minds if the natural growth was not forced, and if the higher training was not either overdone or done with cheap and unsound methods. Among white

Southerners this feeling is widespread and positive. A prominent Southern journal voiced this in a recent editorial.

"The experiment that has been made to give the colored students classical training has not been satisfactory. Even though many were able to pursue the course, most of them did so in a parrot-like way, learning what was taught, but not seeming to appropriate the truth and import of their instruction, and graduating without sensible aim or valuable occupation for their future. The whole scheme has proved a waste of time, efforts, and the money of the state."

While most fair-minded men would recognize this as extreme and overdrawn, still without doubt many are asking, Are there a sufficient number of Negroes ready for college training to warrant the undertaking? Are not too many students prematurely forced into this work? Does it not have the effect of dissatisfying the young Negro with his environment? And do these graduates succeed in real life? Such natural questions cannot be evaded, nor on the other hand must a Nation naturally skeptical as to Negro ability assume an unfavorable answer without careful inquiry and patient openness to conviction. We must not forget that most Americans answer all queries regarding the Negro *a priori*,[11] and that the least that human courtesy can do is to listen to evidence.

The advocates of the higher education of the Negro would be the last to deny the incompleteness and glaring defects of the present system: too many institutions have attempted to do college work, the work in some cases has not been thoroughly done, and quantity rather than quality has sometimes been sought. But all this can be said of higher education throughout the land; it is the almost inevitable incident of educational growth, and leaves the deeper question of the legitimate demand for the higher training of Negroes untouched. And this latter question can be settled in but one way, — by a first-hand study of the facts. If we leave out of view all institutions which have not actually graduated students from a course higher than that of a New England high school, even though they be called colleges; if then we take the thirty-four remaining institutions, we may clear up many misapprehensions by asking searchingly, What kind of institutions are they? what do they teach? and what sort of men do they graduate?

And first we may say that this type of college, including Atlanta, Fisk, and Howard, Wilberforce and Lincoln, Biddle, Shaw, and the rest, is peculiar, almost unique.[12] Through the shining trees that whisper before me as I write, I catch glimpses of a boulder of New England granite, covering a grave, which graduates of Atlanta University have placed there, with this inscription:

> "IN GRATEFUL MEMORY OF THEIR
> FORMER TEACHER AND FRIEND
> AND OF THE UNSELFISH LIFE HE
> LIVED, AND THE NOBLE WORK HE
> WROUGHT; THAT THEY, THEIR
> CHILDREN, AND THEIR CHILD-
> REN'S CHILDREN MIGHT BE
> BLESSED."

This was the gift of New England to the freed Negro: not alms, but a friend; not cash, but character. It was not and is not money these seething millions want, but love and sympathy, the pulse of hearts beating with red blood;—a gift which to-day only their own kindred and race can bring to the masses, but which once saintly souls brought to their favored children in the crusade of the sixties,[13] that finest thing in American history, and one of the few things untainted by sordid greed and cheap vainglory. The teachers in these institutions came not to keep the Negroes in their place, but to raise them out of the defilement of the places where slavery had wallowed them. The colleges they founded were social settlements; homes where the best of the sons of the freedmen came in close and sympathetic touch with the best traditions of New England.[14] They lived and ate together, studied and worked, hoped and harkened in the dawning light. In actual formal content their curriculum was doubtless old-fashioned, but in educational power it was supreme, for it was the contact of living souls.

From such schools about two thousand Negroes have gone forth with the bachelor's degree. The number in itself is enough to put at rest the argument that too large a proportion of Negroes are receiving higher training. If the ratio to population of all Negro students throughout the land, in both college and secondary training, be counted, Commissioner Harris[15] assures us "it must be increased to five times its present average" to equal the average of the land.

Fifty years ago the ability of Negro students in any appreciable numbers to master a modern college course would have been difficult to prove. To-day it is proved by the fact that four hundred Negroes, many of whom have been reported as brilliant students, have received the bachelor's degree from Harvard, Yale, Oberlin, and seventy other leading colleges.[16] Here we have, then, nearly twenty-five hundred Negro graduates, of whom the crucial query must be made, How far did their training fit them for life? It is of course extremely difficult to collect satisfactory data on such a point, — difficult to reach the men, to get trustworthy testimony, and to gauge that testimony by any generally acceptable criterion of success. In 1900, the Conference at Atlanta University undertook to study these graduates, and published the results.[17] First they sought to know what these graduates were doing, and succeeded in getting answers from nearly two-thirds of the living. The direct testimony was in almost all cases corroborated by the reports of the colleges where they graduated, so that in the main the reports were worthy of credence. Fifty-three per cent of these graduates were teachers, — presidents of institutions, heads of normal schools, principals of city school-systems, and the like. Seventeen per cent were clergymen; another seventeen per cent were in the professions, chiefly as physicians. Over six per cent were merchants, farmers, and artisans, and four per cent were in the government civil-service. Granting even that a considerable proportion of the third unheard from are unsuccessful, this is a record of usefulness. Personally I know many hundreds of these graduates, and have corresponded with more than a thousand; through others I have followed carefully the life-work of scores; I have taught some of them and some of the pupils whom they have taught, lived in homes which they have builded, and looked at life through their eyes. Comparing them as a class with my fellow students in New England and in Europe, I cannot hesitate in saying that nowhere have I met men and women with a broader spirit of helpfulness, with deeper devotion to their life-work, or with more consecrated determination to succeed in the face of bitter difficulties than among Negro college-bred men. They have, to be sure, their proportion of ne'er-do-weels, their pedants and lettered fools, but they have a surprisingly small proportion of them; they have not that culture of manner which we instinctively associate with university men, forgetting that in reality it is the heritage from cultured homes, and that no people a generation removed from slavery can escape a certain unpleasant rawness and *gaucherie,*[18] despite the best of training.

With all their larger vision and deeper sensibility, these men have usually been conservative, careful leaders. They have seldom been agitators, have withstood the temptation to head the mob, and have worked steadily and faithfully in a thousand communities in the South. As teachers, they have given the South a commendable system of city schools and large numbers of private normal-schools and academies. Colored college-bred men have worked side by side with white college graduates at Hampton; almost from the beginning the back-bone of Tuskegee's teaching force has been formed of graduates from Fisk and Atlanta. And to-day the institute is filled with college graduates, from the energetic wife of the principal down to the teacher of agriculture, including nearly half of the executive council and a majority of the heads of departments. In the professions, college men are slowly but surely leavening the Negro church, are healing and preventing the devastations of disease, and beginning to furnish legal protection for the liberty and property of the toiling masses. All this is needful work. Who would do it if Negroes did not? How could Negroes do it if they were not trained carefully for it? If white people need colleges to furnish teachers, ministers, lawyers, and doctors, do black people need nothing of the sort?

If it is true that there are an appreciable number of Negro youth in the land capable by character and talent to receive that higher training, the end of which is culture, and if the two and a half thousand who have had something of this training in the past have in the main proved themselves useful to their race and generation, the question then comes, What place in the future development of the South ought the Negro college and college-bred man to occupy? That the present social separation and acute race-sensitiveness must eventually yield to the influences of culture, as the South grows civilized, is clear. But such transformation calls for singular wisdom and patience. If, while the healing of this vast sore is progressing, the races are to live for many years side by side, united in economic effort, obeying a common government, sensitive to mutual thought and feeling, yet subtly and silently separate in many matters of deeper human intimacy,—if this unusual and dangerous development is to progress amid peace and order, mutual respect and growing intelligence, it will call for social surgery at once the delicatest and nicest in modern history. It will demand broad-minded, upright men, both white and black, and in its final accomplishment American civilization will triumph. So far as white men are concerned, this fact is to-day being recognized in the South, and a happy renaissance of university education seems imminent. But the very voices that cry hail to this good work are, strange to relate, largely silent or antagonistic to the higher education of the Negro.

Strange to relate! for this is certain, no secure civilization can be built in the South with the Negro as an ignorant, turbulent proletariat. Suppose we seek to remedy this by making them laborers and nothing more: they are not fools, they have tasted of the Tree of Life, and they will not cease to think, will not cease attempting to read the riddle of the world. By taking away their best equipped teachers and leaders, by slamming the door of opportunity in the faces of their bolder and brighter minds, will you make them satisfied with their lot? or will you not rather transfer their leading from the hands of men taught to think to the hands of untrained demagogues? We ought not to forget that despite the pressure of poverty, and despite the active discouragement and even ridicule of friends, the demand for higher training steadily increases among Negro youth: there were, in the years from 1875 to 1880, 22 Negro graduates from Northern colleges; from 1885 to 1890 there were 43, and from 1895 to 1900, nearly 100 graduates. From Southern Negro colleges there were, in the same three periods, 143, 413, and over 500 graduates. Here, then, is the plain thirst for training; by refusing to give this Talented Tenth[19] the key to knowledge, can any sane man imagine that they will lightly lay aside their yearning and contentedly become hewers of wood and drawers of water?

No. The dangerously clear logic of the Negro's position will more and more loudly assert itself in that day when increasing wealth and more intricate social organization preclude the South from being, as it so largely is, simply an armed camp for intimidating black folk. Such waste of energy cannot be spared if the South is to catch up with civilization. And as the black third of the land grows in thrift and skill, unless skilfully guided in its larger philosophy, it must more and more brood over the red past and the creeping, crooked present, until it grasps a gospel of revolt and revenge and throws its new-found energies athwart the current of advance. Even to-day the masses of the Negroes see all too clearly the anomalies of their position and the moral crookedness of yours. You may marshal strong indictments against them, but their counter-cries, lacking though they be in formal logic, have burning truths within them which you may not wholly ignore, O Southern Gentlemen! If you deplore their presence here, they ask, Who brought us? When you cry, Deliver us from the vision of intermarriage, they answer that legal marriage is infinitely better than systematic concubinage and prostitution. And if in just fury you accuse their vagabonds of violating women, they also in fury quite as just may reply: The wrong which your gentlemen have done against helpless black women in defiance of your own laws is written on the foreheads of two millions of mulattoes, and written in ineffaceable blood. And finally, when you fasten crime upon this race as its peculiar trait, they answer that slavery was the arch-crime, and lynching and lawlessness its twin abortion; that color and race are not crimes, and yet they it is which in this land receives most unceasing condemnation, North, East, South, and West.

I will not say such arguments are wholly justified, — I will not insist that there is no other side to the shield; but I do say that of the nine millions of Negroes in this nation, there is scarcely one out of the cradle to whom these arguments do not daily present themselves in the guise of terrible truth. I insist that the question of the future is how best to keep these millions from brooding over the wrongs of the past and the difficulties of the present, so that all their energies may be bent toward a cheerful striving and co-operation with their white neighbors toward a larger, juster, and fuller future. That one wise method of doing this lies in the closer knitting of the Negro to the great industrial possibilities of the South is a great truth. And this the common schools and the manual training and trade schools are working to accomplish. But these alone are not enough. The foundations of knowledge in this race, as in others, must be sunk deep in the college and university if we would build a solid, permanent structure. Internal problems of social advance must inevitably come, — problems of work and wages, of families and homes, of morals and the true valuing of the things of life; and all these and other inevitable problems of civilization the Negro must meet and solve largely for himself, by reason of his isolation; and can there be any possible solution other than by study and thought and an appeal to the rich experience of the past? Is there not, with such a group and in such a crisis, infinitely more danger to be apprehended from half-trained minds and shallow thinking than from over-education and over-refinement? Surely we have wit enough to found a Negro college so manned and equipped as to steer successfully between the *dilettante* and the fool. We shall hardly induce black men to believe that if their stomachs be full, it matters little about their brains. They already dimly perceive that the paths of peace winding between honest toil and dignified manhood call for the guidance of skilled thinkers, the loving, reverent comradeship between the black lowly and the black men emancipated by training and culture.

The function of the Negro college, then, is clear: it must maintain the standards of popular education, it must seek the social regeneration of the Negro, and it must help in the solution of problems of race contact and co-operation. And finally, beyond all this, it must develop men. Above our modern socialism, and out of the worship of the mass, must persist and evolve that higher individualism which the centres of culture protect; there must come a loftier respect for the sovereign human soul that seeks to know itself and the world about it; that seeks a freedom for expansion and self-development; that will love and hate and labor in its own way, untrammeled alike by old and new. Such souls aforetime have inspired and guided worlds, and if we be not wholly bewitched by our Rhinegold,[20] they shall again. Herein the longing of black men must have respect: the rich and bitter depth of their experience, the unknown treasures of their inner life, the strange rendings of nature they have seen, may give the world new points of view and make their loving, living, and doing precious to all human hearts. And to themselves in these the days that try their souls, the chance to soar in the dim blue air above the smoke is to their finer spirits boon and guerdon for what they lose on earth by being black.

I sit with Shakespeare and he winces not. Across the color line I move arm in arm with Balzac and Dumas, where smiling men and welcoming women glide in gilded halls. From out the caves of evening that swing between the strong-limbed earth and the tracery of the stars, I summon Aristotle and Aurelius and what soul I will, and they come all graciously with no scorn nor condescension. So, wed with Truth, I dwell above the Veil. Is this the life you grudge us, O knightly America? Is this the life you long to change into the dull red hideousness of Georgia? Are you so afraid lest peering from this high Pisgah, between Philistine and Amalekite, we sight the Promised Land?[21]

VII

Of the Black Belt

I am black but comely, O ye daughters of Jerusalem,
As the tents of Kedar, as the curtains of Solomon.
Look not upon me, because I am black,
Because the sun hath looked upon me:
My mother's children were angry with me;
They made me the keeper of the vineyards;
But mine own vineyard have I not kept.

THE SONG OF SOLOMON.

Out of the North the train thundered, and we woke to see the crimson soil of Georgia stretching away bare and monotonous right and left. Here and there lay straggling, unlovely villages, and lean men loafed leisurely at the depots; then again came the stretch of pines and clay. Yet we did not nod, nor weary of the scene; for this is historic ground. Right across our track, three hundred and sixty years ago, wandered the cavalcade of Hernando de Soto,[2] looking for gold and the Great Sea; and he and his foot-sore captives disappeared yonder in the grim forests to the west. Here sits Atlanta, the city of a hundred hills, with something Western, something Southern, and something quite its own, in its busy life. And a little past Atlanta, to the southwest, is the land of the Cherokees,[3] and there, not far from where Sam Hose[4] was crucified, you may stand on a spot which is to-day the centre of the Negro problem,—the centre of those nine million men who are America's dark heritage from slavery and the slave-trade.

Not only is Georgia thus the geographical focus of our Negro population, but in many other respects, both now and yesterday, the Negro problems have seemed to be centered in this State. No other State in the Union can count a million Negroes among its citizens,—a population as large as the slave population of the whole Union in 1800; no other State fought so long and strenuously to gather this host of Africans. Oglethorpe[5] thought slavery against law and gospel; but the circumstances which gave Georgia its first inhabitants were not calculated to furnish citizens overnice in their ideas about rum and slaves. Despite the prohibitions of the trustees, these Georgians, like some of their descendants, proceeded to take the law into their own hands; and so pliant were the judges, and so flagrant the smuggling, and so earnest were the prayers of Whitefield,[6] that by the middle of the eighteenth century all restrictions were swept away, and the slave-trade went merrily on for fifty years and more.

Down in Darien, where the Delegal riots took place some summers ago, there used to come a strong protest against slavery from the Scotch Highlanders; and the Moravians of Ebenezea did not like the system.[7] But not till the Haytian Terror of Toussaint was the trade in men even checked; while the national statute of 1808 did not suffice to stop it.[8] How the Africans poured in!—fifty thousand between 1790 and 1810, and then, from Virginia and from smugglers, two thousand a year for many years more. So the thirty thousand Negroes of Georgia in 1790 were doubled in a decade,—were over a hundred thousand in 1810, had reached two hundred thousand in 1820, and half a million at the time of the war. Thus like a snake the black population writhed upward.

But we must hasten on our journey. This that we pass as we leave Atlanta is the ancient land of the Cherokees,—that brave Indian nation which strove so long for its fatherland, until Fate and the United States Government drove them beyond the Mississippi. If you wish to ride with me you must come into the "Jim Crow Car."[9] There will be no objection,— already four other white men, and a little white girl with her nurse, are in there. Usually the races are mixed in there; but the white coach is all white. Of course this car is not so good as the other, but it is fairly clean and comfortable. The discomfort lies chiefly in the hearts of those four black men yonder—and in mine.

We rumble south in quite a business-like way. The bare red clay and pines of Northern Georgia begin to disappear, and in their place appears a rich rolling land, luxuriant, and here and there well tilled. This is the land of the Creek Indians;[10] and a hard time the Georgians had to seize it. The towns grow more frequent and more interesting, and brand-new cotton mills rise on every side. Below Macon the world grows darker; for now we approach the Black Belt,[11]—that strange land of shadows, at which even slaves paled in the past, and whence come now only faint and half-intelligible murmurs to the world beyond. The "Jim Crow Car" grows larger and a shade better; three rough field-hands and two or three white loafers accompany us, and the newsboy still spreads his wares at one end. The sun is setting, but we can see the great cotton country as we enter it,—the soil now dark and fertile, now thin and gray, with fruit-trees and dilapidated buildings,—all the way to Albany.

At Albany, in the heart of the Black Belt, we stop. Two hundred miles south of Atlanta, two hundred miles west of the Atlantic, and one hundred miles north of the Great Gulf lies Dougherty County, with ten thousand Negroes and two thousand whites. The Flint River winds down from Andersonville, and, turning suddenly at Albany, the county-seat, hurries on to join the Chattahoochee and the sea. Andrew Jackson knew the Flint well, and marched across it once to avenge the Indian Massacre at Fort Mims.[12] That was in 1814, not long before the battle of New Orleans; and by the Creek treaty that followed this campaign, all Dougherty County, and much other rich land, was ceded to Georgia. Still, settlers fought shy of this land, for the Indians were all about, and they were unpleasant neighbors in those days. The panic of 1837, which Jackson bequeathed to Van Buren, turned the planters from the impoverished lands of Virginia, the Carolinas, and east Georgia, toward the West.[13] The Indians were removed to Indian Territory, and settlers poured into these coveted lands to retrieve their broken fortunes. For a radius of a hundred miles about Albany, stretched a great fertile land, luxuriant with forests of pine, oak, ash, hickory, and poplar; hot with the sun and damp with the rich black swamp-land; and here the corner-stone of the Cotton Kingdom was laid.[14]

Albany is to-day a wide-streeted, placid, Southern town, with a broad sweep of stores and saloons, and flanking rows of homes,—whites usually to the north, and blacks to the south. Six days in the week the town looks decidedly too small for itself, and takes frequent and prolonged naps. But on Saturday suddenly the whole county disgorges itself upon the place, and a perfect flood of black peasantry pours through the streets, fills the stores, blocks the sidewalks, chokes the thoroughfares, and takes full possession of the town. They are black, sturdy, uncouth country folk, good-natured and simple, talkative to a degree, and yet far more silent and brooding than the crowds of the Rhine-pfalz, or Naples, or Cracow.[15] They drink considerable quantities of whiskey, but do not get very drunk; they talk and laugh loudly at times, but seldom quarrel or fight. They walk up and down the streets, meet and gossip with friends, stare at the shop windows, buy coffee, cheap candy, and clothes, and at dusk drive home—happy? well no, not exactly happy, but much happier than as though they had not come.

Thus Albany is a real capital,—a typical Southern county town, the centre of the life of ten thousand souls; their point of contact with the outer world, their centre of news and gossip, their market for buying and selling, borrowing and lending, their fountain of justice and law. Once upon a time we knew country life so well and city life so little, that we illustrated city life as that of a closely crowded country district. Now the world has well-nigh forgotten what the country is, and we must imagine a little city of black people scattered far and wide over three hundred lonesome square miles of land, without train or trolley, in the midst of cotton and corn, and wide patches of sand and gloomy soil.

It gets pretty hot in Southern Georgia in July,—a sort of dull, determined heat that seems quite independent of the sun; so it took us some days to muster courage enough to leave the porch and venture out on the long country roads, that we might see this unknown world. Finally we started. It was about ten in the morning, bright with a faint breeze, and we jogged leisurely southward in the valley of the Flint. We passed the scattered box-like cabins of the brick-yard hands, and the long tenement-row facetiously called "The Ark," and were soon in the open country, and on the confines of the great plantations of other days. There is the "Joe Fields place"; a rough old fellow was he, and had killed many a "nigger" in his day. Twelve miles his plantation used to run,—a regular barony. It is nearly all gone now; only straggling bits belong to the family, and the rest has passed to Jews and Negroes. Even the bits which are left are heavily mortgaged, and, like the rest of the land, tilled by tenants. Here is one of them now,—a tall brown man, a hard worker and a hard drinker, illiterate, but versed in farm-lore, as his nodding crops declare. This distressingly new board house is his, and he has just moved out of yonder moss-grown cabin with its one square room.

From the curtains in Benton's house, down the road, a dark comely face is staring at the strangers; for passing carriages are not every-day occurrences here. Benton is an intelligent yellow man with a good-sized family, and manages a plantation blasted by the war and now the broken staff of the widow. He might be well-to-do, they say; but he carouses too much in Albany. And the half-desolate spirit of neglect born of the very soil seems to have settled on these acres. In times past there were cotton-gins and machinery here; but they have rotted away.

The whole land seems forlorn and forsaken. Here are the remnants of the vast plantations of the Sheldons, the Pellots, and the Rensons; but the souls of them are passed. The houses lie in half ruin, or have wholly disappeared; the fences have flown, and the families are wandering in the world. Strange vicissitudes have met these whilom masters. Yonder stretch the wide acres of Bildad Reasor; he died in war-time, but the upstart overseer hastened to wed the widow. Then he went, and his neighbors too, and now only the black tenant remains; but the shadow-hand of the master's grand-nephew or cousin or creditor stretches out of the gray distance to collect the rack-rent remorselessly, and so the land is uncared-for and poor. Only black tenants can stand such a system, and they only because they must. Ten miles we have ridden to-day and have seen no white face.

A resistless feeling of depression falls slowly upon us, despite the gaudy sunshine and the green cotton-fields. This, then, is the Cotton Kingdom, — the shadow of a marvellous dream. And where is the King? Perhaps this is he, — the sweating ploughman, tilling his eighty acres with two lean mules, and fighting a hard battle with debt. So we sit musing, until, as we turn a corner on the sandy road, there comes a fairer scene suddenly in view, — a neat cottage snugly ensconced by the road, and near it a little store. A tall bronzed man rises from the porch as we hail him, and comes out to our carriage. He is six feet in height, with a sober face that smiles gravely. He walks too straight to be a tenant, — yes, he owns two hundred and forty acres. "The land is run down since the boom-days of eighteen hundred and fifty," he explains, and cotton is low. Three black tenants live on his place, and in his little store he keeps a small stock of tobacco, snuff, soap, and soda, for the neighborhood. Here is his gin-house with new machinery just installed. Three hundred bales of cotton went through it last year. Two children he has sent away to school. Yes, he says sadly, he is getting on, but cotton is down to four cents; I know how Debt sits staring at him.

Wherever the King may be, the parks and palaces of the Cotton Kingdom have not wholly disappeared. We plunge even now into great groves of oak and towering pine, with an undergrowth of myrtle and shrubbery. This was the "home-house" of the Thompsons, — slave-barons who drove their coach and four in the merry past. All is silence now, and ashes, and tangled weeds. The owner put his whole fortune into the rising cotton industry of the fifties, and with the falling prices of the eighties he packed up and stole away. Yonder is another grove, with unkempt lawn, great magnolias, and grass-grown paths. The Big House stands in half-ruin, its great front door staring blankly at the street, and the back part grotesquely restored for its black tenant. A shabby, well-built Negro he is, unlucky and irresolute. He digs hard to pay rent to the white girl who owns the remnant of the place. She married a policeman, and lives in Savannah.

Now and again we come to churches. Here is one now,—Shepherd's, they call it,—a great whitewashed barn of a thing, perched on stilts of stone, and looking for all the world as though it were just resting here a moment and might be expected to waddle off down the road at almost any time. And yet it is the centre of a hundred cabin homes; and sometimes, of a Sunday, five hundred persons from far and near gather here and talk and eat and sing. There is a schoolhouse near,—a very airy, empty shed; but even this is an improvement, for usually the school is held in the church. The churches vary from log-huts to those like Shepherd's, and the schools from nothing to this little house that sits demurely on the county line. It is a tiny plank-house, perhaps ten by twenty, and has within a double row of rough unplaned benches, resting mostly on legs, sometimes on boxes. Opposite the door is a square home-made desk. In one corner are the ruins of a stove, and in the other a dim blackboard. It is the cheerfulest schoolhouse I have seen in Dougherty, save in town. Back of the schoolhouse is a lodge-house two stories high and not quite finished. Societies meet there,—societies "to care for the sick and bury the dead"; and these societies grow and flourish.

We had come to the boundaries of Dougherty, and were about to turn west along the county-line, when all these sights were pointed out to us by a kindly old man, black, white-haired, and seventy. Forty-five years he had lived here, and now supports himself and his old wife by the help of the steer tethered yonder and the charity of his black neighbors. He shows us the farm of the Hills just across the county line in Baker,—a widow and two strapping sons, who raised the bales (one need not add "cotton" down here) last year. There are fences and pigs and cows, and the soft-voiced, velvet-skinned young Memnon, who sauntered half-bashfully over to greet the strangers, is proud of his home. We turn now to the west along the county line. Great dismantled trunks of pines tower above the green cotton-fields, cracking their naked gnarled fingers toward the border of living forest beyond. There is little beauty in this region, only a sort of crude abandon that suggests power,—a naked grandeur, as it were. The houses are bare and straight; there are no hammocks or easy-chairs, and few flowers. So when, as here at Rawdon's, one sees a vine clinging to a little porch, and home-like windows peeping over the fences, one takes a long breath. I think I never before quite realized the place of the Fence in civilization. This is the Land of the Unfenced, where crouch on either hand scores of ugly one-room cabins, cheerless and dirty. Here lies the Negro problem in its naked dirt and penury. And here are no fences. But now and then the criss-cross rails or straight palings break into view, and then we know a touch of culture is near. Of course Harrison Gohagen, — a quiet yellow man, young, smooth-faced, and diligent, — of course he is lord of some hundred acres, and we expect to see a vision of well-kept rooms and fat beds and laughing children. For has he not fine fences? And those over yonder, why should they build fences on the rack-rented land? It will only increase their rent.

On we wind, through sand and pines and glimpses of old plantations, till there creeps into sight a cluster of buildings, — wood and brick, mills and houses, and scattered cabins. It seemed quite a village. As it came nearer and nearer, however, the aspect changed: the buildings were rotten, the bricks were falling out, the mills were silent, and the store was closed. Only in the cabins appeared now and then a bit of lazy life. I could imagine the place under some weird spell, and was half-minded to search out the princess. An old ragged black man, honest, simple, and improvident, told us the tale. The Wizard of the North—the Capitalist[16]—had rushed down in the seventies to woo this coy dark soil. He bought a square mile or more, and for a time the field-hands sang, the gins groaned, and the mills buzzed. Then came a change. The agent's son embezzled the funds and ran off with them. Then the agent himself disappeared. Finally the new agent stole even the books, and the company in wrath closed its business and its houses, refused to sell, and let houses and furniture and machinery rust and rot. So the Waters-Loring plantation was stilled by the spell of dishonesty, and stands like some gaunt rebuke to a scarred land.

Somehow that plantation ended our day's journey; for I could not shake off the influence of that silent scene. Back toward town we glided, past the straight and thread-like pines, past a dark tree-dotted pond where the air was heavy with a dead sweet perfume. White slender-legged curlews flitted by us, and the garnet blooms of the cotton looked gay against the green and purple stalks. A peasant girl was hoeing in the field, white-turbaned and black-limbed. All this we saw, but the spell still lay upon us.

How curious a land is this, — how full of untold story, of tragedy and laughter, and the rich legacy of human life; shadowed with a tragic past, and big with future promise! This is the Black Belt of Georgia. Dougherty County is the west end of the Black Belt, and men once called it the Egypt of the Confederacy.[17] It is full of historic interest. First there is the Swamp, to the west, where the Chickasawhatchee flows sullenly southward. The shadow of an old plantation lies at its edge, forlorn and dark. Then comes the pool; pendent gray moss and brackish waters appear, and forests filled with wildfowl. In one place the wood is on fire, smouldering in dull red anger; but nobody minds. Then the swamp grows beautiful; a raised road, built by chained Negro convicts, dips down into it, and forms a way walled and almost covered in living green. Spreading trees spring from a prodigal luxuriance of undergrowth; great dark green shadows fade into the black background, until all is one mass of tangled semi-tropical foliage, marvellous in its weird savage splendor. Once we crossed a black silent stream, where the sad trees and writhing creepers, all glinting fiery yellow and green, seemed like some vast cathedral, — some green Milan builded of wildwood. And as I crossed, I seemed to see again that fierce tragedy of seventy years ago. Osceola,[18] the Indian-Negro chieftain, had risen in the swamps of Florida, vowing vengeance. His war-cry reached the red Creeks of Dougherty, and their war-cry rang from the Chattahoochee to the sea. Men and women and children fled and fell before them as they swept into Dougherty. In yonder shadows a dark and hideously painted warrior glided stealthily on, — another and another, until three hundred had crept into the treacherous swamp. Then the false slime closing about them called the white men from the east. Waist-deep, they fought beneath the tall trees, until the war-cry was hushed and the Indians glided back into the west. Small wonder the wood is red.

Then came the black slaves. Day after day the clank of chained feet marching from Virginia and Carolina to Georgia was heard in these rich swamp lands. Day after day the songs of the callous, the wail of the motherless, and the muttered curses of the wretched echoed from the Flint to the Chickasawhatchee, until by 1860 there had risen in West Dougherty perhaps the richest slave kingdom the modern world ever knew. A hundred and fifty barons commanded the labor of nearly six thousand Negroes, held sway over farms with ninety thousand acres of tilled land, valued even in times of cheap soil at three millions of dollars. Twenty thousand bales of ginned cotton went yearly to England, New and Old; and men that came there bankrupt made money and grew rich. In a single decade the cotton output increased four-fold and the value of lands was tripled. It was the heyday of the *nouveau riche,*[19] and a life of careless extravagance reigned among the masters. Four and six bobtailed thoroughbreds rolled their coaches to town; open hospitality and gay entertainment were the rule. Parks and groves were laid out, rich with flower and vine, and in the midst stood the low wide-halled "big house," with its porch and columns and great fireplaces.

And yet with all this there was something sordid, something forced, —

a certain feverish unrest and recklessness; for was not all this show and tinsel built upon a groan? "This land was a little Hell," said a ragged, brown, and grave-faced man to me. We were seated near a roadside blacksmith-shop, and behind was the bare ruin of some master's home. "I've seen niggers drop dead in the furrow, but they were kicked aside, and the plough never stopped. And down in the guardhouse, there's where the blood ran."

With such foundations a kingdom must in time sway and fall. The masters moved to Macon and Augusta, and left only the irresponsible overseers on the land. And the result is such ruin as this, the Lloyd "home-place": — great waving oaks, a spread of lawn, myrtles and chestnuts, all ragged and wild; a solitary gate-post standing where once was a castle entrance; an old rusty anvil lying amid rotting bellows and wood in the ruins of a blacksmith shop; a wide rambling old mansion, brown and dingy, filled now with the grandchildren of the slaves who once waited on its tables; while the family of the master has dwindled to two lone women, who live in Macon and feed hungrily off the remnants of an earldom. So we ride on, past phantom gates and falling homes, — past the once flourishing farms of the Smiths, the Gandys, and the Lagores, — and find all dilapidated and half ruined, even there where a solitary white woman, a relic of other days, sits alone in state among miles of Negroes and rides to town in her ancient coach each day.

This was indeed the Egypt of the Confederacy, — the rich granary whence potatoes and corn and cotton poured out to the famished and ragged Confederate troops as they battled for a cause lost long before 1861. Sheltered and secure, it became the place of refuge for families, wealth, and slaves. Yet even then the hard ruthless rape of the land began to tell. The red-clay sub-soil already had begun to peer above the loam. The harder the slaves were driven the more careless and fatal was their farming. Then came the revolution of war and Emancipation, the bewilderment of Reconstruction, — and now, what is the Egypt of the Confederacy, and what meaning has it for the nation's weal or woe?

It is a land of rapid contrasts and of curiously mingled hope and pain. Here sits a pretty blue-eyed quadroon hiding her bare feet; she was married only last week, and yonder in the field is her dark young husband, hoeing to support her, at thirty cents a day without board. Across the way is Gatesby, brown and tall, lord of two thousand acres shrewdly won and held. There is a store conducted by his black son, a blacksmith shop, and a ginnery. Five miles below here is a town owned and controlled by one white New Englander. He owns almost a Rhode Island county, with thousands of acres and hundreds of black laborers. Their cabins look better than most, and the farm, with machinery and fertilizers, is much more business-like than any in the county, although the manager drives hard bargains in wages. When now we turn and look five miles above, there on the edge of town are five houses of prostitutes, — two of blacks and three of whites; and in one of the houses of the whites a worthless black boy was harbored too openly two years ago; so he was hanged for rape. And here, too, is the high whitewashed fence of the "stockade," as the county prison is called; the white folks say it is ever full of black crimi-nals, — the black folks say that only colored boys are sent to jail, and they not because they are guilty, but because the State needs criminals to eke out its income by their forced labor.

The Jew is the heir[20] of the slave-baron in Dougherty; and as we ride westward, by wide stretching cornfields and stubby orchards of peach and pear, we see on all sides within the circle of dark forest a Land of Canaan.[21] Here and there are tales of projects for money-getting, born in the swift days of Reconstruction, — "improvement" companies, wine com-panies, mills and factories; nearly all failed, and the Jew fell heir.[22] It is a beautiful land, this Dougherty, west of the Flint. The forests are won-derful, the solemn pines have disappeared, and this is the "Oakey Woods," with its wealth of hickories, beeches, oaks, and palmettos. But a pall of debt hangs over the beautiful land; the merchants are in debt to the wholesalers, the planters are in debt to the merchants, the tenants owe the planters, and laborers bow and bend beneath the burden of it all. Here and there a man has raised his head above these murky waters. We passed one fenced stock-farm, with grass and grazing cattle, that looked very homelike after endless corn and cotton. Here and there are black freeholders: there is the gaunt dull-black Jackson, with his hundred acres. "I says, 'Look up! If you don't look up you can't get up,' " remarks Jack-son, philosophically. And he's gotten up. Dark Carter's neat barns would do credit to New England. His master helped him to get a start, but when the black man died last fall the master's sons immediately laid claim to the estate. "And them white folks will get it, too," said my yellow gossip.

I turn from these well-tended acres with a comfortable feeling that the Negro is rising. Even then, however, the fields, as we proceed, begin to redden and the trees disappear. Rows of old cabins appear filled with renters and laborers, — cheerless, bare, and dirty, for the most part, although here and there the very age and decay makes the scene pic-turesque. A young black fellow greets us. He is twenty-two, and just mar-ried. Until last year he had good luck renting; then cotton fell, and the sheriff seized and sold all he had. So he moved here, where the rent is higher, the land poorer, and the owner inflexible; he rents a forty-dollar mule for twenty dollars a year. Poor lad!—a slave at twenty-two. This plantation, owned now by a Russian Jew,[23] was a part of the famous Bolton estate. After the war it was for many years worked by gangs of Negro convicts, — and black convicts then were even more plentiful than now; it was a way of making Negroes work, and the question of guilt was a minor one. Hard tales of cruelty and mistreatment of the chained freemen are told, but the county authorities were deaf until the free-labor market was nearly ruined by wholesale migration. Then they took the convicts from the plantations, but not until one of the fairest regions of the "Oakey Woods" had been ruined and ravished into a red waste, out of which only a Yankee or a Jew[24] could squeeze more blood from debt-cursed tenants.

No wonder that Luke Black, slow, dull, and discouraged, shuffles to our carriage and talks hopelessly. Why should he strive? Every year finds him deeper in debt. How strange that Georgia, the world-heralded refuge of poor debtors, should bind her own to sloth and misfortune as ruthlessly as ever England did! The poor land groans with its birth-pains, and brings forth scarcely a hundred pounds of cotton to the acre, where fifty years ago it yielded eight times as much. Of this meagre yield the tenant pays from a quarter to a third in rent, and most of the rest in interest on food and supplies bought on credit. Twenty years yonder sunken-cheeked, old black man has labored under that system, and now, turned day-laborer, is supporting his wife and boarding himself on his wages of a dollar and a half a week, received only part of the year.

The Bolton convict farm formerly included the neighboring plantation. Here it was that the convicts were lodged in the great log prison still standing. A dismal place it still remains, with rows of ugly huts filled with surly ignorant tenants. "What rent do you pay here?" I inquired. "I don't know, — what is it, Sam?" "All we make," answered Sam. It is a depressing place, — bare, unshaded, with no charm of past association, only a memory of forced human toil, — now, then, and before the war. They are not happy, these black men whom we meet throughout this region. There is little of the joyous abandon and playfulness which we are wont to associate with the plantation Negro. At best, the natural good-nature is edged with complaint or has changed into sullenness and gloom. And now and then it blazes forth in veiled but hot anger. I remember one big red-eyed black whom we met by the roadside. Forty-five years he had labored on this farm, beginning with nothing, and still having nothing. To be sure, he had given four children a common-school training, and perhaps if the new fence-law had not allowed unfenced crops in West Dougherty he might have raised a little stock and kept ahead. As it is, he is hopelessly in debt, disappointed, and embittered. He stopped us to inquire after the black boy in Albany, whom it was said a policeman had shot and killed for loud talking on the sidewalk. And then he said slowly: "Let a white man touch me, and he dies; I don't boast this,—I don't say it around loud, or before the children,—but I mean it. I've seen them whip my father and my old mother in them cotton-rows till the blood ran; by—" and we passed on.

Now Sears, whom we met next lolling under the chubby oak-trees, was of quite different fibre. Happy?—Well, yes; he laughed and flipped pebbles, and thought the world was as it was. He had worked here twelve years and has nothing but a mortgaged mule. Children? Yes, seven; but they hadn't been to school this year,—couldn't afford books and clothes, and couldn't spare their work. There go part of them to the fields now,— three big boys astride mules, and a strapping girl with bare brown legs. Careless ignorance and laziness here, fierce hate and vindictiveness there;—these are the extremes of the Negro problem which we met that day, and we scarce knew which we preferred.

Here and there we meet distinct characters quite out of the ordinary. One came out of a piece of newly cleared ground, making a wide detour to avoid the snakes. He was an old, hollow-cheeked man, with a drawn and characterful brown face. He had a sort of self-contained quaintness and rough humor impossible to describe; a certain cynical earnestness that puzzled one. "The niggers were jealous of me over on the other place," he said, "and so me and the old woman begged this piece of woods, and I cleared it up myself. Made nothing for two years, but I reckon I've got a crop now." The cotton looked tall and rich, and we praised it. He curtsied low, and then bowed almost to the ground, with an imperturbable gravity that seemed almost suspicious. Then he continued, "My mule died last week,"—a calamity in this land equal to a devastating fire in town,—"but a white man loaned me another." Then he added, eyeing us, "Oh, I gets along with white folks." We turned the conversation. "Bears? deer?" he answered, "well, I should say there were," and he let fly a string of brave oaths, as he told hunting-tales of the swamp. We left him standing still in the middle of the road looking after us, and yet apparently not noticing us.

The Whistle place, which includes his bit of land, was bought soon after the war by an English syndicate, the "Dixie Cotton and Corn Company." A marvellous deal of style their factor put on, with his servants and coach-and-six; so much so that the concern soon landed in inextricable bankruptcy. Nobody lives in the old house now, but a man comes each winter out of the North and collects his high rents. I know not which are the more touching,—such old empty houses, or the homes of the masters' sons. Sad and bitter tales lie hidden back of those white doors,—

tales of poverty, of struggle, of disappointment. A revolution such as that of '63 is a terrible thing;[25] they that rose rich in the morning often slept in paupers' beds. Beggars and vulgar speculators rose to rule over them, and their children went astray. See yonder sad-colored house, with its cabins and fences and glad crops? It is not glad within; last month the prodigal son of the struggling father wrote home from the city for money. Money! Where was it to come from? And so the son rose in the night and killed his baby, and killed his wife, and shot himself dead. And the world passed on.

I remember wheeling around a bend in the road beside a graceful bit of forest and a singing brook. A long low house faced us, with porch and flying pillars, great oaken door, and a broad lawn shining in the evening sun. But the window-panes were gone, the pillars were worm-eaten, and the moss-grown roof was falling in. Half curiously I peered through the unhinged door, and saw where, on the wall across the hall, was written in once gay letters a faded "Welcome."

Quite a contrast to the southwestern part of Dougherty County is the northwest. Soberly timbered in oak and pine, it has none of that half-tropical luxuriance of the southwest. Then, too, there are fewer signs of a romantic past, and more of systematic modern land-grabbing and money-getting. White people are more in evidence here, and farmer and hired labor replace to some extent the absentee landlord and rack-rented tenant. The crops have neither the luxuriance of the richer land nor the signs of neglect so often seen, and there were fences and meadows here and there. Most of this land was poor, and beneath the notice of the slave-baron, before the war. Since then his nephews and the poor whites and the Jews[26] have seized it. The returns of the farmer are too small to allow much for wages, and yet he will not sell off small farms. There is the Negro Sanford; he has worked fourteen years as overseer on the Ladson place, and "paid out enough for fertilizers to have bought a farm," but the owner will not sell off a few acres.

Two children—a boy and a girl—are hoeing sturdily in the fields on the farm where Corliss works. He is smooth-faced and brown, and is fencing up his pigs. He used to run a successful cotton-gin, but the Cotton Seed Oil Trust has forced the price of ginning so low that he says it hardly pays him. He points out a stately old house over the way as the home of "Pa Willis." We eagerly ride over, for "Pa Willis" was the tall and powerful black Moses who led the Negroes for a generation, and led them well. He was a Baptist preacher, and when he died two thousand black people followed him to the grave; and now they preach his funeral sermon each year. His widow lives here,—a weazened, sharp-featured little woman, who curtsied quaintly as we greeted her. Further on lives Jack Delson, the most prosperous Negro farmer in the county. It is a joy to meet him,—a great broad-shouldered, handsome black man, intelligent and jovial. Six hundred and fifty acres he owns, and has eleven black tenants. A neat and tidy home nestled in a flower-garden, and a little store stands beside it.

We pass the Munson place, where a plucky white widow is renting and struggling; and the eleven hundred acres of the Sennet plantation, with its Negro overseer. Then the character of the farms begins to change. Nearly all the lands belong to Russian Jews;[27] the overseers are white, and the cabins are bare board-houses scattered here and there. The rents are high, and day-laborers and "contract" hands abound. It is a keen, hard struggle for living here, and few have time to talk. Tired with the long ride, we gladly drive into Gillonsville. It is a silent cluster of farm-houses standing on the cross-roads, with one of its stores closed and the other kept by a Negro preacher. They tell great tales of busy times at Gillonsville before all the railroads came to Albany; now it is chiefly a memory. Riding down the street, we stop at the preacher's and seat ourselves before the door. It was one of those scenes one cannot soon forget:—a wide, low, little house, whose motherly roof reached over and sheltered a snug little porch. There we sat, after the long hot drive, drinking cool water,—the talkative little storekeeper who is my daily companion; the silent old black woman patching pantaloons and saying never a word; the ragged picture of helpless misfortune who called in just to see the preacher; and finally the neat matronly preacher's wife, plump, yellow, and intelligent. "Own land?" said the wife; "well, only this house." Then she added quietly, "We did buy seven hundred acres up yonder, and paid for it; but they cheated us out of it. Sells was the owner." "Sells!" echoed the ragged misfortune, who was leaning against the balustrade and listening, "he's a regular cheat. I worked for him thirty-seven days this spring, and he paid me in cardboard checks which were to be cashed at the end of the month. But he never cashed them,—kept putting me off. Then the sheriff came and took my mule and corn and furniture—" "Furniture?" I asked; "but furniture is exempt from seizure by law." "Well, he took it just the same," said the hard-faced man.

VIII

Of the Quest of the Golden Fleece

But the Brute said in his breast, "Till the mills I grind have ceased,
The riches shall be dust of dust, dry ashes be the feast!

"On the strong and cunning few
Cynic favors I will strew;
I will stuff their maw with overplus until their spirit dies;
From the patient and the low
I will take the joys they know;
They shall hunger after vanities and still an-hungered go.
Madness shall be on the people, ghastly jealousies arise;
Brother's blood shall cry on brother up the dead and empty skies."

WILLIAM VAUGHN MOODY.

Have you ever seen a cotton-field white with the harvest,—its golden fleece hovering above the black earth like a silvery cloud edged with dark green, its bold white signals waving like the foam of billows from Carolina to Texas across that Black and human Sea? I have sometimes half suspected that here the winged ram Chrysomallus left that Fleece after which Jason and his Argonauts went vaguely wandering into the shadowy East three thousand years ago; and certainly one might frame a pretty and not far-fetched analogy of witchery and dragon's teeth, and blood and armed men, between the ancient and the modern Quest of the Golden Fleece in the Black Sea.[2]

And now the golden fleece is found; not only found, but, in its birthplace, woven. For the hum of the cotton-mills is the newest and most significant thing in the New South today. All through the Carolinas and

117

Georgia, away down to Mexico, rise these gaunt red buildings, bare and homely, and yet so busy and noisy withal that they scarce seem to belong to the slow and sleepy land. Perhaps they sprang from dragons' teeth. So the Cotton Kingdom still lives; the world still bows beneath her sceptre. Even the markets that once defied the *parvenu*[3] have crept one by one across the seas, and then slowly and reluctantly, but surely, have started toward the Black Belt.

To be sure, there are those who wag their heads knowingly and tell us that the capital of the Cotton Kingdom has moved from the Black to the White Belt,—that the Negro of to-day raises not more than half of the cotton crop. Such men forget that the cotton crop has doubled, and more than doubled, since the era of slavery, and that, even granting their contention, the Negro is still supreme in a Cotton Kingdom larger than that on which the Confederacy builded its hopes. So the Negro forms to-day one of the chief figures in a great world-industry; and this, for its own sake, and in the light of historic interest, makes the field-hands of the cotton country worth studying.

We seldom study the condition of the Negro to-day honestly and carefully. It is so much easier to assume that we know it all. Or perhaps, having already reached conclusions in our own minds, we are loth to have them disturbed by facts. And yet how little we really know of these millions,—of their daily lives and longings, of their homely joys and sorrows, of their real shortcomings and the meaning of their crimes! All this we can only learn by intimate contact with the masses, and not by wholesale arguments covering millions separate in time and space, and differing widely in training and culture. To-day, then, my reader, let us turn our faces to the Black Belt of Georgia and seek simply to know the condition of the black farm-laborers of one county there.

Here in 1890 lived ten thousand Negroes and two thousand whites. The country is rich, yet the people are poor. The keynote of the Black Belt is debt; not commercial credit, but debt in the sense of continued inability on the part of the mass of the population to make income cover expense. This is the direct heritage of the South from the wasteful economies of the slave *régime;*[4] but it was emphasized and brought to a crisis by the Emancipation of the slaves. In 1860, Dougherty County had six thousand slaves, worth at least two and a half millions of dollars; its farms were estimated at three millions,—making five and a half millions of property, the value of which depended largely on the slave system, and on the speculative demand for land once marvellously rich but already partially devitalized by careless and exhaustive culture. The war then meant a financial crash; in place of the five and a half millions of 1860, there remained in 1870 only farms valued at less than two millions. With this came increased competition in cotton culture from the rich lands of Texas; a steady fall in the normal price of cotton followed, from about fourteen cents a pound in 1860 until it reached four cents in 1898. Such a financial revolution was it that involved the owners of the cotton-belt in debt. And if things went ill with the master, how fared it with the man?[5]

The plantations of Dougherty County in slavery days were not as imposing and aristocratic as those of Virginia. The Big House[6] was smaller and usually one-storied, and sat very near the slave cabins. Sometimes these cabins stretched off on either side like wings; sometimes only on one side, forming a double row, or edging the road that turned into the plantation from the main thoroughfare. The form and disposition of the laborers' cabins throughout the Black Belt is to-day the same as in slavery days. Some live in the self-same cabins, others in cabins rebuilt on the sites of the old. All are sprinkled in little groups over the face of the land, centering about some dilapidated Big House where the head-tenant or agent lives. The general character and arrangement of these dwellings remains on the whole unaltered. There were in the county, outside the corporate town of Albany, about fifteen hundred Negro families in 1898. Out of all these, only a single family occupied a house with seven rooms; only fourteen have five rooms or more. The mass live in one- and two-room homes.

The size and arrangements of a people's homes are no unfair index of their condition. If, then, we inquire more carefully into these Negro homes, we find much that is unsatisfactory. All over the face of the land is the one-room cabin, — now standing in the shadow of the Big House, now staring at the dusty road, now rising dark and sombre amid the green of the cotton-fields. It is nearly always old and bare, built of rough boards, and neither plastered nor ceiled. Light and ventilation are supplied by the single door and by the square hole in the wall with its wooden shutter. There is no glass, porch, or ornamentation without. Within is a fireplace, black and smoky, and usually unsteady with age. A bed or two, a table, a wooden chest, and a few chairs compose the furniture; while a stray show-bill or a newspaper makes up the decorations for the walls. Now and then one may find such a cabin kept scrupulously neat, with merry steaming fireplace and hospitable door; but the majority are dirty and dilapidated, smelling of eating and sleeping, poorly ventilated, and anything but homes.

Above all, the cabins are crowded. We have come to associate crowding with homes in cities almost exclusively. This is primarily because we have so little accurate knowledge of country life. Here in Dougherty

County one may find families of eight and ten occupying one or two rooms, and for every ten rooms of house accommodation for the Negroes there are twenty-five persons. The worst tenement abominations of New York do not have above twenty-two persons for every ten rooms. Of course, one small, close room in a city, without a yard, is in many respects worse than the larger single country room. In other respects it is better; it has glass windows, a decent chimney, and a trustworthy floor. The single great advantage of the Negro peasant is that he may spend most of his life outside his hovel, in the open fields.

There are four chief causes of these wretched homes: First, long custom born of slavery has assigned such homes to Negroes; white laborers would be offered better accommodations, and might, for that and similar reasons, give better work. Secondly, the Negroes, used to such accommodations, do not as a rule demand better; they do not know what better houses mean. Thirdly, the landlords as a class have not yet come to realize that it is a good-business investment to raise the standard of living among labor by slow and judicious methods; that a Negro laborer who demands three rooms and fifty cents a day would give more efficient work and leave a larger profit than a discouraged toiler herding his family in one room and working for thirty cents. Lastly, among such conditions of life there are few incentives to make the laborer become a better farmer. If he is ambitious, he moves to town or tries other labor; as a tenant-farmer his outlook is almost hopeless, and following it as a makeshift, he takes the house that is given him without protest.

In such homes, then, these Negro peasants live. The families are both small and large; there are many single tenants, — widows and bachelors, and remnants of broken groups. The system of labor and the size of the houses both tend to the breaking up of family groups: the grown children go away as contract hands or migrate to town, the sister goes into service; and so one finds many families with hosts of babies, and many newly married couples, but comparatively few families with half-grown and grown sons and daughters. The average size of Negro families has undoubtedly decreased since the war, primarily from economic stress. In Russia over a third of the bridegrooms and over half the brides are under twenty; the same was true of the antebellum Negroes.[7] To-day, however, very few of the boys and less than a fifth of the Negro girls under twenty are married. The young men marry between the ages of twenty-five and thirty-five; the young women between twenty and thirty. Such postponement is due to the difficulty of earning sufficient to rear and support a family; and it undoubtedly leads, in the country districts, to sexual immorality. The form of this immorality, however, is very seldom that of prostitution, and less frequently that of illegitimacy than one would imagine. Rather, it takes the form of separation and desertion after a family group has been formed. The number of separated persons is thirty-five to the thousand, — a very large number. It would of course be unfair to compare this number with divorce statistics, for many of these separated women are in reality widowed, were the truth known, and in other cases the separation is not permanent. Nevertheless, here lies the seat of greatest moral danger. There is little or no prostitution among these Negroes, and over three-fourths of the families, as found by house-to-house investigation, deserve to be classed as decent people with considerable regard for female chastity. To be sure, the ideas of the mass would not suit New England, and there are many loose habits and notions. Yet the rate of illegitimacy is undoubtedly lower than in Austria or Italy, and the women as a class are modest. The plague-spot in sexual relations is easy marriage and easy separation. This is no sudden development, nor the fruit of Emancipation. It is the plain heritage from slavery. In those days Sam, with his master's consent, "took up" with Mary. No ceremony was necessary, and in the busy life of the great plantations of the Black Belt it was usually dispensed with. If now the master needed Sam's work in another plantation or in another part of the same plantation, or if he took a notion to sell the slave, Sam's married life with Mary was usually unceremoniously broken, and then it was clearly to the master's interest to have both of them take new mates. This widespread custom of two centuries has not been eradicated in thirty years. To-day Sam's grandson "takes up" with a woman without license or ceremony; they live together decently and honestly, and are, to all intents and purposes, man and wife. Sometimes these unions are never broken until death; but in too many cases family quarrels, a roving spirit, a rival suitor, or perhaps more frequently the hopeless battle to support a family, lead to separation, and a broken household is the result. The Negro church has done much to stop this practice, and now most marriage ceremonies are performed by the pastors. Nevertheless, the evil is still deep seated, and only a general raising of the standard of living will finally cure it.

Looking now at the county black population as a whole, it is fair to characterize it as poor and ignorant. Perhaps ten per cent compose the well-to-do and the best of the laborers, while at least nine per cent are thoroughly lewd and vicious. The rest, over eighty per cent, are poor and ignorant, fairly honest and well meaning, plodding, and to a degree shiftless, with some but not great sexual looseness. Such class lines are by no means fixed; they vary, one might almost say, with the price of cotton. The degree of ignorance cannot easily be expressed. We may say, for instance, that nearly two-thirds of them cannot read or write. This but partially expresses the fact. They are ignorant of the world about them, of modern economic organization, of the function of government, of individual worth and possibilities, — of nearly all those things which slavery in self-defence had to keep them from learning. Much that the white boy imbibes from his earliest social atmosphere forms the puzzling problems of the black boy's mature years. America is not another word for Opportunity to *all* her sons.

It is easy for us to lose ourselves in details in endeavoring to grasp and comprehend the real condition of a mass of human beings. We often forget that each unit in the mass is a throbbing human soul. Ignorant it may be, and poverty stricken, black and curious in limb and ways and thought; and yet it loves and hates, it toils and tires, it laughs and weeps its bitter tears, and looks in vague and awful longing at the grim horizon of its life, — all this, even as you and I. These black thousands are not in reality lazy; they are improvident and careless; they insist on breaking the monotony of toil with a glimpse at the great town-world on Saturday; they have their loafers and their rascals; but the great mass of them work continuously and faithfully for a return, and under circumstances that would call forth equal voluntary effort from few if any other modern laboring class. Over eighty-eight per cent of them—men, women, and children— are farmers. Indeed, this is almost the only industry. Most of the children get their schooling after the "crops are laid by," and very few there are that stay in school after the spring work has begun. Child-labor is to be found here in some of its worst phases, as fostering ignorance and stunting physical development. With the grown men of the county there is little variety in work: thirteen hundred are farmers, and two hundred are laborers, teamsters, etc., including twenty-four artisans, ten merchants, twenty-one preachers, and four teachers. This narrowness of life reaches its maximum among the women: thirteen hundred and fifty of these are farm laborers, one hundred are servants and washerwomen, leaving sixty-five housewives, eight teachers, and six seamstresses.

Among this people there is no leisure class.[8] We often forget that in the United States over half the youth and adults are not in the world earning incomes, but are making homes, learning of the world, or resting after the heat of the strife. But here ninety-six per cent are toiling; no one with leisure to turn the bare and cheerless cabin into a home, no old folks to sit beside the fire and hand down traditions of the past; little of careless happy childhood and dreaming youth. The dull monotony of daily toil is broken only by the gayety of the thoughtless and the Saturday trip to town. The toil, like all farm toil, is monotonous, and here there are little machinery and few tools to relieve its burdensome drudgery. But with all this, it is work in the pure open air, and this is something in a day when fresh air is scarce.

The land on the whole is still fertile, despite long abuse. For nine or ten months in succession the crops will come if asked: garden vegetables in April, grain in May, melons in June and July, hay in August, sweet potatoes in September, and cotton from then to Christmas. And yet on two-thirds of the land there is but one crop, and that leaves the toilers in debt. Why is this?

Away down the Baysan road, where the broad flat fields are flanked by great oak forests, is a plantation: many thousands of acres it used to run, here and there, and beyond the great wood. Thirteen hundred human beings here obeyed the call of one, — were his in body, and largely in soul. One of them lives there yet, — a short, stocky man, his dull-brown face seamed and drawn, and his tightly curled hair gray-white. The crops? Just tolerable, he said; just tolerable. Getting on? No — he wasn't getting on at all. Smith of Albany "furnishes" him, and his rent is eight hundred pounds of cotton. Can't make anything at that. Why did n't he buy land? *Humph!* Takes money to buy land. And he turns away. Free! The most piteous thing amid all the black ruin of war-time, amid the broken fortunes of the masters, the blighted hopes of mothers and maidens, and the fall of an empire, — the most piteous thing amid all this was the black freedman who threw down his hoe because the world called him free. What did such a mockery of freedom mean? Not a cent of money, not an inch of land, not a mouthful of victuals, — not even ownership of the rags on his back. Free! On Saturday, once or twice a month, the old master, before the war, used to dole out bacon and meal to his Negroes. And after the first flush of freedom wore off, and his true helplessness dawned on the freedman, he came back and picked up his hoe, and old master still doled out his bacon and meal. The legal form of service was theoretically far different; in practice, task-work or "cropping" was substituted for daily toil in gangs;[9] and the slave gradually became a metayer,[10] or tenant on shares, in name, but a laborer with indeterminate wages in fact.

Still the price of cotton fell, and gradually the landlords deserted their plantations, and the reign of the merchant began. The merchant of the Black Belt is a curious institution, — part banker, part landlord, part contractor, and part despot. His store, which used most frequently to stand at the crossroads and become the centre of a weekly village, has now moved to town; and thither the Negro tenant follows him. The merchant keeps everything, — clothes and shoes, coffee and sugar, pork and meal, canned and dried goods, wagons and ploughs, seed and fertilizer, — and what he has not in stock he can give you an order for at the store across the way. Here, then, comes the tenant, Sam Scott, after he has contracted with some absent landlord's agent for hiring forty acres of land; he fingers his hat nervously until the merchant finishes his morning chat with Colonel Sanders, and calls out, "Well, Sam, what do you want?" Sam wants him to "furnish" him,—*i.e.,* to advance him food and clothing for the year, and perhaps seed and tools, until his crop is raised and sold. If Sam seems a favorable subject, he and the merchant go to a lawyer, and Sam executes a chattel mortgage on his mule and wagon in return for seed and a week's rations. As soon as the green cotton-leaves appear above the ground, another mortgage is given on the "crop." Every Saturday, or at longer intervals, Sam calls upon the merchant for his "rations"; a family of five usually gets about thirty pounds of fat side-pork and a couple of bushels of corn-meal a month. Besides this, clothing and shoes must be furnished; if Sam or his family is sick, there are orders on the druggist and doctor; if the mule wants shoeing, an order on the blacksmith, etc. If Sam is a hard worker and crops promise well, he is often encouraged to buy more,—sugar, extra clothes, perhaps a buggy. But he is seldom encouraged to save. When cotton rose to ten cents last fall, the shrewd merchants of Dougherty County sold a thousand buggies in one season, mostly to black men.

The security offered for such transactions—a crop and chattel mortgage—may at first seem slight. And, indeed, the merchants tell many a true tale of shiftlessness and cheating; of cotton picked at night, mules disappearing, and tenants absconding. But on the whole the merchant of the Black Belt is the most prosperous man in the section. So skilfully and so closely has he drawn the bonds of the law about the tenant, that the black man has often simply to choose between pauperism and crime; he "waives" all homestead exemptions in his contract; he cannot touch his own mortgaged crop, which the laws put almost in the full control of the land-owner and of the merchant. When the crop is growing the merchant watches it like a hawk; as soon as it is ready for market he takes possession of it, sells it, pays the land-owner his rent, subtracts his bill for supplies, and if, as sometimes happens, there is anything left, he hands it over to the black serf for his Christmas celebration.

The direct result of this system is an all-cotton scheme of agriculture and the continued bankruptcy of the tenant. The currency of the Black Belt is cotton. It is a crop always salable for ready money, not usually subject to great yearly fluctuations in price, and one which the Negroes know how to raise. The landlord therefore demands his rent in cotton, and the merchant will accept mortgages on no other crop. There is no use asking the black tenant, then, to diversify his crops,—he cannot under this system. Moreover, the system is bound to bankrupt the tenant. I remember once meeting a little one-mule wagon on the River road. A young black fellow sat in it driving listlessly, his elbows on his knees. His dark-faced wife sat beside him, stolid, silent.

"Hello!" cried my driver,—he has a most impudent way of addressing these people, though they seem used to it,—"what have you got there?"

"Meat and meal," answered the man, stopping. The meat lay uncovered in the bottom of the wagon,—a great thin side of fat pork covered with salt; the meal was in a white bushel bag.

"What did you pay for that meat?"

"Ten cents a pound." It could have been bought for six or seven cents cash.

"And the meal?"

"Two dollars." One dollar and ten cents is the cash price in town. Here was a man paying five dollars for goods which he could have bought for three dollars cash, and raised for one dollar or one dollar and a half.

Yet it is not wholly his fault. The Negro farmer started behind,—started in debt. This was not his choosing, but the crime of this happy-go-lucky nation which goes blundering along with its Reconstruction tragedies, its Spanish war interludes and Philippine matinees, just as though God really were dead.[11] Once in debt, it is no easy matter for a whole race to emerge.

In the year of low-priced cotton, 1898, out of three hundred tenant families one hundred and seventy-five ended their year's work in debt to the extent of fourteen thousand dollars; fifty cleared nothing, and the remaining seventy-five made a total profit of sixteen hundred dollars. The net indebtedness of the black tenant families of the whole county must have been at least sixty thousand dollars. In a more prosperous year the situation is far better; but on the average the majority of tenants end the year even, or in debt, which means that they work for board and clothes. Such an economic organization is radically wrong. Whose is the blame?

The underlying causes of this situation are complicated but discernible. And one of the chief, outside the carelessness of the nation in letting the slave start with nothing, is the widespread opinion among the merchants and employers of the Black Belt that only by the slavery of debt can the Negro be kept at work. Without doubt, some pressure was necessary at the beginning of the free-labor system to keep the listless and lazy at work; and even to-day the mass of the Negro laborers need stricter guardianship than most Northern laborers. Behind this honest and widespread opinion dishonesty and cheating of the ignorant laborers have a good chance to take refuge. And to all this must be added the obvious fact that a slave ancestry and a system of unrequited toil has not improved the efficiency or temper of the mass of black laborers. Nor is this peculiar to Sambo;[12] it has in history been just as true of John and Hans, of Jacques and Pat, of all ground-down peasantries. Such is the situation of the mass of the Negroes in the Black Belt to-day; and they are thinking about it. Crime, and a cheap and dangerous socialism, are the inevitable results of this pondering. I see now that ragged black man sitting on a log, aimlessly whittling a stick. He muttered to me with the murmur of many ages, when he said: "White man sit down whole year; Nigger work day and night and make crop; Nigger hardly gits bread and meat; white man sittin' down gits all. *It's wrong.*" And what do the better classes of Negroes do to improve their situation? One of two things: if any way possible, they buy land; if not, they migrate to town. Just as centuries ago it was no easy thing for the serf to escape into the freedom of town-life, even so to-day there are hindrances laid in the way of county laborers. In considerable parts of all the Gulf States, and especially in Mississippi, Louisiana, and Arkansas, the Negroes on the plantations in the back-country districts are still held at forced labor practically without wages. Especially is this true in districts where the farmers are composed of the more ignorant class of poor whites, and the Negroes are beyond the reach of schools and intercourse with their advancing fellows. If such a peon should run away, the sheriff, elected by white suffrage, can usually be depended on to catch the fugitive, return him, and ask no questions. If he escape to another county, a charge of petty thieving, easily true, can be depended upon to secure his return. Even if some unduly officious person insist upon a trial, neighborly comity will probably make his conviction sure, and then the labor due the county can easily be bought by the master. Such a system is impossible in the more civilized parts of the South, or near the large towns and cities; but in those vast stretches of land beyond the telegraph and the newspaper the spirit of the Thirteenth Amendment is sadly broken.[13] This represents the lowest economic depths of the black American peasant; and in a study of the rise and condition of the Negro freeholder we must trace his economic progress from this modern serfdom.

Even in the better-ordered country districts of the South the free movement of agricultural laborers is hindered by the migration-agent laws.[14] The "Associated Press" recently informed the world of the arrest of a young white man in Southern Georgia who represented the "Atlantic Naval Supplies Company," and who "was caught in the act of enticing hands from the turpentine farm of Mr. John Greer." The crime for which this young man was arrested is taxed five hundred dollars for each county in which the employment agent proposes to gather laborers for work outside the State. Thus the Negroes' ignorance of the labor-market outside his own vicinity is increased rather than diminished by the laws of nearly every Southern State.

Similar to such measures is the unwritten law of the back districts and small towns of the South, that the character of all Negroes unknown to the mass of the community must be vouched for by some white man. This is really a revival of the old Roman idea of the patron under whose protection the new-made freedman was put. In many instances this system has been of great good to the Negro, and very often under the protection and guidance of the former master's family, or other white friends, the freedman progressed in wealth and morality. But the same system has in other cases resulted in the refusal of whole communities to recognize the right of a Negro to change his habitation and to be master of his own fortunes. A black stranger in Baker County, Georgia, for instance, is liable to be stopped anywhere on the public highway and made to state his business to the satisfaction of any white interrogator. If he fails to give a suitable answer, or seems too independent or "sassy," he may be arrested or summarily driven away.

Thus it is that in the country districts of the South, by written or unwritten law, peonage,[15] hindrances to the migration of labor, and a system of white patronage exists over large areas. Besides this, the chance for lawless oppression and illegal exactions is vastly greater in the country than in the city, and nearly all the more serious race disturbances of the last decade have arisen from disputes in the county between master and man,—as, for instance, the Sam Hose affair.[16] As a result of such a situation, there arose, first, the Black Belt; and, second, the Migration to Town. The Black Belt was not, as many assumed, a movement toward fields of labor under more genial climatic conditions; it was primarily a huddling for self-protection,—a massing of the black population for mutual defence in order to secure the peace and tranquillity necessary to economic advance. This movement took place between Emancipation and 1880, and only partially accomplished the desired results. The rush to town since 1880 is the counter-movement of men disappointed in the economic opportunities of the Black Belt.

In Dougherty County, Georgia, one can see easily the results of this experiment in huddling for protection. Only ten per cent of the adult population was born in the county, and yet the blacks outnumber the whites four or five to one. There is undoubtedly a security to the blacks in their very numbers,—a personal freedom from arbitrary treatment, which makes hundreds of laborers cling to Dougherty in spite of low wages and economic distress. But a change is coming, and slowly but surely even here the agricultural laborers are drifting to town and leaving the broad acres behind. Why is this? Why do not the Negroes become land-owners, and build up the black landed peasantry, which has for a generation and more been the dream of philanthropist and statesman?

To the car-window sociologist, to the man who seeks to understand and know the South by devoting the few leisure hours of a holiday trip to unravelling the snarl of centuries,—to such men very often the whole trouble with the black fieldhand may be summed up by Aunt Ophelia's word, "Shiftless!"[17] They have noted repeatedly scenes like one I saw last summer. We were riding along the highroad to town at the close of a long hot day. A couple of young black fellows passed us in a mule-team, with several bushels of loose corn in the rear. One was driving, listlessly bent forward, his elbows on his knees,—a happy-go-lucky, careless picture of irresponsibility. The other was fast asleep in the bottom of the wagon. As we passed we noticed an ear of corn fall from the wagon. They never saw it,—not they. A rod farther on we noted another ear on the ground; and between that creeping mule and town we counted twenty-six ears of corn. Shiftless? Yes, the personification of shiftlessness. And yet follow those boys: they are not lazy; to-morrow morning they 'll be up with the sun; they work hard when they do work, and they work willingly. They have no sordid, selfish, money-getting ways, but rather a fine disdain for mere cash. They 'll loaf before your face and work behind your back with good-natured honesty. They 'll steal a watermelon, and hand you back your lost purse intact. Their great defect as laborers lies in their lack of incentive to work beyond the mere pleasure of physical exertion. They are careless because they have not found that it pays to be careful; they are improvident because the improvident ones of their acquaintance get on about as well as the provident. Above all, they cannot see why they should take unusual pains to make the white man's land better, or to fatten his mule, or save his corn. On the other hand, the white land-owner argues that any attempt to improve these laborers by increased responsibility, or higher wages, or better homes, or land of their own, would be sure to result in failure. He shows his Northern visitor the scarred and wretched land; the ruined mansions, the worn-out soil and mortgaged acres, and says, This is Negro freedom!

Now it happens that both master and man have just enough argument on their respective sides to make it difficult for them to understand each other. The Negro dimly personifies in the white man all his ills and misfortunes; if he is poor, it is because the white man seizes the fruit of his toil; if he is ignorant, it is because the white man gives him neither time nor facilities to learn; and, indeed, if any misfortune happens to him, it is because of some hidden machinations of "white folks." On the other hand, the masters and the masters' sons have never been able to see why the Negro, instead of settling down to be day-laborers for bread and clothes, are infected with a silly desire to rise in the world, and why they are sulky, dissatisifed, and careless, where their fathers were happy and dumb and faithful. "Why, you niggers have an easier time than I do," said a puzzled Albany merchant to his black customer. "Yes," he replied, "and so does yo' hogs."

Taking, then, the dissatisfied and shiftless field-hand as a starting-point, let us inquire how the black thousands of Dougherty have struggled from him up toward their ideal, and what that ideal is. All social struggle is evidenced by the rise, first of economic, then of social classes, among a homogeneous population. To-day the following economic classes are plainly differentiated among these Negroes.

A "submerged tenth" of croppers, with a few paupers; forty per cent who are metayers and thirty-nine per cent of semi-metayers and wage-laborers. There are left five per cent of money-renters and six per cent of freeholders, — the "Upper Ten" of the land. The croppers are entirely without capital, even in the limited sense of food or money to keep them from seed-time to harvest. All they furnish is their labor; the land-owner furnishes land stock, tools, seed, and house; and at the end of the year the laborer gets from a third to a half of the crop. Out of his share, however, comes pay and interest for food and clothing advanced him during the year. Thus we have a laborer without capital and without wages, and an employer whose capital is largely his employees' wages. It is an unsatisfactory arrangement, both for hirer and hired, and is usually in vogue on poor land with hard-pressed owners.

Above the croppers come the great mass of the black population who work the land on their own responsibility, paying rent in cotton and supported by the crop-mortgage system. After the war this system was attractive to the freedmen on account of its larger freedom and its possibilities for making a surplus. But with the carrying out of the crop-lien system, the deterioration of the land, and the slavery of debt, the position of the metayers has sunk to a dead level of practically unrewarded toil. Formerly all tenants had some capital, and often considerable; but absentee land-lordism, rising rack-rent, and falling cotton have stripped them well-nigh of all, and probably not over half of them to-day own their mules. The change from cropper to tenant was accomplished by fixing the rent. If, now, the rent fixed was reasonable, this was an incentive to the tenant to strive. On the other hand, if the rent was too high, or if the land deteriorated, the result was to discourage and check the efforts of the black peasantry. There is no doubt that the latter case is true; that in Dougherty County every economic advantage of the price of cotton in market and of the strivings of the tenant has been taken advantage of by the landlords and merchants, and swallowed up in rent and interest. If cotton rose in price, the rent rose even higher; if cotton fell, the rent remained or followed reluctantly. If a tenant worked hard and raised a large crop, his rent was raised the next year; if that year the crop failed, his corn was confiscated and his mule sold for debt. There were, of course, exceptions to this, — cases of personal kindness and forbearance; but in the vast majority of cases the rule was to extract the uttermost farthing from the mass of the black farm laborers.

The average metayer pays from twenty to thirty per cent of his crop in rent. The result of such rack-rent[18] can only be evil, — abuse and neglect of the soil, deterioration in the character of the laborers, and a widespread sense of injustice. "Wherever the country is poor," cried Arthur Young, "it is in the hands of metayers," and "their condition is more wretched than that of day-laborers."[19] He was talking of Italy a century ago; but he might have been talking of Dougherty County to-day. And especially is that true to-day which he declares was true in France before the Revolution: "The metayers are considered as little better than menial servants, removable at pleasure, and obliged to conform in all things to the will of the landlords." On this low plane half the black population of Dougherty County — perhaps more than half the black millions of this land — are to-day struggling.

A degree above these we may place those laborers who receive money wages for their work. Some receive a house with perhaps a garden-spot; then supplies of food and clothing are advanced, and certain fixed wages are given at the end of the year, varying from thirty to sixty dollars, out of which the supplies must be paid for, with interest. About eighteen per cent of the population belong to this class of semi-metayers, while twenty-two per cent are laborers paid by the month or year, and are either "furnished" by their own savings or perhaps more usually by some merchant who takes his chances of payment. Such laborers receive from thirty-five to fifty cents a day during the working season. They are usually young unmarried persons, some being women; and when they marry they sink to the class of metayers, or, more seldom, become renters.

The renters for fixed money rentals are the first of the emerging classes, and form five per cent of the families. The sole advantage of this small class is their freedom to choose their crops, and the increased responsibility which comes through having money transactions. While some of the renters differ little in condition from the metayers, yet on the whole they are more intelligent and responsible persons, and are the ones who eventually become land-owners. Their better character and greater shrewdness enable them to gain, perhaps to demand, better terms in rents; rented farms, varying from forty to a hundred acres, bear an average rental of about fifty-four dollars a year. The men who conduct such farms do not long remain renters; either they sink to metayers, or with a successful series of harvests rise to be land-owners.

In 1870 the tax-books of Dougherty report no Negroes as landholders. If there were any such at that time, — and there may have been a few, — their land was probably held in the name of some white patron, — a method not uncommon during slavery. In 1875 ownership of land had begun with seven hundred and fifty acres; ten years later this had increased to over sixty-five hundred acres, to nine thousand acres in 1890 and ten thousand in 1900. The total assessed property has in this same period risen from eighty thousand dollars in 1875 to two hundred and forty thousand dollars in 1900.

Two circumstances complicate this development and make it in some respects difficult to be sure of the real tendencies; they are the panic of 1893, and the low price of cotton in 1898.[20] Besides this, the system of assessing property in the country districts of Georgia is somewhat antiquated and of uncertain statistical value; there are no assessors, and each man makes a sworn return to a tax-receiver. Thus public opinion plays a large part, and the returns vary strangely from year to year. Certainly these figures show the small amount of accumulated capital among the Negroes, and the consequent large dependence of their property on temporary prosperity. They have little to tide over a few years of economic depression, and are at the mercy of the cotton-market far more than the whites. And thus the land-owners, despite their marvellous efforts, are really a transient class, continually being depleted by those who fall back into the class of renters or metayers, and augmented by newcomers from the masses. Of the one hundred land-owners in 1898, half had bought their land since 1893, a fourth between 1890 and 1893, a fifth between 1884 and 1890, and the rest between 1870 and 1884. In all, one hundred and eighty-five Negroes have owned land in this county since 1875.

If all the black land-owners who had ever held land here had kept it or left it in the hands of black men, the Negroes would have owned nearer thirty thousand acres than the fifteen thousand they now hold. And yet these fifteen thousand acres are a creditable showing, — a proof of no little weight of the worth and ability of the Negro people. If they had been given an economic start at Emancipation, if they had been in an enlightened and rich community which really desired their best good, then we might perhaps call such a result small or even insignificant. But for a few thousand poor ignorant field-hands, in the face of poverty, a falling market, and social stress, to save and capitalize two hundred thousand dollars in a generation has meant a tremendous effort. The rise of a nation, the pressing forward of a social class, means a bitter struggle, a hard and soul-sickening battle with the world such as few of the more favored classes know or appreciate.

Out of the hard economic conditions of this portion of the Black Belt, only six per cent of the population have succeeded in emerging into peasant proprietorship; and these are not all firmly fixed, but grow and shrink in number with the wavering of the cotton-market. Fully ninety-four per cent have struggled for land and failed, and half of them sit in hopeless serfdom. For these there is one other avenue of escape toward which they have turned in increasing numbers, namely, migration to town. A glance at the distribution of land among the black owners curiously reveals this fact. In 1898 the holdings were as follows: Under forty acres, forty-nine families; forty to two hundred and fifty acres, seventeen families; two hundred and fifty to one thousand acres, thirteen families; one thousand or more acres, two families. Now in 1890 there were forty-four holdings, but only nine of these were under forty acres. The great increase of holdings, then, has come in the buying of small homesteads near town, where their owners really share in the town life; this is a part of the rush to town. And for every landowner who has thus hurried away from the narrow and hard conditions of country life, how many field-hands, how many tenants, how many ruined renters, have joined that long procession? Is it not strange compensation? The sin of the country districts is visited on the town, and the social sores of city life to-day may, here in Dougherty County, and perhaps in many places near and far, look for their final healing without the city walls.

IX

Of the Sons of Master and Man

Life treads on life, and heart on heart;
We press too close in church and mart
To keep a dream or grave apart.

MRS. BROWNING.

The world-old phenomenon of the contact of diverse races of men is to have new exemplification during the new century. Indeed, the characteristic of our age is the contact of European civilization with the world's undeveloped peoples. Whatever we may say of the results of such contact in the past, it certainly forms a chapter in human action not pleasant to look back upon. War, murder, slavery, extermination, and debauchery,—this has again and again been the result of carrying civilization and the blessed gospel to the isles of the sea and the heathen without the law. Nor does it altogether satisfy the conscience of the modern world to be told complacently that all this has been right and proper, the fated triumph of strength over weakness, of righteousness over evil, of superiors over inferiors. It would certainly be soothing if one could readily believe all this; and yet there are too many ugly facts for everything to be thus easily explained away. We feel and know that there are many delicate differences in race psychology, numberless changes that our crude social measurements are not yet able to follow minutely, which explain much of history and social development. At the same time, too, we know that these considerations have never adequately explained or excused the triumph of brute force and cunning over weakness and innocence.

It is, then, the strife of all honorable men of the twentieth century to see that in the future competition of races the survival of the fittest[2] shall mean the triumph of the good, the beautiful, and the true; that we may be able to preserve for future civilization all that is really fine and noble and strong, and not continue to put a premium on greed and impudence and cruelty. To bring this hope to fruition, we are compelled daily to turn more and more to a conscientious study of the phenomena of race-contact, — to a study frank and fair, and not falsified and colored by our wishes or our fears. And we have in the South as fine a field for such a study as the world affords, — a field, to be sure, which the average American scientist deems somewhat beneath his dignity, and which the average man who is not a scientist knows all about, but nevertheless a line of study which by reason of the enormous race complications with which God seems about to punish this nation must increasingly claim our sober attention, study, and thought, we must ask, what are the actual relations of whites and blacks in the South? and we must be answered, not by apology or fault-finding, but by a plain, unvarnished tale.

In the civilized life of to-day the contact of men and their relations to each other fall in a few main lines of action and communication: there is, first, the physical proximity of homes and dwelling-places, the way in which neighborhoods group themselves, and the contiguity of neighborhoods. Secondly, and in our age chiefest, there are the economic relations, — the methods by which individuals cooperate for earning a living, for the mutual satisfaction of wants, for the production of wealth. Next, there are the political relations, the cooperation in social control, in group government, in laying and paying the burden of taxation. In the fourth place there are the less tangible but highly important forms of intellectual contact and commerce, the interchange of ideas through conversation and conference, through periodicals and libraries; and, above all, the gradual formation for each community of that curious *tertium quid*[3] which we call public opinion. Closely allied with this come the various forms of social contact in everyday life, in travel, in theatres, in house gatherings, in marrying and giving in marriage. Finally, there are the varying forms of religious enterprise, of moral teaching and benevolent endeavor. These are the principal ways in which men living in the same communities are brought into contact with each other. It is my present task, therefore, to indicate, from my point of view, how the black race in the South meet and mingle with the whites in these matters of everyday life.

First, as to physical dwelling. It is usually possible to draw in nearly every Southern community a physical color-line on the map, on the one side of which whites dwell and on the other Negroes. The winding and intricacy of the geographical color line varies, of course, in different communities. I know some towns where a straight line drawn through the middle of the main street separates nine-tenths of the whites from nine-tenths of the blacks. In other towns the older settlement of whites has been encircled by a broad band of blacks; in still other cases little settlements or nuclei of blacks have sprung up amid surrounding whites. Usually in cities each street has its distinctive color, and only now and then do the colors meet in close proximity. Even in the country something of this segregation is manifest in the smaller areas, and of course in the larger phenomena of the Black Belt.

All this segregation by color is largely independent of that natural clustering by social grades common to all communities. A Negro slum may be in dangerous proximity to a white residence quarter, while it is quite common to find a white slum planted in the heart of a respectable Negro district. One thing, however, seldom occurs: the best of the whites and the best of the Negroes almost never live in anything like close proximity. It thus happens that in nearly every Southern town and city, both whites and blacks see commonly the worst of each other. This is a vast change from the situation in the past, when, through the close contact of master and house-servant in the patriarchal big house, one found the best of both races in close contact and sympathy,[4] while at the same time the squalor and dull round of toil among the field-hands was removed from the sight and hearing of the family. One can easily see how a person who saw slavery thus from his father's parlors, and sees freedom on the streets of a great city, fails to grasp or comprehend the whole of the new picture. On the other hand, the settled belief of the mass of the Negroes that the Southern white people do not have the black man's best interests at heart has been intensified in later years by this continual daily contact of the better class of blacks with the worst representatives of the white race.

Coming now to the economic relations of the races, we are on ground made familiar by study, much discussion, and no little philanthropic effort. And yet with all this there are many essential elements in the cooperation of Negroes and whites for work and wealth that are too readily overlooked or not thoroughly understood. The average American can easily conceive of a rich land awaiting development and filled with black laborers. To him the Southern problem is simply that of making efficient workingmen out of this material, by giving them the requisite technical skill and the help of invested capital. The problem, however, is by no means as simple as this, from the obvious fact that these workingmen have been trained for centuries as slaves. They exhibit, therefore, all the advantages and defects of such training; they are willing and good-natured, but not self-reliant, provident, or careful. If now the economic development of the South is to be pushed to the verge of exploitation, as seems probable, then we have a mass of workingmen thrown into relentless competition with the workingmen of the world, but handicapped by a training the very opposite to that of the modern self-reliant democratic laborer. What the black laborer needs is careful personal guidance, group leadership of men with hearts in their bosoms, to train them to foresight, carefulness, and honesty. Nor does it require any fine-spun theories of racial differences to prove the necessity of such group training after the brains of the race have been knocked out by two hundred and fifty years of assiduous education in submission, carelessness, and stealing. After Emancipation, it was the plain duty of some one to assume this group leadership and training of the Negro laborer. I will not stop here to inquire whose duty it was, — whether that of the white ex-master who had profited by unpaid toil, or the Northern philanthropist whose persistence brought on the crisis, or the National Government whose edict freed the bondmen; I will not stop to ask whose duty it was, but I insist it was the duty of some one to see that these workingmen were not left alone and unguided, without capital, without land, without skill, without economic organization, without even the bald protection of law, order, and decency, — left in a great land, not to settle down to slow and careful internal development, but destined to be thrown almost immediately into relentless and sharp competition with the best of modern workingmen under an economic system where every participant is fighting for himself, and too often utterly regardless of the rights or welfare of his neighbor.

For we must never forget that the economic system of the South today which has succeeded the old *régime*[5] is not the same system as that of the old industrial North, of England, or of France, with their trades-unions, their restrictive laws, their written and unwritten commercial customs, and their long experience. It is, rather, a copy of that England of the early nineteenth century, before the factory acts, — the England that wrung pity from thinkers and fired the wrath of Carlyle.[6] The rod of empire that passed from the hands of Southern gentlemen in 1865, partly by force, partly by their own petulance, has never returned to them. Rather it has passed to those men who have come to take charge of the industrial exploitation of the New South, — the sons of poor whites fired with a new thirst for wealth and power, thrifty and avaricious Yankees, shrewd and unscrupulous Jews.[7] Into the hands of these men the Southern laborers, white and black, have fallen; and this to their sorrow. For the laborers as such there is in these new captains of industry neither love nor hate, neither sympathy nor romance; it is a cold question of dollars and dividends. Under such a system all labor is bound to suffer. Even the white laborers are not yet intelligent, thrifty, and well trained enough to maintain themselves against the powerful in roads of organized capital. The results among them, even, are long hours of toil, low wages, child labor, and lack of protection against usury and cheating. But among the black laborers all this is aggravated, first, by a race prejudice which varies from a doubt and distrust among the best element of whites to a frenzied hatred among the worst; and, secondly, it is aggravated, as I have said before, by the wretched economic heritage of the freedmen from slavery. With this training it is difficult for the freedman to learn to grasp the opportunities already opened to him, and the new opportunities are seldom given him, but go by favor to the whites.

Left by the best elements of the South with little protection or oversight, he has been made in law and custom the victim of the worst and most unscrupulous men in each community. The crop-lien system which is depopulating the fields of the South is not simply the result of shiftlessness on the part of Negroes, but is also the result of cunningly devised laws as to mortgages, liens, and misdemeanors, which can be made by conscienceless men to entrap and snare the unwary until escape is impossible, further toil a farce, and protest a crime. I have seen, in the Black Belt of Georgia, an ignorant, honest Negro buy and pay for a farm in installments three separate times, and then in the face of law and decency the enterprising Russian Jew[8] who sold it to him pocketed money and deed and left the black man landless, to labor on his own land at thirty cents a day. I have seen a black farmer fall in debt to a white storekeeper, and that storekeeper go to his farm and strip it of every single marketable article, — mules, ploughs, stored crops, tools, furniture, bedding, clocks, looking-glass, — and all this without a warrant, without process of law, without a sheriff or officer, in the face of the law for homestead exemptions, and without rendering to a single responsible person any account or reckoning. And such proceedings can happen, and will happen, in any community where a class of ignorant toilers are placed by custom and race-prejudice beyond the pale of sympathy and race-brotherhood. So long as the best elements of a community do not feel in duty bound to protect and train and care for the weaker members of their group, they leave them to be preyed upon by these swindlers and rascals.

This unfortunate economic situation does not mean the hindrance of all advance in the black South, or the absence of a class of black landlords and mechanics who, in spite of disadvantages, are accumulating property and making good citizens. But it does mean that this class is not nearly so large as a fairer economic system might easily make it, that those who survive in the competition are handicapped so as to accomplish much less than they deserve to, and that, above all, the *personnel* of the successful class is left to chance and accident, and not to any intelligent culling or reasonable methods of selection. As a remedy for this, there is but one possible procedure. We must accept some of the race prejudice in the South as a fact, — deplorable in its intensity, unfortunate in results, and dangerous for the future, but nevertheless a hard fact which only time can efface. We cannot hope, then, in this generation, or for several generations, that the mass of the whites can be brought to assume that close sympathetic and self-sacrificing leadership of the blacks which their present situation so eloquently demands. Such leadership, such social teaching and example, must come from the blacks themselves. For some time men doubted as to whether the Negro could develop such leaders; but to-day no one seriously disputes the capability of individual Negroes to assimilate the culture and common sense of modern civilization, and to pass it on, to some extent at least, to their fellows. If this is true, then here is the path out of the economic situation, and here is the imperative demand for trained Negro leaders of character and intelligence, — men of skill, men of light and leading, college-bred men, black captains of industry, and missionaries of culture; men who thoroughly comprehend and know modern civilization, and can take hold of Negro communities and raise and train them by force of precept and example, deep sympathy, and the inspiration of common blood and ideals. But if such men are to be effective they must have some power, — they must be backed by the best public opinion of these communities, and able to wield for their objects and aims such weapons as the experience of the world has taught are indispensable to human progress.[9]

Of such weapons the greatest, perhaps, in the modern world is the power of the ballot; and this brings me to a consideration of the third form of contact between whites and blacks in the South, — political activity.

In the attitude of the American mind toward Negro suffrage can be traced with unusual accuracy the prevalent conceptions of government. In the fifties we were near enough the echoes of the French Revolution to believe pretty thoroughly in universal suffrage. We argued, as we thought then rather logically, that no social class was so good, so true, and so disinterested as to be trusted wholly with the political destiny of its neighbors; that in every state the best arbiters of their own welfare are the persons directly affected; consequently that it is only by arming every hand with a ballot, — with the right to have a voice in the policy of the state, — that the greatest good to the greatest number could be attained.[10] To be sure, there were objections to these arguments, but we thought we had answered them tersely and convincingly; if some one complained of the ignorance of voters, we answered, "Educate them." If another complained of their venality, we replied, "Disfranchise them or put them in jail." And, finally, to the men who feared demagogues and the natural perversity of some human beings we insisted that time and bitter experience would teach the most hardheaded. It was at this time that the question of Negro suffrage in the South was raised. Here was a defenceless people suddenly made free. How were they to be protected from those who did not believe in their freedom and were determined to thwart it? Not by force, said the North; not by government guardianship, said the South; then by the ballot, the sole and legitimate defence of a free people, said the Common Sense of the Nation. No one thought, at the time, that the ex-slaves could use the ballot intelligently or very effectively; but they did think that the possession of so great power by a great class in the nation would compel their fellows to educate this class to its intelligent use.

Meantime, new thoughts came to the nation: the inevitable period of moral retrogression and political trickery that ever follows in the wake of war overtook us. So flagrant became the political scandals that reputable men began to leave politics alone, and politics consequently became disreputable. Men began to pride themselves on having nothing to do with their own government, and to agree tacitly with those who regarded public office as a private perquisite. In this state of mind it became easy to wink at the suppression of the Negro vote in the South, and to advise self-respecting Negroes to leave politics entirely alone. The decent and reputable citizens of the North who neglected their own civic duties grew hilarious over the exaggerated importance with which the Negro regarded the franchise. Thus it easily happened that more and more the better class of Negroes followed the advice from abroad and the pressure from home, and took no further interest in politics, leaving to the careless and the venal of their race the exercise of their rights as voters. The black vote that still remained was not trained and educated, but further debauched by open and unblushing bribery, or force and fraud; until the Negro voter was thoroughly inoculated with the idea that politics was a method of private gain by disreputable means.

And finally, now, to-day, when we are awakening to the fact that the perpetuity of republican institutions on this continent depends on the purification of the ballot, the civic training of voters, and the raising of voting to the plane of a solemn duty which a patriotic citizen neglects to his peril and to the peril of his children's children,—in this day, when we are striving for a renaissance of civic virtue, what are we going to say to the black voter of the South? Are we going to tell him still that politics is a disreputable and useless form of human activity? Are we going to induce the best class of Negroes to take less and less interest in government, and to give up their right to take such an interest, without a protest? I am not saying a word against all legitimate efforts to purge the ballot of ignorance, pauperism, and crime. But few have pretended that the present movement for disfranchisement in the South is for such a purpose; it has been plainly and frankly declared in nearly every case that the object of the disfranchising laws is the elimination of the black man from politics.

Now, is this a minor matter which has no influence on the main question of the industrial and intellectual development of the Negro? Can we establish a mass of black laborers and artisans and landholders in the South who, by law and public opinion, have absolutely no voice in shaping the laws under which they live and work? Can the modern organization of industry, assuming as it does free democratic government and the power and ability of the laboring classes to compel respect for their welfare, — can this system be carried out in the South when half its laboring force is voiceless in the public councils and powerless in its own defence? To-day the black man of the South has almost nothing to say as to how much he shall be taxed, or how those taxes shall be expended; as to who shall execute the laws, and how they shall do it; as to who shall make the laws, and how they shall be made. It is pitiable that frantic efforts must be made at critical times to get law-makers in some States even to listen to the respectful presentation of the black man's side of a current controversy. Daily the Negro is coming more and more to look upon law and justice, not as protecting safeguards, but as sources of humiliation and oppression. The laws are made by men who have little interest in him; they are executed by men who have absolutely no motive for treating the black people with courtesy or consideration; and, finally, the accused law-breaker is tried, not by his peers, but too often by men who would rather punish ten innocent Negroes than let one guilty one escape.

I should be the last one to deny the patent weaknesses and shortcomings of the Negro people; I should be the last to withhold sympathy from the white South in its efforts to solve its intricate social problems. I freely acknowledge that it is possible, and sometimes best, that a partially undeveloped people should be ruled by the best of their stronger and better neighbors for their own good, until such time as they can start and fight the world's battles alone. I have already pointed out how sorely in need of such economic and spiritual guidance the emancipated Negro was, and I am quite willing to admit that if the representatives of the best white Southern public opinion were the ruling and guiding powers in the South to-day the conditions indicated would be fairly well fulfilled. But the point I have insisted upon, and now emphasize again, is that the best opinion of the South to-day is not the ruling opinion. That to leave the Negro helpless and without a ballot to-day is to leave him, not to the guidance of the best, but rather to the exploitation and debauchment of the worst; that this is no truer of the South than of the North, — of the North than of Europe: in any land, in any country under modern free competition, to lay any class of weak and despised people, be they white, black, or blue, at the political mercy of their stronger, richer, and more resourceful fellows, is a temptation which human nature seldom has withstood and seldom will withstand.

Moreover, the political status of the Negro in the South is closely connected with the question of Negro crime. There can be no doubt that crime among Negroes has sensibly increased in the last thirty years, and that there has appeared in the slums of great cities a distinct criminal class among the blacks. In explaining this unfortunate development, we must note two things: (1) that the inevitable result of Emancipation was to increase crime and criminals, and (2) that the police system of the South was primarily designed to control slaves. As to the first point, we must not forget that under a strict slave system there can scarcely be such a thing as crime. But when these variously constituted human particles are suddenly thrown broadcast on the sea of life, some swim, some sink, and some hang suspended, to be forced up or down by the chance currents of a busy hurrying world. So great an economic and social revolution as swept the South in '63 meant a weeding out among the Negroes of the incompetents and vicious, the beginning of a differentiation of social grades.[11] Now a rising group of people are not lifted bodily from the ground like an inert solid mass, but rather stretch upward like a living plant with its roots still clinging in the mould. The appearance, therefore, of the Negro criminal was a phenomenon to be awaited; and while it causes anxiety, it should not occasion surprise.

Here again the hope for the future depended peculiarly on careful and delicate dealing with these criminals. Their offences at first were those of laziness, carelessness, and impulse, rather than of malignity or ungoverned viciousness. Such misdemeanors needed discriminating treatment, firm but reformatory, with no hint of injustice, and full proof of guilt. For such dealing with criminals, white or black, the South had no machinery, no adequate jails or reformatories; its police system was arranged to deal with blacks alone, and tacitly assumed that every white man was *ipso facto*[12] a member of that police. Thus grew up a double system of justice, which erred on the white side by undue leniency and the practical immunity of red-handed criminals, and erred on the black side by undue severity, injustice, and lack of discrimination. For, as I have said, the police system of the South was originally designed to keep track of all Negroes, not simply of criminals; and when the Negroes were freed and the whole South was convinced of the impossibility of free Negro labor, the first and almost universal device was to use the courts as a means of reënslaving the blacks. It was not then a question of crime, but rather one of color, that settled a man's conviction on almost any charge. Thus Negroes came to look upon courts as instruments of injustice and oppression, and upon those convicted in them as martyrs and victims.

When, now, the real Negro criminal appeared, and instead of petty stealing and vagrancy we began to have highway robbery, burglary, murder, and rape, there was a curious effect on both sides the color-line: the Negroes refused to believe the evidence of white witnesses or the fairness of white juries, so that the greatest deterrent to crime, the public opinion of one's own social caste, was lost, and the criminal was looked upon as crucified rather than hanged. On the other hand, the whites, used to being careless as to the guilt or innocence of accused Negroes, were swept in moments of passion beyond law, reason, and decency. Such a situation is bound to increase crime, and has increased it. To natural viciousness and vagrancy are being daily added motives of revolt and revenge which stir up all the latent savagery of both races and make peaceful attention to economic development often impossible.

But the chief problem in any community cursed with crime is not the punishment of the criminals, but the preventing of the young from being trained to crime. And here again the peculiar conditions of the South have prevented proper precautions. I have seen twelve-year-old boys working in chains on the public streets of Atlanta, directly in front of the schools, in company with old and hardened criminals; and this indiscriminate mingling of men and women and children makes the chain-gangs perfect schools of crime and debauchery. The struggle for reformatories, which has gone on in Virginia, Georgia, and other States, is the one encouraging sign of the awakening of some communities to the suicidal results of this policy.

It is the public schools, however, which can be made, outside the homes, the greatest means of training decent self-respecting citizens. We have been so hotly engaged recently in discussing trade-schools and the higher education that the pitiable plight of the public-school system in the South has almost dropped from view. Of every five dollars spent for public education in the State of Georgia, the white schools get four dollars and the Negro one dollar; and even then the white public-school system, save in the cities, is bad and cries for reform. If this is true of the whites, what of the blacks? I am becoming more and more convinced, as I look upon the system of common-school training in the South, that the national government must soon step in and aid popular education in some way. To-day it has been only by the most strenuous efforts on the part of the thinking men of the South that the Negro's share of the school fund has not been cut down to a pittance in some half-dozen States; and that movement not only is not dead, but in many communities is gaining strength. What in the name of reason does this nation expect of a people, poorly trained and hard pressed in severe economic competition, without political rights, and with ludicrously inadequate common-school facilities? What can it expect but crime and listlessness, offset here and there by the dogged struggles of the fortunate and more determined who are themselves buoyed by the hope that in due time the country will come to its senses?

I have thus far sought to make clear the physical, economic, and political relations of the Negroes and whites in the South, as I have conceived them, including, for the reasons set forth, crime and education. But after all that has been said on these more tangible matters of human contact, there still remains a part essential to a proper description of the South which it is difficult to describe or fix in terms easily understood by strangers. It is, in fine, the atmosphere of the land, the thought and feeling, the thousand and one little actions which go to make up life. In any community or nation it is these little things which are most elusive to the grasp and yet most essential to any clear conception of the group life taken as a whole. What is thus true of all communities is peculiarly true of the South, where, outside of written history and outside of printed law, there has been going on for a generation as deep a storm and stress[13] of human souls, as intense a ferment of feeling, as intricate a writhing of spirit, as ever a people experienced. Within and without the sombre veil of color vast social forces have been at work, — efforts for human betterment, movements toward disintegration and despair, tragedies and comedies in social and economic life, and a swaying and lifting and sinking of human hearts which have made this land a land of mingled sorrow and joy, of change and excitement and unrest.

The centre of this spiritual turmoil has ever been the millions of black freedmen and their sons, whose destiny is so fatefully bound up with that of the nation. And yet the casual observer visiting the South sees at first little of this. He notes the growing frequency of dark faces as he rides along,—but otherwise the days slip lazily on, the sun shines, and this little world seems as happy and contented as other worlds he has visited. Indeed, on the question of questions—the Negro problem—he hears so little that there almost seems to be a conspiracy of silence; the morning papers seldom mention it, and then usually in a far-fetched academic way, and indeed almost every one seems to forget and ignore the darker half of the land, until the astonished visitor is inclined to ask if after all there *is* any problem here. But if he lingers long enough there comes the awakening: perhaps in a sudden whirl of passion which leaves him gasping at its bitter intensity; more likely in a gradually dawning sense of things he had not at first noticed. Slowly but surely his eyes begin to catch the shadows of the color-line: here he meets crowds of Negroes and whites; then he is suddenly aware that he cannot discover a single dark face; or again at the close of a day's wandering he may find himself in some strange assembly, where all faces are tinged brown or black, and where he has the vague, uncomfortable feeling of the stranger. He realizes at last that silently, resistlessly, the world about flows by him in two great streams: they ripple on in the same sunshine, they approach and mingle their waters in seeming carelessness,—then they divide and flow wide apart. It is done quietly; no mistakes are made, or if one occurs, the swift arm of the law and of public opinion swings down for a moment, as when the other day a black man and a white woman were arrested for talking together on Whitehall Street in Atlanta.

Now if one notices carefully one will see that between these two worlds, despite much physical contact and daily intermingling, there is almost no community of intellectual life or point of transference where the thoughts and feelings of one race can come into direct contact and sympathy with the thoughts and feelings of the other. Before and directly after the war, when all the best of the Negroes were domestic servants in the best of the white families, there were bonds of intimacy, affection, and sometimes blood relationship, between the races. They lived in the same home, shared in the family life, often attended the same church, and talked and conversed with each other. But the increasing civilization of the Negro since then has naturally meant the development of higher classes: there are increasing numbers of ministers, teachers, physicians, merchants, mechanics, and independent farmers, who by nature and training are the aristocracy and leaders of the blacks. Between them, however, and the best element of the whites, there is little or no intellectual commerce. They go to separate churches, they live in separate sections, they are strictly separated in all public gatherings, they travel separately, and they are beginning to read different papers and books. To most libraries, lectures, concerts, and museums, Negroes are either not admitted at all, or on terms peculiarly galling to the pride of the very classes who might otherwise be attracted. The daily paper chronicles the doings of the black world from afar with no great regard for accuracy; and so on, throughout the category of means for intellectual communication, — schools, conferences, efforts for social betterment, and the like, — it is usually true that the very representatives of the two races, who for mutual benefit and the welfare of the land ought to be in complete understanding and sympathy, are so far strangers that one side thinks all whites are narrow and prejudiced, and the other thinks educated Negroes dangerous and insolent. Moreover, in a land where the tyranny of public opinion and the intolerance of criticism is for obvious historical reasons so strong as in the South, such a situation is extremely difficult to correct. The white man, as well as the Negro, is bound and barred by the color-line, and many a scheme of friendliness and philanthropy, of broad-minded sympathy and generous fellowship between the two has dropped still-born because some busybody has forced the color-question to the front and brought the tremendous force of unwritten law against the innovators.

It is hardly necessary for me to add very much in regard to the social contact between the races. Nothing has come to replace that finer sympathy and love between some masters and house servants which the radical and more uncompromising drawing of the color-line in recent years has caused almost completely to disappear. In a world where it means so much to take a man by the hand and sit beside him, to look frankly into his eyes and feel his heart beating with red blood; in a world where a social cigar or a cup of tea together means more than legislative halls and magazine articles and speeches, — one can imagine the consequences of the almost utter absence of such social amenities between estranged races, whose separation extends even to parks and street-cars.

Here there can be none of that social going down to the people, — the opening of heart and hand of the best to the worst, in generous acknowledgment of a common humanity and a common destiny. On the other hand, in matters of simple almsgiving, where there can be no question of social contact, and in the succor of the aged and sick, the South, as if stirred by a feeling of its unfortunate limitations, is generous to a fault. The black beggar is never turned away without a good deal more than a crust, and a call for help for the unfortunate meets quick response. I remember, one cold winter, in Atlanta, when I refrained from contributing to a public relief fund lest Negroes should be discriminated against,

I afterward inquired of a friend: "Were any black people receiving aid?" "Why," said he, "they were *all* black."

And yet this does not touch the kernel of the problem. Human advancement is not a mere question of almsgiving, but rather of sympathy and cooperation among classes who would scorn charity. And here is a land where, in the higher walks of life, in all the higher striving for the good and noble and true, the color-line comes to separate natural friends and co-workers; while at the bottom of the social group, in the saloon, the gambling-hell, and the brothel, that same line wavers and disappears.

I have sought to paint an average picture of real relations between the sons of master and man in the South. I have not glossed over matters for policy's sake, for I fear we have already gone too far in that sort of thing. On the other hand, I have sincerely sought to let no unfair exaggerations creep in. I do not doubt that in some Southern communities conditions are better than those I have indicated; while I am no less certain that in other communities they are far worse.

Nor does the paradox and danger of this situation fail to interest and perplex the best conscience of the South. Deeply religious and intensely democratic as are the mass of the whites, they feel acutely the false position in which the Negro problems place them. Such an essentially honest-hearted and generous people cannot cite the caste-levelling precepts of Christianity, or believe in equality of opportunity for all men, without coming to feel more and more with each generation that the present drawing of the color-line is a flat contradiction to their beliefs and professions. But just as often as they come to this point, the present social condition of the Negro stands as a menace and a portent before even the most open-minded: if there were nothing to charge against the Negro but his blackness or other physical peculiarities, they argue, the problem would be comparatively simple; but what can we say to his ignorance, shiftlessness, poverty, and crime? can a self-respecting group hold anything but the least possible fellowship with such persons and survive? and shall we let a mawkish sentiment sweep away the culture of our fathers or the hope of our children? The argument so put is of great strength, but it is not a whit stronger than the argument of thinking Negroes: granted, they reply, that the condition of our masses is bad; there is certainly on the one hand adequate historical cause for this, and unmistakable evidence that no small number have, in spite of tremendous disadvantages, risen to the level of American civilization. And when, by proscription and prejudice, these same Negroes are classed with and treated like the lowest of their people, simply *because* they are Negroes, such a policy not only discourages thrift and intelligence among black men, but puts a direct premium on the very things you complain of,—inefficiency and crime. Draw lines of crime, of incompetency, of vice, as tightly and uncompromisingly as you will, for these things must be proscribed; but a color-line not only does not accomplish this purpose, but thwarts it.

In the face of two such arguments, the future of the South depends on the ability of the representatives of these opposing views to see and appreciate and sympathize with each other's position,—for the Negro to realize more deeply than he does at present the need of uplifting the masses of his people, for the white people to realize more vividly than they have yet done the deadening and disastrous effect of a color-prejudice that classes Phillis Wheatley and Sam Hose in the same despised class.[14]

It is not enough for the Negroes to declare that color-prejudice is the sole cause of their social condition, nor for the white South to reply that their social condition is the main cause of prejudice. They both act as reciprocal cause and effect, and a change in neither alone will bring the desired effect. Both must change, or neither can improve to any great extent. The Negro cannot stand the present reactionary tendencies and unreasoning drawing of the color-line indefinitely without discouragement and retrogression. And the condition of the Negro is ever the excuse for further discrimination. Only by a union of intelligence and sympathy across the color-line in this critical period of the Republic shall justice and right triumph,—

> "That mind and soul according well,
> May make one music as before,
> But vaster."[15]

X

Of the Faith of the Fathers

Dim face of Beauty haunting all the world,
  Fair face of Beauty all too fair to see,
Where the lost stars adown the heavens are hurled, —
    There, there alone for thee
    May white peace be.

Beauty, sad face of Beauty, Mystery, Wonder,
  What are these dreams to foolish babbling men
Who cry with little noises 'neath the thunder
    Of Ages ground to sand,
    To a little sand.

FIONA MACLEOD.

It was out in the country, far from home, far from my foster home, on a dark Sunday night. The road wandered from our rambling log-house up the stony bed of a creek, past wheat and corn, until we could hear dimly across the fields a rhythmic cadence of song, — soft, thrilling, powerful, that swelled and died sorrowfully in our ears. I was a country school-teacher then, fresh from the East, and had never seen a Southern Negro revival. To be sure, we in Berkshire were not perhaps as stiff and formal as they in Suffolk[2] of olden time; yet we were very quiet and subdued, and I know not what would have happened those clear Sabbath mornings had some one punctuated the sermon with a wild scream, or interrupted the long prayer with a loud Amen! And so most striking to me, as I approached the village and the little plain church perched aloft, was the air of intense excitement that possessed that mass of black folk. A sort of suppressed terror hung in the air and seemed to seize us, — a pythian madness, a demoniac possession, that lent terrible reality to song and word. The black and massive form of the preacher swayed and quivered as the words crowded to his lips and flew at us in singular eloquence. The people moaned and fluttered, and then the gaunt-cheeked brown woman beside me suddenly leaped straight into the air and shrieked like a lost soul, while round about came wail and groan and outcry, and a scene of human passion such as I had never conceived before.

Those who have not thus witnessed the frenzy of a Negro revival in the untouched backwoods of the South can but dimly realize the religious feeling of the slave; as described, such scenes appear grotesque and funny, but as seen they are awful. Three things characterized this religion of the slave,—the Preacher,[3] the Music, and the Frenzy. The Preacher is the most unique personality developed by the Negro on American soil. A leader, a politician, an orator, a "boss," an intriguer, an idealist,—all these he is, and ever, too, the centre of a group of men, now twenty, now a thousand in number. The combination of a certain adroitness with deep-seated earnestness, of tact with consummate ability, gave him his preeminence, and helps him maintain it. The type, of course, varies according to time and place, from the West Indies in the sixteenth century to New England in the nineteenth, and from the Mississippi bottoms to cities like New Orleans or New York.

The Music of Negro religion is that plaintive rhythmic melody, with its touching minor cadences, which, despite caricature and defilement, still remains the most original and beautiful expression of human life and longing yet born on American soil. Sprung from the African forests, where its counterpart can still be heard, it was adapted, changed, and intensified by the tragic soul-life of the slave, until, under the stress of law and whip, it became the one true expression of a people's sorrow, despair, and hope.

Finally the Frenzy or "Shouting,"[4] when the Spirit of the Lord passed by, and, seizing the devotee, made him mad with supernatural joy, was the last essential of Negro religion and the one more devoutly believed in than all the rest. It varied in expression from the silent rapt countenance or the low murmur and moan to the mad abandon of physical fervor,— the stamping, shrieking, and shouting, the rushing to and fro and wild waving of arms, the weeping and laughing, the vision and the trance. All this is nothing new in the world, but old as religion, as Delphi and Endor.[5] And so firm a hold did it have on the Negro, that many generations firmly believed that without this visible manifestation of the God there could be no true communion with the Invisible.

These were the characteristics of Negro religious life as developed up to the time of Emancipation. Since under the peculiar circumstances of the black man's environment they were the one expression of his higher life, they are of deep interest to the student of his development, both socially and psychologically. Numerous are the attractive lines of inquiry that here group themselves. What did slavery mean to the African savage? What was his attitude toward the World and Life? What seemed to him good and evil, — God and Devil? Whither went his longings and strivings, and wherefore were his heart-burnings and disappointments? Answers to such questions can come only from a study of Negro religion as a development, through its gradual changes from the heathenism[6] of the Gold Coast to the institutional Negro church of Chicago.

Moreover, the religious growth of millions of men, even though they be slaves, cannot be without potent influence upon their contemporaries. The Methodists and Baptists of America owe much of their condition to the silent but potent influence of their millions of Negro converts. Especially is this noticeable in the South, where theology and religious philosophy are on this account a long way behind the North, and where the religion of the poor whites is a plain copy of Negro thought and methods. The mass of "gospel" hymns which has swept through American churches and well-nigh ruined our sense of song consists largely of debased imitations of Negro melodies made by ears that caught the jingle but not the music, the body but not the soul, of the Jubilee songs.[7] It is thus clear that the study of Negro religion is not only a vital part of the history of the Negro in America, but no uninteresting part of American history.

The Negro church of to-day is the social centre of Negro life in the United States, and the most characteristic expression of African character. Take a typical church in a small Virginian town: it is the "First Baptist" — a roomy brick edifice seating five hundred or more persons, tastefully finished in Georgia pine, with a carpet, a small organ, and stained-glass windows. Underneath is a large assembly room with benches. This building is the central club-house of a community of a thousand or more Negroes. Various organizations meet here, — the church proper, the Sunday-school, two or three insurance societies, women's societies, secret societies, and mass meetings of various kinds. Entertainments, suppers, and lectures are held beside the five or six regular weekly religious services. Considerable sums of money are collected and expended here, employment is found for the idle, strangers are introduced, news is disseminated and charity distributed. At the same time this social, intellectual, and economic centre is a religious centre of great power. Depravity, Sin, Redemption, Heaven, Hell, and Damnation are preached twice a Sunday with much fervor, and revivals take place every year after the crops are laid by; and few indeed of the community have the hardihood to withstand conversion. Back of this more formal religion, the Church often stands as a real conserver of morals, a strengthener of family life, and the final authority on what is Good and Right.

Thus one can see in the Negro church to-day, reproduced in microcosm, all that great world from which the Negro is cut off by color-prejudice and social condition. In the great city churches the same tendency is noticeable and in many respects emphasized. A great church like the Bethel of Philadelphia[8] has over eleven hundred members, an edifice seating fifteen hundred persons and valued at one hundred thousand dollars, an annual budget of five thousand dollars, and a government consisting of a pastor with several assisting local preachers, an executive and legislative board, financial boards and tax collectors; general church meetings for making laws; subdivided groups led by class leaders, a company of militia, and twenty-four auxiliary societies. The activity of a church like this is immense and far-reaching, and the bishops who preside over these organizations throughout the land are among the most powerful Negro rulers in the world.

Such churches are really governments of men, and consequently a little investigation reveals the curious fact that, in the South, at least, practically every American Negro is a church member. Some, to be sure, are not regularly enrolled, and a few do not habitually attend services; but, practically, a proscribed people must have a social centre, and that centre for this people is the Negro church. The census of 1890 showed nearly twenty-four thousand Negro churches in the country, with a total enrolled membership of over two and a half millions, or ten actual church members to every twenty-eight persons, and in some Southern States one in every two persons. Besides these there is the large number who, while not enrolled as members, attend and take part in many of the activities of the church. There is an organized Negro church for every sixty black families in the nation, and in some States for every forty families, owning, on an average, a thousand dollars' worth of property each, or nearly twenty-six million dollars in all.

Such, then, is the large development of the Negro church since Emancipation. The question now is, What have been the successive steps of this social history and what are the present tendencies? First, we must realize that no such institution as the Negro church could rear itself without definite historical foundations. These foundations we can find if we remember that the social history of the Negro did not start in America. He was brought from a definite social environment, — the polygamous clan life under the headship of the chief and the potent influence of the priest. His religion was nature-worship, with profound belief in invisible surrounding influences, good and bad, and his worship was through incantation and sacrifice. The first rude change in this life was the slave ship and the West Indian sugar-fields. The plantation organization replaced the clan and tribe, and the white master replaced the chief with far greater and more despotic powers. Forced and long-continued toil became the rule of life, the old ties of blood relationship and kinship disappeared, and instead of the family appeared a new polygamy and polyandry,[9] which, in some cases, almost reached promiscuity. It was a terrific social revolution, and yet some traces were retained of the former group life, and the chief remaining institution was the Priest or Medicineman. He early appeared on the plantation and found his function as the healer of the sick, the interpreter of the Unknown, the comforter of the sorrowing, the supernatural avenger of wrong, and the one who rudely but picturesquely expressed the longing, disappointment, and resentment of a stolen and oppressed people. Thus, as bard,[10] physician, judge, and priest, within the narrow limits allowed by the slave system, rose the Negro preacher, and under him the first Afro-American institution, the Negro church. This church was not at first by any means Christian nor definitely organized; rather it was an adaptation and mingling of heathen rites among the members of each plantation, and roughly designated as Voodooism.[11] Association with the masters, missionary effort and motives of expediency gave these rites an early veneer of Christianity, and after the lapse of many generations the Negro church became Christian.

Two characteristic things must be noticed in regard to this church. First, it became almost entirely Baptist and Methodist in faith; secondly, as a social institution it antedated by many decades the monogamic Negro home. From the very circumstances of its beginning, the church was confined to the plantation, and consisted primarily of a series of disconnected units; although, later on, some freedom of movement was allowed, still this geographical limitation was always important and was one cause of the spread of the decentralized and democratic Baptist faith among the slaves. At the same time, the visible rite of baptism appealed strongly to their mystic temperament. To-day the Baptist Church is still largest in membership among Negroes, and has a million and a half communicants. Next in popularity came the churches organized in connection with the white neighboring churches, chiefly Baptist and Methodist, with a few Episcopalian and others. The Methodists still form the second greatest denomination, with nearly a million members. The faith of these two leading denominations was more suited to the slave church from the prominence they gave to religious feeling and fervor. The Negro membership in other denominations has always been small and relatively unimportant, although the Episcopalians and Presbyterians are gaining among the more intelligent classes to-day, and the Catholic Church is making headway in certain sections. After Emancipation, and still earlier in the North, the Negro churches largely severed such affiliations as they had had with the white churches, either by choice or by compulsion. The Baptist churches became independent, but the Methodists were compelled early to unite for purposes of episcopal government. This gave rise to the great African Methodist Church, the greatest Negro organization in the world, to the Zion Church and the Colored Methodist, and to the black conferences and churches in this and other denominations.[12]

The second fact noted, namely, that the Negro church antedates the Negro home, leads to an explanation of much that is paradoxical in this communistic institution and in the morals of its members. But especially it leads us to regard this institution as peculiarly the expression of the inner ethical life of a people in a sense seldom true elsewhere. Let us turn, then, from the outer physical development of the church to the more important inner ethical life of the people who compose it. The Negro has already been pointed out many times as a religious animal, — a being of that deep emotional nature which turns instinctively toward the supernatural. Endowed with a rich tropical imagination and a keen, delicate appreciation of Nature, the transplanted African lived in a world animate with gods and devils, elves and witches; full of strange influences, — of Good to be implored, of Evil to be propitiated. Slavery, then, was to him the dark triumph of Evil over him. All the hateful powers of the Underworld were striving against him, and a spirit of revolt and revenge filled his heart. He called up all the resources of heathenism to aid, — exorcism and witchcraft, the mysterious Obi worship with its barbarous rites, spells, and blood-sacrifice even, now and then, of human victims.[13] Weird midnight orgies and mystic conjurations were invoked, the witch-woman and the voodoo-priest became the centre of Negro group life, and that vein of vague superstition which characterizes the unlettered Negro even to-day was deepened and strengthened.

In spite, however, of such success as that of the fierce Maroons, the Danish blacks, and others, the spirit of revolt gradually died away under the untiring energy and superior strength of the slave masters. By the middle of the eighteenth century the black slave had sunk, with hushed murmurs, to his place at the bottom of a new economic system, and was unconsciously ripe for a new philosophy of life. Nothing suited his condition then better than the doctrines of passive submission embodied in the newly learned Christianity. Slave masters early realized this, and cheerfully aided religious propaganda within certain bounds. The long system of repression and degradation of the Negro tended to emphasize the elements in his character which made him a valuable chattel: courtesy became humility, moral strength degenerated into submission, and the exquisite native appreciation of the beautiful became an infinite capacity for dumb suffering. The Negro, losing the joy of this world, eagerly seized upon the offered conceptions of the next; the avenging Spirit of the Lord enjoining patience in this world, under sorrow and tribulation until the Great Day when He should lead His dark children home,—this became his comforting dream. His preacher repeated the prophecy, and his bards sang,—

> "Children, we all shall be free
> When the Lord shall appear!"[14]

This deep religious fatalism, painted so beautifully in "Uncle Tom,"[15] came soon to breed, as all fatalistic faiths will, the sensualist side by side with the martyr. Under the lax moral life of the plantation, where marriage was a farce, laziness a virtue, and property a theft, a religion of resignation and submission degenerated easily, in less strenuous minds, into a philosophy of indulgence and crime. Many of the worst characteristics of the Negro masses of to-day had their seed in this period of the slave's ethical growth. Here it was that the Home was ruined under the very shadow of the Church, white and black; here habits of shiftlessness took root, and sullen hopelessness replaced hopeful strife.

With the beginning of the abolition movement and the gradual growth of a class of free Negroes came a change. We often neglect the influence of the freedman before the war, because of the paucity of his numbers and the small weight he had in the history of the nation. But we must not forget that his chief influence was internal,—was exerted on the black world; and that there he was the ethical and social leader. Huddled as he was in a few centres like Philadelphia, New York, and New Orleans, the masses of the freedmen sank into poverty and listlessness; but not all of them. The free Negro leader early arose and his chief characteristic was intense earnestness and deep feeling on the slavery question. Freedom became to him a real thing and not a dream. His religion became darker and more intense, and into his ethics crept a note of revenge, into his songs a day of reckoning close at hand. The "Coming of the Lord" swept this side of Death, and came to be a thing to be hoped for in this day. Through fugitive slaves and irrepressible discussion this desire for freedom seized the black millions still in bondage, and became their one ideal of life. The black bards caught new notes, and sometimes even dared to sing, —

> "O Freedom, O Freedom, O Freedom over me!
> Before I'll be a slave
> I'll be buried in my grave,
> And go home to my Lord
> And be free."[16]

For fifty years Negro religion thus transformed itself and identified itself with the dream of Abolition, until that which was a radical fad in the white North and an anarchistic plot in the white South had become a religion to the black world. Thus, when Emancipation finally came, it seemed to the freedman a literal Coming of the Lord. His fervid imagination was stirred as never before, by the tramp of armies, the blood and dust of battle, and the wail and whirl of social upheaval. He stood dumb and motionless before the whirlwind: what had he to do with it? Was it not the Lord's doing, and marvellous in his eyes? Joyed and bewildered with what came, he stood awaiting new wonders till the inevitable Age of Reaction swept over the nation and brought the crisis of to-day.

It is difficult to explain clearly the present critical stage of Negro religion. First, we must remember that living as the blacks do in close contact with a great modern nation, and sharing, although imperfectly, the soul-life of that nation, they must necessarily be affected more or less directly by all the religious and ethical forces that are to-day moving the United States. These questions and movements are, however, overshadowed and dwarfed by the (to them) all-important question of their civil, political, and economic status. They must perpetually discuss the "Negro Problem," — must live, move, and have their being in it, and interpret all else in its light or darkness. With this come, too, peculiar problems of their inner life, — of the status of women, the maintenance of Home, the training of children, the accumulation of wealth, and the prevention of crime. All this must mean a time of intense ethical ferment, of religious heart-searching and intellectual unrest. From the double life every American Negro must live, as a Negro and as an American as swept on by the current of the nineteenth while yet struggling in the eddies of the fifteenth century, — from this must arise a painful self-consciousness, an almost morbid sense of personality and a moral hesitancy which is fatal to self-confidence. The worlds within and without the Veil of Color are changing, and changing rapidly, but not at the same rate, not in the same way; and this must produce a peculiar wrenching of the soul, a peculiar sense of doubt and bewilderment. Such a double life, with double thoughts, double duties, and double social classes, must give rise to double words and double ideals, and tempt the mind to pretence or to revolt, to hypocrisy or to radicalism.

In some such doubtful words and phrases can one perhaps most clearly picture the peculiar ethical paradox that faces the Negro of to-day and is tingeing and changing his religious life. Feeling that his rights and his dearest ideals are being trampled upon, that the public conscience is ever more deaf to his righteous appeal, and that all the reactionary forces of prejudice, greed, and revenge are daily gaining new strength and fresh allies, the Negro faces no enviable dilemma. Conscious of his impotence, and pessimistic, he often becomes bitter and vindictive; and his religion, instead of a worship, is a complaint and a curse, a wail rather than a hope, a sneer rather than a faith. On the other hand, another type of mind, shrewder and keener and more tortuous too, sees in the very strength of the anti-Negro movement its patent weaknesses, and with Jesuitic casuistry[17] is deterred by no ethical considerations in the endeavor to turn this weakness to the black man's strength. Thus we have two great and hardly reconcilable streams of thought and ethical strivings; the danger of the one lies in anarchy, that of the other in hypocrisy. The one type of Negro stands almost ready to curse God and die, and the other is too often found a traitor to right and a coward before force; the one is wedded to ideals remote, whimsical, perhaps impossible of realization; the other forgets that life is more than meat and the body more than raiment. But, after all, is not this simply the writhing of the age translated into black, — the triumph of the Lie which to-day, with its false culture, faces the hideousness of the anarchist assassin?

To-day the two groups of Negroes, the one in the North, the other in the South, represent these divergent ethical tendencies, the first tending toward radicalism, the other toward hypocritical compromise. It is no idle regret with which the white South mourns the loss of the old-time Negro, — the frank, honest, simple old servant who stood for the earlier religious age of submission and humility. With all his laziness and lack of many elements of true manhood, he was at least open-hearted, faithful, and sincere. To-day he is gone, but who is to blame for his going? Is it not those very persons who mourn for him? Is it not the tendency, born of Reconstruction and Reaction, to found a society on lawlessness and deception, to tamper with the moral fibre of a naturally honest and straightforward people until the whites threaten to become ungovernable tyrants and the blacks criminals and hypocrites? Deception is the natural defence of the weak against the strong, and the South used it for many years against its conquerors; to-day it must be prepared to see its black proletariat turn that same two-edged weapon against itself. And how natural this is! The death of Denmark Vesey and Nat Turner[18] proved long since to the Negro the present hopelessness of physical defence. Political defence is becoming less and less available, and economic defence is still only partially effective. But there is a patent defence at hand, the defence of deception and flattery, of cajoling and lying. It is the same defence which the Jews[19] of the Middle Age used and which left its stamp on their character for centuries. To-day the young Negro of the South who would succeed cannot be frank and outspoken, honest and self-assertive, but rather he is daily tempted to be silent and wary, politic and sly; he must flatter and be pleasant, endure petty insults with a smile, shut his eyes to wrong; in too many cases he sees positive personal advantage in deception and lying. His real thoughts, his real aspirations, must be guarded in whispers; he must not criticize, he must not complain. Patience, humility, and adroitness must, in these growing black youth, replace impulse, manliness, and courage. With this sacrifice there is an economic opening, and perhaps peace and some prosperity. Without this there is riot, migration, or crime. Nor is this situation peculiar to the Southern United States, — is it not rather the only method by which undeveloped races have gained the right to share modern culture? The price of culture is a Lie.

✸On the other hand, in the North the tendency is to emphasize the radicalism of the Negro. Driven from his birthright in the South by a situation at which every fibre of his more outspoken and assertive nature revolts, he finds himself in a land where he can scarcely earn a decent living amid the harsh competition and the color discrimination. At the same time, through schools and periodicals, discussions and lectures, he is intellectually quickened and awakened. The soul, long pent up and dwarfed, suddenly expands in new-found freedom. What wonder that every tendency is to excess, — radical complaint, radical remedies, bitter denunciation or angry silence. Some sink, some rise. The criminal and the sensualist leave the church for the gambling-hell and the brothel, and fill the slums of Chicago and Baltimore; the better classes segregate themselves from the group-life of both white and black, and form an aristocracy, cultured but pessimistic, whose bitter criticism stings while it points out no way of escape. They despise the submission and subserviency of the Southern Negroes, but offer no other means by which a poor and oppressed minority can exist side by side with its masters. Feeling deeply and keenly the tendencies and opportunities of the age in which they live, their souls are bitter at the fate which drops the Veil between; and the very fact that this bitterness is natural and justifiable only serves to intensify it and make it more maddening.

Between the two extreme types of ethical attitude which I have thus sought to make clear wavers the mass of the millions of Negroes, North and South; and their religious life and activity partake of this social conflict within their ranks. Their churches are differentiating,—now into groups of cold, fashionable devotees, in no way distinguishable from similar white groups save in color of skin; now into large social and business institutions catering to the desire for information and amusement of their members, warily avoiding unpleasant questions both within and without the black world, and preaching in effect if not in word: *Dum vivimus, vivamus.*[20]

But back of this still broods silently the deep religious feeling of the real Negro heart, the stirring, unguided might of powerful human souls who have lost the guiding star of the past and are seeking in the great night a new religious ideal. Some day the Awakening will come, when the pent-up vigor of ten million souls shall sweep irresistibly toward the Goal, out of the Valley of the Shadow of Death,[21] where all that makes life worth living—Liberty, Justice, and Right—is marked "For White People Only."

XI

Of the Passing of the First-Born

O sister, sister, thy first-begotten,
The hands that cling and the feet that follow,
The voice of the child's blood crying yet,
Who hath remembered me? who hath forgotten?
Thou hast forgotten, O summer swallow,
But the world shall end when I forget.

S<small>WINBURNE</small>.

"Unto you a child is born,"[2] sang the bit of yellow paper that fluttered into my room one brown October morning. Then the fear of fatherhood mingled wildly with the joy of creation; I wondered how it looked and how it felt,—what were its eyes, and how its hair curled and crumpled itself. And I thought in awe of her,—she who had slept with Death to tear a man-child from underneath her heart, while I was unconsciously wandering. I fled to my wife and child, repeating the while to myself half wonderingly, "Wife and child? Wife and child?"—fled fast and faster than boat and steamcar, and yet must ever impatiently await them; away from the hard-voiced city, away from the flickering sea into my own Berkshire Hills that sit all sadly guarding the gates of Massachusetts.

Up the stairs I ran to the wan mother and whimpering babe, to the sanctuary on whose altar a life at my bidding had offered itself to win a life, and won. What is this tiny formless thing, this new-born wail from an unknown world,—all head and voice? I handle it curiously, and watch perplexed its winking, breathing, and sneezing. I did not love it then; it seemed a ludicrous thing to love; but her I loved, my girl-mother, she whom now I saw unfolding like the glory of the morning—the transfigured woman.

Through her I came to love the wee thing, as it grew and waxed strong; as its little soul unfolded itself in twitter and cry and half-formed word, and as its eyes caught the gleam and flash of life. How beautiful he was, with his olive-tinted flesh and dark gold ringlets, his eyes of mingled blue and brown, his perfect little limbs, and the soft voluptuous roll which the blood of Africa had moulded into his features! I held him in my arms, after we had sped far away to our Southern home,—held him, and glanced at the hot red soil of Georgia and the breathless city of a hundred hills, and felt a vague unrest. Why was his hair tinted with gold? An evil omen was golden hair in my life. Why had not the brown of his eyes crushed out and killed the blue?—for brown were his father's eyes, and his father's father's. And thus in the Land of the Color-line I saw, as it fell across my baby, the shadow of the Veil.

Within the Veil was he born, said I; and there within shall he live,—a Negro and a Negro's son. Holding in that little head—ah, bitterly!—the unbowed pride of a hunted race, clinging with that tiny dimpled hand—ah, wearily!—to a hope not hopeless but unhopeful, and seeing with those bright wondering eyes that peer into my soul a land whose freedom is to us a mockery and whose liberty a lie. I saw the shadow of the Veil as it passed over my baby, I saw the cold city towering above the blood-red land. I held my face beside his little cheek, showed him the star-children and the twinkling lights as they began to flash, and stilled with an even-song the unvoiced terror of my life.

So sturdy and masterful he grew, so filled with bubbling life so tremulous with the unspoken wisdom of a life but eighteen months distant from the All-life,—we were not far from worshipping this revelation of the divine, my wife and I. Her own life builded and moulded itself upon the child; he tinged her every dream and idealized her every effort. No hands but hers must touch and garnish those little limbs; no dress or frill must touch them that had not wearied her fingers; no voice but hers could coax him off to Dreamland, and she and he together spoke some soft and unknown tongue and in it held communion. I too mused above his little white bed; saw the strength of my own arm stretched onward through the ages through the newer strength of his; saw the dream of my black fathers stagger a step onward in the wild phantasm of the world; heard in his baby voice the voice of the Prophet that was to rise within the Veil.

And so we dreamed and loved and planned by fall and winter, and the full flush of the long Southern spring, till the hot winds rolled from the fetid Gulf, till the roses shivered and the still stern sun quivered its awful light over the hills of Atlanta. And then one night the little feet pattered wearily to the wee white bed, and the tiny hands trembled; and a warm flushed face tossed on the pillow, and we knew baby was sick. Ten days he lay there,—a swift week and three endless days, wasting, wasting away. Cheerily the mother nursed him the first days, and laughed into the little eyes that smiled again. Tenderly then she hovered round him, till the smile fled away and Fear crouched beside the little bed.

Then the day ended not, and night was a dreamless terror, and joy and sleep slipped away. I hear now that Voice at midnight calling me from dull and dreamless trance,—crying, "The Shadow of Death! The Shadow of Death!"[3] Out into the starlight I crept, to rouse the gray physician,—the Shadow of Death, the Shadow of Death. The hours trembled on; the night listened; the ghastly dawn glided like a tired thing across the lamplight. Then we two alone looked upon the child as he turned toward us with great eyes, and stretched his string-like hands,—the Shadow of Death! And we spoke no word, and turned away.

He died at eventide, when the sun lay like a brooding sorrow above the western hills, veiling its face; when the winds spoke not, and the trees, the great green trees he loved, stood motionless. I saw his breath beat quicker and quicker, pause, and then his little soul leapt like a star that travels in the night and left a world of darkness in its train. The day changed not; the same tall trees peeped in at the windows, the same green grass glinted in the setting sun. Only in the chamber of death writhed the world's most piteous thing—a childless mother.

I shirk not. I long for work. I pant for a life full of striving. I am no coward, to shrink before the rugged rush of the storm, nor even quail before the awful shadow of the Veil. But hearken, O Death! Is not this my life hard enough,—is not that dull land that stretches its sneering web about me cold enough,—is not all the world beyond these four little walls pitiless enough, but that thou must needs enter here,—thou, O Death? About my head the thundering storm beat like a heartless voice, and the crazy forest pulsed with the curses of the weak; but what cared I, within my home beside my wife and baby boy? Wast thou so jealous of one little coign of happiness that thou must needs enter there,— thou, O Death?

A perfect life was his, all joy and love, with tears to make it brighter,— sweet as a summer's day beside the Housatonic. The world loved him; the women kissed his curls, the men looked gravely into his wonderful eyes, and the children hovered and fluttered about him. I can see him now, changing like the sky from sparkling laughter to darkening frowns, and then to wondering thoughtfulness as he watched the world. He knew no color-line, poor dear,—and the Veil, though it shadowed him, had not yet darkened half his sun. He loved the white matron, he loved his black nurse; and in his little world walked souls alone, uncolored and unclothed. I—yea, all men—are larger and purer by the infinite breadth of that one little life. She who in simple clearness of vision sees beyond the stars said when he had flown, "He will be happy There; he ever loved beautiful things." And I, far more ignorant, and blind by the web of mine own weaving, sit alone winding words and muttering, "If still he be, and he be There, and there be a There, let him be happy, O Fate!"[4]

Blithe was the morning of his burial, with bird and song and sweet-smelling flowers. The trees whispered to the grass, but the children sat with hushed faces. And yet it seemed a ghostly unreal day,—the wraith of Life. We seemed to rumble down an unknown street behind a little white bundle of posies, with the shadow of a song in our ears. The busy city dinned about us; they did not say much, those pale-faced hurrying men and women; they did not say much,—they only glanced and said, "Niggers!"

We could not lay him in the ground there in Georgia, for the earth there is strangely red; so we bore him away to the northward, with his flowers and his little folded hands. In vain, in vain!—for where, O God! beneath thy broad blue sky shall my dark baby rest in peace,—where Reverence dwells, and Goodness, and a Freedom that is free?

All that day and all that night there sat an awful gladness in my heart,— nay, blame me not if I see the world thus darkly through the Veil,[5]—and my soul whispers ever to me, saying, "Not dead, not dead, but escaped; not bond, but free." No bitter meanness now shall sicken his baby heart till it die a living death, no taunt shall madden his happy boyhood. Fool that I was to think or wish that this little soul should grow choked and deformed within the Veil! I might have known that yonder deep unworldly look that ever and anon floated past his eyes was peering far beyond this narrow Now. In the poise of his little curl-crowned head did there not sit all that wild pride of being which his father had hardly crushed in his own heart? For what, forsooth, shall a Negro want with pride amid the stud-ied humiliations of fifty million fellows? Well sped, my boy, before the world had dubbed your ambition insolence, had held your ideals unat-tainable, and taught you to cringe and bow. Better far this nameless void that stops my life than a sea of sorrow for you.

Idle words; he might have borne his burden more bravely than we,— aye, and found it lighter too, some day; for surely, surely this is not the end. Surely there shall yet dawn some mighty morning to lift the Veil and set the prisoned free. Not for me,—I shall die in my bonds,—but for fresh young souls who have not known the night and waken to the morn-ing; a morning when men ask of the workman, not "Is he white?" but "Can he work?" When men ask artists, not "Are they black?" but "Do they know?" Some morning this may be, long, long years to come. But now there wails, on that dark shore within the Veil, the same deep voice, *Thou shalt forego!*[6] And all have I foregone at that command, and with small complaint,—all save that fair young form that lies so coldly wed with death in the nest I had builded.

If one must have gone, why not I? Why may I not rest me from this restlessness and sleep from this wide waking? Was not the world's alem-bic, Time, in his young hands, and is not my time waning? Are there so many workers in the vineyard that the fair promise of this little body could lightly be tossed away? The wretched of my race that line the alleys of the nation sit fatherless and unmothered; but Love sat beside his cradle, and in his ear Wisdom waited to speak. Perhaps now he knows the All-love, and needs not to be wise. Sleep, then, child,—sleep till I sleep and waken to a baby voice and the ceaseless patter of little feet—above the Veil.

XII

Of Alexander Crummell

Then from the Dawn it seemed there came, but faint
As from beyond the limit of the world,
Like the last echo born of a great cry,
Sounds, as if some fair city were one voice
Around a king returning from his wars.

TENNYSON.

This is the history of a human heart,—the tale of a black boy who many long years ago began to struggle with life that he might know the world and know himself. Three temptations he met on those dark dunes that lay gray and dismal before the wonder-eyes of the child: the temptation of Hate, that stood out against the red dawn; the temptation of Despair, that darkened noonday; and the temptation of Doubt, that ever steals along with twilight. Above all, you must hear of the vales he crossed,—the Valley of Humiliation and the Valley of the Shadow of Death.[2]

I saw Alexander Crummell first at a Wilberforce commencement season, amid its bustle and crush. Tall, frail, and black he stood, with simple dignity and an unmistakable air of good breeding. I talked with him apart, where the storming of the lusty young orators could not harm us. I spoke to him politely, then curiously, then eagerly, as I began to feel the fineness of his character,—his calm courtesy, the sweetness of his strength, and his fair blending of the hope and truth of life. Instinctively I bowed before this man, as one bows before the prophets of the world. Some seer he seemed, that came not from the crimson Past or the gray

To-come, but from the pulsing Now,—that mocking world which seemed to me at once so light and dark, so splendid and sordid. Four-score years had he wandered in this same world of mine, within the Veil.

He was born with the Missouri Compromise and lay a-dying amid the echoes of Manila and El Caney:[3] stirring times for living, times dark to look back upon, darker to look forward to. The black-faced lad that paused over his mud and marbles seventy years ago saw puzzling vistas as he looked down the world. The slave-ship still groaned across the Atlantic, faint cries burdened the Southern breeze, and the great black father whispered mad tales of cruelty into those young ears. From the low door-way the mother silently watched her boy at play, and at nightfall sought him eagerly lest the shadows bear him away to the land of slaves.[4]

So his young mind worked and winced and shaped curiously a vision of Life; and in the midst of that vision ever stood one dark figure alone,— ever with the hard, thick countenance of that bitter father, and a form that fell in vast and shapeless folds. Thus the temptation of Hate grew and shadowed the growing child,—gliding stealthily into his laughter, fading into his play, and seizing his dreams by day and night with rough, rude turbulence. So the black boy asked of sky and sun and flower the never-answered Why? and loved, as he grew, neither the world nor the world's rough ways.

Strange temptation for a child, you may think; and yet in this wide land to-day a thousand thousand dark children brood before this same temptation, and feel its cold and shuddering arms. For them, perhaps, some one will some day lift the Veil,—will come tenderly and cheerily into those sad little lives and brush the brooding hate away, just as Beriah Green[5] strode in upon the life of Alexander Crummell. And before the bluff, kind-hearted man the shadow seemed less dark. Beriah Green had a school in Oneida County, New York, with a score of mischievous boys. "I'm going to bring a black boy here to educate," said Beriah Green, as only a crank and an abolitionist would have dared to say. "Oho!" laughed the boys. "Ye-es," said his wife; and Alexander came. Once before, the black boy had sought a school, had travelled, cold and hungry, four hundred miles up into free New Hampshire, to Canaan. But the godly farmers hitched ninety yoke of oxen to the abolition schoolhouse and dragged it into the middle of the swamp. The black boy trudged away.[6]

The nineteenth was the first century of human sympathy,—the age when half wonderingly we began to descry in others that transfigured spark of divinity which we call Myself; when clodhoppers and peasants, and tramps and thieves, and millionaires and—sometimes—Negroes, became throbbing souls whose warm pulsing life touched us so nearly that we half gasped with surprise, crying, "Thou too! Hast Thou seen Sorrow and the dull waters of Hopelessness? Hast Thou known Life?" And then all helplessly we peered into those Other-worlds, and wailed, "O World of Worlds, how shall man make you one?"

So in that little Oneida school there came to those schoolboys a revelation of thought and longing beneath one black skin, of which they had not dreamed before. And to the lonely boy came a new dawn of sympathy and inspiration. The shadowy, formless thing—the temptation of Hate, that hovered between him and the world—grew fainter and less sinister. It did not wholly fade away, but diffused itself and lingered thick at the edges. Through it the child now first saw the blue and gold of life,— the sun-swept road that ran 'twixt heaven and earth until in one far-off wan wavering line they met and kissed. A vision of life came to the growing boy,—mystic, wonderful. He raised his head, stretched himself, breathed deep of the fresh new air. Yonder, behind the forests, he heard strange sounds; then glinting through the trees he saw, far, far away, the bronzed hosts of a nation calling,—calling faintly, calling loudly. He heard the hateful clank of their chains, he felt them cringe and grovel, and there rose within him a protest and a prophecy. And he girded himself to walk down the world.

A voice and vision called him to be a priest,—a seer to lead the uncalled out of the house of bondage. He saw the headless host turn toward him like the whirling of mad waters,—he stretched forth his hands eagerly, and then, even as he stretched them, suddenly there swept across the vision the temptation of Despair.[7]

They were not wicked men,—the problem of life is not the problem of the wicked,—they were calm, good men, Bishops of the Apostolic Church of God, and strove toward righteousness. They said slowly, "It is all very natural—it is even commendable; but the General Theological Seminary of the Episcopal Church cannot admit a Negro." And when that thin, half-grotesque figure still haunted their doors, they put their hands kindly, half sorrowfully, on his shoulders, and said, "Now,—of course, we—we know how *you* feel about it; but you see it is impossible,—that is—well—it is premature. Sometime, we trust—sincerely trust—all such distinctions will fade away; but now the world is as it is."[8]

This was the temptation of Despair; and the young man fought it doggedly. Like some grave shadow he flitted by those halls, pleading, arguing, half angrily demanding admittance, until there came the final *No;* until men hustled the disturber away, marked him as foolish, unreasonable, and injudicious, a vain rebel against God's law. And then from that

Vision Splendid all the glory faded slowly away, and left an earth gray and stern rolling on beneath a dark despair. Even the kind hands that stretched themselves toward him from out the depths of that dull morning seemed but parts of the purple shadows. He saw them coldly, and asked, "Why should I strive by special grace when the way of the world is closed to me?" All gently yet, the hands urged him on, — the hands of young John Jay,[9] that daring father's daring son; the hands of the good folk of Boston, that free city. And yet, with a way to the priesthood of the Church open at last before him, the cloud lingered there; and even when in old St. Paul's the venerable Bishop raised his white arms above the Negro deacon — even then the burden had not lifted from that heart, for there had passed a glory from the earth.[10]

And yet the fire through which Alexander Crummell went did not burn in vain. Slowly and more soberly he took up again his plan of life. More critically he studied the situation. Deep down below the slavery and servitude of the Negro people he saw their fatal weaknesses, which long years of mistreatment had emphasized. The dearth of strong moral character, of unbending righteousness, he felt, was their great shortcoming, and here he would begin. He would gather the best of his people into some little Episcopal chapel and there lead, teach, and inspire them, till the leaven spread, till the children grew, till the world hearkened, till — till — and then across his dream gleamed some faint after-glow of that first fair vision of youth — only an after-glow, for there had passed a glory from the earth.

One day — it was in 1842, and the springtide was struggling merrily with the May winds of New England — he stood at last in his own chapel in Providence, a priest of the Church.[11] The days sped by, and the dark young clergyman labored; he wrote his sermons carefully; he intoned his prayers with a soft, earnest voice; he haunted the streets and accosted the wayfarers; he visited the sick, and knelt beside the dying. He worked and toiled, week by week, day by day, month by month. And yet month by month the congregation dwindled, week by week the hollow walls echoed more sharply, day by day the calls came fewer and fewer, and day by day the third temptation sat clearer and still more clearly within the Veil; a temptation, as it were, bland and smiling, with just a shade of mockery in its smooth tones. First it came casually, in the cadence of a voice: "Oh, colored folks? Yes." Or perhaps more definitely: "What do you *expect?*" In voice and gesture lay the doubt — the temptation of Doubt. How he hated it, and stormed at it furiously! "Of course they are capable," he cried; "of course they can learn and strive and achieve — " and "Of course," added the temptation softly, "they do nothing of the sort." Of all the three temptations, this one struck the deepest. Hate? He had outgrown so childish a thing. Despair? He had steeled his right arm against it, and fought it with the vigor of determination. But to doubt the worth of his life-work,—to doubt the destiny and capability of the race his soul loved because it was his; to find listless squalor instead of eager endeavor; to hear his own lips whispering, "They do not care; they cannot know; they are dumb driven cattle,—why cast your pearls before swine?"—this, this seemed more than man could bear; and he closed the door, and sank upon the steps of the chancel, and cast his robe upon the floor and writhed.

The evening sunbeams had set the dust to dancing in the gloomy chapel when he arose. He folded his vestments, put away the hymn-books, and closed the great Bible. He stepped out into the twilight, looked back upon the narrow little pulpit with a weary smile, and locked the door. Then he walked briskly to the Bishop, and told the Bishop what the Bishop already knew. "I have failed," he said simply. And gaining courage by the confession, he added: "What I need is a larger constituency. There are comparatively few Negroes here, and perhaps they are not of the best. I must go where the field is wider, and try again." So the Bishop sent him to Philadelphia, with a letter to Bishop Onderdonk.[12]

Bishop Onderdonk lived at the head of six white steps,—corpulent, red-faced, and the author of several thrilling tracts on Apostolic Succession. It was after dinner, and the Bishop had settled himself for a pleasant season of contemplation, when the bell must needs ring, and there must burst in upon the Bishop a letter and a thin, ungainly Negro. Bishop Onderdonk read the letter hastily and frowned. Fortunately, his mind was already clear on this point; and he cleared his brow and looked at Crummell. Then he said, slowly and impressively: "I will receive you into this diocese on one condition: no Negro priest can sit in my church convention, and no Negro church must ask for representation there."

I sometimes fancy I can see that tableau: the frail black figure, nervously twitching his hat before the massive abdomen of Bishop Onderdonk; his threadbare coat thrown against the dark woodwork of the book-cases, where Fox's "Lives of the Martyrs" nestled happily beside "The Whole Duty of Man."[13] I seem to see the wide eyes of the Negro wander past the Bishop's broadcloth to where the swinging glass doors of the cabinet glow in the sunlight. A little blue fly is trying to cross the yawning keyhole. He marches briskly up to it, peers into the chasm in a surprised sort of way, and rubs his feelers reflectively; then he essays its depths, and, finding it bottomless, draws back again. The dark-faced priest finds himself wondering if the fly too has faced its Valley of Humiliation, and if it will plunge into it, — when lo! it spreads its tiny wings and buzzes merrily across, leaving the watcher wingless and alone.

Then the full weight of his burden fell upon him. The rich walls wheeled away, and before him lay the cold rough moor winding on through life, cut in twain by one thick granite ridge, — here, the Valley of Humiliation; yonder, the Valley of the Shadow of Death. And I know not which be darker, — no, not I. But this I know: in yonder Vale of the Humble stand to-day a million swarthy men, who willingly would

> ". . . bear the whips and scorns of time,
> The oppressor's wrong, the proud man's contumely,
> The pangs of despised love, the law's delay,
> The insolence of office, and the spurns
> That patient merit of the unworthy takes,"[14]

all this and more would they bear did they but know that this were sacrifice and not a meaner thing. So surged the thought within that lone black breast. The Bishop cleared his throat suggestively; then, recollecting that there was really nothing to say, considerately said nothing, only sat tapping his foot impatiently. But Alexander Crummell said, slowly and heavily: "I will never enter your diocese on such terms." And saying this, he turned and passed into the Valley of the Shadow of Death. You might have noted only the physical dying, the shattered frame and hacking cough; but in that soul lay deeper death than that. He found a chapel in New York, — the church of his father; he labored for it in poverty and starvation, scorned by his fellow priests. Half in despair, he wandered across the sea, a beggar with outstretched hands.[15] Englishmen clasped them, — Wilberforce and Stanley, Thirwell and Ingles, and even Froude and Macaulay; Sir Benjamin Brodie bade him rest awhile at Queen's College in Cambridge, and there he lingered, struggling for health of body and mind, until he took his degree in '53.[16] Restless still and unsatisfied, he turned toward Africa, and for long years, amid the spawn of the slave-smugglers, sought a new heaven and a new earth.[17]

So the man groped for light; all this was not Life, — it was the world-wandering of a soul in search of itself, the striving of one who vainly sought his place in the world, ever haunted by the shadow of a death that is more than death, — the passing of a soul that has missed its duty. Twenty years he wandered, — twenty years and more; and yet the hard rasping question kept gnawing within him, "What, in God's name, am I on earth for?" In the narrow New York parish his soul seemed cramped and smothered. In the fine old air of the English University he heard the millions wailing over the sea. In the wild fever-cursed swamps of West Africa he stood helpless and alone.

You will not wonder at his weird pilgrimage,—you who in the swift whirl of living, amid its cold paradox and marvellous vision, have fronted life and asked its riddle face to face. And if you find that riddle hard to read, remember that yonder black boy finds it just a little harder; if it is difficult for you to find and face your duty, it is a shade more difficult for him; if your heart sickens in the blood and dust of battle, remember that to him the dust is thicker and the battle fiercer. No wonder the wanderers fall! No wonder we point to thief and murderer, and haunting prostitute, and the never-ending throng of unhearsed dead! The Valley of the Shadow of Death gives few of its pilgrims back to the world.

But Alexander Crummell it gave back. Out of the temptation of Hate, and burned by the fire of Despair, triumphant over Doubt, and steeled by Sacrifice against Humiliation, he turned at last home across the waters, humble and strong, gentle and determined. He bent to all the gibes and prejudices, to all hatred and discrimination, with that rare courtesy which is the armor of pure souls. He fought among his own, the low, the grasping, and the wicked, with that unbending righteousness which is the sword of the just. He never faltered, he seldom complained; he simply worked, inspiring the young, rebuking the old, helping the weak, guiding the strong.[18]

So he grew, and brought within his wide influence all that was best of those who walk within the Veil. They who live without knew not nor dreamed of that full power within, that mighty inspiration which the dull gauze of caste decreed that most men should not know. And now that he is gone, I sweep the Veil away and cry, Lo! the soul to whose dear memory I bring this little tribute. I can see his face still, dark and heavy-lined beneath his snowy hair; lighting and shading, now with inspiration for the future, now in innocent pain at some human wickedness, now with sorrow at some hard memory from the past. The more I met Alexander Crummell, the more I felt how much that world was losing which knew so little of him. In another age he might have sat among the elders of the land in purple-bordered toga; in another country mothers might have sung him to the cradles.

He did his work,—he did it nobly and well; and yet I sorrow that here he worked alone, with so little human sympathy. His name to-day, in this broad land, means little, and comes to fifty million ears laden with no incense of memory or emulation. And herein lies the tragedy of the age: not that men are poor, — all men know something of poverty; not that men are wicked, — who is good? not that men are ignorant, — what is Truth? Nay, but that men know so little of men.[19]

He sat one morning gazing toward the sea. He smiled and said, "The gate is rusty on the hinges." That night at star-rise a wind came moaning out of the west to blow the gate ajar, and then the soul I loved fled like a flame across the Seas, and in its seat sat Death.

I wonder where he is to-day? I wonder if in that dim world beyond, as he came gliding in, there rose on some wan throne a King, — a dark and pierced Jew, who knows the writhings of the earthly damned, saying, as he laid those heart-wrung talents down, "Well done!" while round about the morning stars sat singing.[20]

XIII

Of the Coming of John

What bring they 'neath the midnight,
   Beside the River-sea?
They bring the human heart wherein
   No nightly calm can be;
That droppeth never with the wind,
   Nor drieth with the dew;
O calm it, God; thy calm is broad
   To cover spirits too.
     The river floweth on.

MRS. BROWNING.

Carlisle Street runs westward from the centre of Johnstown, across a great black bridge, down a hill and up again, by little shops and meat-markets, past single-storied homes, until suddenly it stops against a wide green lawn. It is a broad, restful place, with two large buildings outlined against the west. When at evening the winds come swelling from the east, and the great pall of the city's smoke hangs wearily above the valley, then the red west glows like a dreamland down Carlisle Street, and, at the tolling of the supper-bell, throws the passing forms of students in dark silhouette against the sky. Tall and black, they move slowly by, and seem in the sinister light to flit before the city like dim warning ghosts. Perhaps they are; for this is Wells Institute, and these black students have few dealings with the white city below.

And if you will notice, night after night, there is one dark form that ever hurries last and late toward the twinkling lights of Swain Hall, — for Jones is never on time. A long, straggling fellow he is, brown and hard-haired, who seems to be growing straight out of his clothes, and walks with a half-apologetic roll. He used perpetually to set the quiet dining-room into waves of merriment, as he stole to his place after the bell had tapped for prayers; he seemed so perfectly awkward. And yet one glance at his face made one forgive him much, — that broad, good-natured smile in which lay no bit of art or artifice, but seemed just bubbling good-nature and genuine satisfaction with the world.

He came to us from Altamaha, away down there beneath the gnarled oaks of Southeastern Georgia, where the sea croons to the sands and the sands listen till they sink half drowned beneath the waters, rising only here and there in long, low islands. The white folk of Altamaha voted John a good boy, — fine plough-hand, good in the rice-fields, handy everywhere, and always good-natured and respectful. But they shook their heads when his mother wanted to send him off to school. "It'll spoil him, — ruin him," they said; and they talked as though they knew. But full half the black folk followed him proudly to the station, and carried his queer little trunk and many bundles. And there they shook and shook hands, and the girls kissed him shyly and the boys clapped him on the back. So the train came, and he pinched his little sister lovingly, and put his great arms about his mother's neck, and then was away with a puff and a roar into the great yellow world that flamed and flared about the doubtful pilgrim.[2] Up the coast they hurried, past the squares and palmettos of Savannah, through the cotton-fields and through the weary night, to Millville, and came with the morning to the noise and bustle of Johnstown.

And they that stood behind, that morning in Altamaha, and watched the train as it noisily bore playmate and brother and son away to the world, had thereafter one ever-recurring word, — "When John comes." Then what parties were to be, and what speakings in the churches; what new furniture in the front room, — perhaps even a new front room; and there would be a new schoolhouse, with John as teacher; and then perhaps a big wedding; all this and more — when John comes. But the white people shook their heads.

At first he was coming at Christmas-time, — but the vacation proved too short; and then, the next summer, — but times were hard and schooling costly, and so, instead, he worked in Johnstown. And so it drifted to the next summer, and the next, — till playmates scattered, and mother grew gray, and sister went up to the Judge's kitchen to work. And still the legend lingered, — "When John comes."

Up at the Judge's they rather liked this refrain; for they too had a John—a fair-haired, smooth-faced boy, who had played many a long summer's day to its close with his darker namesake. "Yes, sir! John is at Princeton, sir," said the broad-shouldered gray-haired Judge every morning as he marched down to the post-office. "Showing the Yankees what a Southern gentleman can do," he added; and strode home again with his letters and papers. Up at the great pillared house they lingered long over the Princeton letter,—the Judge and his frail wife, his sister and growing daughters. "It'll make a man of him," said the Judge, "college is the place." And then he asked the shy little waitress, "Well, Jennie, how's your John?" and added reflectively, "Too bad, too bad your mother sent him off,—it will spoil him." And the waitress wondered.

Thus in the far-away Southern village the world lay waiting, half consciously, the coming of two young men, and dreamed in an inarticulate way of new things that would be done and new thoughts that all would think. And yet it was singular that few thought of two Johns,—for the black folk thought of one John, and he was black; and the white folk thought of another John, and he was white. And neither world thought the other world's thought, save with a vague unrest.

Up in Johnstown, at the Institute, we were long puzzled at the case of John Jones. For a long time the clay seemed unfit for any sort of moulding. He was loud and boisterous, always laughing and singing, and never able to work consecutively at anything. He did not know how to study; he had no idea of thoroughness; and with his tardiness, carelessness, and appalling good-humor, we were sore perplexed. One night we sat in faculty-meeting, worried and serious; for Jones was in trouble again. This last escapade was too much, and so we solemnly voted "that Jones, on account of repeated disorder and inattention to work, be suspended for the rest of the term."

It seemed to us that the first time life ever struck Jones as a really serious thing was when the Dean told him he must leave school. He stared at the gray-haired man blankly, with great eyes. "Why,—why," he faltered, "but—I have n't graduated!" Then the Dean slowly and clearly explained, reminding him of the tardiness and the carelessness, of the poor lessons and neglected work, of the noise and disorder, until the fellow hung his head in confusion. Then he said quickly, "But you won't tell mammy and sister,—you won't write mammy, now will you? For if you won't I'll go out into the city and work, and come back next term and show you something." So the Dean promised faithfully, and John shouldered his little trunk, giving neither word nor look to the giggling boys, and walked down Carlisle Street to the great city, with sober eyes and a set and serious face.

Perhaps we imagined it, but someway it seemed to us that the serious look that crept over his boyish face that afternoon never left it again. When he came back to us he went to work with all his rugged strength. It was a hard struggle, for things did not come easily to him, — few crowding memories of early life and teaching came to help him on his new way; but all the world toward which he strove was of his own building, and he builded slow and hard. As the light dawned lingeringly on his new creations, he sat rapt and silent before the vision, or wandered alone over the green campus peering through and beyond the world of men into a world of thought. And the thoughts at times puzzled him sorely; he could not see just why the circle was not square, and carried it out fifty-six decimal places one midnight, — would have gone further, indeed, had not the matron rapped for lights out. He caught terrible colds lying on his back in the meadows of nights, trying to think out the solar system; he had grave doubts as to the ethics of the Fall of Rome, and strongly suspected the Germans of being thieves and rascals, despite his text-books; he pondered long over every new Greek word, and wondered why this meant that and why it couldn't mean something else, and how it must have felt to think all things in Greek. So he thought and puzzled along for himself, — pausing perplexed where others skipped merrily, and walking steadily through the difficulties where the rest stopped and surrendered.

Thus he grew in body and soul, and with him his clothes seemed to grow and arrange themselves; coat sleeves got longer, cuffs appeared, and collars got less soiled. Now and then his boots shone, and a new dignity crept into his walk. And we who saw daily a new thoughtfulness growing in his eyes began to expect something of this plodding boy. Thus he passed out of the preparatory school into college, and we who watched him felt four more years of change, which almost transformed the tall, grave man who bowed to us commencement morning. He had left his queer thought-world and come back to a world of motion and of men. He looked now for the first time sharply about him, and wondered he had seen so little before. He grew slowly to feel almost for the first time the Veil that lay between him and the white world; he first noticed now the oppression that had not seemed oppression before, differences that erstwhile seemed natural, restraints and slights that in his boyhood days had gone unnoticed or been greeted with a laugh. He felt angry now when men did not call him "Mister," he clenched his hands at the "Jim Crow" cars,[3] and chafed at the color-line that hemmed in him and his. A tinge of sarcasm crept into his speech, and a vague bitterness into his life; and he sat long hours wondering and planning a way around these crooked things. Daily he found himself shrinking from the choked and narrow life of his native town. And yet he always planned to go back to Altamaha, — always planned to work there. Still, more and more as the day approached he hesitated with a nameless dread; and even the day after graduation he seized with eagerness the offer of the Dean to send him North with the quartette during the summer vacation, to sing for the Institute. A breath of air before the plunge, he said to himself in half apology.

It was a bright September afternoon, and the streets of New York were brilliant with moving men. They reminded John of the sea, as he sat in the square and watched them, so changelessly changing, so bright and dark, so grave and gay. He scanned their rich and faultless clothes, the way they carried their hands, the shape of their hats; he peered into the hurrying carriages. Then, leaning back with a sigh, he said, "This is the World." The notion suddenly seized him to see where the world was going; since many of the richer and brighter seemed hurrying all one way. So when a tall, light-haired young man and a little talkative lady came by, he rose half hesitatingly and followed them. Up the street they went, past stores and gay shops, across a broad square, until with a hundred others they entered the high portal of a great building.

He was pushed toward the ticket-office with the others, and felt in his pocket for the new five-dollar bill he had hoarded. There seemed really no time for hesitation, so he drew it bravely out, passed it to the busy clerk, and received simply a ticket but no change. When at last he realized that he had paid five dollars to enter he knew not what, he stood stock-still amazed. "Be careful," said a low voice behind him; "you must not lynch the colored gentleman simply because he's in your way," and a girl looked up roguishly into the eyes of her fair-haired escort. A shade of annoyance passed over the escort's face. "You *will* not understand us at the South," he said half impatiently, as if continuing an argument. "With all your professions, one never sees in the North so cordial and intimate relations between white and black as are everyday occurrences with us. Why, I remember my closest play-fellow in boyhood was a little Negro named after me, and surely no two, — *well!*" The man stopped short and flushed to the roots of his hair, for there directly beside his reserved orchestra chairs sat the Negro he had stumbled over in the hallway. He hesitated and grew pale with anger, called the usher and gave him his card, with a few peremptory words, and slowly sat down. The lady deftly changed the subject.

All this John did not see, for he sat in a half-maze minding the scene about him; the delicate beauty of the hall, the faint perfume, the moving myriad of men, the rich clothing and low hum of talking seemed all a part of a world so different from his, so strangely more beautiful than anything he had known, that he sat in dreamland, and started when, after a hush, rose high and clear the music of Lohengrin's swan.[4] The infinite beauty of the wail lingered and swept through every muscle of his frame, and put it all a-tune. He closed his eyes and grasped the elbows of the chair, touching unwittingly the lady's arm. And the lady drew away. A deep longing swelled in all his heart to rise with that clear music out of the dirt and dust of that low life that held him prisoned and befouled. If he could only live up in the free air where birds sang and setting suns had no touch of blood! Who had called him to be the slave and butt of all? And if he had called, what right had he to call when a world like this lay open before men?

Then the movement changed, and fuller, mightier harmony swelled away. He looked thoughtfully across the hall, and wondered why the beautiful gray-haired woman looked so listless, and what the little man could be whispering about. He would not like to be listless and idle, he thought, for he felt with the music the movement of power within him. If he but had some master-work, some life-service, hard,—aye, bitter hard, but without the cringing and sickening servility, without the cruel hurt that hardened his heart and soul. When at last a soft sorrow crept across the violins, there came to him the vision of a far-off home,—the great eyes of his sister, and the dark drawn face of his mother. And his heart sank below the waters, even as the sea-sand sinks by the shores of Altamaha, only to be lifted aloft again with that last ethereal wail of the swan that quivered and faded away into the sky.

It left John sitting so silent and rapt that he did not for some time notice the usher tapping him lightly on the shoulder and saying politely, "Will you step this way, please, sir?" A little surprised, he arose quickly at the last tap, and, turning to leave his seat, looked full into the face of the fair-haired young man. For the first time the young man recognized his dark boyhood playmate, and John knew that it was the Judge's son. The white John started, lifted his hand, and then froze into his chair; the black John smiled lightly, then grimly, and followed the usher down the aisle. The manager was sorry, very, very sorry,—but he explained that some mistake had been made in selling the gentleman a seat already disposed of; he would refund the money, of course,—and indeed felt the matter keenly, and so forth, and—before he had finished John was gone, walking hurriedly across the square and down the broad streets, and as he passed the park he buttoned his coat and said, "John Jones, you're a natural-born fool." Then he went to his lodgings and wrote a letter, and tore it up; he wrote another, and threw it in the fire. Then he seized a scrap of paper and wrote: "Dear Mother and Sister—I am coming—John."

"Perhaps," said John, as he settled himself on the train, "perhaps I am to blame myself in struggling against my manifest destiny[5] simply because it looks hard and unpleasant. Here is my duty to Altamaha plain before me; perhaps they'll let me help settle the Negro problems there,—perhaps they won't. 'I will go in to the King, which is not according to the law; and if I perish, I perish.' "[6] And then he mused and dreamed, and planned a life-work; and the train flew south.

Down in Altamaha, after seven long years, all the world knew John was coming. The homes were scrubbed and scoured,—above all, one; the gardens and yards had an unwonted trimness, and Jennie bought a new gingham. With some finesse and negotiation, all the dark Methodists and Presbyterians were induced to join in a monster welcome at the Baptist Church; and as the day drew near, warm discussions arose on every corner as to the exact extent and nature of John's accomplishments. It was noontide on a gray and cloudy day when he came. The black town flocked to the depot, with a little of the white at the edges,—a happy throng, with "Good-mawnings" and "Howdys" and laughing and joking and jostling. Mother sat yonder in the window watching; but sister Jennie stood on the platform, nervously fingering her dress,—tall and lithe, with soft brown skin and loving eyes peering from out a tangled wilderness of hair. John rose gloomily as the train stopped, for he was thinking of the "Jim Crow" car; he stepped to the platform, and paused: a little dingy station, a black crowd gaudy and dirty, a half-mile of dilapidated shanties along a straggling ditch of mud. An overwhelming sense of the sordidness and narrowness of it all seized him; he looked in vain for his mother, kissed coldly the tall, strange girl who called him brother, spoke a short, dry word here and there; then, lingering neither for hand-shaking nor gossip, started silently up the street, raising his hat merely to the last eager old aunty, to her open-mouthed astonishment. The people were distinctly bewildered. This silent, cold man,—was this John? Where was his smile and hearty handgrasp? " 'Peared kind o' down in the mouf," said the Methodist preacher thoughtfully. "Seemed monstus stuck up," complained a Baptist sister. But the white postmaster from the edge of the crowd expressed the opinion of his folks plainly. "That damn Nigger," said he, as he shouldered the mail and arranged his tobacco, "has gone North and got plum full o' fool notions; but they won't work in Altamaha." And the crowd melted away.

The meeting of welcome at the Baptist Church was a failure. Rain spoiled the barbecue, and thunder turned the milk in the ice-cream.

When the speaking came at night, the house was crowded to overflowing. The three preachers had especially prepared themselves, but somehow John's manner seemed to throw a blanket over everything,—he seemed so cold and preoccupied, and had so strange an air of restraint that the Methodist brother could not warm up to his theme and elicited not a single "Amen"; the Presbyterian prayer was but feebly responded to, and even the Baptist preacher, though he wakened faint enthusiasm, got so mixed up in his favorite sentence that he had to close it by stopping fully fifteen minutes sooner than he meant. The people moved uneasily in their seats as John rose to reply. He spoke slowly and methodically. The age, he said, demanded new ideas;[7] we were far different from those men of the seventeenth and eighteenth centuries,—with broader ideas of human brotherhood and destiny. Then he spoke of the rise of charity and popular education, and particularly of the spread of wealth and work. The question was, then, he added reflectively, looking at the low discolored ceiling, what part the Negroes of this land would take in the striving of the new century. He sketched in vague outline the new Industrial School that might rise among these pines, he spoke in detail of the charitable and philanthropic work that might be organized, of money that might be saved for banks and business. Finally he urged unity, and deprecated especially religious and denominational bickering. "To-day," he said, with a smile, "the world cares little whether a man be Baptist or Methodist, or indeed a churchman at all, so long as he is good and true. What difference does it make whether a man be baptized in river or wash-bowl, or not at all? Let's leave all that littleness, and look higher."[8] Then, thinking of nothing else, he slowly sat down. A painful hush seized that crowded mass. Little had they understood of what he said, for he spoke an unknown tongue, save the last word about baptism; that they knew, and they sat very still while the clock ticked. Then at last a low suppressed snarl came from the Amen corner, and an old bent man arose, walked over the seats, and climbed straight up into the pulpit. He was wrinkled and black, with scant gray and tufted hair; his voice and hands shook as with palsy; but on his face lay the intense rapt look of the religious fanatic. He seized the Bible with his rough, huge hands; twice he raised it inarticulate, and then fairly burst into the words, with rude and awful eloquence. He quivered, swayed, and bent; then rose aloft in perfect majesty, till the people moaned and wept, wailed and shouted, and a wild shrieking arose from the corners where all the pent-up feeling of the hour gathered itself and rushed into the air. John never knew clearly what the old man said; he only felt himself held up to scorn and scathing denunciation for trampling on the true Religion, and he realized with amazement that all unknowingly he had put rough, rude hands on something this little world held sacred. He arose silently, and passed out into the night. Down toward the sea he went, in the fitful starlight, half conscious of the girl who followed timidly after him. When at last he stood upon the bluff, he turned to his little sister and looked upon her sorrowfully, remembering with sudden pain how little thought he had given her. He put his arm about her and let her passion of tears spend itself on his shoulder.

Long they stood together, peering over the gray unresting water.

"John," she said, "does it make every one — unhappy when they study and learn lots of things?"

He paused and smiled. "I am afraid it does," he said.

"And, John, are you glad you studied?"

"Yes," came the answer, slowly but positively.

She watched the flickering lights upon the sea, and said thoughtfully, "I wish I was unhappy, — and — and," putting both arms about his neck, "I think I am, a little, John."

It was several days later that John walked up to the Judge's house to ask for the privilege of teaching the Negro school. The Judge himself met him at the front door, stared a little hard at him, and said brusquely, "Go 'round to the kitchen door, John, and wait." Sitting on the kitchen steps, John stared at the corn, thoroughly perplexed. What on earth had come over him? Every step he made offended some one. He had come to save his people, and before he left the depot he had hurt them. He sought to teach them at the church, and had outraged their deepest feelings. He had schooled himself to be respectful to the Judge, and then blundered into his front door. And all the time he had meant right, — and yet, and yet, somehow he found it so hard and strange to fit his old surroundings again, to find his place in the world about him. He could not remember that he used to have any difficulty in the past, when life was glad and gay. The world seemed smooth and easy then. Perhaps, — but his sister came to the kitchen door just then and said the Judge awaited him.

The Judge sat in the dining-room amid his morning's mail, and he did not ask John to sit down. He plunged squarely into the business. "You've come for the school, I suppose. Well, John, I want to speak to you plainly. You know I'm a friend to your people. I've helped you and your family, and would have done more if you hadn't got the notion of going off. Now I like the colored people, and sympathize with all their reasonable aspirations; but you and I both know, John, that in this country the Negro must remain subordinate, and can never expect to be the equal of white men. In their place, your people can be honest and respectful; and God knows, I'll do what I can to help them. But when they want to reverse nature, and rule white men, and marry white women, and sit in my parlor, then, by God! we'll hold them under if we have to lynch every Nigger in the land. Now, John, the question is, are you, with your education and Northern notions, going to accept the situation and teach the darkies to be faithful servants and laborers as your fathers were, — I knew your father, John, he belonged to my brother, and he was a good Nigger. Well—well, are you going to be like him, or are you going to try to put fool ideas of rising and equality into these folks' heads, and make them discontented and unhappy?"

"I am going to accept the situation, Judge Henderson," answered John, with a brevity that did not escape the keen old man. He hesitated a moment, and then said shortly, "Very well, —we'll try you awhile. Good-morning."

It was a full month after the opening of the Negro school that the other John came home, tall, gay, and headstrong. The mother wept, the sisters sang. The whole white town was glad. A proud man was the Judge, and it was a goodly sight to see the two swinging down Main Street together. And yet all did not go smoothly between them, for the younger man could not and did not veil his contempt for the little town, and plainly had his heart set on New York. Now the one cherished ambition of the Judge was to see his son mayor of Altamaha, representative to the legislature, and—who could say?—governor of Georgia. So the argument often waxed hot between them. "Good heavens, father," the younger man would say after dinner, as he lighted a cigar and stood by the fireplace, "you surely don't expect a young fellow like me to settle down permanently in this—this God-forgotten town with nothing but mud and Negroes?" "I did," the Judge would answer laconically; and on this particular day it seemed from the gathering scowl that he was about to add something more emphatic, but neighbors had already begun to drop in to admire his son, and the conversation drifted.

"Heah that John is livenin' things up at the darky school," volunteered the postmaster, after a pause.

"What now?" asked the Judge, sharply.

"Oh, nothin' in particulah, —just his almighty air and uppish ways. B'lieve I did heah somethin' about his givin' talks on the French Revolution, equality, and such like. He's what I call a dangerous Nigger."[9]

"Have you heard him say anything out of the way?"

"Why, no, —but Sally, our girl, told my wife a lot of rot. Then, too, I don't need to heah: a Nigger what won't say 'sir' to a white man, or—"

"Who is this John?" interrupted the son.

"Why, it's little black John, Peggy's son, —your old play-fellow."

The young man's face flushed angrily, and then he laughed.

"Oh," said he, "it's the darky that tried to force himself into a seat beside the lady I was escorting—"

But Judge Henderson waited to hear no more. He had been nettled all day, and now at this he rose with a half-smothered oath, took his hat and cane, and walked straight to the schoolhouse.

For John, it had been a long, hard pull to get things started in the rickety old shanty that sheltered his school. The Negroes were rent into factions for and against him, the parents were careless, the children irregular and dirty, and books, pencils, and slates largely missing. Nevertheless, he struggled hopefully on, and seemed to see at last some glimmering of dawn. The attendance was larger and the children were a shade cleaner this week. Even the booby class in reading showed a little comforting progress. So John settled himself with renewed patience this afternoon.

"Now, Mandy," he said cheerfully, "that's better; but you must n't chop your words up so: 'If—the—man—goes.' Why, your little brother even would n't tell a story that way, now would he?"

"Naw, suh, he cain't talk."

"All right; now let 's try again: 'If the man—' "

"John!"

The whole school started in surprise, and the teacher half arose, as the red, angry face of the Judge appeared in the open doorway.

"John, this school is closed. You children can go home and get to work. The white people of Altamaha are not spending their money on black folks to have their heads crammed with impudence and lies. Clear out! I'll lock the door myself."

Up at the great pillared house the tall young son wandered aimlessly about after his father's abrupt departure. In the house there was little to interest him; the books were old and stale, the local newspaper flat, and the women had retired with headaches and sewing. He tried a nap, but it was too warm. So he sauntered out into the fields, complaining disconsolately, "Good Lord! how long will this imprisonment last!" He was not a bad fellow,—just a little spoiled and self-indulgent, and as headstrong as his proud father. He seemed a young man pleasant to look upon, as he sat on the great black stump at the edge of the pines idly swinging his legs and smoking. "Why, there is n't even a girl worth getting up a respectable flirtation with," he growled. Just then his eye caught a tall, willowy figure hurrying toward him on the narrow path. He looked with interest at first, and then burst into a laugh as he said, "Well, I declare, if it is n't Jennie, the little brown kitchen-maid! Why, I never noticed before what a trim little body she is. Hello, Jennie! Why, you have n't kissed me since I came home," he said gaily. The young girl stared at him in surprise and confusion, — faltered something inarticulate, and attempted to pass. But a wilful mood had seized the young idler, and he caught at her arm. Frightened, she slipped by; and half mischievously he turned and ran after her through the tall pines.

Yonder, toward the sea, at the end of the path, came John slowly, with his head down. He had turned wearily homeward from the schoolhouse; then, thinking to shield his mother from the blow, started to meet his sister as she came from work and break the news of his dismissal to her. "I'll go away," he said slowly; "I'll go away and find work, and send for them. I cannot live here longer." And then the fierce, buried anger surged up into his throat. He waved his arms and hurried wildly up the path.

The great brown sea lay silent. The air scarce breathed. The dying day bathed the twisted oaks and mighty pines in black and gold. There came from the wind no warning, not a whisper from the cloudless sky. There was only a black man hurrying on with an ache in his heart, seeing neither sun nor sea, but starting as from a dream at the frightened cry that woke the pines, to see his dark sister struggling in the arms of a tall and fair-haired man.

He said not a word, but, seizing a fallen limb, struck him with all the pent-up hatred of his great black arm; and the body lay white and still beneath the pines, all bathed in sunshine and in blood. John looked at it dreamily, then walked back to the house briskly, and said in a soft voice, "Mammy, I'm going away, — I'm going to be free."

She gazed at him dimly and faltered, "No'th, honey, is yo' gwine No'th agin?"

He looked out where the North Star glistened pale above the waters, and said, "Yes, mammy, I'm going — North."

Then, without another word, he went out into the narrow lane, up by the straight pines, to the same winding path, and seated himself on the great black stump, looking at the blood where the body had lain. Yonder in the gray past he had played with that dead boy, romping together under the solemn trees. The night deepened; he thought of the boys at Johnstown. He wondered how Brown had turned out, and Carey? And Jones, — Jones? Why, *he* was Jones, and he wondered what they would all say when they knew, when they knew, in that great long dining-room with its hundreds of merry eyes. Then as the sheen of the starlight stole over him, he thought of the gilded ceiling of that vast concert hall, and heard stealing toward him the faint sweet music of the swan. Hark! was it music, or the hurry and shouting of men? Yes, surely! Clear and high the faint sweet melody rose and fluttered like a living thing, so that the very earth trembled as with the tramp of horses and murmur of angry men.

He leaned back and smiled toward the sea, whence rose the strange melody, away from the dark shadows where lay the noise of horses galloping, galloping on. With an effort he roused himself, bent forward, and looked steadily down the pathway, softly humming the "Song of the Bride,"

"Freudig geführt, ziehet dahin."[10]

Amid the trees in the dim morning twilight he watched their shadows dancing and heard their horses thundering toward him, until at last they came sweeping like a storm, and he saw in front that haggard white-haired man, whose eyes flashed red with fury. Oh, how he pitied him,—pitied him,—and wondered if he had the coiling twisted rope. Then, as the storm burst round him, he rose slowly to his feet and turned his closed eyes toward the Sea.

And the world whistled in his ears.

XIV

The Sorrow Songs

I walk through the churchyard
    To lay this body down;
I know moon-rise, I know star-rise;
I walk in the moonlight, I walk in the starlight;
I'll lie in the grave and stretch out my arms,
I'll go to judgment in the evening of the day,
And my soul and thy soul shall meet that day,
    When I lay this body down.

Negro Song.

They that walked in darkness sang songs in the olden days—Sorrow Songs—for they were weary at heart. And so before each thought that I have written in this book I have set a phrase, a haunting echo of these weird old songs in which the soul of the black slave spoke to men. Ever since I was a child these songs have stirred me strangely. They came out of the South unknown to me, one by one, and yet at once I knew them as of me and of mine. Then in after years when I came to Nashville I saw the great temple builded of these songs towering over the pale city. To me Jubilee Hall[2] seemed ever made of the songs themselves, and its bricks were red with the blood and dust of toil. Out of them rose for me morning, noon, and night, bursts of wonderful melody, full of the voices of my brothers and sisters, full of the voices of the past.

Little of beauty has America given the world save the rude grandeur God himself stamped on her bosom; the human spirit in this new world has expressed itself in vigor and ingenuity rather than in beauty. And so by fateful chance the Negro folk-song—the rhythmic cry of the slave—stands to-day not simply as the sole American music, but as the most beautiful expression of human experience born this side the seas. It has been neglected, it has been, and is, half despised, and above all it has been persistently mistaken and misunderstood; but notwithstanding, it still remains as the singular spiritual heritage of the nation and the greatest gift of the Negro people.

Away back in the thirties the melody of these slave songs stirred the nation, but the songs were soon half forgotten. Some, like "Near the lake where drooped the willow," passed into current airs and their source was forgotten; others were caricatured on the "minstrel" stage[3] and their memory died away. Then in war-time came the singular Port Royal experiment[4] after the capture of Hilton Head, and perhaps for the first time the North met the Southern slave face to face and heart to heart with no third witness. The Sea Islands of the Carolinas, where they met, were filled with a black folk of primitive type, touched and moulded less by the world about them than any others outside the Black Belt. Their appearance was uncouth, their language funny, but their hearts were human and their singing stirred men with a mighty power. Thomas Wentworth Higginson[5] hastened to tell of these songs, and Miss McKim[6] and others urged upon the world their rare beauty. But the world listened only half credulously until the Fisk Jubilee Singers[7] sang the slave songs so deeply into the world's heart that it can never wholly forget them again.

There was once a blacksmith's son born at Cadiz, New York, who in the changes of time taught school in Ohio and helped defend Cincinnati from Kirby Smith. Then he fought at Chancellorsville and Gettysburg[8] and finally served in the Freedman's Bureau at Nashville. Here he formed a Sunday-school class of black children in 1866, and sang with them and taught them to sing. And then they taught him to sing, and when once the glory of the Jubilee songs passed into the soul of George L. White,[9] he knew his life-work was to let those Negroes sing to the world as they had sung to him. So in 1871 the pilgrimage of the Fisk Jubilee Singers began. North to Cincinnati they rode,—four half-clothed black boys and five girl-women,—led by a man with a cause and a purpose. They stopped at Wilberforce, the oldest of Negro schools, where a black bishop blessed them. Then they went, fighting cold and starvation, shut out of hotels, and cheerfully sneered at, ever northward; and ever the magic of their song kept thrilling hearts, until a burst of applause in the Congregational Council at Oberlin revealed them to the world.[10] They came to New York and

Henry Ward Beecher dared to welcome them,[11] even though the metro-
politan dailies sneered at his "Nigger Minstrels." So their songs conquered till they sang across the land and across the sea, before Queen
and Kaiser, in Scotland and Ireland, Holland and Switzerland. Seven
years they sang, and brought back a hundred and fifty thousand dollars
to found Fisk University.

Since their day they have been imitated — sometimes well, by the
singers of Hampton and Atlanta, sometimes ill, by straggling quartettes.
Caricature has sought again to spoil the quaint beauty of the music, and
has filled the air with many debased melodies which vulgar ears scarce
know from the real. But the true Negro folk-song still lives in the hearts
of those who have heard them truly sung and in the hearts of the Negro
people.

What are these songs, and what do they mean? I know little of music
and can say nothing in technical phrase, but I know something of men,
and knowing them, I know that these songs are the articulate message
of the slave to the world. They tell us in these eager days that life was joyous to the black slave, careless and happy. I can easily believe this of
some, of many. But not all the past South, though it rose from the dead,
can gainsay the heart-touching witness of these songs. They are the
music of an unhappy people, of the children of disappointment; they tell
of death and suffering and unvoiced longing toward a truer world, of misty
wanderings and hidden ways.

The songs are indeed the siftings of centuries; the music is far more
ancient than the words, and in it we can trace here and there signs of
development. My grandfather's grandmother was seized by an evil Dutch
trader two centuries ago;[12] and coming to the valleys of the Hudson and
Housatonic, black, little, and lithe, she shivered and shrank in the harsh
north winds, looked longingly at the hills, and often crooned a heathen
melody to the child between her knees, thus:

13

Do ba - na co - ba, ge - ne me, ge - ne me!

Do ba - na co - ba, ge - ne me, ge - ne me!

Ben d' nu - li, nu - li, nu - li, nu - li, ben d' le.

The child sang it to his children and they to their children's children, and so two hundred years it has travelled down to us and we sing it to our children, knowing as little as our fathers what its words may mean, but knowing well the meaning of its music.

This was primitive African music; it may be seen in larger form in the strange chant which heralds "The Coming of John":

"You may bury me in the East,
You may bury me in the West,
But I 'll hear the trumpet sound in that morning,"[14]

—the voice of exile.

Ten master songs, more or less, one may pluck from this forest of melody—songs of undoubted Negro origin and wide popular currency, and songs peculiarly characteristic of the slave. One of these I have just mentioned. Another whose strains begin this book is "Nobody knows the trouble I've seen." When, struck with a sudden poverty, the United States refused to fulfil its promises of land to the freedmen, a brigadier-general went down to the Sea Islands to carry the news. An old woman on the outskirts of the throng began singing this song; all the mass joined with her, swaying. And the soldier wept.

The third song is the cradle-song of death which all men know,— "Swing low, sweet chariot,"—whose bars begin the life story of "Alexander Crummell." Then there is the song of many waters, "Roll, Jordan, roll," a mighty chorus with minor cadences. There were many songs of the fugitive like that which opens "The Wings of Atalanta," and the more familiar "Been a-listening." The seventh is the song of the End and the Beginning—"My Lord, what a mourning! when the stars begin to fall"; a strain of this is placed before "The Dawn of Freedom." The song of groping—"My way's cloudy"—begins "The Meaning of Progress"; the ninth is the song of this chapter—"Wrestlin' Jacob, the day is a-breaking,"—a pæan of hopeful strife. The last master song is the song of songs—"Steal away"[15]—sprung from "The Faith of the Fathers."

There are many others of the Negro folk-songs as striking and characteristic as these, as, for instance, the three strains in the third, eighth, and ninth chapters; and others I am sure could easily make a selection on more scientific principles. There are, too, songs that seem to me a step removed from the more primitive types: there is the maze-like medley, "Bright sparkles," one phrase of which heads "The Black Belt"; the Easter carol, "Dust, dust and ashes"; the dirge, "My mother's took her flight and gone home"; and that burst of melody hovering over "The Passing of the First-Born"—"I hope my mother will be there in that beautiful world on high."

These represent a third step in the development of the slave song, of which "You may bury me in the East" is the first, and songs like "March on" (chapter six) and "Steal away" are the second. The first is African music, the second Afro-American, while the third is a blending of Negro music with the music heard in the foster land. The result is still distinctively Negro and the method of blending original, but the elements are both Negro and Caucasian. One might go further and find a fourth step in this development, where the songs of white America have been distinctively influenced by the slave songs or have incorporated whole phrases of Negro melody, as "Swanee River" and "Old Black Joe."[16] Side by side, too, with the growth has gone the debasements and imitations—the Negro "minstrel" songs, many of the "gospel" hymns, and some of the contemporary "coon" songs,[17]—a mass of music in which the novice may easily lose himself and never find the real Negro melodies.

In these songs, I have said, the slave spoke to the world. Such a message is naturally veiled and half articulate. Words and music have lost each other and new and cant phrases of a dimly understood theology have displaced the older sentiment. Once in a while we catch a strange word of an unknown tongue, as the "Mighty Myo," which figures as a river of death; more often slight words or mere doggerel are joined to music of singular sweetness. Purely secular songs are few in number, partly because many of them were turned into hymns by a change of words, partly because the frolics were seldom heard by the stranger, and the music less often caught. Of nearly all the songs, however, the music is distinctly sorrowful. The ten master songs I have mentioned tell in word and music of trouble and exile, of strife and hiding; they grope toward some unseen power and sigh for rest in the End.

The words that are left to us are not without interest, and, cleared of evident dross, they conceal much of real poetry and meaning beneath conventional theology and unmeaning rhapsody. Like all primitive folk, the slave stood near to Nature's heart. Life was a "rough and rolling sea" like the brown Atlantic of the Sea Islands; the "Wilderness" was the home of God, and the "lonesome valley" led to the way of life. "Winter 'll soon be over," was the picture of life and death to a tropical imagination. The sudden wild thunderstorms of the South awed and impressed the Negroes,—at times the rumbling seemed to them "mournful," at times imperious:

"My Lord calls me,
He calls me by the thunder,
The trumpet sounds it in my soul."[18]

The monotonous toil and exposure is painted in many words. One sees
the ploughmen in the hot, moist furrow, singing:

"Dere 's no rain to wet you,
Dere 's no sun to burn you,
Oh, push along, believer,
I want to go home."[19]

The bowed and bent old man cries, with thrice-repeated wail:

"O Lord, keep me from sinking down,"

and he rebukes the devil of doubt who can whisper:

"Jesus is dead and God's gone away."[20]

Yet the soul-hunger is there, the restlessness of the savage, the wail of
the wanderer, and the plaint is put in one little phrase:

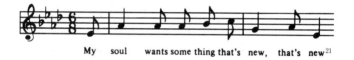

My   soul   wants some thing that's new,   that's new[21]

Over the inner thoughts of the slaves and their relations one with
another the shadow of fear ever hung, so that we get but glimpses here
and there, and also with them, eloquent omissions and silences. Mother
and child are sung, but seldom father; fugitive and weary wanderer call
for pity and affection, but there is little of wooing and wedding; the rocks
and the mountains are well known, but home is unknown. Strange blending of love and helplessness sings through the refrain:

"Yonder 's my ole mudder,
Been waggin' at de hill so long;
'Bout time she cross over,
Git home bime-by."[22]

Elsewhere comes the cry of the "motherless" and the "Farewell, farewell,
my only child."

Love-songs are scarce and fall into two categories—the frivolous and
light, and the sad. Of deep successful love there is ominous silence, and in
one of the oldest of these songs there is a depth of history and meaning:

Poor Ro - sy, poor gal; Poor Ro - sy, poor gal; Ro - sy break my poor heart. Heav'n shall - a - be my home.[23]

A black woman said of the song, "It can't be sung without a full heart and a troubled sperrit." The same voice sings here that sings in the German folk-song:

"Jetz Geh i' an's brunele, trink' aber net."[24]

Of death the Negro showed little fear, but talked of it familiarly and even fondly as simply a crossing of the waters, perhaps — who knows? — back to his ancient forests again. Later days transfigured his fatalism, and amid the dust and dirt the toiler sang:

"Dust, dust and ashes, fly over my grave,
But the Lord shall bear my spirit home."[25]

The things evidently borrowed from the surrounding world undergo characteristic change when they enter the mouth of the slave. Especially is this true of Bible phrases. "Weep, O captive daughter of Zion," is quaintly turned into "Zion, weep-a-low," and the wheels of Ezekiel[26] are turned every way in the mystic dreaming of the slave, till he says:

"There's a little wheel a-turnin' in-a-my heart."[27]

As in olden time, the words of these hymns were improvised by some leading minstrel of the religious band. The circumstances of the gathering, however, the rhythm of the songs, and the limitations of allowable thought, confined the poetry for the most part to single or double lines, and they seldom were expanded to quatrains or longer tales, although there are some few examples of sustained efforts, chiefly paraphrases of the Bible. Three short series of verses have always attracted me, — the one that heads this chapter, of one line of which Thomas Wentworth Higginson has fittingly said, "Never, it seems to me, since man first lived and suffered was his infinite longing for peace uttered more plaintively." The second and third are descriptions of the Last Judgment, — the one a late improvisation, with some traces of outside influence:

"Oh, the stars in the elements are falling,
And the moon drips away into blood,
And the ransomed of the Lord are returning unto God,
Blessed be the name of the Lord."[28]

And the other earlier and homelier picture from the low coast lands:

"Michael, haul the boat ashore,
Then you 'll hear the horn they blow,
Then you 'll hear the trumpet sound,
Trumpet sound the world around,
Trumpet sound for rich and poor,
Trumpet sound the Jubilee,
Trumpet sound for you and me."[29]

Through all the sorrow of the Sorrow Songs there breathes a hope —
a faith in the ultimate justice of things. The minor cadences of despair
change often to triumph and calm confidence. Sometimes it is faith in life,
sometimes a faith in death, sometimes assurance of boundless justice in
some fair world beyond. But whichever it is, the meaning is always clear:
that sometime, somewhere, men will judge men by their souls and not
by their skins. Is such a hope justified? Do the Sorrow Songs sing true?

The silently growing assumption of this age is that the probation of
races is past, and that the backward races of today are of proven inefficiency and not worth the saving. Such an assumption is the arrogance of
peoples irreverent toward Time and ignorant of the deeds of men. A
thousand years ago such an assumption, easily possible, would have
made it difficult for the Teuton to prove his right to life. Two thousand
years ago such dogmatism, readily welcome, would have scouted the idea
of blond races ever leading civilization. So wofully unorganized is sociological knowledge that the meaning of progress, the meaning of "swift"
and "slow" in human doing, and the limits of human perfectability, are
veiled, unanswered sphinxes on the shores of science. Why should
Æschylus have sung two thousand years before Shakespeare was born?[30]
Why has civilization flourished in Europe, and flickered, flamed, and
died in Africa? So long as the world stands meekly dumb before such
questions, shall this nation proclaim its ignorance and unhallowed prejudices by denying freedom of opportunity to those who brought the Sorrow Songs to the Seats of the Mighty?

Your country? How came it yours? Before the Pilgrims[31] landed we
were here. Here we have brought our three gifts and mingled them with
yours: a gift of story and song — soft, stirring melody in an ill-harmonized
and unmelodious land; the gift of sweat and brawn to beat back the wilder-

ness, conquer the soil, and lay the foundations of this vast economic empire two hundred years earlier than your weak hands could have done it; the third, a gift of the Spirit. Around us the history of the land has centred for thrice a hundred years; out of the nation's heart we have called all that was best to throttle and subdue all that was worst; fire and blood, prayer and sacrifice, have billowed over this people, and they have found peace only in the altars of the God of Right. Nor has our gift of the Spirit been merely passive. Actively we have woven ourselves with the very warp and woof of this nation,—we fought their battles, shared their sorrow, mingled our blood with theirs, and generation after generation have pleaded with a headstrong, careless people to despise not Justice, Mercy, and Truth, lest the nation be smitten with a curse. Our song, our toil, our cheer, and warning have been given to this nation in blood-brotherhood. Are not these gifts worth the giving? Is not this work and striving? Would America have been America without her Negro people?

Even so is the hope that sang in the songs of my fathers well sung. If somewhere in this whirl and chaos of things there dwells Eternal Good, pitiful yet masterful, then anon in His good time America shall rend the Veil and the prisoned shall go free. Free, free as the sunshine trickling down the morning into these high windows of mine, free as yonder fresh young voices welling up to me from the caverns of brick and mortar below—swelling with song, instinct with life, tremulous treble and darkening bass. My children, my little children, are singing to the sunshine, and thus they sing:

And the traveller girds himself, and sets his face toward the Morning, and goes his way.

The Afterthought

Hear my cry, O God the Reader, vouchsafe that this my book fall not still-born into the world-wilderness. Let there spring, Gentle One, from out its leaves vigor of thought and thoughtful deed to reap the harvest wonderful. (Let the ears of a guilty people tingle with truth, and seventy millions sigh for the righteousness which exalteth nations, in this drear day when human brotherhood is mockery and a snare.) Thus in Thy good time may infinite reason turn the tangle straight, and these crooked marks on a fragile leaf be not indeed.[1]

THE END

NOTES

In assembling the annotations for the Bedford Books edition of *The Souls of Black Folk,* we have relied particularly on the following sources, in addition to a variety of encyclopedic references and the work of other scholars.

The W. E. B. Du Bois Papers are housed at the University of Massachusetts Amherst. They are cited in these notes as Du Bois Papers.

Aptheker, Herbert. *The Literary Legacy of W. E. B. Du Bois.* New York: Kraus International, 1989.

Elbert, Monica, ed. Notes to *The Souls of Black Folk,* by W. E. B. Du Bois. New York: Penguin, 1989.

Foner, Eric. *Reconstruction: America's Unfinished Revolution, 1863–1877.* New York: Harper and Row, 1989.

Gates, Henry Louis Jr., ed. Introduction to *The Souls of Black Folk,* by W. E. B. Du Bois. New York: Bantam, 1989.

Huggins, Nathan I., ed. Notes to *The Souls of Black Folk,* by W. E. B. Du Bois. New York: Vintage, 1990.

Lewis, David Levering. *W. E. B. Du Bois: Biography of a Race, 1868–1919.* New York: Henry Holt, 1993.

Moses, Wilson Jeremiah. *Alexander Crummell: A Study of Civilization and Its Discontents.* New York: Oxford University Press, 1969.

Raboteau, Albert J. *Slave Religion: The "Invisible Institution" in the Antebellum South.* New York: Oxford University Press, 1978.

Salzman, Jack, David Lionel Smith, and Cornel West, eds. *The Encyclopedia of African-American Culture and History.* 5 vols. New York: Macmillan, 1996.

Sundquist, Eric J. *To Wake the Nations: Race in the Making of American Literature.* Cambridge: Harvard University Press, 1993.

"The Forethought"

[1]Du Bois proclaimed for the first time publicly that "the problem of the twentieth century is the problem of the color-line" in an address in London to the first Pan-African conference, July 1900.

[2]Booker T. Washington.

[3]The metaphor of the Veil recurs throughout *Souls,* where it acquires multiple meanings. For biblical uses of the veil, see Exodus 34.33–35; 2 Corinthians 13.13–18; Matthew 27.51; Hebrews 6.19, 10.20; and Isaiah 25.7.

[4]In the 1953 Blue Heron Press edition of *Souls,* the last sentence of this paragraph reads: "All this I have ended with a tale twice told but seldom written, and a chapter of song."

I. "Of Our Spiritual Strivings"

[1]The verse is Arthur Symons, "The Crying of Waters." The music is a Negro spiritual, "Nobody Knows the Trouble I've Seen." In every chapter but the last, Du Bois uses this structure of epigraphs: a passage of verse (usually from an American or European poet, but in one case from the Bible and in another from the *Rubaiyat of Omar Khayyam*), followed by a bar of music from the songs of American slaves. On the significance of this structure, especially the choice and origins of the spirituals, see Sundquist, *To Wake the Nations,* 490–539.

[2]Mechanicsville was a Civil War battle fought on June 26, 1862, just east of Richmond, Virginia.

[3]Housatonic is the river that flows through Great Barrington, Massachusetts.

[4]In a composition he wrote as an undergraduate at Harvard, Du Bois may have expressed resentment that had been prompted by this childhood experience. Entitled "The American Girl," the essay describes the girl as an "eye-sore" whose face is "more shrewd than intelligent, arrogant than dignified, silly than pleasant, and pretty than beautiful." See Herbert

Aptheker, ed., *Against Racism: Unpublished Essays, Papers, Addresses, 1887–1961, W. E. B. Du Bois* (Amherst: University of Massachusetts Press, 1985), 20. "The shades of the prison-house closed round us all" explicitly echoes William Wordsworth's ode "Intimations Of Immortality From Recollections Of Early Childhood," lines 67–68. See chapter 12, note 10.

⁵The figure of the seventh son carries multiple meanings. Apparently revising Hegel's philosophy of history, Du Bois adds the Negro to Hegel's story of six world-historical peoples (see pp. 12–13). In African American folklore, the seventh son is said to be distinguished in some way, to be able to see ghosts, and to make a good doctor. See Newbell Niles Puckett, *Folk Beliefs of the Southern Negro* (New York: Dover, 1969); Elsie Clews Parsons, *Folk-Lore of the Sea Islands, South Carolina* (Cambridge, Mass.: American Folklore Society, 1923); and Melville Herskovitz, *The Myth of the Negro Past* (1941; reprint, Boston: Beacon Press, 1958).

⁶In African American folklore, a child born with a caul, a veil-like membrane that sometimes covers the head at birth, is said to be lucky, to be able to tell fortunes, and to be a "double-sighted" seer of ghosts. In some West African folk traditions, a child born with a caul is thought to possess a special personality endowed with spiritual potency. For biblical allusions to the veil, see "The Forethought," note 3. Also see the sources in note 5 of this chapter.

⁷For an introduction to the literature on double consciousness, see Dickson D. Bruce Jr., "W. E. B. Du Bois and the Idea of Double Consciousness," *American Literature* 64 (June 1992): 299–309. Also see page 26, note 21.

⁸Du Bois in this passage echoes the most prominent philosophers and poets writing in the European romantic tradition (such as William Blake, Samuel Taylor Coleridge, Friedrich Schiller, and Georg Wilhelm Friedrich Hegel) by promoting the creation of a unified self that synthesizes and preserves diverse elements. Though the American Negro was captured in Africa and forced into slavery in America, he knows no nostalgia for an African "self" that was untainted by the experience of America. Rather, his is a quest for a better, truer, and more encompassing self, the search for a mode of integrity that merges his African and newly acquired American identities yet retains them as distinct. On the romantic philosophers and poets, see M. H. Abrams, *Natural Supernaturalism* (New York: Norton, 1971).

⁹Du Bois envisions blacks in America as the Old Testament Jews (Israelites) who have yet to escape the land of their captivity (Egypt) and enter the promised land (Canaan). On the late-nineteenth-century tradition of African American religious and political thought that gives rise to this imagery, see David W. Wills, "Exodus Piety: African-American Religion in an Age of Immigration," in *Minority Faiths and the American Protestant Mainstream,* ed. David O'Brien and Jonathan Sarns (forthcoming).

¹⁰From the Negro spiritual "Shout, O Children!"

¹¹Shakespeare, *Macbeth*, 3.4.102–3.

¹²The Ku Klux Klan is the white fraternal terrorist organization created in 1866 by Confederate veterans in Pulaski, Tennessee. Its members altered the Greek word for circle, *kuklos,* and invented their name. During Reconstruction in the South, the Klan engaged in widespread violence against blacks and their white Republican supporters.

¹³Carpetbaggers were northern politicians and businessmen who moved to the South after the Civil War, allegedly to exploit the devastation of the South and the political vacuum left by the defeat of the Confederacy.

¹⁴The Fifteenth Amendment to the U.S. Constitution passed Congress in February 1869 and was ratified by the states in March 1870. It provided that voting rights "shall not be denied . . . on account of race, color, or previous condition of servitude." The Fifteenth Amendment was a moderate measure; it did not specifically outlaw qualifications tests for the right to vote. But it did represent the federal government's key role as guarantor of rights during Reconstruction.

¹⁵In the disputed presidential election of 1876, Republican Rutherford B. Hayes defeated Democrat Samuel J. Tilden. In three southern states, Louisiana, Florida, and South Carolina, the voting returns were disputed, with fraud and intimidation charged by both sides. The election was settled by a congressional committee that declared Hayes the winner in the three contested states as well as by a political compromise (known as the Compromise of

1877) between the two parties. The "revolution" refers to southern Democratic threats to secede from the Union or march on Washington, D.C., early in the crisis. This "revolution" also represented the abandonment of the freedpeople in the South by the Republican Party.

[16]See 1 Corinthians 13.12: "For now we see through a glass, darkly; but then face to face: now I know in part; but then shall I know even as also I am known."

[17]Du Bois alludes to the belief, prevalent in the nineteenth century, that there exist several races of human beings that can be ranked hierarchically. For example, Count Arthur de Gobineau, in his *Essay on the Inequality of Human Races* (1853–1855), held that the white race possessed qualities (such as love of freedom, honor, and spirituality) that made it superior to the yellow and black races.

[18]Toussaint L'Ouverture (1746–1803) was the leader of the Haitian revolution of 1791. A former slave, he became a brilliant general, led the forces that overthrew French rule in Sainte Domingue, and established himself as ruler of the new government by 1796. Toussaint was eventually captured by the French and died in France in 1803.

[19]Literally in English, "storm and stress," the term *Sturm und Drang* was used for a literary movement in Germany during the last quarter of the eighteenth century. In general, the writings of the Sturm und Drang movement were intensely personal, emphasizing emotional experience and spiritual struggle. The work that perhaps best captures the spirit of the movement is Johann Wolfgang von Goethe's novel *Die Leiden des Jungen Werthers* (The Sorrows of Young Werther), published in 1774.

[20]Appealing to the necessity of self-defense to justify an extension of the franchise was common in the nineteenth century and echoed utilitarian arguments for democracy made by philosophers Jeremy Bentham and James Mill. On Bentham's and Mill's views, see C. B. McPherson, *The Life and Times of Liberal Democracy* (Oxford: Oxford University Press, 1977), 23–43.

[21]Du Bois echoes the commencement speech he delivered at Harvard in June 1890, "Jefferson Davis as a Representative of Civilization." The speech describes the contrast between the brutal civilization of Jefferson Davis, president of the Confederacy, and the personal submissiveness of the Negro. See Aptheker, *Against Racism,* 14–16. Also see page 125 in chapter 8 of *Souls.*

II. "Of the Dawn of Freedom"

[1]The verse is James Russell Lowell, "The Present Crisis," stanza 8. The music is a Negro spiritual, "My Lord What a Mourning!"

[2]The Thirteenth (1865), Fourteenth (1866), and Fifteenth (1870) Amendments to the U.S. Constitution. The Thirteenth abolished slavery; the Fourteenth defined U.S. citizenship and provided "equal protection of the laws"; and the Fifteenth provided the right to vote for black males.

[3]The Freedmen's Bureau, officially created by Congress in March 1865 as the Bureau of Refugees, Freedmen, and Abandoned Lands, was the first large federal agency of social welfare in American history. Its work included provision of food, shelter, and medical aid to the destitute (black and white in the devastated South), the education of the freedpeople, the negotiation of new labor arrangements between ex-slaves and ex-masters, and the establishment of judicial procedures (courts) to secure freedpeople's rights. The bureau lasted until 1872. Congress cut off its budget in 1869, except for education, which lasted only one more year. The hundreds of bureau agents, mostly northerners, were not always zealous in their support of freedpeople's rights, but the freedpeople themselves came to see the agency as their protector. The bureau was always a controversial symbol of the challenge and meaning of Reconstruction.

[4]Benjamin F. Butler (1818–1893) was a Massachusetts politician and Civil War general. At Fortress Monroe, Virginia, in May 1861, Butler declared the slaves who entered his lines "contraband of war." The idea of slaves as confiscated enemy property caught on. John C. Frémont (1813–1880) was a western explorer, Republican candidate for president in 1856, and Civil War general. In Missouri in August 1861, Frémont issued a proclamation that all

slaves escaping to his lines were free. Frémont acted without authority, and President Lincoln countermanded the order.

[5]Henry W. Halleck (1815–1872), a Union general, succeeded Frémont in Missouri.

[6]Simon Cameron (1799–1889), former U.S. senator from Pennsylvania, was secretary of war in Lincoln's cabinet in 1861.

[7]The "long-headed man with care-chiselled face" is Abraham Lincoln. The Emancipation Proclamation, freeing all slaves in those southern "states in rebellion," took effect on January 1, 1863.

[8]The Second Confiscation Act, passed by Congress on July 17, 1862, freed virtually all slaves liberated by the Union forces and empowered the president to enlist black soldiers.

[9]Edward L. Pierce (1829–1897), a Boston abolitionist, went south during the war to work with the freedpeople in their adjustment to free labor. Salmon P. Chase (1808–1873), former U.S. senator from Ohio and secretary of the treasury in 1861–1862, appointed Pierce as the government agent in charge of cotton production and the freedpeople at Port Royal, South Carolina, in the sea islands. The Port Royal Experiment (1862–1865) was the effort to resume cotton production among the freed blacks on Hilton Head Island; it was conducted jointly by New England missionaries, federal government agents, the Union army, and private entrepreneurs.

[10]These were the contraband camps, established especially along the Virginia coast and in the Mississippi River Valley. For thousands, the contraband camps became the initial entry into free labor practices and a slow but certain embrace of a new sense of dignity. See Ira Berlin et al., eds., *Freedom: A Documentary History of Emancipation, 1861–1867,* ser. 1, vol. 3 (New York: Cambridge University Press, 1990), 674–98.

[11]Freedmen's Aid societies were northern philanthropic groups, largely private and often affiliated with churches, that organized material aid and the initial educational opportunities for the freedpeople during the Civil War.

[12]In July 1839 Africans aboard the slave ship *La Amistad* mutinied off the coast of Cuba. Led by Joseph Cinque, the mutineers killed the ship's captain and ordered the Spanish sailors to sail back to Africa. But a meandering course landed them in New London, Connecticut. Abolitionists took up the *Amistad* rebels' cause when they were imprisoned. In American federal courts, the mutineers eventually won their case, and in November 1841, some thirty-five Africans sailed from New York to return to Sierra Leone.

[13]John A. Dix (1798–1879), Nathaniel P. Banks (1816–1894), John Eaton Jr. (1829–?), and Rufus Saxton, Jr. (1824–1908) were Union officers in charge of freedpeople's affairs in the occupied South during or at the end of the war.

[14]The "Conqueror" is Union General William Tecumseh Sherman (1820–1891), who led the "march to the sea," from Atlanta to Savannah, November 4–December 22, 1864.

[15]"Bitter sufferers" is Du Bois's label for the "Conquered" white southerners. The term "Lost Cause," is at least as old as Edward A. Pollard's book *The Lost Cause: A New Southern History of the War of the Confederates* (New York: Treat and Company, 1867). The "Lost Cause" came to indicate a web of ideas and rituals—a public memory, a type of civil religion, and later a widespread literary phenomenon—that allowed southerners, and some northerners, to believe that the Confederacy had never really been defeated on the battlefield and that it had fought for noble political and racial values, such as state sovereignty and white supremacy.

[16]General Sherman, very conservative on racial matters, opposed the enlistment of black troops. But when thousands of refugee freedpeople followed his army during the march to the sea, he issued Field Order 15, setting aside exclusively for freed slaves a stretch of rich coastal land from Charleston, South Carolina to Jacksonville, Florida. Some twenty thousand black families took advantage of this opportunity during the summer of 1865, but by fall 1865, President Andrew Johnson countermanded the order and returned the land to its former owners.

[17]William Pitt Fessenden (1806–1869), a former U.S. senator from Maine, was secretary of the treasury in 1864–1865. Oliver Otis Howard (1830–1909), a professional soldier, former mathematics professor at West Point, and Union general in the Civil War, became commissioner of the Freedmen's Bureau in May 1865. He helped to found (1867) and served as president (1869–1874) of Howard University in Washington, D.C. He was investigated

and exonerated by a court of inquiry in 1874 for the many accusations of corruption in the Freedmen's Bureau. Howard was widely known at the end of the war as the "Christian General"; he conceived of and conducted the bureau as part of his sense of Christian mission.

[18]Charles Sumner (1811–1874), an abolitionist and a U.S. senator from Massachusetts, was a leader of the Radical Republicans during the early years of Reconstruction and an ardent advocate of black suffrage and civil rights.

[19]Du Bois may be referring to language in General Howard's Circular 13, issued on July 28, 1865. If so, he has some dates wrong. But in this paragraph and in what follows, Du Bois effectively captures the complex circumstances Howard and the Freedmen's Bureau faced in 1865. Du Bois admired the missionary zeal of the bureau at the same time he criticized the results of its work.

[20]Du Bois makes the simple but important point that the bureau was placed under the auspices of the army and the War Department. As much as humanitarian assistance, its work was seen as an official part of the reestablishment of order in the South.

[21]Du Bois implies a "crusade" of the scale of the eight major medieval Christian Crusades. Saint Louis is Louis IX of France, who led the Sixth Crusade to the Holy Land and was canonized in 1297.

[22]Here, perhaps, Du Bois begins to explain why the less dramatic social history of Reconstruction has not caught the popular historical imagination as have the battles and leaders of the Civil War itself.

[23]Lyman Trumbull (1813–1896), U.S. senator from Illinois, led the effort to extend the life and authority of the Freedmen's Bureau. The bill passed Congress on February 19, 1866, and was vetoed by President Andrew Johnson. Congress overrode Johnson's veto on July 16, 1865.

[24]Andrew Johnson (1808–1875), Lincoln's successor as president, eventually locked horns with the Republicans in Congress over control of Reconstruction policy. Johnson was an ardent states' rightist and opponent of black rights. Johnson's monumental political and constitutional struggle with Congress over Reconstruction and the fate of the freedmen led to his impeachment in 1868 (he was the only president to be impeached), although he was acquitted in his Senate trial.

[25]By using the language "government of men," Du Bois captures some of the reasons why the Freedmen's Bureau was so controversial in Reconstruction America. It was a severe test of political philosophy, of human wills, and of attitudes about race. It was a test of just what Americans believed "government" owed its people and just who was included in "the people."

[26]The concept of "failure" and why and how the Freedmen's Bureau and Reconstruction policy may have failed have long been part of popular perception and historians' debates about Reconstruction. See Foner, *Reconstruction,* 602–12. Also see W. E. B. Du Bois, *Black Reconstruction in America, 1860–1880* (New York: Atheneum, 1935), 708, where Du Bois writes that "the attempt to make black men American citizens was in a certain sense all a failure, but a splendid failure."

[27]"Clasping hands across the bloody chasm" became a common slogan of sectional reunion by the 1880s and 1890s, especially at Blue-Gray soldiers' reunions. The slogan was used at least as early as Horace Greeley's campaign for the presidency on the Liberal Republican ticket in 1872. Here Du Bois gives the figure of clasping hands a different and subversive meaning.

[28]*Toto coelo:* Latin, literally, "by the whole heaven," that is, "by an immense distance" or "diametrically."

[29]The slogan "forty acres and a mule" came to represent the freedpeople's expectations of receiving land from the Union army or the federal government at the end of the war. It may have taken root with Sherman's Field Order 15 in January 1865. A "forty-acre program" was called for in the act of March 3, 1865, that created the Freedmen's Bureau. A Freedmen's Bureau circular, issued June 10, 1865, provided for the "location of such refugees and freedmen as may desire it on homes of forty (40) acres." The program was formalized

as a policy in General Howard's Circular 13, issued on July 28, 1865, which instructed bureau staff to "set apart" lands for the freedmen in forty-acre plots. See William S. McFeely, *Yankee Stepfather: General O. O. Howard and the Freedmen* (New Haven: Yale University Press, 1968), 98–106.

[30]Edmund A. Ware (1837–1885), educator and clergyman, was appointed by General Howard as superintendent of education for Georgia in 1867. He founded Atlanta University (1865), a black college for the freedpeople, where Du Bois would eventually teach from 1897 to 1910. Samuel Armstrong (1839–1893), born to missionary parents in Hawaii, became a Union officer and commander of a black regiment during the Civil War. He was the founder and guiding force of Hampton Institute (1868) in Virginia and a mentor to Booker T. Washington. Erastus M. Cravath (1833–1900), a clergyman, educator, and abolitionist, helped found Fisk University (1866) in Nashville, Tennessee, and served as its principal beginning in 1875. Du Bois attended Fisk as an undergraduate in 1887–1890.

[31]Du Bois refers here to the slave codes of 1865, passed by southern state legislatures before they were disbanded by Congress under Radical Reconstruction in 1866–1867.

[32]William W. Belknap (1829–1890), secretary of war under Ulysses S. Grant. Belknap was the subject of a major scandal—he had received bribes for the sale of trading posts in Indian territory in the West—in 1876. He was impeached by the House of Representatives and resigned his office promptly.

[33]The Freedmen's Savings and Trust Company was incorporated by Congress in 1865. It failed in 1874 under its final president, Frederick Douglass. The bank was never adequately capitalized, and the federal government failed over time to provide it with the subsidies it needed to become a viable lending and savings institution for the freedpeople.

[34]Garrett Davis (1815–1882), a Democratic senator from Kentucky, staunchly opposed measures to improve freedpeople's lives.

[35]Serious readers at the turn of the century would not find many writers explaining the "legacies" of emancipation and Reconstruction in quite these terms.

[36]The "King's Highway" was the main trans-Jordanian route from Ezion-Geber on the Gulf of Aqaba to Syria in biblical times. See Numbers 20.17, 21.22.

III. *"Of Mr. Booker T. Washington and Others"*

[1]The verse is Lord Byron, "Childe Harold's Pilgrimage," Canto 2, stanza 74, line 710; stanza 76, lines 720–21. The music is a Negro spiritual, "A Great Camp Meeting in the Promised Land."

[2]The historical "moment" Du Bois captures here is the Gilded Age of the 1880s and 1890s.

[3]Industrial schools, as well as a variety of other self-improvement efforts, had been widely discussed at antebellum black conventions, especially one held in Rochester, New York, in July 1853. See, for example, Frederick Douglass, "The Industrial College," *Frederick Douglass's Paper,* January 2, 1854, in *Life and Writings of Frederick Douglass,* ed. Philip S. Foner (New York: International Publishers, 1950), 2:272–75. Indeed, much of the debate over the purpose and character of black education, which became central to the Du Bois–Washington dispute in the early twentieth century, had been publicly addressed, often with similar controversy, among black leaders of the pre–Civil War generation.

[4]Joseph C. Price (1854–1893) was born in Elizabeth, North Carolina, the son of a slave father and a free mother. Price graduated from Lincoln University in Pennsylvania in 1881 and became an A.M.E. Zion minister and a pioneering black educator in North Carolina. He founded Zion Wesley College in 1882 and Livingstone College in Salisbury, North Carolina, in 1885. A captivating orator, successful fundraiser among wealthy whites, and a proponent of liberal arts education, Price was seen as offering an alternative to the educational leadership of Booker T. Washington until his early death at age forty. In *The Crisis,* March 22, 1922, Du Bois declared that had Price lived, Livingstone College would have been the "black Harvard."

[5]Washington founded Tuskegee Institute as a normal school (what today is called a sec-

ondary school) in 1881 in Tuskegee, Alabama. He served as principal until his death in 1915. The institute grew into a college of industrial education and training for southern black schoolteachers and became the most prominent and successful black educational institution.

[6]The "Atlanta Compromise" was the most famous speech of Washington's life, delivered at the Cotton States Exposition in Atlanta on September 18, 1895. Washington argued that blacks should stay in the South, "cast down their buckets" where they were, pursue economic self-development and industrial education, and renounce political and civil rights in the Jim Crow South. The speech is reprinted as chapter 14 in Washington's autobiography, *Up from Slavery* (1901).

[7]Jefferson Davis (1808–1889) was president of the Confederate States of America during the Civil War. He was a veteran of the Mexican War (1846–48) and had been secretary of war (1853–57) and a U.S. senator from Mississippi (1847–51, 1857–61).

[8]Socrates (469?–399 B.C.) was a Greek philosopher, founder of the Socratic method of philosophical inquiry. St. Francis of Assisi (1182–1226) founded the order of Franciscan monks in Assisi, Italy. He completely embraced poverty, attempting in every way possible to model Christ's life. His writings endure as expressions of love and human kindness.

[9]Washington met and dined with President Theodore Roosevelt at the White House on October 16, 1901. See Louis Harlan, *Booker T. Washington: The Wizard of Tuskegee, 1901–1915* (New York: Oxford University Press, 1984), 2:304–24.

[10]By "hushing of the criticism" Du Bois refers to the growing concern by 1903 that Washington's power extended to paying "hush money" to certain black newspaper editors to make them conform to Washington's point of view on many issues. Hence the accusation by some black intellectuals and activists that Washington operated as a type of "boss politician" through the "Tuskegee Machine."

[11]Maroons were guerrilla bands of escaped slaves in the West Indies and in Central and South America in the eighteenth century. They formed colonies, often in mountainous regions as in Jamaica, and in some cases became formidable military forces. Cato of Stono was one of the leaders of the first major slave rebellion in the colonial American South. The rebellion occurred along the Stono River in South Carolina in 1739.

[12]Phillis Wheatley (c. 1753–1784), a poet, was born in West Africa, brought to America at age eight, and sold to John Wheatley of Boston. Her first book of verse, *Poems on Various Subjects, Religious and Moral,* was published in London in 1773. She is widely regarded as the first African American writer-poet of distinction. Crispus Attucks (1723–1770) was an escaped slave, a dockworker, a black patriot, and one of the victims killed in the Boston Massacre on March 5, 1770. Peter Salem (c. 1750–1816) was a Massachusetts slave who gained his freedom by fighting in the American forces in the Revolution, especially at the Battle of Bunker Hill, June 17, 1775. Salem Poor (1747–?) was a free black who also fought in the American forces in the Revolution. Benjamin Banneker (1731–1806) was a free black born in Maryland; he became a prominent mathematician, scientist, and architect and published an almanac for farmers (1792–1802). James C. Derham (c. 1762–?) was born a slave in Philadelphia, learned the art of medicine from his owner-physician, bought his own freedom in 1783, and established a successful medical practice in New Orleans. Paul Cuffe (1759–1817) was born in Boston of an African father and an American Indian mother. He became a ship captain and merchant seaman out of Nantucket and an early proponent of black emigration to Africa.

[13]Gabriel Prosser (d. 1800) was a slave who led an unsuccessful insurrection conspiracy in Richmond, Virginia, in 1800. The revolt was betrayed by fellow slaves as well as ruined by thunderstorms. Prosser and other leaders were executed. Denmark Vesey (d. 1822) was an ex-slave from Haiti who led an aborted rebellion in Charleston, South Carolina, in 1822. Betrayed, he and other leaders were executed or deported. Nat Turner (1800–1831) was the leader of the bloodiest slave insurrection in North America, which occurred in Southampton County, Virginia, in August 1831. A religious visionary, his *Confessions* became an important part of the lore and literature of the antebellum crisis over slavery. Turner's rebellion, which killed nearly sixty whites in forty-eight hours, contradicted the myth of the contented slave in southern society.

[14]The African Methodist Episcopal Church. See page 213, note 12.

[15]David Walker (1785–1830) was a black abolitionist born free in North Carolina who achieved an education by unknown means. He moved to Boston by the mid-1820s and wrote *An Appeal to the Coloured Citizens of the World* (1829), one of the earliest and most militant antislavery documents. The *Appeal* drew upon the natural rights tradition, the Bible, and concepts of black nationalist self-reliance to warn America of its doom if slavery was not abolished. Walker was found dead outside his clothing shop in 1830.

[16]James Forten (1766–1842) was a Revolutionary War veteran and a wealthy black sailmaker and abolitionist in Philadelphia. He is known as the earliest black philanthropist, as the author of some of the earliest antislavery petitions and public letters, and as a cofounder of the American Anti-Slavery Society (1833). Robert Purvis (1810–1898) was a black Philadelphia businessman, the son-in-law of James Forten. He was active in founding the American Anti-Slavery Society and became one of the leading abolitionists and proponents of black civil rights in the antebellum period. Shad is either Abraham D. Shadd (1801–1882), a free black leader in Wilmington, Delaware, and a staunch opponent of colonization, or Shadd's even more prominent daughter Mary Ann Shadd (1823–1893), who traveled north, became a teacher and an abolitionist, moved to Canada, edited the *Provincial Freeman,* and led an emigration campaign in the 1850s to induce fugitive slaves to move to Canada. James G. Barbadoes (1796–1841) was a free black, a Boston clothier and barber, and a cofounder of the American Anti-Slavery Society. He led an unsuccessful emigration campaign to Jamaica in 1840–1841. Alexander Du Bois was Du Bois's paternal grandfather; born in the Bahamas, a free person of color, he lived much of his life as a small merchant and ship steward in New Haven, Connecticut. Young Will Du Bois first met his grandfather in August 1883 in New Bedford, Massachusetts. Alexander Du Bois had been for a time the treasurer of St. Luke's Episcopal Church in New Haven, when Alexander Crummell was its pastor (c. 1840). For the ways in which Du Bois used his grandfather as a means to construct a half-mythical family past, see Lewis, *W. E. B. Du Bois,* 40–47.

[17]Charles Lenox Remond (1810–1873) was a Boston black abolitionist and a prominent traveling lecturer. He belonged to the Garrisonian wing of the American Anti-Slavery Society, a radical faction devoted to abolition and black civil rights. William Cooper Nell (1816–1874), a Boston black abolitionist and staunch Garrisonian, led the campaign to integrate the Boston schools in the 1840s and wrote a pioneering history, *Colored Patriots of the American Revolution* (1855). William Wells Brown (1814–1884) was a fugitive slave who became a lecturer and the author of a novel, *Clotel, or the President's Daughter* (1853), and a work of history, *The Black Man: His Antecedents, His Genius, and His Achievements* (1863). Frederick Douglass (1818–1895) was a slave, abolitionist, orator, editor, and author of three prominent slave narratives. The most famous of his books was the first, the *Narrative of the Life of Frederick Douglass, An American Slave* (1845). Douglass edited his own newspaper for sixteen years (1847–1863) and became the most important black leader and thinker of the nineteenth century. In his voluminous lectures and writings Douglass was a leading proponent of the integrationist vision of African American destiny. He insisted on American citizenship and civil and political rights for blacks throughout his life.

[18]John Brown's raid, in October 1859, was a pivotal event in the coming of the Civil War. Brown was a white abolitionist who led a small guerrilla band in the capture of the federal arsenal at Harpers Ferry, Virginia. He was captured and later executed in a celebrated hanging in November 1859, but the raid had great symbolic and real significance in the crisis of disunion in 1860–1861.

[19]Robert Brown Elliot (1841–1884) was a black politician and newspaper editor educated in Boston and London. He was elected to numerous offices in South Carolina during Reconstruction, including the U.S. Congress. John Mercer Langston (1829–1897) was a slave, born in Virginia, freed by his owner, and educated at Oberlin College in Ohio. He was elected Virginia's first black congressman during Reconstruction and became dean of the Howard University Law School. Blanche K. Bruce (1841–1898) was a slave who escaped in 1861 and was educated in the North. He moved to Mississippi during

Reconstruction, became a planter, and was elected the first black U.S. senator as a member of the Republican Party. Alexander Crummell (1819–1898) was a black Episcopal clergyman and theologian. Denied admission to major American colleges, he was educated at Cambridge University in England. He became a missionary to Africa and lived in Liberia (1853–1871). When Crummell returned to America he became rector of St. Luke's Church in Washington, D.C., and helped found the American Negro Academy. Daniel Alexander Payne (1811–1893) was a black educator, founder of Wilberforce College in 1863, a prominent religious writer, and bishop of the AME Church. By "Reconstruction politicians," Du Bois refers generally to the nearly four hundred blacks who served in all levels of state government in the South, as well as in the U.S. Congress, during Reconstruction.

[20]The Revolution of 1876: See page 197, note 15.

[21]The term "silent suffrage" refers to the fact that most black leaders in the nineteenth century lacked elective sanction from their people because the vast majority of blacks could not vote.

[22]A "gospel of Work and Money" may refer to Andrew Carnegie's *Gospel of Wealth,* a book published in 1900 that celebrated business enterprise, laissez-faire individualism, moneymaking, and philanthropy.

[23]As a result of the Spanish-American War in 1898, the United States gained overseas possessions in Hawaii and the Philippines.

[24]Archibald H. Grimké (1849–1930) and his brother, Francis J. Grimké (1850–1937), were born slaves in South Carolina. They were the nephews of Sarah Grimké, one of the early female abolitionists. Archibald became a lawyer, a prominent writer, and the leader of the NAACP's Washington, D.C., branch. Francis became a prominent minister and was active in the affairs of Howard University in Washington, D.C. Kelly Miller (1863–1939) was born the son of a Confederate soldier and a slave mother. He became a mathematics and sociology professor at Howard University and a noted essayist on black history and sociology. John Wesley Edward Bowen (1855–1933) was a Methodist minister and educator. He received a Ph.D. in religion from Boston University in 1887 and taught at Gammon Theological Seminary in Atlanta, Georgia.

[25]This paragraph forms, perhaps, the heart of Du Bois's emerging attack on Washington's leadership; it addresses Washington's educational philosophy and the question of civil and political rights. It also anticipates some of Du Bois's other writings in the struggle against Washington, especially "The Parting of the Ways," *World Today* 6 (April 1904): 521–23, and "The Niagara Movement: Address to the Country," published as a pamphlet in 1906.

[26]"Thinking classes" refers to Du Bois's concept of the "Talented Tenth," the idea that an educated black elite (10 percent) ought to lead and provide an uplifting example for the masses of the race. Also see page 100. Possibly he first formally named this concept in "Of the Training of Black Men," *Atlantic Monthly* 90 (September 1902): 296, which he revised as chapter 6 of *Souls.*

[27]Here Du Bois states succinctly his sense that the nature of sectional reconciliation was at stake in the debates over Washington's leadership.

[28]Du Bois demonstrates that he does not believe in collective guilt, yet he believes that the nation as a whole should assume responsibility for the deeds of the past. His generosity toward the white South is especially interesting given the sour state of race relations in 1903.

[29]Charles Aycock (1859–1912) was governor of North Carolina (1901–1905) and an educational reformer. John Tyler Morgan (1824–1907) was a white supremacist U.S. senator from Alabama (1876–1907). Thomas Nelson Page (1853–1922) was a white southern novelist, essayist, and popular short story writer who did much to create the romanticized "plantation school" of American literature. Benjamin R. Tillman (1847–1919) was a populist orator, a virulent white supremacist governor of South Carolina (1890–1894), and a U.S. senator (1894–1918).

[30]Joshua was Moses' minister. After Moses' death God spoke directly to Joshua and called on him to lead the children of Israel over the River Jordan. See Joshua 1–3.

[31]The preamble of the Declaration of Independence, 1776.

IV. "Of the Meaning of Progress"

[1]The verse is Friedrich Schiller, "Die Jungfrau von Orleans" (The Maid of Orleans), 4.1: "If you want to announce your power / Select those, that free of sin / Live in your eternal house! / Send forth your spirits / The eternal ones, the pure—/ That do not feel, nor cry! / Not the tender maiden send / Nor the shepherdess of gentle soul" (translation courtesy of Karin B. H. Beckett). The music is a Negro spiritual, "My Way's Cloudy."

[2]Du Bois taught school in Alexandria, Tennessee, for two summers, in 1886 and 1887.

[3]In these passages Du Bois has become himself the New England "school ma'am" of Reconstruction lore, whom he celebrated in chapter 2.

[4]Sharecropping was the post–Civil War practice by which farmers paid for their tenancy with a "share" of their annual crop (usually one-half), either because they could not or they opted not to pay cash rent. This system became the primary mode of black agricultural labor and life in the South during the last third of the nineteenth century.

[5]Cicero's *pro Archia Poeta* is the Roman orator's speech justifying literature as a great art and the honor due the writer by society.

[6]According to the autobiography Du Bois wrote near the end of his life, he had his first sexual experience with Josie's mother. He wrote: "as teacher in the rural districts of East Tennessee, I was literally raped by the unhappy wife who was my landlady." See *The Autobiography of W. E. B. Du Bois: A Soliloquy on Viewing My Life from the Last Decade of Its First Century* (New York: International Publishers, 1968), 280. On this encounter also see Lewis, *Du Bois,* 71.

[7]A Jim Crow car was a train car designated for blacks only.

V. "Of the Wings of Atalanta"

[1]The verse is John Greenleaf Whittier, "Howard at Atlanta," stanza 6. General Oliver Otis Howard commanded one corps of Sherman's army that captured Atlanta in September 1864. The music is a Negro spiritual, "The Rocks and the Mountains."

[2]In remarkably lyrical prose, Du Bois refers to the destruction and revival of Atlanta, the "City of a Hundred Hills." The campaign and siege of Atlanta during the Civil War occurred May 1 to September 8, 1864. The city fell to General Sherman's Union army on September 1, one of the turning points in the war. Much of the city was burned.

[3]*Réclame:* public acclaim or showmanship.

[4]This passage could have been read by white southerners as a sympathetic characterization of the "Lost Cause." (See p. 199, n. 15).

[5]Lachesis was one of the Three Fates in Greek mythology, the disposer of lots, who assigned to each person his or her destiny and determined the length of the thread of life.

[6]Mercury was Jupiter's messenger, graceful and swift, with wings on his hat and sandals. He was the god of commerce and the market and was often seen as a shrewd thief; hence, perhaps, Du Bois's association of Mercury with New England. Mercury was the Roman equivalent of the Greek god Hermes.

[7]Boeotia was a province in Greece where the city of Thebes was located. It means "heifer's land."

[8]Atalanta was a beautiful maiden in Greek mythology, abandoned by her father on a mountainside because she was not a son. Atalanta was protected by animals, raised by hunters, and grew to be a great hunter and the swiftest runner. None could beat her in a footrace until she met Hippomenes, who distracted her during their race by rolling three magnificent golden apples in her path. Hippomenes's reward for his conquest was marriage to Atalanta.

[9]*Bourse:* in French, literally, a purse, but here it means a stock exchange or place of financial speculation.

[10]Third Estate: During the era of European feudalism, the first estate (or level of society) was the clergy, the second estate the nobility, and the third estate the common people.

[11]Pluto was the Greek god of the underworld and the giver of wealth that is derived from underground. Du Bois associates him with the North, the nation's major source of industrial wealth.

[12]Ceres (Roman equivalent for the Greek goddess Demeter) was the goddess of corn, grain, and the harvest. Du Bois associates her with the American West, the heartland and a granary.

[13]Apollo was the son of Zeus, the master musician who played the golden lyre on Mount Olympus. He was the archer-god, the arrows from whose bow could reach great distances, and the god of many noble virtues such as light, truth, healing, and divine guidance. Du Bois associates the demise of the knightly southern gentleman with Apollo.

[14]Venus (the Roman equivalent of the Greek goddess Aphrodite) was goddess of love and beauty who beguiled all, gods and men alike.

[15]*Parvenu* is one who has recently attained a position of wealth or power but lacks the prestige, dignity, or manner appropriate to it.

[16]"Cracker" is a derogatory, slang term for a poor white southerner.

[17]Mammonism is the pursuit of material goods and wealth with a debasing influence.

[18]Dido, a figure of Roman mythology, was the founder and queen of Carthage on the northern coast of Africa. Aeneas, son of Venus, landed lost and shipwrecked on the shores of Carthage after fleeing Troy ("Troy divine") in the wake of the Trojans' defeat. Through the conniving of the gods, Dido and Aeneas fell in love, but Aeneas was called by Jupiter to his destiny in Italy. Dido cursed the Trojans and committed suicide after Aeneas departed.

[19]Pharaohs were the monarchs of ancient Egypt. Plato (427–347 B.C.) was a Greek philosopher, the most brilliant student of Socrates, and the founder of a school of philosophy (his Academy) in 386 B.C. in an olive grove in Athens. *Trivium* and *quadrivium* refer to the method of dividing academic disciplines in medieval universities. Of the seven liberal arts, the *trivium* was the lower three: grammar, logic, and rhetoric. The *quadrivium* was the upper four: arithmetic, music, geometry, and astronomy.

[20]Du Bois refers to four major universities: Oxford in England, Leipzig in eastern Germany, and Yale and Columbia in the United States.

[21]Parnassus is a high mountain in Greece near Delphi. Delphi was a place sacred to Apollo and the Muses, and the site of the oracle of Apollo.

[22]Johann Wolfgang von Goethe, *Faust,* line 1549. "Renounce shalt thou, thou shalt renounce." In this section Faust laments life's limitations. Renunciation, he says, is life's "everlasting song."

[23]Academus was Plato's school of philosophy, founded in Athens in 386 B.C., the ancient root of Western universities. Cambridge University is a prestigious university in England.

[24]The sixth, seventh, and eighth commandments: "thou shalt not kill . . . commit adultery . . . or steal." See Deuteronomy 5.17–19.

[25]In Greek mythology the Hesperides were the daughters of Atlas and Hesperis; they guarded the golden apples presented by Gaea, the earth goddess, to Hera. The Boeotian lovers are Atalanta and Hippomenes (see note 8).

[26]These are all prominent southern universities. Trinity, in Durham, North Carolina, later became Duke University.

VI. *"Of the Training of Black Men"*

[1]The verse is "The Rubaiyat of Omar Khayyam," stanza 44, translated by Edward Fitzgerald. The music is a Negro spiritual, "March On."

[2]Jamestown was the first permanent English settlement in North America, founded in 1607. The first slave ship arrived at Jamestown in 1619.

[3]*Tertium quid:* Latin for a "third something," an intermediate component.

[4]*Dilettante:* a person with a superficial interest in the arts or knowledge.

[5]*Zeitgeist:* German for the moral, intellectual, and cultural spirit of an era.

[6]Samuel Johnson (1709–1784), English poet, essayist, and lexicographer, most famous for his *Dictionary of the English Language* and *Lives of the Poets.*

[7]Harvard University, in Cambridge, Massachusetts, founded in 1630, is America's oldest institution of higher learning.

[8]The "missionaries of '68" were the northern teachers in the freedmen's schools during the early years of Reconstruction.

⁹Tuskegee Institute, founded by Booker T. Washington. See page 201, note 5.

¹⁰Fisk University was founded in 1866 in Nashville, Tennessee. Hampton Institute was founded as a school for freedmen in 1868 by Samuel Armstrong, Civil War general, commander of black troops, and eventual mentor to Booker T. Washington. Spelman Seminary, now College, founded in 1881 by two New England women, Sophia Packard and Harriet Giles, was the first college in America for black women.

¹¹*a priori:* without regard for empirical experience or evidence. Du Bois suggests that most Americans' reasoning about the Negro is based on racial prejudice, not on a careful appraisal of available evidence.

¹²Atlanta University was founded in 1865, Howard in 1867. Wilberforce University in Ohio was founded in 1856 by the African Methodist Episcopal Church and named for the famous British abolitionist William Wilberforce. Lincoln University, in Oxford, Pennsylvania, was founded in 1854 by the American Colonization Society and devoted to classical education for blacks. It was the first college founded in America for blacks. Biddle University, in Charlotte, North Carolina, was founded in 1867 by the Presbyterian Church as a school for the religious education of black men. It was named for its original benefactor, Mary Biddle, and its name was changed in 1921 to Johnson C. Smith University. Shaw University, in Raleigh, North Carolina, was founded in 1865 by Baptists, one of the first medical schools for blacks.

¹³The "crusade of the sixties" is Du Bois's description of the missionary spirit of the teachers in the freedmen's schools and of those workers in the Freedmen's Bureau who sought to secure black civil and political rights between 1865 and 1869.

¹⁴Du Bois's celebration of the efforts of New England schoolteachers and the founders of black colleges reflects his own autobiographical attachments to the "best traditions of New England." See his first formal autobiography, *Dusk of Dawn: An Essay toward an Autobiography of a Race Concept* (New York: Harcourt, Brace, 1940), chaps. 2 and 3.

¹⁵William Torrey Harris, U.S. commissioner of education (1889–1906). He had been superintendent of the St. Louis, Missouri, school system (1867–1880).

¹⁶Oberlin College, founded in Oberlin, Ohio, in 1833, was a pioneer as the first college to institute coeducation, one of the first to admit black students, and a prominent abolitionist institution.

¹⁷Du Bois refers here to the fifth Atlanta University conference, "The College-Bred Negro" (1900). Such conferences resulted in his numerous Atlanta University Studies, conducted as sociological surveys. For the 1900 conference, nearly half of the 2,600 living men and women graduates of black colleges responded to questionnaires about the nature of their education and their lives. The results were a stunning revelation to Americans who noticed. In February 1901, Du Bois testified in Washington, D.C., before the U.S. Industrial Commission, at least one member of which was astonished to learn that "Colored men" had college degrees. In June 1898, Du Bois delivered a commencement address at Fisk University entitled "Careers Open to College-Bred Negroes." See Lewis, *Du Bois,* 221.

¹⁸*gaucherie:* French for lack of social grace and experience.

¹⁹Talented Tenth: See page 204, note 26.

²⁰Rhine-gold: in German mythology, stashes of gold watched over by Rhine river valley maidens and later possessed by the Nibelungen, a race of dwarfs, and Siegfried, a Scandinavian prince. Du Bois may also be alluding to *Das Rheingold,* the first part of Richard Wagner's four-part opera, *Der Ring des Nibelungen* (The Ring of the Nibelung), first performed in Munich in September 1869.

²¹William Shakespeare (1564–1616), Elizabethan poet and playwright. Honoré de Balzac (1799–1850), French novelist. Alexandre Dumas (1802–1870), French dramatist and novelist of mixed racial ancestry. Aristotle (384–322), Greek philosopher. Marcus Aurelius (121–180), Stoic philosopher and Roman emperor from 161 to 180. Pisgah: a mountain looking east from the Jordan River, from which Moses viewed the Promised Land. Philistine: southeastern Palestine, the region of an ancient, warlike tribe. Amalekite: member of a nomadic tribe hostile to the Israelites in their journey over Jordan to the Promised Land in the Old Testament.

VII. "Of the Black Belt"

[1]The verse is Song of Solomon 1.5–6. The music is a Negro spiritual, "Bright Sparkles in the Churchyard."

[2]Hernando de Soto (1500?–1542), Spanish explorer and conquistador. In 1539–1542, he journeyed through southeastern North America in search of gold.

[3]Cherokees are the American Indian tribe whose ancestral lands were in western North Carolina and northern Georgia.

[4]Sam Hose was a farmworker from Palmetto, Georgia, a few miles from Atlanta. In April 1899 he was accused of murdering his employer in a dispute over wages. He escaped and while at large was accused of raping the employer's wife. After capture, he confessed to the murder but not the rape. A white mob of two thousand men, women, and children lynched and burned Hose, taking "souvenirs" of the body and the tree. Hose's knuckles were put on display in a store window in Atlanta. This event, followed in May by the death of his son Burghardt from diphtheria, shocked and depressed Du Bois.

[5]James Edward Oglethorpe (1696–1785), English philanthropist and founder of the colony of Georgia.

[6]George Whitefield (1714–1770), English evangelist and revivalist preacher, toured Georgia in 1738, advocating a lifting of restrictions on the slave trade; he favored lenient treatment of slaves while defending the institution of slavery.

[7]The Delegal riots occurred in Darien, Georgia, on August 23, 1899. Hundreds of blacks who had heard rumors of a lynching assembled and blocked the removal of a prisoner from the jail. Many were tried for insurrection, and twenty-one were sentenced to convict farms for a year. Scotch Highlanders, immigrants from Scotland, settled in Georgia at the end of the eighteenth century. Antislavery Moravians settled in Ebenezer (1734) and New Ebenezer (1736), near Savannah.

[8]Toussaint L'Ouverture; see page 198, note 18. The national statute of 1808 is the act of Congress, March 2, 1807, prohibiting the importation of slaves into the United States after January 1, 1808.

[9]Jim Crow Car: See page 205, note 7 (chapter 4).

[10]The Creeks are an American Indian tribe whose ancestral lands were in Georgia, Alabama, and part of Florida.

[11]The term "Black Belt" came into use especially after the Civil War to designate portions of the South where the black population was most numerous and where, during slavery, the slave population was most dense. The region includes the states of the Deep South—South Carolina, Georgia, Alabama, Mississippi, and southern Louisiana. The term has also been used to describe the region of fertile black soil in those same states. In his *Up from Slavery* (1901), Booker T. Washington defined "Black Belt": "So far as I can learn, the term was first used to designate a part of the country which was distinguished by the colour of the soil. The part of the country possessing this thick, dark, and naturally rich soil was, of course, the part of the South where the slaves were most profitable, and, consequently, where they were taken in the largest numbers. Later, and especially since the war, the term seems to be used wholly in a political sense—that is, to designate the counties where the black people outnumber the white" (Booker T. Washington, *Up from Slavery* [1901; reprint, New York: Oxford University Press, 1995], 63). Du Bois uses "Black Belt" in what Washington called the "political sense."

[12]Creek Indians massacred white settlers at Fort Mims, Alabama, August 30, 1813. Andrew Jackson (1767–1845), born in Tennessee, was president of the United States (1829–1839). As a major general of the militia, he led U.S. troops against the Creek Indians in 1813–1814 during the War of 1812.

[13]The panic of 1837 was an economic depression that began with a wave of bank failures in May 1837. The economic crisis lasted in the South for seven years; hence Du Bois's notion that President Andrew Jackson "bequeathed" it to his successor, Martin Van Buren.

[14]The term "Cotton Kingdom" was used at least as early as the 1850s to describe the supremacy of cotton production in southern agriculture as well as the wealth and political power that white Southerners derived from a monopoly on world cotton production in the

mid-nineteenth century. Use of this term persisted into the late nineteenth and early twentieth centuries as a regional designation for the Deep South.

[15]The Rhinepfalz is a region along the Rhine River in southwestern Germany. Naples is a city on the western coast of Italy, south of Rome. Cracow (Krakow) is a city in Poland.

[16]"The Wizard of the North—the Capitalist—" may be a reference to the *Wizard of Oz*, an allegory about the populist movement of the 1890s. Those who had allegedly "rushed down in the seventies" are the carpetbaggers of Reconstruction lore, northerners who relocated in the South after the Civil War.

[17]Egypt of the Confederacy: Du Bois's use of the biblical "Egypt" reflects his sense that the Old South had been a place of bondage for blacks and that the "Black Belt" of the turn of the century was still a place of enduring bondage and exploitation.

[18]Osceola (1800–1838) was a Seminole Indian chief who was part black. He was born in Georgia, welcomed numerous fugitive slaves into his people in Florida, and led them against U.S. forces in the Seminole War of 1835.

[19]*nouveau riche:* French for newly rich.

[20]"The Jew is the heir" is changed to "Immigrants are heirs" in the 1953 edition. This reference to Jews, and several to follow, were eventually the subject of objection and some controversy. Probably in 1905, Jacob Schiff and Rabbi Stephen S. Wise raised questions about Du Bois's use of "Jews" in ways that implied anti-Semitism. Du Bois had written to Schiff seeking funding for a new black periodical. In the ninth edition, published in December 1911, Du Bois made only one change in the original text: "a Yankee or a Jew" became "a Yankee and his like" (p. 113 in this edition). Through all the succeeding editions of *Souls*, Du Bois made no changes until the fiftieth-anniversary edition in 1953. In February 1953, Du Bois wrote to his close friend, and soon to be editor of his papers, Herbert Aptheker, indicating that he wanted the several references to Jews changed in the new edition. "As I re-read these words today," Du Bois said, "I see that . . . harm might come if they were allowed to stand as they are. First of all, I am not at all sure that the foreign exploiters to whom I referred in my study of the Black Belt, were in fact Jews. I took the word of my informants, and I am now wondering if in fact Russian Jews in any number were in Georgia at the time. But even if they were, what I was condemning was the exploitation and not the race nor religion. And I did not, when writing, realize that by stressing the name of the group instead of what some members of the group may have done, I was unjustly maligning a people in exactly the same way my folk were then and are now falsely accused" (Du Bois to Herbert Aptheker, Seattle, Washington, February 27, 1953, W. E. B. Du Bois Papers, Box 360; reprinted on p. 265 in this volume).

In a memorandum in June 1953, to Howard Fast, who presided over the publication of the fiftieth-anniversary edition at the Blue Heron Press, Du Bois reflected on the essays in *Souls*. "They outline a phase of my spiritual development," he said. "My social and economic philosophy was then as I now see it immature, and my outlook on race provincial." Du Bois said that he had not changed the passages about Jews because he "had no conscious desire to malign Jews." He left the words to stand because he "did not realize until the horrible massacre of German Jews, how even unconscious repetition of current folklore such as the concept of Jews as more guilty of exploitation than others, had helped the Hitlers of the world." At that point (June 1953), Du Bois had resolved to let the language stand as in the original, "believing that other references to Jews in this very book and my evident personal indebtedness to Jewish culture will absolve me from blame of unfairness." At the very least, he concluded, "the case but illustrates how easy it is, especially in race relations, inadvertently to give a totally wrong impression." See memo, Du Bois "To Howard Fast, for repub. of *Souls of Black Folk,*" New York, June 1953, Du Bois Papers, reel 69. The memo contains a penciled note, "not used," suggesting that Du Bois never sent it to Fast.

Later that summer, Du Bois changed his mind and made eight emendations regarding his use of the term "Jew." Each is indicated in our notes. Moreover, Du Bois wrote an extraordinary memorandum to the Blue Heron Press, dated March 16, 1953 (Du Bois Papers, reel 69), indicating that the following be added to the end of chapter 7:

In the foregoing chapter, "Jews" have been mentioned five times, and the late Jacob Schiff once complained that this gave an impression of anti-Semitism. This at the time I stoutly denied; but as I read the passages again in the light of subsequent history, I see how I laid myself open to this possible misapprehension. What, of course, I meant to condemn was exploitation of black labor and that it was in this county and at that time in part a matter of immigrant Jews, was incidental and not essential. My inner sympathy with the Jewish people was expressed better in the last paragraph of page 227 [the final paragraph of chapter 12, "Of Alexander Crummell"]. But this illustrates how easily one slips into unconscious condemnation of a whole group.

This addition, however, for reasons unknown, was not included in the 1953 edition. Du Bois seems to have experienced some confusion and indecision in evaluating his use of "Jews" in the original edition. He clearly regretted it and amended the language. Perhaps he was struggling to maintain the original literary integrity of the text; perhaps he was also embarrassed to be confronting at age eighty-five his relatively youthful uses of language. Undoubtedly, in the post-Holocaust world of 1953, any reference to Jews read very differently than it would have in 1903. What is clear is that Du Bois's thinking and writing about Jews in 1903 reflected a larger turn-of-the-century anti-Semitic discourse which he had learned or absorbed as a part of his nineteenth-century education. On Du Bois's revisions, see Herbert Aptheker, *The Literary Legacy of W. E. B. Du Bois* (White Plains, N.Y.: Kraus International, 1989), 78–83; and *The Souls of Black Folk,* ed. Henry Louis Gates, Jr. (1903; reprint, New York: Bantam, 1989), xxvi–xxix. On nineteenth-century anti-Semitism, see George L. Mosse, *Toward the Final Solution: A History of European Racism* (Madison: University of Wisconsin Press, 1985); and Zygmunt Bauman, *Modernity and the Holocaust* (Ithaca: Cornell University Press, 1989).

[21]The Land of Canaan is the Promised Land of the Old Testament. See Exodus 6.1–5. For one of the fullest expressions of the promise of the new land of Canaan, see Deuteronomy 11.5–32. Du Bois suggests the same promise for the "beautiful land" of Dougherty County. Also see page 197, note 9.

[22]"Nearly all failed, and the Jew fell heir" is changed to "most failed, and foreigners fell heir" in the 1953 edition.

[23]"Russian Jew" is changed to "foreigner" in the 1953 edition.

[24]"A Yankee or a Jew" is changed to "A Yankee or an immigrant" in the 1953 edition.

[25]"A revolution such as that of '63" refers to emancipation.

[26]"Nephews and the poor whites and the Jews" is changed to "poor relations and foreign immigrants" in the 1953 edition.

[27]Du Bois kept this reference to Jews in the 1953 edition. Why he chose not to change it is not clear.

VIII. *"Of the Quest of the Golden Fleece"*

[1]The verse is William Vaughn Moody, "The Brute." The music is a Negro spiritual, "Children You'll Be Called On."

[2]Here Du Bois recalls the Greek myth of Jason, who in his ship the *Argo* and in the company of his Argonauts traveled to the land of Aeetes in search of a golden fleece. To win the fleece, Jason was required to yoke two brazen-footed, fire-breathing bulls; to plow the field of Ares and sow it with dragon's teeth; to defeat the armed men who sprang from these teeth; and to conquer the sleepless dragon that guarded the tree on which the fleece had been suspended. Jason accomplished these deeds with the help of the "witchery" of Medea, Aeetes' daughter, whom he later married.

[3]*Parvenu:* See page 206, note 15.

[4]*Régime:* a system of rule or management.

[5]Throughout this chapter Du Bois addresses the conflict between "master and man." In chapter 9, he directs his attention to the social and political legacies of this conflict.

[6]On a slave plantation, the Big House was the house in which the master and his family resided.

[7] In this chapter and the next, Du Bois compares southern blacks and Russian peasants and makes interesting use of the term "serfdom." The Russian serfs were emancipated in 1861, while American slaves were emancipated in 1863–1865. For a comparative history of slavery and serfdom, see Peter Kolchin, *Unfree Labor: American Slavery and Russian Serfdom* (Cambridge: Harvard University Press, 1987). For a comparative literary perspective on Du Bois and the Russian writer Fyodor Dostoevsky, see Dale E. Peterson, "Notes from the Underworld: Dostoevsky, Du Bois, and the Discovery of Ethnic Soul," *Massachusetts Review* 35 (Summer 1994): 225–49.

[8] In using the phrase *leisure class,* Du Bois may be presupposing his readers' familiarity with Thorstein Veblen's economics classic of 1899, *The Theory of the Leisure Class.* Although he does not mention Veblen by name, Du Bois uses terms ("making homes," "learning of the world") that echo Veblen's characterization of leisure. For a discussion of some affinities between Du Bois's and Veblen's conceptions of sociological inquiry, see Shamoon Zamir, *Dark Voices: W. E. B. Du Bois and American Thought, 1888–1903* (Chicago: University of Chicago Press, 1995).

[9] For a brief description of the sharecropping system, which Du Bois here calls "cropping" and elsewhere "crop-mortgage," see page 205, note 4 (chapter 4).

[10] *Metayer:* another word for sharecropper.

[11] For brief accounts of Reconstruction, the Spanish-American War, and U.S. involvement in the Philippines, see page 198, note 3, and page 204, note 23. Nineteenth-century writers who discussed the death of God include Heinrich Heine, G. W. F. Hegel, and, most famously, Friedrich Nietzsche. The first occurrence of the phrase *"Gott ist todt"* (God is dead) in Nietzsche's books is in the *Die Fröhliche Wissenschaft* (The Gay Science), published in 1882.

[12] The name Sambo was used in the American South to refer to African Americans; it is often associated with the racist idea that African Americans are lazy, irresponsible, and prone to infantile behavior.

[13] The Thirteenth Amendment (1865) to the Constitution abolished slavery.

[14] Migration-agent laws are state restrictions on labor agents' ability to entice workers to move from one state to another. Such laws were part of a structure designed to keep black laborers confined to rural, agricultural districts.

[15] Peonage was a practice in which black debtors could be forced to sign labor contracts, held in stockades, and hunted if they escaped. Revelations of widespread practices like peonage emerged from the South in 1903.

[16] Sam Hose: See page 208, note 4.

[17] Aunt Ophelia is an allusion to the character of the same name, sometimes called Miss Ophelia, in Harriet Beecher Stowe's classic novel *Uncle Tom's Cabin* (1852). Aunt Ophelia is a Vermont-born abolitionist who nevertheless has many racial prejudices about blacks to overcome during the course of the novel.

[18] Rack rent is an excessive or unreasonably high rent, or a rent equal (or nearly equal) to the full value of the land.

[19] Arthur Young published *Travels in France during the Years 1787, 1788 and 1789* in 1792. For the second passage which Du Bois cites from this extended and vivid portrait of France just before the Revolution, see *Travels in France during the Years 1787, 1788 and 1789,* ed. Constantia Maxwell (Cambridge: Cambridge University Press, 1950), 297. We have not been able to locate the source of the first passage.

[20] The panic of 1893 was an economic depression that hit the United States in May and June 1893, when the New York Stock Exchange crashed and the U.S. gold reserve collapsed. The collapse led to widespread economic distress, unemployment, and plummeting agricultural prices throughout most of the 1890s.

IX. "Of the Sons of Master and Man"

[1] The verse is Elizabeth Barrett Browning, "A Vision of Poets," lines 820–22. The music is a Negro spiritual, "I'm a Rolling."

[2]"Survival of the fittest" was a favorite catchphrase of a group of nineteenth-century sociological theories known as "social Darwinism." Misappropriating language from Charles Darwin's *On the Origin of Species* (1859), social Darwinists held that human beings, no less than plants and animals, compete for survival and for social success. According to the social Darwinists, individuals who became rich and powerful were the "fittest"; individuals who fell into the lower socioeconomic classes were said to be the least fit. See Richard Hofstadter, *Social Darwinism in American Thought* (1944; reprint, Boston: Beacon Press, 1955).

[3]*Tertium quid:* See page 206, note 3.

[4]Sympathy is a recurrent and central theme in chapter 9. For an account of the connections between Du Bois's notion of sympathy and discussions of sympathy in the writings of Adam Smith, William James, and Franz Boas, see Zamir, *Dark Voices.* For an analysis of the role the concept of sympathy plays in this chapter, as well as elsewhere in *Souls,* see Gooding-Williams, "Du Bois's Counter-Sublime, *Massachusetts Review* 35 (Spring-Summer 1994): 203–6."

[5]*Régime:* See page 210, note 4.

[6]Thomas Carlyle (1795–1881) was a Scottish essayist and historian. As a social critic, he commented on the dangers of industrialization, the harsh living conditions of British workers, and the vices of democracy. Carlyle's best-known books include *Sartor Resartus* (1833–1834) and *On Heroes, Hero Worship, and the Heroic in History* (1841). See Zamir, *Dark Voices,* for an account of the young Du Bois's admiration for Carlyle.

[7]"Shrewd and unscrupulous Jews" is changed to "and unscrupulous immigrants" in the 1953 edition.

[8]"The enterprising Russian Jew" is changed to "the enterprising American" in the 1953 edition.

[9]In this paragraph, Du Bois echoes Matthew Arnold's discussion of "great men of culture" in *Culture and Anarchy* (1869). "The great men of culture," wrote Arnold, an English poet and critic, "are those who have had a passion for diffusing, for making prevail, for carrying from one end of society to the other, the best knowledge, the best ideas of their time; who have laboured to make . . . [knowledge] . . . a true source . . . of sweetness and light." Du Bois again echoes Arnold in the final paragraph of "The Development of a People" (reprinted on p. 238 in this volume), when he argues that "the college of to-day stands for the transmission from age to age of all that is best in the world's deeds, thoughts and traditions" (p. 254). For a discussion of the affinities between Du Bois's and Arnold's concepts of culture, see Houston A. Baker Jr., "The Black Man of Culture: W. E. B. Du Bois and *The Souls of Black Folk,"* in *Long Black Song: Essays in Black American Literature and Culture* (Charlottesville: University of Virginia Press, 1972).

[10]"The greatest good to the greatest number" is a catchphrase of nineteenth-century utilitarianism. Here, as in chapter 1, Du Bois adduces a standard utilitarian argument for democracy (see p. 198, note 20).

[11]Du Bois refers in this sentence to the consequences of the Emancipation Proclamation, which took effect on January 1, 1863.

[12]*ipso facto:* Latin for "by the very fact."

[13]storm and stress: See page 198, note 19.

[14]Phillis Wheatley and Sam Hose: See page 202, note 12, and page 208, note 4.

[15]Alfred, Lord Tennyson, *In Memoriam,* lines 27–28.

X. *"Of the Faith of the Fathers"*

[1]The verse is by Fiona Macleod (pen name for William Sharp), "Dim Face of Beauty." The music is a Negro spiritual, "Steal Away Home." The tradition is that the song evolved among American slaves who, resisting the sermons and services of white preachers who exhorted them to be obedient to their masters, retreated to their quarters or to the seclusion of brush arbors ("hush harbors") and conducted their own forms of worship. See Albert J. Raboteau, *Slave Religion: The "Invisible Institution" in the Antebellum South* (New York: Oxford University Press, 1978), 212–19, 359 n 1.

[2]Berkshire is the county in western Massachusetts where Du Bois was born and raised.

Suffolk is a county in England. Du Bois refers here to the stiffness of the Congregationalism he experienced growing up in Great Barrington. The first southern Negro revival he witnessed was in Wilson County, Tennessee (see chap. 4).

[3]Du Bois overestimates neither the uniqueness nor the significance of the slave preacher in the development of African American Christianity. On the origins and multiple roles of the slave preacher, see Raboteau, *Slave Religion,* 231–39. Du Bois helped pioneer the study of the black church, in both its pre- and its post-emancipation forms. The Negro church was the subject of a major conference, and of the eighth Atlanta University Study, published in the same year as *Souls.* See W. E. B. Du Bois, ed., *The Negro Church* (Atlanta: Atlanta University Press, 1903). That volume includes analyses of the African origins of black religion in America as well as comprehensive statistical treatments of every denomination of black churches. On early preachers, see 30–37. "Of the Faith of the Fathers" was originally published in *The New World: A Quarterly Review of Religion, Ethics and Theology* 9 (December 1900): 614–25, and was therefore a forerunner of *The Negro Church.*

[4]"Frenzy" is Du Bois's word for the religious tradition of spirit possession. On the nature and development of spirit possession in both West African cosmology and worship practice, as well as in African American slave religion, see Raboteau, *Slave Religion,* 10–11, 63–73. "Shouting" refers to a religious dance form of clearly African origin that survived among American slaves. This dance form was known as the "ring shout." Often conducted outdoors, the ring shout was a group dance, a circular movement, in which ecstatic religious behavior (spirit possession) was encouraged. On the extended significance of the ring shout in African American culture, see Sterling Stuckey, *Slave Culture: Nationalist Theory and the Foundations of Black America* (New York: Oxford University Press, 1987), 11–97.

[5]Delphi is the shrine of Apollo on Mount Parnassus in ancient Greece. Endor was the spirit woman (witch) who, at the request of King Saul, summoned the ghost of the prophet Samuel, who in turn foretold the defeat of the Israelites at the hands of the Philistines. Endor cooked a meal for the doomed Saul and his servants. 1 Samuel 28.3–25.

[6]Heathenism is that which is judged to be a strange or uncivilized religious belief or practice. Du Bois here may simply mean non-Christian. In characterizing West African religion as heathen, Du Bois joins a larger Western discourse about the character of non-Western religious traditions.

[7]"Gospel" hymns were a musical form that evolved from the Protestant urban revival movement of the 1850s. Typically, gospel songs exhibited greater stylistic complexity than the older spirituals. Here Du Bois seems to be using the phrase "Jubilee songs" as a general description of black sacred and folk music.

[8]Mother Bethel African Methodist Episcopal Church in Philadelphia was the first urban, denominational black church in America, founded in 1794. See below, note 12.

[9]Polygamy is the practice of men having two or more wives. Polyandry is the practice of women having two or more husbands.

[10]A bard is a folk or tribal poet-singer who recites the epic tales and sings the heroic songs of his or her people. One scholar of *Souls* has suggested that this entire text might be seen as Du Bois's own performance as the bard of African American culture in the early twentieth century. See Sundquist, *To Wake the Nations,* 525–39.

[11]Voodooism was an organized cult of religious practices and a system of magic with clear African origins. In the New World, voodoo took root especially in Haiti, where it was called *vaudau,* and merged African spirit traditions and Catholicism. In Haiti, followers of *vaudau* stress devotion to land, to family, and to spirits that are worshiped in elaborate ceremonies that may include singing, dancing, and drumming. Voodoo took root in the American South, especially in New Orleans. Sometimes called "Hoodoo" or "conjure" in North America, it became a system of magic, divination, herbalism, and the use of signs. Spirit possession is the key African element that survived in voodoo's many forms. On voodoo, see Raboteau, *Slave Religion,* 25–27, 75–80.

[12]The African Methodist Episcopal Church (AME) was founded in Philadelphia by Richard Allen, a former slave and itinerant Methodist preacher, in 1787. Allen and other blacks first formed the Free African Society of Philadelphia to achieve autonomy in their

religious lives, rejected the segregation and racism of the traditional Methodist Church, and then built Mother Bethel African Methodist Episcopal Church in 1794. Allen was elected the AME's first bishop in 1816. By 1864, the AME had 50,000 members in 1,600 congregations, mostly in the North. By 1880, those numbers had swelled to 387,566 and 2,051, with many new congregations founded in the South during Reconstruction. From 1890 to 1916, the AME grew from 494,777 to 548,355 members, and from 2,481 to 6,636 congregations.

The African Methodist Episcopal Zion Church (AMEZ) emerged as an offshoot of the AME in the 1820s. AMEZ preachers and members were inspired by a somewhat more activist and evangelical purpose than the larger AME. By 1896 the AMEZ church numbered 350,000 members.

The Colored Methodist Episcopal Church (CME) was founded in 1870 in Jackson, Tennessee, by former slaves who had been members of the Methodist Episcopal Church in the South and broke away from the church of their former masters. The CME eventually founded some twenty-one schools and four colleges in the South.

[13]Obi was a religious practice or a form of sorcery of African origin. It took root in Jamaica, where it is known as *obeah*. According to early observations of slave practices in Jamaica, *"obeah* men" used magic for evil purposes on other people. *Obeah* was important among Jamaican slaves because it supported rebellion, provided protection against thieves, and assisted in the detection of guilt. See Raboteau, *Slave Religion,* 33–34. Du Bois uses the term "obi" as a broad generalization. See his discussion of *obeah* in *The Negro Church,* 5–6.

[14]From the Negro spiritual "Children, We All Shall Be Free."

[15]Uncle Tom is the title character in Harriet Beecher Stowe's *Uncle Tom's Cabin* (1852).

[16]From the Negro spiritual "O Freedom."

[17]Jesuitic casuistry: A Jesuit is a member of a Roman Catholic religious order, the Society of Jesus; casuistry is the resolution of moral issues through the interpretation of ethical principles or religious doctrine. This disparaging use of the expression implies a person who is equivocating, unethical, and crafty.

[18]Denmark Vesey and Nat Turner: See page 202, note 13.

[19]"The Jews" is changed to "peasants" in the 1953 edition.

[20]*Dum vivimus, vivamus:* Latin for "While we live, let us live."

[21]"Valley of the Shadow of Death" is from Psalms 23.4: "Yea, though I walk through the valley of the shadow of death, I will fear no evil: for thou art with me; thy rod and thy staff they comfort me." Also see Isaiah 9.2 and Jeremiah 2.6.

XI. *"Of the Passing of the First-Born"*

[1]The verse is Algernon C. Swinburne, "Itylus," final stanza. The music is a Negro spiritual, "I Hope My Mother Will Be There."

[2]Du Bois's "Unto you a child is born" echoes Isaiah 9.6: "For unto us a child is born, unto us a son is given: and the government shall be upon his shoulder: and his name shall be called Wonderful, Counsellor, The mighty God, the everlasting Father, The Prince of Peace." While teaching at Wilberforce College, Du Bois met Nina Gomer, a student at Wilberforce. They were married May 12, 1896, in Cedar Rapids, Iowa, Nina's hometown. On October 2, 1897, their son Burghardt Gomer Du Bois was born in Great Barrington, Massachusetts, where Nina had gone to give birth. Burghardt died of diphtheria in Atlanta on May 24, 1899, four months short of his second birthday. This chapter is Du Bois's elegy to his son.

[3]The Shadow of Death: See page 214, note 21.

[4]In these lines, argues Arnold Rampersad, "doubt completely infects [Du Bois's] vision of his son's future." According to Rampersad, "Of the Passing of the First-Born" is a bitter parody of the traditional Christian elegy (such as Milton's *Lycidas*) in which the central mourner, a black man, can find no consolation. See Arnold Rampersad, "Slavery and the Literary Imagination: Du Bois's *The Souls of Black Folk,"* in *Slavery and the Literary Imagination: Selected Papers from the English Institute, 1987,* ed. Deborah E. McDowell and Arnold Rampersad (Baltimore: Johns Hopkins University Press, 1989).

[5]"Darkly, through the Veil": See page 198, note 16.

6. *"Thou shalt forego"*: Du Bois's translation of Goethe's "sollst entbehren," which can also be translated "Thou shalt renounce." See page 206, note 22.

XII. *"Of Alexander Crummell"*

[1]The verse is Alfred, Lord Tennyson, "The Passing of Arthur," lines 457–61. The music is a Negro spiritual, "Swing Low, Sweet Chariot."

[2]For a brief description of Crummell's career, see page 203, note 19. For a comprehensive biographical treatment of Crummell's life, on which we have relied for most of these notes, see Wilson Jeremiah Moses, *Alexander Crummell: A Study of Civilization and Its Discontents* (New York: Oxford University Press, 1989). In this first paragraph, Du Bois tacitly refers to John Bunyan's classic allegory *The Pilgrim's Progress*, which was published in 1678 and 1684. Echoing Bunyan's depiction of the life and journey of Christian, Bunyan's protagonist, Du Bois represents Crummell's career as fraught with temptations (specifically, hate, despair, and doubt) and as leading Crummell, like Christian, into a "Valley of Humiliation" and a "Valley of the Shadow of Death" (also see p. 214, note 21). Du Bois's allusions to *The Pilgrim's Progress* are significant, for they suggest that his "history of a human heart" is the history of the heart of a Protestant pilgrim. For further discussion of the significance of these allusions, see Stanley Brodwin, "The Veil Transcended: Form and Meaning in W. E. B. Du Bois' *The Souls of Black Folk*," *Journal of Black Studies* (March 1972): 313, and Gooding-Williams, "Du Bois's Counter-Sublime," 203–6.

[3]After a bitter debate from December 1819 to March 1820, the U.S. Congress passed the Missouri Compromise, which admitted Missouri to the Union as a slave state and Maine as a free state and excluded slavery from all the lands of the Louisiana Purchase north of 36°30′ (except for Missouri). Manila (in the Philippines) and El Caney (in Cuba) were Spanish-American War battles in 1898.

[4]Boston Crummell, Alexander Crummell's father and an oysterman, is said to have been descended from Temne chiefs in West Africa in what is now Sierra Leone. Alexander Crummell believed that his father had been kidnapped into slavery when a child of about twelve or thirteen years of age. According to one account, the senior Crummell arrived in the United States at the age of thirteen and was brought up in the Episcopal Church. Alexander Crummell's mother, Charity Hicks, was a free-born black woman born in Jericho, Long Island. She accompanied her son to Liberia in November 1865.

[5]Beriah Green founded the Oneida Institute in Whitesboro, New York. Crummell became a member of the sophomore class at Oneida in February 1836.

[6]With his two childhood friends Henry Highland Garnet and Thomas S. Sidney, Crummell enrolled in 1835 in the Noyes Academy (a school founded by abolitionists and open to students of both races) in Canaan, New Hampshire. On August 10, 1835, a mob hostile to the presence of blacks at Noyes and to the abolitionist activities of Noyes students hitched the academy building to ninety yoke of oxen and hauled it off into a swamp. Shortly thereafter, Crummell, Garnet, and Sidney quit New Hampshire and returned to New York.

[7]In this paragraph and in the preceding one, Du Bois seems to be describing the experience of religious conversion that Crummell underwent while attending the Oneida Institute. The figure of "stretched forth hands" echoes Psalms 68.31: "Princes shall come out of Egypt; Ethiopia shall soon stretch out her hand to God." As Wilson Moses has shown, Ethiopianism (the idea that black people are destined to create a glorious civilization in Africa or elsewhere) is a recurrent motif in African American politics and letters. See Wilson Jeremiah Moses, *The Wings of Ethiopia* (Ames: Iowa State University Press, 1990).

[8]Here Du Bois refers to an incident of 1838 in which Benjamin T. Onderdonk, the Episcopal bishop of New York, denied Crummell admission to the Episcopal Church's General Theological Seminary. For a detailed account of this incident, see Moses, *Alexander Crummell*, 22–30.

[9]John Jay was the grandson and namesake of the first chief justice of the U.S. Supreme Court. He was the son of the abolitionist William Jay.

[10]In St. Paul's Episcopal Cathedral in Boston on May 30, 1842, Crummell was ordained to the diaconate by Bishop Griswold. In St. Paul's Church in Philadelphia in 1844, he was

ordained to the Episcopal priesthood by Bishop Lee of Delaware. Du Bois appears to allude to the first of these events. Du Bois's phrase, "for there had passed a glory from the earth," and his reference in the same paragraph to "that Vision Splendid" draw on the language of William Wordsworth's famous ode "Intimations Of Immortality From Recollections Of Early Childhood," lines 18 and 73. See chapter 1, note 4.

[11]Crummell had become a lay reader for the small black congregation of Christ Church in Providence, Rhode Island, in 1841.

[12]Du Bois refers to Bishop Henry U. Onderdonk of Philadelphia, the brother of Bishop Benjamin T. Onderdonk of New York.

[13]John Foxe's *Actes and Monuments* (also known as the *Book of Martyrs*) was published in 1563; it is a history of the Protestant Church and its martyrs and a source on which John Bunyan seems to have relied in composing *The Pilgrim's Progress. The Whole Duty of Man* (1658) is a Protestant devotional text of anonymous authorship that discusses human beings' duties to God and to each other.

[14]Shakespeare, *Hamlet,* 3.1.70–74.

[15]In 1845 Crummell returned to New York City, where he became rector of the Church of the Messiah. In 1848 he traveled to England, where in 1849 he began his studies at Cambridge University.

[16]Each of the seven Englishmen mentioned here were associates or supporters of Crummell during his years in Great Britain. Samuel Wilberforce (1805–1873) was an Anglican bishop, the son of William Wilberforce, the abolitionist and opponent of the slave trade (also see p. 207, note 12). Stanley is possibly Arthur Penrhyn (1815–1881), an English author and clergyman, dean of Westminster. Connop Thirwell (1797–1875) was a historian of Greece and Rome and an Anglican bishop. Ingles is probably John Inglis, the Anglican bishop of Nova Scotia, who died in London in 1850. James Anthony Froude (1818–1894) was an English religious historian and biographer, author of the twelve-volume *History of England from the Fall of Wolsey to the Defeat of the Spanish Armada.* Thomas Babington Macaulay (1800–1859), the son of Zachary Macaulay, an abolitionist, became an eminent historian and statesman and wrote the great Whiggish work *The History of England from the Accession of James the Second.* Brodie is likely to be Sir Benjamin Collins Brodie (1783–1862), a well-known English physiologist and surgeon.

[17]Between 1853 and 1872 Crummell lived in Liberia for close to sixteen years. During this period, he traveled twice to the United States. He returned permanently to the United States in 1872. Du Bois's allusion to "a new heaven and a new earth" echoes Revelation 21.1.

[18]For Crummell's career in America after his return from Africa, see Moses, *Alexander Crummell,* chaps. 11–14.

[19]For a discussion of the theme of tragedy in this chapter, see Gooding-Williams, "Du Bois's Counter-Sublime."

[20]In the last sentence, Du Bois echoes the parable of the talents from Matthew 25.14–30.

XIII. "Of the Coming of John"

[1]The verse is Elizabeth Barrett Browning, "Romance of the Ganges," stanza 2, lines 10–18. The music is a Negro spiritual, "You May Bury Me in the East" (also known as "I'll Hear the Trumpet Sound"). The title of this chapter, "Of the Coming of John," explicitly recalls the biblical coming of John the Baptist (Matthew 3.1 and Luke 3.3). For a brief discussion of the connection between Du Bois's black John and John the Baptist, see Stanley Brodwin, "The Veil Transcended," 316–18.

[2]Du Bois returns to the theme of the pilgrim, familiar from chapter 12.

[3]"Jim Crow" cars: See page 205, note 7 (chapter 4).

[4]In this and the following paragraph, Du Bois depicts John listening to the prelude to Richard Wagner's opera *Lohengrin.* In "Opera and the Negro Problem," an essay that appeared in the *Pittsburgh Courier* on October 31, 1936, Du Bois remarked that *Lohengrin* was one of the few operas he knew by long acquaintance and that he had heard it performed six or eight times in different lands and languages.

[5]"Manifest destiny" was a phrase that expressed the claim that it was the providential mission, or destiny, of Anglo-Saxon Americans to conquer, control, and develop the North American continent.

[6]Esther 4.16. On the eve of his twenty-fifth birthday, Du Bois recorded his thoughts regarding his life and future. He concludes his remarks by citing the same biblical passage that black John cites: "These are my plans: to make a name in science, to make a name in literature and thus to raise my race. Or perhaps to raise a visible empire in Africa thro' England, France, or Germany. I wonder what will be the outcome? Who knows? I will go unto the king— which is not according to the law and if I perish I perish" (see Aptheker, *Against Racism,* 29).

[7]Here, perhaps, Du Bois alludes to Alexander Crummell's Harpers Ferry address of 1885, "The Need for New Ideas and New Aims for a New Era." See *Africa and America* (1891; reprint, New York: Negro Universities Press, 1969).

[8]Here, ironically, Du Bois's John the Baptist appears as John the "anti-Baptist," a John who slights the significance of baptism.

[9]By linking "talks on the French Revolution" to "a dangerous Nigger," Du Bois recalls the panic that seized many white Americans when, in August 1791, black slaves on the island of Sainte Domingue, inspired by the egalitarian ideals of the French Revolution, rose up to kill their masters. See also page 198, note 18.

[10]In quoting the "Song of the Bride" from Wagner's *Lohengrin,* Du Bois substitutes "freudig" (joyfully) for "treulich" (faithfully). The verse translated is "joyfully led, move on."

XIV. *"The Sorrow Songs"*

[1]The verse is from the Negro spiritual "Lay This Body Down." The music is from the Negro spiritual "Wrestlin' Jacob."

Du Bois did not rely on firsthand experience alone to write "The Sorrow Songs." The two songs that provide the epigraph and the bar of music for this chapter appear side by side in an early article by Thomas Wentworth Higginson, "Negro Spirituals," *Atlantic Monthly* 19 (June 1867). Virtually all the songs and lyrics Du Bois uses in his epigraphs and throughout this essay (including his mini-canon of "ten master songs") can be found in several collections and ethnographies available at the turn of the century. The sources from which Du Bois worked are likely to include M. F. Armstrong and Helen W. Ludlow, *Hampton and Its Students, with Fifty Cabin and Plantation Songs,* arranged by Thomas P. Fenner (New York: Putnam's, 1874); J. B. T. Marsh, *The Story of the Jubilee Singers with Their Songs,* rev. ed. (1872; Boston: Houghton Mifflin, 1880); William Francis Allen, Charles Pickard Ware, and Lucy McKim, *Slave Songs of the United States* (1867; reprint, New York: Arno Press, 1971); and Lucy McKim, "Songs of the Port Royal Contrabands," *Dwight's Journal of Music,* November 8, 1862, reprinted in Bruce Jackson, ed., *The Negro and His Folklore in Nineteenth Century Periodicals* (Austin: University of Texas Press, 1967).

A remarkable feature of "The Sorrow Songs," especially Du Bois's use of bars of music without identifying lyrics, is that for many blacks, particularly members of the educated and emerging middle class, the spirituals had become a source of ambivalence, reminders of the slave past they wished to put to rest. In this book, Du Bois boldly honors slave music as a way of rehabilitating African American folk culture. The lyrics remain hidden until the final chapter of *Souls,* a device that modeled the slaves' clandestine creation and expression of this music. The slave songs were a source of autonomous religious faith, an explanation of this world and the next, and a mode of community survival and resistance.

There are many modern analyses of the slave songs. See especially Eileen Southern, *The Music of Black Americans: A History* (New York: Norton, 1971), 150–216; Lawrence W. Levine, *Black Culture and Black Consciousness: Afro-American Folk Thought from Slavery to Freedom* (New York: Oxford University Press, 1977), 3–55. On Du Bois's use of the songs, see Sundquist, *To Wake the Nations,* 490–539.

[2]Jubilee Hall is a building at Fisk University in Nashville, completed in 1875, the year Fisk graduated its first class. The building was financed by proceeds from the Fisk Jubilee Singers' national and European tours. (See note 7 in this chapter.)

[3]The "minstrel" stage refers to the tradition of popular entertainment that emerged in the 1840s. White performers in blackface sang and spoke in black dialects, usually drawing their themes and lyrics from racial stereotypes. Minstrelsy became the first uniquely American form of show business and stage entertainment.

[4]Port Royal Experiment: See page 199, note 9.

[5]Thomas Wentworth Higginson (1823–1911), a Massachusetts abolitionist, became the white commander of a black regiment, the First South Carolina Volunteers, in the Civil War. He wrote the classic *Army Life in a Black Regiment* (1870) and one of the first important studies of slave music, "The Spirituals," in 1867. (See note 1 in this chapter.)

[6]Lucy McKim Garrison (1842–1877), daughter of abolitionist James Miller McKim, collected and recorded the lyrics of slave songs in South Carolina during the Civil War. (See note 1 in this chapter.)

[7]The Fisk Jubilee Singers were the choral group founded at Fisk University in 1867. The group began to achieve fame by 1871 after an appearance at Oberlin College in Ohio. The original eleven members sang anthems, traditional ballads, operatic excerpts, and temperance songs and were most popular for their revival of the spirituals in stylized form. The choir toured the United States, England, and Europe.

[8]Edmund Kirby Smith (1824–1893) was the Confederate general who led an invasion of Kentucky in September and October 1862 that threatened Cincinnati. Chancellorsville was a Civil War battle fought near Fredericksburg, Virginia, May 2–3, 1863. Gettysburg was the pivotal battle of the Civil War fought in southern Pennsylvania, July 1–3, 1863.

[9]George L. White, the treasurer and vocal music teacher at Fisk University, founded the Fisk Jubilee Singers.

[10]At a meeting of the National Council of Congregational Churches, part of the American Missionary Association, at Oberlin College on November 15, 1871, the Fisk Jubilee Singers received their first great publicity.

[11]Henry Ward Beecher (1813–1887), brother of Harriet Beecher Stowe, was pastor of Plymouth Church in Brooklyn, New York. His invitation to and endorsement of the Fisk Jubilee Singers furthered their success in 1872.

[12]Du Bois's maternal grandfather was Othello Burghardt. Othello's grandfather was Tom Burghardt. Little is known of Othello's grandmother, Tom Burghardt's wife, who is the "grandfather's grandmother" referred to in this passage.

[13]The African geographic or ethnic origin of this melody has not been determined. David Levering Lewis tried to locate its roots without full success. The "best hypothesis," he states, is that it may have been a "Wolof song from Senegambia about confinement or captivity" (Lewis, *W. E. B. Du Bois,* 14, 585 n 7).

[14]From the Negro spiritual "You May Bury Me in the East," also called "I'll Hear the Trumpet Sound."

[15]On the significance of "Steal Away," see page 212, note 1.

[16]"Swanee River" and "Old Black Joe" are famous songs by the nineteenth century's most prominent songwriter, Stephen Foster. Many of Foster's songs became staples of the minstrel stage. See Southern, *Music of Black Americans,* 93.

[17]"Coon" songs were a form of minstrel song that was especially derogatory toward blacks, depicting a character called Zip Coon who often could not stop laughing.

[18]From the Negro spiritual "Steal Away."

[19]From the Negro spiritual "There's No Rain to Wet You."

[20]From the Negro spiritual "Keep Me from Sinking Down."

[21]From the Negro spiritual "My Soul Wants Something That's New."

[22]From the Negro spiritual "O'er the Crossing."

[23]From the Negro spiritual "Poor Rosy."

[24]From the German (Schwäbian) folk song "Jetzt gang I ans Brünnele." The line translates: "Now I'm going to the well, but I will not drink." The song is one of broken or lost love and of death.

[25]From the Negro spiritual "Dust and Ashes."

[26] From Ezekiel 1.15–28. Also see Isaiah 52.2.

[27] From the Negro spiritual "There's a Little Wheel a-Turnin'."

[28] An adaptation of the Negro spiritual "My Lord, What a Mourning!"

[29] From the Negro spiritual "Michael, Row the Boat Ashore."

[30] Aeschylus was the oldest of the three great tragic poets and playwrights of ancient Greece. On Shakespeare, see page 207, note 21.

[31] The Pilgrims landed at Plymouth Rock, Massachusetts, in 1620, and formed the first English colony in New England. The first Africans landed in North America, probably as slaves, possibly as indentured servants, in Jamestown, Virginia, on a Dutch ship in 1619.

[32] From the Negro spiritual "Let Us Cheer the Weary Traveler."

"The Afterthought"

[1] Du Bois echoes Ecclesiastes 7.13: "Consider the work of God: for who can make that straight, which he hath made crooked?"

PART TWO

Selected Photographs, Essays, and Correspondence

The Great Barrington, Massachusetts High School graduation class of 1884. Du Bois, at far left, was sixteen years old in this photograph. Special Collections and Archives, W. E. B. Du Bois Library, University of Massachusetts Amherst.

The Fisk University graduation of class of 1888, Nashville, Tennessee. The twenty-year-old Du Bois is second from left. His commencement oration was on the German national leader, Otto von Bismarck. Special Collections and Archives W. E. B. Du Bois Library, University of Massachusetts Amherst.

The Harvard University commencement speakers, Cambridge Massachusetts, June, 1890. Du Bois is at far right. He delivered a commencement oration entitled "Jefferson Davis as a Representative of Civilization." Special Collections and Archives, W. E. B. Du Bois Library, University of Massachusetts Amherst.

Du Bois and Nina Gomer Du Bois, with son Burghardt, who died at less than two years of age in Atlanta, May, 1899. Chapter 11 of *Souls,* "Of the Passing of the First-Born," is based on Burghardt's death. Du Bois met Nina Gomer while she was a student at Wilberforce University in Ohio. Nina grew up in Cedar Rapids, Iowa; she and DuBois were married there in 1896. Special Collections and Archives, W. E. B. Du Bois Library, University of Massachusetts Amherst.

Du Bois at the Paris Exposition Universelle, spring, 1900, where he received a grand prize for his exhibit on black economic development in America. Shortly after the Paris Exposition Du Bois attended the First Pan-African Congress in London. Special Collections and Archives, W. E. B. Du Bois Library, University of Massachusetts Amherst.

Du Bois in his office, Atlanta University, 1909. Du Bois wrote all of the essays in *Souls* while living in Atlanta between 1897 and 1903. Special Collections and Archives, W. E. B. Du Bois Library, University of Massachusetts Amherst.

The first page of the original manuscript of chapter 13, "Of the Coming of John," *The Souls of Black Folk*. Special Collections and Archives, W. E. B. Du Bois Library, University of Massachusetts Amherst.

Du Bois in Berlin to receive an honorary degree from Humboldt University, 1958, at age ninety. Special Collections and Archives, W. E. B. DuBois Library. University of Massachusetts Amherst.

Essays by W. E. B. Du Bois

The Conservation of Races

1897

Du Bois was twenty-nine years old when he delivered this address on March 5, 1897, in Washington, D.C., at the founding meeting of the American Negro Academy. The essay was published later that year as the second of the academy's "occasional papers." In "The Conservation of Races," Du Bois attempts to develop a sociohistorical concept of racial identity and argues that sociohistorical explanation can account for the distinctive character of a race's spiritual message to humanity. As one of the founding papers of the American Negro Academy, it may have been crafted in deference to Alexander Crummell and other elders in the organization. But it also represents Du Bois's developing thought shortly before he began to write the articles that later became The Souls of Black Folk. *Du Bois's essay may be read as a philosophical prologue to his explanation of African American spirituality in* Souls.

The American Negro has always felt an intense personal interest in discussions as to the origins and destinies of races: primarily because back of most discussions of race with which he is familiar, have lurked certain assumptions as to his natural abilities, as to his political, intellectual and moral status, which he felt were wrong. He has, consequently, been led to deprecate and minimize race distinctions, to believe intensely that out of one blood God created all nations, and to speak of human

---

"The Conservation of Races," Eric J. Sundquist, ed., *The Oxford W. E. B. Du Bois Reader* (New York: Oxford University Press, 1996), 38–47.

brotherhood as though it were the possibility of an already dawning tomorrow.

Nevertheless, in our calmer moments we must acknowledge that human beings are divided into races; that in this country the two most extreme types of the world's races have met, and the resulting problem as to the future relations of these types is not only of intense and living interest to us, but forms an epoch in the history of mankind.

It is necessary, therefore, in planning our movements, in guiding our future development, that at times we rise above the pressing, but smaller questions of separate schools and cars, wage-discrimination and lynch law, to survey the whole question of race in human philosophy and to lay, on a basis of broad knowledge and careful insight, those large lines of policy and higher ideals which may form our guiding lines and boundaries in the practical difficulties of everyday. For it is certain that all human striving must recognize the hard limits of natural law, and that any striving, no matter how intense and earnest, which is against the constitution of the world, is vain. The question, then, which we must seriously consider is this: what is the real meaning of race; what has, in the past, been the law of race development, and what lessons has the past history of race development to teach the rising Negro people?

When we thus come to inquire into the essential difference of races we find it hard to come at once to any definite conclusion. Many criteria of race differences have in the past been proposed, as color, hair, cranial measurements and language. And manifestly, in each of these respects, human beings differ widely. They vary in color, for instance, from the marble-like pallor of the Scandinavian to the rich, dark brown of the Zulu, passing by the creamy Slav, the yellow Chinese, the light brown Sicilian and the brown Egyptian. Men vary, too, in the texture of hair from the obstinately straight hair of the Chinese to the obstinately tufted and frizzled hair of the Bushman. In measurement of heads, again, men vary; from the broad-headed Tartar to the medium-headed European and the narrow-headed Hottentot; or, again in language, from the highly-inflected Roman tongue to the monosyllabic Chinese. All these physical characteristics are patent enough, and if they agreed with each other it would be very easy to classify mankind. Unfortunately for scientists, however, these criteria of race are most exasperatingly intermingled. Color does not agree with texture of hair, for many of the dark races have straight hair; nor does color agree with the breadth of the head, for the yellow Tartar has a broader head than the German; nor, again, has the science of language as yet succeeded in clearing up the relative authority of these various and contradictory criteria.

The final word of science, so far, is that we have at least two, perhaps three, great families of human beings—the whites and Negroes, possibly the yellow race. That other races have arisen from the intermingling of the blood of these two. This broad division of the world's races which men like [Thomas Henry] Huxley and [Friedrich] Raetzel have introduced as more nearly true than the old five-race scheme of [Johann-Friedrich] Blumenbach, is nothing more than an acknowledgement that, so far as purely physical characteristics are concerned, the differences between men do not explain all the differences of their history. It declares, as Darwin himself said, that great as is the physical unlikeness of the various races of men, their likenesses are greater, and upon this rests the whole scientific doctrine of human brotherhood.

Although the wonderful developments of human history teach that the grosser physical differences of color, hair and bone go but a short way toward explaining the different roles which groups of men have played in human progress, yet there are differences—subtle, delicate and elusive, though they may be—which have silently but definitely separated men into groups. While these subtle forces have generally followed the natural cleavage of common blood, descent and physical peculiarities, they have at other times swept across and ignored these. At all times, however, they have divided human beings into races, which, while they perhaps transcend scientific definition, nevertheless, are clearly defined to the eye of the historian and sociologist.

If this be true, then the history of the world is the history, not of individuals, but of groups, not of nations, but of races, and he who ignores or seeks to override the race idea in human history ignores and overrides the central thought of all history. What, then, is a race? It is a vast family of human beings, generally of common blood and language, always of common history, traditions and impulses, who are both voluntarily and involuntarily striving together for the accomplishment of certain more or less vividly conceived ideals of life.

Turning to real history, there can be no doubt, first, as to the widespread, nay, universal, prevalence of the race idea, the race spirit, the race ideal, and as to its efficiency as the vastest and most ingenious invention for human progress. We, who have been reared and trained under the individualistic philosophy of the Declaration of Independence and the laissez-faire philosophy of Adam Smith, are loath to see and loath to acknowledge this patent fact of human history. We see the Pharaohs, Caesars, Toussaints and Napoleons of history and forget the vast races of which they were but epitomized expressions. We are apt to think in our American impatience, that while it may have been true in the past that closed race groups made history, that here in conglomerate America *nous avons changé tout cela* — we have changed all that, and have no need of this ancient instrument of progress. This assumption of which the Negro people are especially fond cannot be established by a careful consideration of history.

We find upon the world's stage today eight distinctly differentiated races, in the sense in which history tells us the word must be used. They are the Slavs of Eastern Europe, the Teutons of middle Europe, the English of Great Britain and America, the Romance nations of Southern and Western Europe, the Negroes of Africa and America, the Semitic people of Western Asia and Northern Africa, the Hindoos of Central Asia and the Mongolians of Eastern Asia. There are, of course, other minor race groups, [such] as the American Indians, the Esquimaux and the South Sea Islanders; these larger races, too, are far from homogeneous; the Slav includes the Czech, the Magyar, the Pole and the Russian; the Teuton includes the German, the Scandinavian and the Dutch; the English include the Scotch, the Irish and the conglomerate American. Under Romance nations the widely-differing Frenchman, Italian, Sicilian and Spaniard are comprehended. The term Negro is, perhaps, the most indefinite of all, combining the Mulattoes and Zamboes of America and the Egyptians, Bantus and Bushmen of Africa. Among the Hindoos are traces of widely differing nations, while the great Chinese, Tartar, Korean and Japanese families fall under the one designation — Mongolian.

The question now is: What is the real distinction between these nations? Is it the physical differences of blood, color and cranial measurements? Certainly we must all acknowledge that physical differences play a great part, and that, with wide exceptions and qualifications, these eight great races of today follow the cleavage of physical race distinctions; the English and Teuton represent the white variety of mankind; the Mongolian, the yellow; the Negroes, the black. Between these are many crosses and mixtures, where Mongolian and Teuton have blended into the Slav, and other mixtures have produced the Romance nations and the Semites. But while race differences have followed mainly physical race lines, yet no mere physical distinctions would really define or explain the deeper differences — the cohesiveness and continuity of these groups. The deeper differences are spiritual, psychical, differences — undoubtedly based on the physical, but infinitely transcending them. The forces that bind together the Teuton nations are, then, first, their race identity and common blood; secondly, and more important, a common history, common laws and religion, similar habits of thought and a conscious striving together for certain ideals of life. The whole process which has brought about these race differentiations has been a growth, and the great characteristic of this growth has been the differentiation of spiritual and mental differences between great races of mankind and the integration of physical differences.

The age of nomadic tribes of closely related individuals represents the maximum of physical differences. They were practically vast families, and there were as many groups as families. As the families came together to form cities the physical differences lessened, purity of blood was replaced by the requirement of domicile, and all who lived within the city bounds became gradually to be regarded as members of the group; i.e., there was a slight and slow breaking down of physical barriers. This, however, was accompanied by an increase of the spiritual and social differences between cities. This city became husbandmen; this, merchants; another, warriors; and so on. The *ideals of life* for which the different cities struggled were different.

When at last cities began to coalesce into nations there was another breaking down of barriers which separated groups of men. The larger and broader differences of color, hair and physical proportions were not by any means ignored, but myriads of minor differences disappeared, and the sociological and historical races of men began to approximate the present division of races as indicated by physical researches. At the same time the spiritual and psychical differences of race groups which constituted the nations became deep and decisive. The English nation stood for constitutional liberty and commercial freedom; the German nation for science and philosophy; the Romance nations stood for literature and art, and the other race groups are striving, each in its own way, to develop for civilization its particular message, its particular ideal, which shall help to guide the world nearer and nearer that perfection of human life for which we all long, that "one far-off Divine event."

This has been the function of the race differences up to the present time. What shall be its function in the future? Manifestly some of the great races of today—particularly the Negro race—have not as yet given to civilization the full spiritual message which they are capable of giving. I will not say that the Negro race has as yet given no message to the world, for it is still a mooted question among scientists as to just how far Egyptian civilization was Negro in its origin; if it was not wholly Negro, it was certainly very closely allied. Be that as it may, however, the fact still remains that the full, complete Negro message of the whole Negro race has not as yet been given to the world: that the messages and ideal of the yellow race have not been completed, and that the striving of the mighty Slavs has but begun.

The question is, then: how shall this message be delivered; how shall these various ideals be realized? The answer is plain: by the development of these race groups, not as individuals, but as races. For the development of Japanese genius, Japanese literature and art, Japanese spirit, only Japanese, bound and welded together, Japanese inspired by one vast ideal, can work out in its fullness the wonderful message which Japan has for the nations of the earth. For the development of Negro genius, of Negro literature and art, of Negro spirit, only Negroes bound and welded together, Negroes inspired by one vast ideal, can work out in its fullness the great message we have for humanity. We cannot reverse history; we are subject to the same natural laws as other races, and if the Negro is ever to be a factor in the world's history—if among the gaily-colored banners that deck the broad ramparts of civilization is to hang one uncompromising black, then it must be placed there by black hands, fashioned by black heads and hallowed by the travail of two hundred million black hearts beating in one glad song of jubilee.

For this reason, the advance guard of the Negro people—the eight million people of Negro blood in the United States of America—must soon come to realize that if they are to take their just place in the van of Pan-Negroism, then their destiny is *not* absorption by the white Americans. That if in America it is to be proven for the first time in the modern world that not only are Negroes capable of evolving individual men like Toussaint the Saviour, but are a nation stored with wonderful possibilities of culture, then their destiny is not a servile imitation of Anglo-Saxon culture, but a stalwart originality which shall unswervingly follow Negro ideals.

It may, however, be objected here that the situation of our race in America renders this attitude impossible; that our sole hope of salvation lies in our being able to lose our race identity in the commingled blood of the nation; and that any other course would merely increase the friction of races which we call race prejudice, and against which we have so long and so earnestly fought.

Here, then, is the dilemma, and it is a puzzling one, I admit. No Negro who has given earnest thought to the situation of his people in America has failed, at some time in life, to find himself at these crossroads; has failed to ask himself at some time: what, after all, am I? Am I an American or am I a Negro? Can I be both? Or is it my duty to cease to be a Negro as soon as possible and be an American? If I strive as a Negro, am I not perpetuating the very cleft that threatens and separates black and white America? Is not my only possible practical aim the subduction of all that is Negro in me to the American? Does my black blood place upon me any more obligation to assert my nationality than German, or Irish or Italian blood would?

It is such incessant self-questioning, and the hesitation that arises from it, that is making the present period a time of vacillation and contradiction for the American Negro; combined race action is stifled, race responsibility is shirked, race enterprises languish, and the best blood, the best talent, the best energy of the Negro people cannot be marshaled to do the bidding of the race. They stand back to make room for every rascal and demagogue who chooses to cloak his selfish devilry under the veil of race pride.

Is this right? Is it rational? Is it good policy? Have we in America a distinct mission as a race—a distinct sphere of action and an opportunity for race development, or is self-obliteration the highest end to which Negro blood dare aspire?

If we carefully consider what race prejudice really is, we find it, historically, to be nothing but the friction between different groups of people; it is the difference in aim, in feeling, in ideals of two different races; if, now, this difference exists touching territory, laws, language, or even religion, it is manifest that these people cannot live in the same territory without fatal collision; but if, on the other hand, there is substantial agreement in laws, language and religion; if there is a satisfactory adjustment of economic life, then there is no reason why, in the same country and on the same street, two or three great national ideals might not thrive and develop, that men of different races might not strive together for their race ideals as well, perhaps even better, than in isolation.

Here, it seems to me, is the reading of the riddle that puzzles so many of us. We are Americans, not only by birth and by citizenship, but by our political ideals, our language, our religion. Farther than that, our Americanism does not go. At that point, we are Negroes, members of a vast historic race that from the very dawn of creation has slept, but half awakening in the dark forests of its African fatherland. We are the first fruits of this new nation, the harbinger of that black tomorrow which is yet destined to soften the whiteness of the Teutonic today. We are that people whose subtle sense of song has given America its only American music, its only American fairy tales, its only touch of pathos and humor amid its mad money-getting plutocracy. As such, it is our duty to conserve our physical powers, our intellectual endowments, our spiritual ideals; as a race we must strive by race organization, by race solidarity, by race unity to the realization of that broader humanity which freely recognizes differences in men, but sternly deprecates inequality in their opportunities of development.

For the accomplishment of these ends we need race organizations: Negro colleges, Negro newspapers, Negro business organizations, a Negro school of literature and art, and an intellectual clearing house, for all these products of the Negro mind, which we may call a Negro Academy. Not only is all this necessary for positive advance, it is absolutely imperative for negative defense. Let us not deceive ourselves at our situation in this country. Weighted with a heritage of moral iniquity from our past history, hard pressed in the economic world by foreign immigrants and native prejudice, hated here, despised there and pitied everywhere; our one haven of refuge is ourselves, and but one means of advance, our own belief in our great destiny, our own implicit trust in our ability and worth.

There is no power under God's high heaven that can stop the advance of eight thousand thousand honest, earnest, inspired and united people. But—and here is the rub—they *must* be honest, fearlessly criticizing their own faults, zealously correcting them; they must be *earnest*. No people that laughs at itself, and ridicules itself, and wishes to God it was anything but itself ever wrote its name in history; it *must* be inspired with the Divine faith of our black mothers, that out of the blood and dust of battle will march a victorious host, a mighty nation, a peculiar people, to speak to the nations of earth a Divine truth that shall make them free. And such a people must be united; not merely united for the organized theft of political spoils, not united to disgrace religion with whoremongers and ward-heelers; not united merely to protest and pass resolutions, but united to stop the ravages of consumption among the Negro people, united to keep black boys from loafing, gambling and crime; united to guard the purity of black women and to reduce that vast army of black prostitutes that is today marching to hell; and united in serious organizations, to determine by careful conference and thoughtful interchange of opinion the broad lines of policy and action for the American Negro.

This is the reason for being which the American Negro Academy has. It aims at once to be the epitome and expression of the intellect of the black-blooded people of America, the exponent of the race ideals of one of the world's great races. As such, the Academy must, if successful, be:

a. Representative in character.
b. Impartial in conduct.
c. Firm in leadership.

It must be representative in character; not in that it represents all interests or all factions, but in that it seeks to comprise something of the *best* thought, the most unselfish striving and the highest ideals. There are scattered in forgotten nooks and corners throughout the land, Negroes of some considerable training, of high minds, and high motives, who are unknown to their fellows, who exert far too little influence. These the Negro Academy should strive to bring into touch with each other and to give them a common mouthpiece.

The Academy should be impartial in conduct; while it aims to exalt the people it should aim to do so by truth—not by lies, by honesty—not by flattery. It should continually impress the fact upon the Negro people that they must not expect to have things done for them—they *must do for themselves;* that they have on their hands a vast work of self-reformation to do, and that a little less complaint and whining, and a little more dogged work and manly striving would do us more credit and benefit than a thousand Force or Civil Rights bills.

Finally, the American Negro Academy must point out a practical path of advance to the Negro people; there lie before every Negro today hundreds of questions of policy and right which must be settled and which each one settles now, not in accordance with any rule, but by impulse or individual preference; for instance: what should be the attitude of Negroes toward the educational qualification for voters? What should be our attitude toward separate schools? How should we meet discriminations on railways and in hotels? Such questions need not so much specific answers for each part as a general expression of policy, and nobody should be better fitted to announce such a policy than a representative honest Negro Academy.

All this, however, must come in time after careful organization and long conference. The immediate work before us should be practical and have direct bearing upon the situation of the Negro. The historical work of collecting the laws of the United States and of the various states of the Union with regard to the Negro is a work of such magnitude and importance that no body but one like this could think of undertaking it. If we could accomplish that one task we would justify our existence.

In the field of sociology an appalling work lies before us. First, we must unflinchingly and bravely face the truth, not with apologies, but with solemn earnestness. The Negro Academy ought to sound a note of warning that would echo in every black cabin in the land: *unless we conquer our present vices they will conquer us;* we are diseased, we are developing criminal tendencies, and an alarmingly large percentage of our men and women are sexually impure. The Negro Academy should stand and proclaim this over the housetops, crying with Garrison: *I will not equivocate, I will not retreat a single inch, and I will be heard.* The Academy should seek to gather about it the talented, unselfish men, the pure and noble-minded women, to fight an army of devils that disgraces our manhood and our womanhood. There does not stand today upon God's earth a race more capable in muscle, in intellect, in morals, than the American Negro, if he will bend his energies in the right direction; if he will

> Burst his birth's invidious bar
> And grasp the skirts of happy chance,
> And breast the blows of circumstance,
> And grapple with his evil star.

In science and morals, I have indicated two fields of work for the Academy. Finally, in practical policy, I wish to suggest the following *Academy Creed:*

1. We believe that the Negro people, as a race, have a contribution to make to civilization and humanity, which no other race can make.
2. We believe it the duty of the Americans of Negro descent, as a body, to maintain their race identity until this mission of the Negro people is accomplished, and the ideal of human brotherhood has become a practical possibility.
3. We believe that, unless modern civilization is a failure, it is entirely feasible and practicable for two races in such essential political, economic and religious harmony as the white and colored people of America, to develop side by side in peace and mutual happiness, the peculiar contribution which each has to make to the culture of their common country.
4. As a means to this end we advocate, not such social equality between these races as would disregard human likes and dislikes, but such a social equilibrium as would, throughout all the complicated relations of life, give due and just consideration to culture, ability, and moral worth, whether they be found under white or black skins.
5. We believe that the first and greatest step toward the settlement of the present friction between the races — commonly called the Negro problem — lies in the correction of the immorality, crime and laziness among the Negroes themselves, which still remains as a heritage from slavery. We believe that

only earnest and long continued efforts on our own part can
cure these social ills.

6. We believe that the second great step toward a better adjustment
   of the relations between the races should be a more impartial
   selection of ability in the economic and intellectual world, and a
   greater respect for personal liberty and worth, regardless of
   race. We believe that only earnest efforts on the part of the white
   people of this country will bring much needed reform in these
   matters.

7. On the basis of the foregoing declaration, and firmly believing
   in our high destiny, we, as American Negroes, are resolved to
   strive in every honorable way for the realization of the best and
   highest aims, for the development of strong manhood and
   pure womanhood, and for the rearing of a race ideal in America
   and Africa, to the glory of God and the uplifting of the Negro
   people.

The Development of a People
1904

*Du Bois was thirty-six years old when "The Development of a People" first
appeared in the April 1904 issue of the* International Journal of Ethics,
exactly one year after the publication of The Souls of Black Folk. *This little-
known but striking essay sets forth a developmental theory of "human
advancement historically considered" and applies that theory to the history
of the Negro people. With a narrative sweep that extends from the origins of
the slave trade in the European Renaissance to the "civilization of the twentieth century," Du Bois depicts African Americans as struggling to cope with
"the demands and meaning of the modern culture" into which slavery and
emancipation have thrust them. Reprising many of the themes evident in*
Souls —*progress, duality, the weight of history, the relationship of material
circumstances to spiritual life, the nature of leadership, the nature of culture, and the experience of journeying into the South —this essay provides
an appropriate postscript to the book.*

"The Development of a People," Herbert Aptheker, ed., *Writings by W. E. B. Du Bois in
Periodicals Edited by Others,* vol. 1, *1891–1909* (Millwood, N.Y.: Kraus-Thompson, 1982),
203–15.

In the realm of physical health the teachings of Nature, with its stern mercy and merciful punishment, are showing men gradually to avoid the mistake of unhealthful homes, and to clear fever and malaria away from parts of earth otherwise so beautiful. Death that arises from foul sewage, bad plumbing or vitiated air we no longer attribute to "Acts of God," but to "Misdeeds of Man," and so work to correct this loss. But if we have escaped Mediaevalism to some extent in the care of physical health, we certainly have not in the higher realm of the economic and spiritual development of people. Here the world rests, and is largely contented to rest, in a strange fatalism. Nations and groups and social classes are born and reared, reel sick unto death, or tear forward in frenzied striving. We sit and watch and moralize, and judge our neighbors or ourselves foredoomed to failure or success, not because we know or have studied the causes of a people's advance, but rather because we instinctively dislike certain races, and instinctively like our own.

This attitude cannot long prevail. The solidarity of human interests in a world which is daily becoming physically smaller, cannot afford to grope in darkness as to the causes and incentives to human advance when the advance of all depends increasingly on the advance of each. Nor is it enough here to have simply the philanthropic impulse — simply a rather blind and aimless desire to do good.

If then we would grapple intelligently with the greater problems of human development in society, we must sit and study and learn even when the mad impulse of aimless philanthropy is striving within, and we find it easier to labor blindly, rather than to wait intelligently.

In no single set of human problems is this striving after intelligence, after real facts and clear thinking, more important than in answering the many questions that concern the American Negro. And especially is this true since the basic axiom upon which all intelligent and decent men, North and South, white and black, must agree, is that the best interests of every single American demand that *every Negro make the best of himself.*

But what is good and better and best in the measure of human advance? and how shall we compare the present with the past, nation with nation, and group with group, so as to gain real intelligent insight into conditions and needs, and enlightened guidance? Now this is extremely difficult in matters of human development, because we are so ignorant of the ordinary facts relating to conditions of life, and because, above all, criteria of life and the objects of living are so diverse.

And yet the desire for clear judgment and rational advance, even in so intricate a problem as that of the races in the United States, is not hopeless. First of all, the most hopeful thing about the race problem to-day is, that people are beginning to recognize its intricacy and be justly suspicious of any person who insists that the race problem is simply this or simply that—realizing that it is not simply anything. It is as complex as human nature, and you do well to distrust the judgment of any man who thinks, however honestly, that any one simple remedy will cure evils that arise from the whirling wants and longings and passions of writhing human souls.

Not only do we to-day recognize the Negro problems as intricate, but we are beginning to see that they are pressing—asking, *demanding* solution; not to be put off by half measures, not answered by being handed down in thinly disguised yet even larger form to our children. With these intricate and pressing problems before us, we ask searchingly and often for the light; and here again we are baffled. An honest gentleman from the South informs us that there are fully as many illiterate Negroes to-day in the South as there were at Emancipation. We gasp with astonishment, and as we are asking "Where then is all our money and effort gone?" another gentleman from the South, apparently just as honest, tells us that whereas nine-tenths of the Negroes in 1870 could *not* read and write, to-day fully three-fifths of them *can;* or, again, the Negroes themselves exult over the ownership of three hundred million dollars worth of real estate, while the critic points out that the Negroes are a burden to the South, since forming a third of the population they own but one-twenty-fifth of the property.

Such seemingly contradictory propositions and others even more glaring, we hear every day, and it is small wonder that persons without leisure to weigh the evidence find themselves curiously in the dark at times and anxious for reliable interpretation of the real facts.

Much of this befogging of the situation is apparent rather than real. As a matter of fact, the statements referred to are not at all contradictory. There are to-day more illiterate Negroes than in 1870, but there are six times as many who can read and write. The real underlying problem is dynamic, not static. Is the educational movement in the right direction, and is it as rapid as is safe? or, in other words, What is satisfactory advance in education? Ought a people to learn to read and write in one generation or in a hundred years? How far can we hasten the growth of intelligence, avoiding stagnation on the one hand, and abnormal forcing on the other? Or take the question of property ownership; it is probably true that only a twenty-fifth of the total property of the South belongs to the Negro, and that the Negro property of the land exceeds three hundred million. Here, again, brute figures mean little, and the comparison between black and white is misleading. The basic question is, How soon after a social revolution like emancipation ought one reasonably to expect the appearance of habits of thrift and the accumulation of property? Moreover, how far is the accumulating of wealth indicative of general advance in moral habits and sound character, or how far is it independent of them or in spite of them?

In other words, if we are to judge intelligently or clearly of the development of a people, we must allow ourselves neither to be dazzled by figures nor misled by inapt comparisons, but we must seek to know what human advancement historically considered has meant and what it means to-day, and from such criteria we may then judge the condition, development and needs of the group before us. I want then to mention briefly the steps which groups of men have usually taken in their forward struggling, and to ask which of these steps the Negroes of the United States have taken and how far they have gone. In such comparisons we cannot, unfortunately, have the aid of exact statistics, for actual measurement of social phenomena is peculiar to the Nineteenth century—that is, to an age when the culture Nations were full-grown, and we can only roughly indicate conditions in the days of their youth. A certain youth and childhood is common to all men in their mingled striving. Everywhere, glancing across the seas of human history, we note it. The average American community of to-day has grown by a slow, intricate and hesitating advance through four overlapping eras. First, there is the struggle for sheer physical existence—a struggle still waging among the submerged tenth, but settled for a majority of the community long years ago. Above this comes the accumulation for future subsistence—the saving and striving and transmuting of goods for use in days to come—a stage reached to-day tentatively for the middle classes and to an astounding degree by a few. Then in every community there goes on from the first, but with larger and larger emphasis as the years fly, some essay to train the young into the tradition of the fathers—their religion, thought and tricks of doing. And, finally, as the group meets other groups and comes into larger spiritual contact with nations, there is that transference and sifting and accumulation of the elements of human culture which makes for wider civilization and higher development. These four steps of subsistence, accumulation, education and culture-contact are not disconnected, discreet [*sic*] stages. No nation ever settles its problems of poverty and then turns to educating children; or first accumulates its wealth and then its culture. On the contrary, in every stage of a nation's growing all these efforts are present, and we designate any particular age of a people's development as (for instance) a struggle for existence, because, their conscious effort is more largely expended in this direction than in others; but despite this we all know, or ought to know, that no growing nation can spend its whole effort on to-day's food lest accumulation and training of children and learning of their neighbors—lest all these things so vitally necessary to advance be neglected, and the people, full-bellied though they be, stagnate and die because in one mighty struggle to live they forget the weightier objects of life.

We all know these very obvious truths, and yet despite ourselves certain mechanical conceptions of society creep into our everyday thought. We think of growing men as cogs in some vast factory—we would stop these wheels and set these others going, hasten that department and retard this; but this conception applied to struggling men is mischievously wrong. You cannot stop the education of children in order to feed their fathers; the children continue to grow—something they are bound to learn. What then shall it be: truth, or half-truth, good or bad? So, too, a people may be engaged in the pressing work of accumulating and saving for future needs—storing grain and cotton, building houses, leveling land; but all the time they are learning something from inevitable contact with men and nations and thoughts—you cannot stop this learning; you cannot postpone it. What then shall this learning—this contact with culture—be? a lesson of fact or fable? of growth or debauchery? the inspiration of the schools or the degradation of the slums? Something it must be, but what? The growth of society is an ever-living, many-sided, bundle of activities, some of which are emphasized at different ages, none of which can be neglected without peril, all of which demand guidance and direction. As they receive this, the nation grows; as they do not, it stagnates and dies.

Whence now must the guidance and direction come? It can come only from four great sources: the precepts of parents, the sight of Seers, the opinion of the majority, and the tradition of the grandfathers; or, in other words, a nation or group of people can be taught the things it must learn in its family circles, at the feet of teachers and preachers, by contact with surrounding society, by reverence for the dead Hand—for that mighty accumulation of customs and traditions handed down generation after generation.

And thus I come to the center of my theme. How far do these great means of growth operate among American Negroes and influence their development in the main lines of human advancement?

Let me take you journeying across mountains and meadows, threading the hills of Maryland, gliding over the broad fields of Virginia, climbing the blue ridge of Carolina and seating ourselves in the cotton kingdom. I would not like you to spend a day or a month here in this little town;

I should much rather you would spend ten years, if you are really studying the problem; for casual visitors get casual ideas, and the problems
here are the growth of centuries.

From the depot and the cluster of doubtful houses that form the town,
pale crimson fields with tell-tale gullies stretch desolately away. The
whole horizon looks shabby, and there is a certain awful leisure in the
air that makes a westerner wonder when work begins. A neglected and
uncertain road wanders up from the depot, past several little stores and
a post-office, and then stops hesitatingly and melts away into crooked
paths across the washed-out cotton fields. But I do not want you to see
so much of the physical as of the spiritual town, and first you must see
the color line. It stands at the depot with "waiting room for white people"
and "waiting room for colored people," and then the uninitiated might lose
sight of it; but it is there, there and curiously wandering, but continuous
and never ending. And in that little town, as in a thousand others, they
have an eleventh commandment, and it reads "Thou shalt not Cross the
Line." Men may at times break the sixth commandment and the seventh,
and it makes but little stir. But when the eleventh is broken, *the world
heaves.* And yet you must not think the town inhabited by anything inhu-
man. Simple, good hearted folks are there—generosity and hospitality,
politeness and charity, dim strivings and hard efforts—a human world,
aye, even lovable at times; and one cannot argue about that strange line—
it is simply so.

Were you there in person I could not take you easily across the line
into the world I want to study. But in spirit let me lead you across. In one
part of the town are sure to be clustered the majority of the Negro cabins; there is no strict physical separation; on some streets whites and
blacks are neighbors, and yet the general clustering by color is plain. I
want to take you among the houses of the colored people, and I start not
with the best, but with the worst: a little one-room box with a family of
eight. The cabin is dirty, ill-smelling and cheerless; the furniture is scanty,
old and worn. The man works when he has no whiskey to drink, which
is comparatively seldom. The woman washes and squanders and squanders and washes. I am not sure that the couple were ever married formally, but still they'll stick together in all probability for life, despite their
quarreling. There are five children, and the nameless child of the eldest
daughter makes the last member of the family. Three of the children can
spell and read a bit, but there's little need of it. The rest of the family are
in ignorance, dark and dense. Here is a problem of home and family. One
shudders at it almost hopelessly, or flares in anger and says: why do these
people live like animals? Why don't they work and strive to do? If the

stranger be from the North he looks suspiciously at the color line and shakes his head. If he be from the South he looks at it thankfully and stamps his foot. And these two attitudes are in some respects typical. We look around for the forces keeping this family down, or with fatalistic resignation conclude that nothing better is to be expected of black people. Exactly the same attitude with which the man of a century or so ago fought disease: looked about for the witch, or wondered at the chastening of the Lord; but withal continued to live in the swamps. There are forces in the little town to keep Negroes down, but they do not wholly explain the condition of this family. There are differences in human capabilities, but that they are not based on color can be seen in a dozen Negro homes up the street. What we have in degraded homes like this is a plain survival from the past.

What was slavery and the slave trade? Turn again with me even at the risk of hearing a twice-told tale and, as we have journeyed in space to this little southern town, so journey again in time, back through that curious crooked way along which civilization has wandered looking for the light. There was the nineteenth century—a century of material prosperity, of systematic catering to human wants, that men might eat, drink, be clothed and transported through space. And with this came the physical freeing of the soul through the wonders of science and the spread of democracy. Such a century was a legitimate offspring of the eighteenth century, of the years from 1700 to 1800, when our grandfathers' grandfathers lived— that era of revolution and heart searching that gave the world George Washington and the French Revolution. Behind the eighteenth century looms the age of Louis XIV of France, an age of mighty leaders: Richelieu, Gustavus Adolphus, and Oliver Cromwell. Thus we come back on the world's way, through three centuries of imperialism, revolution and commercial democracy, to two great centuries which prepared Europe for the years from 1600 to 1900—the century of the Protestant Reformation and the century of the Renaissance. The African Slave trade was the child of the Renaissance. We do not realize this; we think of the slave trade as a thing apart, the incident of a decade or a century, and yet let us never forget that from the year 1442, when Antonio Gonzales first looked upon the river of Gold, until 1807, when Great Britain first checked the slave trade, for three hundred and sixty-five years Africa was surrendered wholly to the cruelty and rapacity of the Christian man-dealer, and for full five hundred years and more this frightful heart disease of the Dark Continent destroyed the beginnings of Negro civilization, overturned governments, murdered men, disrupted families and poisoned the civilized world. Do you want an explanation of the degradation of this pitiful little nest perched in the crimson soil of Georgia? Ask your fathers and your father's fathers, for they know. Nay, you need not go back even to their memories.

In 1880 a traveler crossed Africa from Lake Nyassa to Lake Tanganyika. He saw the southern end of the lake peopled with large and prosperous villages. The next traveler who followed in 1890 found not a solitary human being—nothing but burned homes and bleaching skeletons. He tells us that the Wa-Nkonde tribe to which these people belonged, was, until this event, one of the most prosperous tribes in East Central Africa. Their people occupied a country of exceptional fertility and beauty. Three rivers, which never failed in the severest drought, ran through their territory, and their crops were the richest and most varied in the country. They possessed herds of cattle and goats; they fished in the lake with nets; they wrought iron into many-patterned spear-heads with exceptional ingenuity and skill; and that even artistic taste had begun to develop among them was evident from the ornamental work of their huts, which were unique for clever construction and beauty of design. This people, in short, by their own inherent ability and the natural resources of their country, were on the high road to civilization. Then came the overthrow. Arab traders mingled with them, settled peacefully among them, obeyed their laws, and gained their confidence. The number of the traders slowly increased; the power of the chief was slowly undermined, until, at last, with superior weapons and reinforcements, every vestige of the tribe was swept away and their lands laid in red ruins. Fourteen villages they razed from the ground and, finally, seizing more slaves than they could transport, drove the rest into the tall dry grass and set it on fire; and in the black forest was silence.

This took place in the nineteenth century during your lives, in the midst of modern missionary effort. But worse was the tale of the eighteenth century and the seventeenth century and the sixteenth century, and this whole dark crime against a human race began in 1442 when the historic thirty Negroes landed in Lisbon.

Systematic man-hunting was known in ancient times, but it subsided as civilization advanced, until the Mohammedan fanatics swept across Africa. Arabian slavery, however, had its mitigations. It was patriarchal house service; the slave might hope to rise and, once admitted to the household of faith, he became in fact, and not merely in theory, a man and a brother. The domestic slavery of the African tribes represented that first triumph of humanity that leads the savage to spare his foe's life and use his labor. Such slaves could and did rise to freedom and preferment; they became parts of the new tribe. It was left to Christian slavery to improve on all this—to make slavery a rigid unending caste by adding to bondage the prejudice of race and color. Marauding bands traversed the forests, fell upon native villages, slew the old and young and drove the rest in herds to the slave market; tribe was incited against tribe, and nation against nation. As Mr. Stanley tells us,

> While a people were thus subject to capture and expatriation, it was clearly impossible that any intellectual or moral progress could be made. The greater number of those accessible from the coast were compelled to study the best methods of avoiding the slaver and escaping his force and his wiles; the rest only thought of the arts of kidnapping their innocent and unsuspecting fellow creatures. Yet, contradictory as it may appear to us, there were not wanting at the same time zealous men who devoted themselves to Christianity. In Angola, Congo and Mozambique, and far up the Zambesi, missionaries erected churches and cathedrals, appointed bishops and priests who converted and baptized; while at the mouth of the Congo, the Niger and the Zambesi their countrymen built slave barracoons, and anchored their murderous slave ships. Europeans legalized and sanctioned the slave trade; the public conscience of the period approved it; the mitred heads of the church blessed the slave gangs as they marched to the shore, and the tax-collector received the levy per head as lawful revenue.

The development of the trade depended largely upon the commercial nations, and, as they put more and more ruthless enterprise into the traffic, it grew and flourished. First came the Portuguese as the world's slave trader, secured in their monopoly by the Bull of Demarcation issued by Pope Alexander VI. Beginning in 1442 they traded a hundred and fifty years, until Portugal was reduced to a province of Spain in 1580 and her African settlements neglected. Immediately the thrifty Dutch began to monopolize the trade, and held it for a century, until Oliver Cromwell deprived them of it. The celebrated Dutch West India Company intrigued with native states and gained a monopoly of the trade in Negroes from 1630 to 1668. They whirled a stream of cargoes over the great seas, filled the West Indies, skirted the coasts of America and, sailing up the curving river to Jamestown, planted the Negro problems in Virginia in 1619. Then the English scented gain and bestirred themselves mightily.

Two English slave ships sailed from Plymouth in the middle of the sixteenth century, but the great founder of the English slave trade was Sir John Hawkins. Queen Elizabeth had some scruples at the trade in human beings, and made Hawkins promise to seize only those who were willing to go with him—a thing which he easily promised and easily forgot. This Sir John Hawkins was a strange product of his times. Brave, ruthless, cruel and religious: a pirate, a man-stealer and a patriot. He sailed to Africa in the middle of the sixteenth century, and immediately saw profits for English gain. He burned villages, murdered the natives and stole slaves, and then, urging his crew to love one another and serve God daily, he sailed merrily westward to the Spanish West Indies in the good ship called the "Jesus," and compelled the Spaniards to buy slaves at the muzzle of his guns.

Thus the English slave trade began under Queen Elizabeth, was encouraged under James I, who had made the translation of our Bible, and renewed by Oliver Cromwell, the great Puritan, who fought for it and seized the island of Jamaica as a slave market. So kings, queens and countries encouraged the trade, and the English soon became the world's greatest slave traders. New manufactures suitable to the trade were introduced into England, and the trade brought so much gold to Great Britain that they named the pieces "guineas" after the slave coast. Four million dollars a year went from England, in the eighteenth century, to buy slaves. Liverpool, the city where the trade centered, had, in 1783, nine hundred slave ships in the trade, and in eleven years they carried $76,000,000 worth of slaves to America, and they did this on a clear profit of $60,000,000.

These vast returns seduced the conscience of Europe. [Samuel] Boswell, the biographer of Dr. Johnson, called the slave trade "an important necessary branch of commerce," and probably the best people of England were of this opinion, and were surprised and indignant when [Thomas] Clarkson and [William] Wilberforce began their campaign.

Gradually aroused by repeated and seemingly hopeless assaults, the conscience of England awoke and forbade the trade, in 1807, after having guided and cherished it for one hundred and fifty years. She called for aid from America, and America apparently responded in the statutes of 1808. But, true to her reputation as the most lawless nation on earth, America made no attempt to enforce the law in her own territory for a generation, and, after that, refused repeatedly and doggedly to prevent the slave trade of the world from sailing peacefully under the American flag for fifty years—up until the very outbreak of the civil war. Thus, from 1442 to 1860, nearly half a millennium, the Christian world fattened on the stealing of human souls.

Nor was there any pretence of charity in the methods of their doing. The capture of the slaves was organized deceit, murder and force; the shipping of them was far worse than the modern shipping of horses and cattle. Of this middle passage across the sea in slow sailing ships, with brutal sailors and little to eat, it has often been said "that never in the world before was so much wretchedness condensed in so little room."

The Negroes, naked and in irons, were chained to each other hand and foot, and stowed so close that they were not allowed more than a foot and a half each. Thus, crammed together like herrings in a barrel, they contracted putrid and fatal disorders, so that those who came to inspect them in the morning had frequently to pick dead slaves out of their rows and unchain their corpses from the bodies of their wretched mates. Blood and filth covered the floors, the hot air reeked with contagion, and the death rate among the slaves often reached fifty per cent, not to speak of the decimation when once they reached the West Indian plantations.

The world will never know the exact number of slaves transported to America. Several thousand came in the fifteenth century, tens of thousands in the sixteenth, and hundreds of thousands in the seventeenth. In the eighteenth century more than two and one-half millions of slaves were transported, and in 1790 Negroes were crossing the ocean at the rate of sixty thousand a year. Dunbar thinks that nearly fifteen millions were transported in all.

Such was the traffic that revolutionized Africa. Instead of man-hunting being an incident of tribal wars, war became the incident of man-hunting. From the Senegal to St. Paul de Loanda winding, beaten tracks converged to the sea from every corner of the Dark Continent, covered with the blood of the foot-sore, lined with the bleaching bones of the dead, and echoing with the wails of the conquered, the bereaved and the dying. The coast stood bristling with forts and prisons to receive the human cattle. Across the blue waters of the Atlantic two hundred and fifty ships a year hurried to the west, with their crowded, half-suffocated cargoes. And during all this time Martin Luther had lived and died, Calvin had preached, Raphael had painted and Shakespeare and Milton sung; and yet for four hundred years the coasts of Africa and America were strewn with the dying and the dead, four hundred years the sharks followed the scurrying ships, four hundred years Ethiopia stretched forth her hands unto God. All this you know, all this you have read many a time. I tell it again, lest you forget.

What was slavery to the slave trade? Not simply forced labor, else we are all in bondage. Not simply toil without pay, even that is not unknown in America. No, the dark damnation of slavery in America was the destruction of the African family and of all just ideals of family life. No one pretends that the family life of African tribes had reached modern standards — barbarous nations have barbarous ideals. But this does not mean that they have no ideals at all. The patriarchal clan-life of the Africans, with its polygamy protected by custom, tradition and legal penalty, was infinitely superior to the shameless promiscuity of the West Indian plantations, the unhallowed concubinage of Virginia, or the prostitution of

Louisiana. And these ideals slavery broke and scattered and flirted to the winds and left ignorance and degradation in their train.

When the good New England clergyman thought it a shame that slaves should herd like animals, without a legal marriage bond, he devised a quaint ceremony for them in which Sally promised Bob to cleave to him. For life? Oh no. As long as "God in his providence" kept them on the same plantation. This was in New England where there was a good deal more conscience than in Georgia. What ideal of family life could one reasonably expect Bob and Sally to have? The modern American family (considering the shame of divorce) has not reached perfection; yet it is the result of long training and carefully fostered ideals and persistent purging of the socially unfit.

As I study this family in the little southern town, in all its degradation and uncleanness, I cannot but see a plain case of cause and effect. If you degrade people the result is degradation, and you have no right to be surprised at it. Nor am I called upon to apologize for these people, or to make fun of their dumb misery. For their condition there is an apology due, witness High Heaven; but not from me.

Upon the town we have visited, upon the state, upon this section, the awful incubus of the past broods like a writhing sorrow, and when we turn our faces from that past, we turn it not to forget but to remember; viewing degradation with fear and not contempt, with awe and not criticism, bowing our head and straining willing ears to the iron voice

> . . . of Nature merciful and stern.
> I teach by killing, let others learn.

But the Negroes of the South are not all upon this low level. From this Nadir they stretch slowly, resolutely upward, by infinite gradation, helped now by the hand of a kindly master or a master's son, now by the sacrifice of friends; always by the ceaseless energy of a people who will never submit to burial alive.

Look across the street of your little southern town: here is a better house — a mother and father, two sons and a girl. They are hard-working people and good people. They read and write a little and, though they are slow and good natured, they are seldom idle. And yet they are unskilled, without foresight, always in debt and living from hand to mouth. Hard pressed they may sink into crime; encouraged they may rise to comfort, but never to wealth. Why? Because they and their fathers have been trained this way. What does a slave know of saving? What can he know of forethought? What could he learn even of skill, save in exceptional cases? In other words, slavery must of necessity send into the world of work a mass of unskilled laborers who have no idea of what thrift means; who have been a part of a great economic organization but had nothing to do with its organizing; and so when they are suddenly called to take a place in a greater organization, in which free individual initiative is a potent factor, they cannot, for they do not know how; they lack skill and, more than that, they lack ideals!

And so we might go on: past problems of work and wages, of legal protection, of civil rights and of education, up to this jaunty, little yellow house on a cross street with a flower-bed struggling sturdily with the clay, with vines and creepers and a gleam of white curtains and a decorous parlor. If you enter this house you may not find it altogether up to your ideals. A Dutch housekeeper would find undiscovered corners, and a fastidious person might object to the general scheme of decoration. And yet, compared with the homes in the town, white or black, the house is among the best. It may be the home of a Negro butcher who serves both sides the color line, or of a small grocer, a carpenter, a school teacher or a preacher. Whatever this man may be, he is a leader in a peculiar sense — the ideal-maker in his group of people. The white world is there, but it is the other side of the color line; it is seen distinctly and from afar. Of white and black there is no mingling in church and school, in general gatherings. The black world is isolated and alone; it gets its ideals, its larger thoughts, its notions of life, from these local leaders; they set the tone to that all-powerful spiritual world that surrounds and envelopes the souls of men; their standards of living, their interpretation of sunshine and rain and human hearts, their thoughts of love and labor, their aspirations and dim imaginings — all that makes life *life*.

Not only does this group leader guide a mass of men isolated in space, but also isolated in time. For we must remember that not only did slavery overthrow the Negro family and teach few lessons of thrift and foresight; it also totally broke a nation from all its traditions of the past in every realm of life. I fear I cannot impress upon you the full meaning of such a revolution. A nation that breaks suddenly with its past is almost fatally crippled. No matter how crude or imperfect that past may be, with all its defects, it is the foundation upon which generations to come must build. Beauty and finish and architectural detail are not required of it, but the massive weight of centuries of customs and traditions it must have. The slave trade, a new climate, a new economic regime, a new language and a new religion separated the American Negro as completely from his fatherland as it is possible for human agencies to do. The result is curious. There is a certain swaying in the air, a tilting and a crumbling, a vast difficulty of adjustment — of making the new ideas of work and wealth, of authority and right, fit in and hitch themselves to something gone; to the authority of the fathers, the customs of the past in a nation without grandfathers. So, then, the Negro group leader not only sets present standards, but he supplies in a measure the lack of past standards, and his leading is doubly difficult, since with Emancipation there came a second partial breaking with the past. The leader of the masses must discriminate between the good and bad in the past; he must keep the lesson of work and reject the lesson of concubinage; he must add more lessons of moral rectitude to the old religious fervor; he must, in fine, stand to this group in the light of the interpreter of the civilization of the twentieth century to the minds and hearts of people who, from sheer necessity, can but dimly comprehend it. And this man—I care not what his vocation may be—preacher, teacher, physician, or artisan, this person is going to solve the Negro problem; for that problem is at bottom the clash of two different standards of culture, and this priest it is who interprets the one to the other.

Let me for a moment recapitulate. In the life of advancing peoples there must go on simultaneously a struggle for existence, accumulation of wealth, education of the young, and a development in culture and the higher things of life. The more backward the nation the larger sum of effort goes into the struggle for existence; the more forward the nation the larger and broader is the life of the spirit. For guidance, in taking these steps in civilization, the nation looks to four sources: the precepts of parents, the sight of seers, the opinion of the majority and the traditions of the past.

Here, then, is a group of people in which every one of these great sources of inspiration is partially crippled: the family group is struggling to recover from the debauchery of slavery; and the number of the enlightened leaders must necessarily be small; the surrounding and more civilized white majority is cut off from its natural influence by the color line; and the traditions of the past are either lost, or largely traditions of evil and wrong.

Any one looking the problem squarely in the face might conclude that it was unjust to expect progress, or the signs of progress, until many generations had gone by. Indeed, we must not forget that those people who claimed to know the Negro best, freely and confidently predicted during the abolition controversy—

1. That free Negroes would not, and could not, work effectively.
2. That the freedman who did work, would not save.
3. That it was impossible to educate Negroes.
4. That no members of the race gave signs of ability and leadership.
5. That the race was morally degenerate.

Not only was this said, it was sincerely and passionately believed, by honorable men who, with their forefathers, had lived with the Negro three hundred years. And yet to-day the Negro in one generation forms the chief laboring force of the most rapidly developing part of the land. He owns twelve million acres of land, two hundred and fifty million dollars worth of farm property, and controls as owner or renter five hundred millions. Nearly three-fifths of the Negroes have learned to read and write. An increasing number have given evidence of ability and thoughtfulness—not, to be sure, of transcendent genius, but of integrity, large knowledge and common-sense. And finally there can be to-day no reasonable dispute but that the number of efficient, law-abiding and morally upright black people in this land is far larger than it ever was before, and is daily growing. Now these obvious and patent facts do not by any means indicate the full solution of the problem. There are still hosts of idle and unreliable Negro laborers; the race still, as a whole, has not learned the lesson of thrift and saving; fully seventy-five per cent are still fairly designated as ignorant. The number of group leaders of ability and character is far behind the demand, and the development of a trustworthy upper class has, as is usually true, been accompanied by the differentiation of a dangerous class of criminals.

What the figures of Negro advancement mean is, that the development has been distinctly and markedly in the right direction, and that, given justice and help, no honest man can doubt the outcome. The giving of justice means the recognition of desert wherever it appears; the right to vote on exactly the same terms as other people vote; the right to the equal use of public conveniences and the educating of youth in the public schools. On these points, important as they are, I will not dwell. I am more interested here in asking how these struggling people may be actually helped. I conceive that such help may take any one of four forms:—

1. Among a people deprived of guiding traditions, they may be furnished trained guidance in matters of civilization and ideals of living.
2. A people whose family life is not strongly established must have put before them and brought home to them the morals of sane and sanitary living.
3. The mass of Negro children must have the keys of knowledge put into their hands by good elementary schools.
4. The Negro youth must have the opportunity to learn the technical skill of modern industry.

All these forms of help are important. No one of them can be neglected without danger of increasing complications as time flies, and each one of them are lines of endeavor in which the Negro cannot be reasonably expected to help himself without aid from others. For instance, it cannot be seriously expected that a race of freedmen would have the skill necessary for modern industry. They cannot teach themselves what they themselves do not know, and consequently a legitimate and crying need of the south is the establishment of industrial schools. The public school system is one of the foundation stones of free republican government. Negro children, as well as other children, have a right to ask of the nation knowledge of reading, writing and the rules of number, together with some conception of the world in time and space. Not one Negro child in three is to-day receiving any such training or has any chance to receive it, and a decent public school system in the South, aided by the national government, is something that must come in the near future, if you expect the race problem to be settled.

Here then are two great needs: public schools and industrial schools. How are schools of any sort established? By furnishing teachers. Given properly equipped teachers and your schools are a foregone success; without them, I care not how much you spend on buildings and equipment, the schools are a failure. It is here that Negro colleges, like Atlanta University, show their first usefulness.

But, in my list of ways in which the Negro may legitimately be helped to help himself, I named two other avenues of aid, and I named them first because to my mind they are even of more importance than popular education. I mean the moral uplift of a people. Now moral uplift comes not primarily from schools, but from strong home life and high social ideals. I have spoken of the Negroes' deficiency in these lines and the reason of that deficiency. Here, then, is a chance for help, but how? Not by direct teaching, because that is often ineffective and it is precluded in the South by the color line. It can be done, to my mind, only by group leadership; by planting in every community of Negroes black men with ideals of life and thrift and civilization, such as must in time filter through the masses and set examples of moral living and correct thinking to the great masses of Negroes who spend but little of their life in schools. After all the education of men comes but in small degree from schools; it comes mostly from the fireside, from companionships, from your social set, from the opinion of each individual's little world. This is even more true of the Negro. His world is smaller. He is shut in to himself by prejudice; he has, by reason of his poverty, little time for school. If he is to learn, he must learn from his group leaders, his daily companions, his social surroundings, his own dark world of striving, longing and dreaming. Here, then, you must plant the seed of civilization. Here you must place men educated, not merely in the technique of teaching or skill of hand, but above and beyond that into a thorough understanding of their age and the demands and meaning of modern culture. In so far as the college of to-day stands for the transmission from age to age of all that is best in the world's deeds, thoughts and traditions, in so far it is a crying necessity that a race, ruthlessly torn from its traditions and trained for centuries awry, should receive back through the higher culture of its gifted children some of the riches of the great system of culture into which it has been thrust. If the meaning of modern life cannot be taught at Negro hearthsides because the parents themselves are untaught, then its ideals can be forced into the centres of Negro life only by the teaching of higher institutions of learning and the agency of thoroughly educated men.

The Souls of Black Folk
1904

Published in 1904, more than a year and a half after the publication of The Souls of Black Folk, *this short piece seems to have served as Du Bois's personal explanation of what he had tried to accomplish in the book. It reads like an apologia, even a response to some of his reviewers. Here Du Bois claims a certain "narrowness" as well as "clearness of vision," an "African" outlook and a perspective of "English restraint." He worries that the diverse essays in* Souls *lack cohesiveness and unity. Yet he reflects on the writer's struggle to forge meaning out of feeling and experience and stresses that a "tone of self-revelation" informs the entire work. The piece represents the author searching to explain his work and makes an intriguing companion to the book.*

One who is born with a cause is predestined to a certain narrowness of view, and at the same time to some clearness of vision within his limits with which the world often finds it well to reckon. My book has many of

"The Souls of Black Folk," *Independent,* November 17, 1904.

the defects and some of the advantages of this situation. Because I am a negro I lose something of that breadth of view which the more cosmopolitan races have, and with this goes an intensity of feeling and conviction which both wins and repels sympathy, and now enlightens, now puzzles.

The Souls of Black Folk is a series of fourteen essays written under various circumstances and for different purposes during a period of seven years. It has, therefore, considerable, perhaps too great, diversity. There are bits of history and biography, some description of scenes and persons, something of controversy and criticism, some statistics and a bit of storytelling. All this leads to rather abrupt transitions of style, tone and viewpoint and, too, without doubt, to a distinct sense of incompleteness and sketchiness.

On the other hand, there is a unity in the book, not simply the general unity of the larger topic, but a unity of purpose in the distinctively subjective note that runs in each essay. Through all the book runs a personal and intimate tone of self-revelation. In each essay I sought to speak from within— to depict a world as we see it who dwell therein. In thus giving up the usual impersonal and judicial attitude of the traditional author I have lost in authority but gained in vividness. The reader will, I am sure, feel in reading my words peculiar warrant for setting his judgment against mine, but at the same time some revelation of how the world looks to me cannot easily escape him.

This is not saying that the style and workmanship of the book make its meaning altogether clear. A clear central message it has conveyed to most readers, I think, but around this center there has lain a penumbra of vagueness and half-veiled allusion which has made these and others especially impatient. How far this fault is in me and how far it is in the nature of the message I am not sure. It is difficult, strangely difficult, to translate the finer feelings of men into words. The Thing itself sits clear before you; but when you have dressed it out in periods it seems fearfully uncouth and inchoate. Nevertheless, as the feeling is deep the greater the impelling force to seek to express it. And here the feeling was deep.

In its larger aspects the style is tropical—African. This needs no apology. The blood of my fathers spoke through me and cast off the English restraint of my training and surroundings. The resulting accomplishment is a matter of taste. Sometimes I think very well of it and sometimes I do not.

Correspondence about
The Souls of Black Folk,
1903–1957

Every author dreams of being read carefully, of affecting the ideas and emotions of his or her readers. Du Bois received many letters over the years admiring or criticizing *Souls*. We reprint a small selection of them here, in some cases with Du Bois's response, as a means of expanding the context within which the book can be interpreted. These letters demonstrate the range of ways *Souls* has been read by blacks and whites, the famous and the ordinary, within the United States and abroad.

Ida B. Wells-Barnett to Du Bois
Chicago, Illinois
May 30, 1903

Ida B. Wells-Barnett (1862–1931), a well-known journalist, feminist, and antilynching campaigner, describes a meeting at the home of Mrs. Celia Parker Woolley in Chicago (a gathering much like that of a book club), attended by numerous whites and eight blacks. A spirited discussion of Souls *became a forum for airing views on the developing dispute between Du Bois and Booker T. Washington.*

Reprinted from Herbert Aptheker, ed., *The Correspondence of W. E. B. Du Bois* (Amherst: University of Massachusetts Press, 1973–1978), 1:55–56.

Chicago, Ill., May 30th, 1903.

Dear Prof. DuBois:—

Your note of April 23rd did not especially call for a reply so I did not send one. I meant though to write you about a Conference which we had over your book at the home of Mrs. Celia Parker Woolley, a very good friend of the race. She had a company of some of the most literary folks here among white folks, at her home one Sunday evening about three weeks ago, and then she had Dr. and Mrs. Bentley; Mr. Lloyd Wheeler, Prof. [Monroe] Work, Mr. and Mrs. Laing-Williams, your humble servant and her better half, all there to do the discussing.

Mrs. Bentley had a fine review about which she had doubtless told you. Most of the others, save my husband and myself, confined their reviews solely to your criticisms of Booker T. and thought the book was weak because of them. Of course you know our sentiments. There was not much time for the white side of the audience to present its view but they too took the same view. Of one thing I am very certain, the discussion stimulated a curiosity to read the book.

But I feel sure you have heard about all this. My main object for writing now is to tell you that Mrs. Woolley, than whom there is not a truer friend of the race, seemed a little hurt that you had not acknowledged the receipt of a little book of her own which she had sent you. It is called "The Western Slope" and I am quite sure that while you may have overlooked its modest proportions in the press and stress of your own multitudinous work, it would need only a hint to have you duly look it up, and send the donor a cordial note of thanks both for what she has said for our race in it, as well as the work she is trying to do to convert her friends to your view of the subject in your own book.

I lunched with Miss Jane Addams at Hull House Wednesday and found that she too was disappointed at not seeing you when she was in Atlanta recently. She said she did not blame you for not making your exhibit before the conference. But she tried to get a personal audience with you herself and failed. She said she wrote asking you to call, and that she telephoned over to the University requesting the same thing but that you did not come nor did she hear from you. I do not need to tell you who Miss Addams is. I assured her there must be some mistake, either you did not get the message or they refused to take your card up if you called at the hotel. I am sure that in your leisure moments you will find time to write her a note, to let her know that the silence was not intentional on your part.

We are still reading your book with the same delighted appreciation. I am arranging myself for a meeting of our best brained, to have a discussion thereon, within the next two weeks. Am only sorry that you cannot be present with us.

Yours truly,
I. B. W.-B.

Caroline Pemberton to Du Bois

Philadelphia, Pennsylvania, December 12, 1903

A northerner with strong socialist sympathies, Caroline Pemberton was deeply moved by Souls, *but she criticizes Du Bois for overlooking the "relations of the colored man to the labor problem." Later in life, Du Bois himself would gradually move toward a deeper analysis of class in American society.*

My Dear Mr. Du Bois,

I must write and try to tell you how deeply your book "The Souls of Black Folk" has stirred me, and how strongly I agree with your conclusions on higher education and your estimate of Booker T. Washington. I am glad you have had the courage to voice the dissatisfaction that your race justly feels with his gospel of materialism. I wish I could have a talk with you on the many problems touched on, — I wish I could tell you how the music of your race pierces my heart when I hear its genuine melodies and not the white man's cheap imitations, — or worse still, — the Negro's imitation of the white man's imitations, — a whole tragedy in itself! Your book is a cry, a passionate appeal to the hearts & brains of the white race. It will touch many hearts, — but, — I do not say this in discouragement, — it is not thro the benevolent or the tenderhearted that your mission is to be accomplished & your race reach its destiny.

It is such a long story,—there is no use beginning it now—but there is one phase of the whole "problem" that you overlook, & that is the relation of the colored man to the labor problem. You do not seem to be aware that the white laborers of the North are facing the same alternative of starvation,—or submission and unceasing, unrecompensed toil. Don't you know that America is either on the verge of a terrible conflict between capital & labor,—or the establishment of a vast military & industrial despotism? Everything up here is turmoil, rebellion, mutterings, wrong & oppression. It is all part of the same game—the suppression of the laborer white or black. Your people furnish a larger percentage of laborers in proportion to your numbers than the whites do. The door of opportunity is closing on all the working class,—it shuts with a bang on yours. You comprise the working class of the South,—hence you must be kept down. The class hatred is concealed under race hatred. I do not say that race hatred does not exist separate & apart from class hatred,—but the fact that the white man wants your unrecompensed toil is largely the reason of his race prejudice,—the reason why he hates the sight of an educated color man,—a colored teacher or doctor or lawyer. It is just one more prisoner escaped from the stockade of unrequited toil!

Up here, we have become accustomed to a more hypocritical attitude to labor,—but we are fast losing the glamour and tearing off the mask. The Capitalists here want to establish the old relations of master & slave in all except name, between those who toil for a daily wage & those who pocket the profits the toiler has created. We are a little less crude & barbarous in our methods, that is all. You will live to see an attempt to disfranchise white laborers the moment they gain the courage to vote against their masters,—as your working class has heroically, gratefully & blindly done, since the war. Nonetheless, I deeply sympathize with you & yours, & with the educated colored Class that you represent. There is nothing analogous to *you* up north here among the whites. I see one mistake you all make,—however—it is in thinking the white man's culture is the only culture and his "Civilization" the only real "Civilization." What he boasts of as "Civilization" is a hideous mockery,—a nightmare of horrors,—child labor, toiling women in mills, slums full of misery; jails, almshouses, brothels, and palaces full of degenerates! We all know some change is coming; what will it be?

Yours cordially,
Caroline H. Pemberton

D. Tabak to Du Bois

This remarkable letter by a Jewish immigrant living in New York City attests to the capacity of Souls *to convey to its readers a sense of transcendent tragedy. The twenty-four-year-old immigrant, who describes himself as a "Russian Jew" and as "white colored," seems to have felt a strange combination of guilt and personal affinity in reading the book. The letter is also remarkable for the sense of class and gender identity it conveys.*

Educator W.E.B. DuBois, Atlanta University.

Most dear sir:

I took a stroll one day when I saw "The Souls of Black Folk" lying upon a book shelf in a corner of DeLancy Street. The name attracted me. I consequently bought it, went home and read it—when I suddenly found myself a-crying.

I was over powered by a peculiar pain that was so much akin to bliss, indignation stirring my blood, yet, somehow, being glad of that—growing furious at times, overcome with shame and disgrace, yet, from underneath all this, up swelled a keen sense of inner delight. Heavens who could describe in adequate terms that Satanic blending of both pain of a bleeding heart and joy og [*sic*] the gods? But lo, all this inner agitation culminated to "tears, idle tears."

I creid [*sic*] so feminine-like. And I am a man. A man lacking in manners, perhaps, but not in manhood. I am fast reaching my maturity. Am 24. A Russian Jew. Adverse circumstances have brought me to this country where more than one eight of the entire population is being hated and persecuted and lynched and denied all rights a thousand times more cruel than we Jews are in Russia. Believe me, Mr. DuBois, that when I Read your "Coming of John" I was ashamed of being white colored. I envied all ye despised and abused. Not that I like being treated that way but I want to be in the right, to be aggrieved in a direct way even rather than be the aggressor in an indirect way. And to think that the treatment meted out to negroes is in the face of the fact that they are the very ones who actually gave their life's blood to the upbuilding of the economic and industrial welfare of the nation is—what is it?—it baffles invective.

How I admire your self possession!

When I was younger I used to think that the thing held most dear in

---

Reprinted from Du Bois Papers, University of Massachusetts Amherst, reel 3. The letter is undated, but it is located with letters from 1905.

this world was life and limb. That in order to save a life from death or a limb from injury everyone will readily leave everything else behind and rush to assist towards that end. When first I saw a man being bruised and clubbed with a number of people looking on calmly I was puzzled. I simply could not understand it. And to this day I still believe the principle cause of that seemingly eternal tragedy of Cian [*sic*] vs. Abel to be a mere blunder of the heart — a simple misunderstanding which only needs to be cleared up. . . .

How genuinely glad one feels in obeying nature's law to love his fellowmen. Why it is all so simple, and pleasant and conducive to all good things. We all love. Indeed we all love to love. But some of us — a good many of us — lo, I must say the most of us — do not as yet know themselves.

Fore and After-thought.

If I transgressed upon any of the accepted ways of writing I know you will not mind. If I failed in any degree to pay the respects due to a man of your position and learning I know you will pass that by. How do I know it? By intuition. I feel you are bigger than ordinary. That there is not the slightest touch of vanity about you that I a poor, ignorant workingman can address you as my equal, that you are able to discern my beating heart aflame with love and sympathy to all nature's children.

My desire to write you something broke through my natural shyness and conscious ignorance of style and form. So then, it must have been an overwhelming desire. O, if I could but pray — how fervently I should pray that you keep up the noble work you do. I only wish with all my heart that you may live to see those ghastly social injustices to be completely and forever abolished.

Yours, for the right to live,
D. Tabak
120 S. 1st Street.
Brooklyn.

Du Bois to William James
June 12, 1906

William James (1842–1910), professor, philosopher of pragmatism, and pioneer of psychology, had been one of Du Bois's teachers and mentors while Du Bois was a student at Harvard in the early 1890s. In this letter, Du Bois responds to James's claim that Souls *is too despairing, arguing that he was not wedded to the "minor key."*

Reprinted from Du Bois Papers, University of Massachusetts Amherst, reel 2.

Dear Professor James:

It was very kind of you to read my book & write me so appreciative a letter. You must not think I am personally wedded to the "minor key" business — on the contrary I am tuned to a most aggressive & unquenchable hopefulness. I wanted in this case simply to reveal fully the other side to the world. Mrs. Du Bois joins me in regards to yourself and Mrs. James, and in wishes for a pleasant & restful summer.

W.E.B. Du Bois

Hallie E. Queen to Du Bois

Ithaca, New York
February 11, 1907

Hallie E. Queen, one of only a few black undergraduates at Cornell University, helped to organize what became a Du Bois Club on her campus. Her descriptions of readings of specific chapters among her group, as well as the hopeful tone with which she speaks of the "Veil . . . lifting," must have been gratifying to Du Bois. This letter also provides an interesting, if small, window onto issues of "race on campus," circa 1907.

Ithaca, N.Y., Feb. 11, 1907.

My dear Mr. Du Bois,

I know that I am taking an unpardonable license in addressing you but I thought that you would be glad to know of a movement which has been started at Cornell and which concerns you in a peculiarly intimate manner. Let me say at the beginning that I am one of two colored girl students at Cornell, being now a Junior. Some weeks ago a movement was started to make a study of your works. From what I can understand, it originated in the mind of a Philadelphia white girl who had heard you speak before the Ethical Culture Society. At any rate, I was asked to be a member of the Club, as yet unnamed. Altho your works have been so widespread I am sure that you will be pleased at this new departure on the part of a set

Reprinted from Herbert Aptheker, ed., *The Correspondence of W. E. B. Du Bois* (Amherst: University of Massachusetts Press, 1973–1978), 1:125–26.

of young persons at a University which is hardly noted for its broadness of view.

The Co-Operative Society, the Students' Store, immediately received a large order for your "Souls of Black Folk," with which we began our work. A copy of the book was sent to the wife of Ambassador Andrew D. White (who lives on the Campus) and others were sent to other persons whom we wish to be prepared when we call upon them to help us in any way.

Up to date we have read and discussed three essays—The "Passing of the First Born," "The Coming of John" and "Our Spiritual Strivings." Because of my peculiar connection with the literary department of Cornell I was chosen critic of the Club. May I tell you just a few things that have been said? One of the girls, a Senior from Massachusetts said that the paragraph on page 217 was the most beautiful picture of maternity that she had ever seen. Another said that "Our Spiritual Strivings" reminded her of the One hundred and thirty seventh Psalm—"By the rivers of Babylon"—comparisons of "The Passing of the First Born" with the work of the two Van Dykes and others seldom gave the other writers cause for pride. It was a significant thing that the papers were not actuated by any fanatical sympathy as they generally were kept apart from any racial suggestions.

Your book is in our Library presented by Henry W. Sage and constantly referred to by Dean Walter Willcox of the College of Arts and Sciences.

When we came to study the "Coming of John," things took a different turn. Then all of the pent up sympathy was expressed and I am glad to tell you, Mr. Du Bois, that I believe that the discussion of that one essay has done much toward broadening the racial spirit at Cornell, that is, the best kind of racial spirit.

Now, Mr. Du Bois, will you pardon me for thus occupying your time? I was so full of it—it has meant so much to me that I wanted to tell you. We have thirty one people at Cornell—we have over thirty thousand American white students. As soon as our Club, of which I am at present the only Negro member, becomes incorporated and named, we will want you to know more about it, and all of these peoples will know. Surely the "Veil" is lifting; surely the day is not so far off. The horizon is broadening here—somewhere the Sun is already high.

Again hoping you will pardon me, and thanking you in the name of the Club, for your book, I am

Very respectfully yours
(Miss) Hallie E. Queen

W. D. Hooper to Du Bois
Athens, Georgia, September 2, 1909

Du Bois to W. D. Hooper
October 11, 1909

*This exchange between Du Bois and a University of Georgia Latin profes-
sor is a fascinating communication across the color line. Hooper's plea of
innocence stimulates a stinging response.*

Athens, Ga., September 2nd, 1909.

Prof W. E. B. DuBois
Dear Sir:—
    I have just read the tragedy which you call "The Souls of Black Folk,"
and I cannot refrain from writing to tell you how profoundly it has affected
me. It is faint praise—but even the pure English was very refreshing in
this day of slovenliness.
    The pathetic part of the whole thing is what you stress repeatedly—
that the control of the South is not in the hands of its best people. The
problem is the problem of the lower class whites, and the more enlightened are utterly powerless. I have long grieved over your own position,
and wished that there could be some alleviation, and known that there
could be none. I have, however, wanted you to know that my skirts at least
are clean. I have never wittingly wronged one of your race in any way. I
have never defrauded one of them of money, I have never insulted one
of them, I have never given even a slight to one of them. I have been careful to train my children to respect their feelings in every way, and have
punished them for offenses in this respect which I should else have
passed over. And I have been able to be of service to many of them in more
ways than in the matter of money. The Principal of the city schools here
has had regular teaching from me in both Latin and German, and I have
been able also to help others. Of course I voted against disfranchisement.
    This is a small thing, but your book has put me on the defensive.
These things I have done and left undone, and yet my whole training and

Reprinted from Herbert Aptheker, ed., *The Correspondence of W. E. B. Du Bois* (Amherst:
University of Massachusetts Press, 1973–1978), 1:152–53.

environment have been such that I cannot break away from the other things of which you complain—I should not use the word, because the book is notably free from complaint. You, in turn, must look as leniently as you can on feelings which have been made part of us, and we must labor together, in all ways to lighten the gloom. And with it all rest assured that many of us feel most deeply the pathos of your own position.

> Yours very truly,
> W. D. Hooper

> Atlanta, Ga., October 11, 1909

Mr. W. D. Hooper
My dear Sir:

I have read your very kind letter of Sept. 2nd again and again with increasing interest and sympathy. I have taken the liberty to read it to some of my friends and they have been both moved and encouraged. I thank you for your frank words and I want to say two things in answer to them which I will trust will not sound ungracious. First, whenever an aristocracy allows the mob to rule the fault is not with the mob; and secondly, Comrade, you and I can never be satisfied with sitting down before a great human problem and saying nothing can be done. We must do something. That is the reason we are on Earth.

Again thanking you for your kind words, I beg to remain

> Very sincerely yours,
> W. E. B. Du Bois

Du Bois to Herbert Aptheker

Seattle, Washington
February 27, 1953

In this letter Du Bois discusses his references to Jews in Souls *and describes five places in the text where he wishes to make changes in the forthcoming fiftieth-anniversary edition. Du Bois also admits that the use of language, regardless of one's intention, may result in "unjustly maligning a people." Du Bois made the prescribed changes in the 1953 edition. A close associate*

Reprinted from Du Bois Papers, University of Massachusetts Amherst, box 360.

of Du Bois in the 1950s, Aptheker, a renowned scholar of African American history, edited and published many volumes of Du Bois's work in the 1970s and 1980s.

Dear Mr. Aptheker:

Shirley and I have had fifteen days of perfect sunshine in California; I have spoken eight times and Shirley eleven, to very sympathetic audiences, on "Africa" and on "Peace." We are now ending with talks in Seattle and Portland. We reach New York, March 5.

In Los Angeles, a friend gave me a copy of *Souls of Black Folk.* I have had a chance to read it in part for the first time in years. I find in chapters VII, VIII and IX, five incidental references to Jews. I recall that years ago, Jacob Schiff wrote me criticising these references and that I denied any thought of race or religious prejudice and promised to go over the passages in future editions. The editions however succeeded each other without any consultation with me, and evidently the matter slipped my mind.

As I re-read these words today, I see that there harm might come if they were allowed to stand as they are. First of all, I am not at all sure that the foreign exploiters to whom I referred in my study of the Black Belt, were in fact Jews. I took the word of my informants, and I am now wondering if in fact Russian Jews in any number were in Georgia at the time. But even if they were, what I was condemning was the exploitation and not the race nor religion. And I did not, when writing, realize that by stressing the name of the group instead of what some members of the group may have done, I was unjustly maligning a people in exactly the same way my folk were then and are now falsely accused.

In view of this and because of the even greater danger of injustice now than then, I want in the even[t] of re-publication to change these passages. How this can best be done I am not sure; but I am going to think it over and when I return, I hope you will have some suggestions. The passages which I have noted are on pp. 126, 127, 132, 133 and 170. I think there was one other, but I have not yet found it. Please think this over and give me your advice.

Our love to you, your wife and daughter from both of us,

Sincerely yours,
W.E.B. Du Bois

Langston Hughes to Du Bois
New York City
May 22, 1956

In this letter Langston Hughes, the great African American poet, reflects on his many readings of Souls *and speaks, in his way, for several generations of writers.*

May 22, 1956

Dr. W. E. B. Du Bois,
31 Grace Court,
Brooklyn 2, New York.

Dear Dr. Du Bois,

I have just read again your *The Souls of Black Folk* — for perhaps the tenth time — the first time having been some forty years ago when I was a child in Kansas. Its beauty and passion and power are as moving and as meaningful as ever.

My very best regards to Shirley and continued good wishes to you both,

Sincerely,
Langston Hughes

Reprinted from Du Bois Papers, University of Massachusetts Amherst, reel 71.

A Du Bois Chronology (1868–1963)

1868 William Edward Burghardt Du Bois born, February 23, in Great Barrington, Massachusetts, a small town in the Berkshire Hills in the southwestern corner of the state, the only child of Alfred Du Bois and Mary Sylvina Burghardt. Father abandons family, never returns.

1869–1873 Mother works as domestic servant.

1872 Grandfather Othello Burghardt dies. Du Bois moves with mother from a South Egremont farm into Great Barrington.

1874–1878 Attends public school, extraordinary as a student, advances a grade.

1879 Grandmother Sally Burghardt dies. Mother experiences a paralytic stroke. Moves with mother to rooms above the railroad station in Great Barrington.

1880–1882 Attends high school, lives with mother in four rooms at rear of a widow's house. Does odd jobs, including selling *New York Globe,* a black weekly newspaper. Buys five-volume Macaulay's *History of England.*

1883 Becomes an occasional correspondent and reporter for *Springfield Republican* and *New York Globe.* Travels to New Bedford, Massachusetts, to meet his grandfather Alexander Du Bois and attends a West Indian emancipation celebration on August 1, a gathering of three thousand blacks.

1884 Graduates from high school, the only black in a class of thirteen. Aspires to attend Harvard, but mother's poverty and other factors prevent the opportunity. Works for a year as a timekeeper for a contractor building a granite mansion in Great Barrington.

1885 Mother dies, March 23. Local teachers and ministers arrange a scholarship to send him to Fisk University in Nashville, Tennessee. Enters Fisk as a sophomore, edits college newspaper, studies German, Greek, Latin, classical literature, philosophy, ethics, chemistry, and physics.

1886–1887 Teaches for two summers in small town of Alexandria, in eastern Tennessee, hears black folk songs and spirituals for the first time.

1888–1889   Graduates with B.A. from Fisk, gives commencement oration on Bismarck. Enters Harvard College as a junior, rents a room from a black woman in Cambridge, rather than living in dormitory. Studies philosophy with William James and George Santayana, economics with Frank Taussig, and history with Albert Bushnell Hart. Rejected by Harvard Glee Club, develops personal ties with and lectures in the local black community.

1890   Receives B.A. in philosophy from Harvard. Wins second prize in oratorical competition, delivers one of five commencement orations, "Jefferson Davis as a Representative of Civilization." Accepted to graduate school at Harvard.

1891   Receives M.A. in history, begins to apply for funding for study in Europe.

1892   After initial rejection, a second appeal to the Slater Fund for the Education of Negroes secures grant to study at the Friedrich Wilhelm University in Berlin, Germany.

1893   Studies history, economics, and politics. Travels throughout Germany and several European countries, attends opera and symphony, writes a thesis on agricultural economics in the American South. On twenty-fifth birthday, writes a meditation on his destiny.

1894   Denied a third-year grant to study in Berlin, returns to United States. Accepts teaching job in classics at Wilberforce University, a black college in Xenia, Ohio.

1895   Becomes first black to receive Ph.D. from Harvard, with dissertation in history called *The Suppression of the African Slave Trade to the United States of America, 1638–1870.*

1896   *Suppression* published as a book, the first volume in Harvard Historical Monograph series. Marries Nina Gomer, a student at Wilberforce from Cedar Rapids, Iowa. Moves with Nina to Philadelphia, where the University of Pennsylvania hires him to study Philadelphia's black community.

1897   Delivers "The Conservation of Races" as a founding member of the American Negro Academy. Takes professorship in history and economics at Atlanta University, begins broad study of black social life that will culminate in the sixteen *Atlanta University Studies*, published between 1898 and 1914.

1899   Son Burghardt dies of diphtheria in Atlanta. A poor black man, Sam Hose, lynched near Atlanta. Publishes *The Philadelphia Negro.*

1900   Receives grand prize for exhibit on black economic development at the Paris Exposition. Attends Pan-African conference in London; delivers the line "The problem of the twentieth century is the problem of the color line" for first time. Daughter Yolande born October 21 in Great Barrington.

1901   *Atlantic Monthly* publishes "The Freedmen's Bureau," which becomes chapter 2 of *Souls.*

1903 Publishes *The Souls of Black Folk,* achieves widest acclaim yet. Book goes through six printings by 1905. Publishes essay "The Talented Tenth." Leads opposition to Booker T. Washington's accommodationism.

1904 Carnegie Hall conference of black leadership held. Du Bois and Washington speak, outlining their differing social philosophies.

1905 Founding of the Niagara Movement at a meeting of twenty-nine black leaders in Fort Erie, Ontario; the organization is devoted to protest for black civil and political rights.

1906 Conducts sociological study of Loundes County, Alabama. White mobs attack and kill blacks in Atlanta, inspiring the poem "A Litany of Atlanta."

1907–1910 Founds and edits monthly journal *Horizon.* Niagara Movement meetings dwindle in size; final gathering in 1909.

1909 Publishes biography *John Brown.*

1910 Founding of National Association for the Advancement of Colored People. Du Bois hired as director of publications and research, elected as sole black member of NAACP board of directors. Moves to New York to edit and write for *The Crisis,* the publication of the NAACP.

1911 Attends Universal Races Congress in London, a meeting devoted to refutation of racial theories. Publishes first novel, *The Quest of the Silver Fleece.*

1912 Endorses Democrat Woodrow Wilson for president.

1913 Designs major exposition in New York to commemorate fiftieth anniversary of emancipation; writes and produces *The Star of Ethiopia,* a pageant celebrating black history (performed several times in three other cities in succeeding years). Circulation of *Crisis* reaches 30,000.

1915 Publishes *The Negro,* a survey of African and African American history. Joins NAACP campaign against D. W. Griffith's film *The Birth of a Nation.* Booker T. Washington dies.

1916 Writes open letter to President Wilson protesting segregation policies in federal government. Endorses Republican Charles Evans Hughes for president.

1917 Works for separate training camp for black officers in U.S. military, acknowledging no alternative. Urges blacks to seek jobs in war industries. Marches on Fifth Avenue in NAACP silent parade against lynching.

1918 Threatened with prosecution by Justice Department if he does not cease open criticism of racism in U.S. military. Offered commission by War Department as special military intelligence adviser on racial problems. Writes "Close Ranks" editorial in July *Crisis,* arguing that blacks should support the war, preserve democracy abroad, and delay protesting lack of democracy at home. Controversy ensues among blacks over editorial; War Department commission withdrawn. Goes to France to investigate treatment of black troops.

1919 Helps organize First Pan-African Congress in Paris. Accused by members of Congress of inciting race riots in America. Publishes essay in *Crisis* on blacks in the war in Europe; issue sells 106,000 copies.

1920 Publishes *Darkwater: Voices from within the Veil,* collection of essays modeled on form of *The Souls of Black Folk.* Creates *The Brownies' Book,* a magazine for black children; lasts until 1921.

1921 Leads Second Pan-African Congress in London, Brussels, and Paris. Writes articles critical of Marcus Garvey and the Universal Negro Improvement Association.

1922 Works for Dyer antilynching bill in Congress, which passes House of Representatives and is blocked in Senate.

1923 Awarded Spingarn Medal by NAACP. Organizes Third Pan-African Congress in London, Paris, and Lisbon.

1924 Travels to Liberia, Sierra Leone, Guinea, and Senegal in Africa. Publishes *The Gift of Black Folk: The Negroes in the Making of America.* Endorses Progressive candidate Robert La Follette for president. Writes "A Lunatic or a Traitor" in *Crisis,* condemning Marcus Garvey.

1925 Publishes "The Negro Mind Reaches Out" in Alain Locke's *The New Negro: An Interpretation,* an important book of the Harlem Renaissance.

1926 Creates Krigwa Players, a Harlem theater group. Visits the Soviet Union; returns impressed with the Bolshevik Revolution.

1928 Daughter Yolande marries poet Countee Cullen in Harlem; wedding attended by three thousand people; marriage ends within a year. Publishes novel *Dark Princess: A Romance.*

1929 To save *Crisis* from financial failure, receives $5,000 subsidy from NAACP; subsidy opposed by acting secretary, Walter White.

1930–1931 Internal dispute in NAACP deepens over debt-ridden *Crisis;* Du Bois tries to limit power of board of directors over magazine.

1933 Begins to change position on integration; advocates increased black separatism and economic and social self-reliance. Relinquishes editorship of *Crisis* to George Streator and Roy Wilkins. Accepts one-year professorship at Atlanta University; teaches seminar on Marx and the Negro.

1934 Writes editorials advocating voluntary black segregation and institution building. Resigns from *Crisis* and NAACP. Accepts faculty appointment in sociology at Atlanta University. Tries to revive Atlanta Studies; travels through segregated South to conduct research. Although lacking sufficient funds, begins work on projected multivolume *Encyclopedia of the Negro.*

1935 Publishes *Black Reconstruction in America,* the major historical work of his career; the book eventually helps stimulate a fundamental reinterpretation of the post–Civil War era.

1936–1937 Writes weekly column for the *Pittsburgh Courier,* lasting until January 1938. Travels to Europe, Russia, and, via Trans-Siberian Railroad, to China and Japan. Spends five months in Germany in 1936, reporting on rise of Nazism; observes Hitler's socialist methods, denounces persecution of Jews.

1938 Delivers autobiographical address "A Pageant in Seven Decades, 1868–1938," at Atlanta University on seventieth birthday.

1939 Revised version of *The Negro* published as *Black Folk Then and Now.*

1940 Autobiography, *Dusk of Dawn,* published. Founds *Phylon,* an international magazine of black affairs; writes for the journal until 1944.

1941–1942 Conducts broad sociological study of southern blacks.

1943–1944 Leads two Atlanta conferences with limited funding. Atlanta University forces him to retire; receives pension for five years. Offered position with NAACP as director of special research; reluctant to work with Walter White and to return to organization, but accepts and moves back to New York.

1945 Begins writing column for *Chicago Defender,* continues until 1948. Attends San Francisco meeting that drafts United Nations charter; criticizes charter for failure to oppose colonialism. Helps organize Fifth Pan-African Congress in Manchester, England, in October; meets Kwame Nkrumah and Jomo Kenyatta, leaders of budding independence movements in Africa. Wife, Nina, suffers stroke, is hospitalized for eight months. First introductory volume of *Encyclopedia of the Negro* and *Color and Democracy: Colonies and Peace,* an anticolonial critique of the post–World War II world, published.

1946 Calls twenty organizations to New York to draft petition to United Nations on behalf of African American civil rights.

1947 Edits and writes introduction for *An Appeal to the World,* an NAACP-sponsored essay collection designed to influence world opinion on behalf of blacks' struggle against injustice in America. In a hearing before UN Commission on Human Rights, Soviet Union supports the initiative in *Appeal,* while United States opposes it. Publishes *The World and Africa.*

1948 Bitter dispute with Walter White and NAACP ends in Du Bois's dismissal from organization when his memorandum critical of NAACP board of directors appears in *New York Times.* Supports Progressive candidate Henry Wallace for president. Remains highly critical of U.S. foreign policy.

1949 Works for and addresses conferences on world peace in New York, Paris, and Moscow as cold war intensifies.

1950 Nina Gomer Du Bois dies in Baltimore, July 1, and is buried in Great Barrington. Elected chairman of the Peace Information Center, which advocates banning nuclear weapons; U.S. Justice Department considers the organization an "agent of a foreign principal"; organization effectively disbands.

Runs for U.S. Senate from New York as the American Labor Party candidate; receives 4 percent of vote statewide and 15 percent in Harlem.

1951 Marries forty-five-year-old writer, teacher, and civil rights activist Shirley Graham. Indicted along with four other officers of the Peace Information Center, as alleged agents of foreign interests. Fingerprinted and briefly handcuffed at arraignment in Washington, D.C. Speaking tour and fundraising campaign for legal expenses raises $35,000. Trial in Washington, D.C., November 8–13, ends in acquittal.

1952 Left-wing political views continue to cause deep rift between Du Bois and the black mainstream, especially the NAACP. Department of State refuses to issue him a passport on grounds that his foreign travel is not in national interest; later demands that he sign a statement declaring he is not a member of the Communist Party. Du Bois refuses. *In Battle for Peace,* an account of his indictment and trial, published.

1953 Eulogizes Joseph Stalin in *National Guardian.* Reads the Twenty-Third Psalm at the funeral of Julius and Ethel Rosenberg, executed as Soviet agents.

1954 Reacts with joy and surprise to Supreme Court decision in *Brown v. Board of Education* outlawing segregation in schools; comments, "I have seen the impossible happen."

1956 Declares support for Martin Luther King Jr. in Montgomery, Alabama, bus boycott. Invited to speak in People's Republic of China; passport refused. Challenges William Faulkner to debate on segregation in Mississippi; Faulkner declines.

1957 Publishes *The Ordeal of Mansart,* first volume of *Black Flame* trilogy of historical novels, intended as a saga of black life in America from Reconstruction to the 1950s. Refused passport to attend independence ceremonies in Ghana.

1958 Ninetieth birthday celebration attended by two thousand people in New York. Begins work on *The Autobiography of W. E. B. Du Bois,* published in 1968. Supreme Court ruling allows him to obtain passport. Begins world tour in August; visits England, France, Belgium, Czechoslovakia, East Germany, and Soviet Union. Receives honorary degree from Humboldt University in East Berlin.

1959 Meets with Nikita Khrushchev. Travels to China, meets Mao Zedong and Zhou Enlai. Receives International Lenin Prize. *Mansart Builds a School,* second volume of *Black Flame* trilogy, published.

1960 Travels to Ghana and Nigeria to attend celebrations of independence and inaugurations.

1961 Daughter Yolande dies of heart attack in Baltimore in March. Accepts invitation from Kwame Nkrumah to move to Ghana and revive the *Encyclopedia Africana* project. Applies for membership in the Communist Party of the United States; departs for Ghana in October.

1962   Undergoes prostate surgery in Accra and Bucharest. Travels to China.

1963   Becomes citizen of Ghana. Turns ninety-five on February 23. Dies in Accra, August 27, on eve of civil rights march on Washington. Buried with state funeral in Accra, August 29. At Lincoln Memorial in Washington on August 28, Roy Wilkins, executive secretary of NAACP, breaks from his text to announce Du Bois's death. "Regardless of the fact that in his later years Dr. Du Bois chose another path," Wilkins tells the huge crowd, "it is incontrovertible that at the dawn of the twentieth century his was the voice calling you to gather here today in this cause." An aged, weeping black woman in the crowd is heard to say: "It's like Moses. God had written that he should never enter the promised land."

In the preparation of this chronology we have relied on many sources, especially the similar chronologies in Nathan I. Huggins, ed., *W. E. B. Du Bois: Writings* (New York: Library of America, 1986); Arnold Rampersad, ed., *The Souls of Black Folk* (New York: Everyman's Library, 1993); and David Levering Lewis, *W. E. B. Du Bois: The Biography of a Race, 1869–1819* (New York: Holt, 1993).

Questions for Consideration

1. Explain Du Bois's concept of "double-consciousness" and discuss some of the ways he uses that concept throughout the book. In what ways does Du Bois see the idea of "twoness" as a strength or a weakness for African Americans?

2. Compare at least three passages in which Du Bois uses the figure of the Veil. To what extent, if any, does the significance of this figure alter from one context to another? As a metaphor, what does it stand for?

3. Write a brief introduction to one of the chapters in *Souls*, showing how the musical and literary epigraphs that begin the chapter inform what follows.

4. Analyze Du Bois's concept of race as he first explores it in "The Conservation of Races" and then as it emerges in *Souls*. Is his conception of race biological? Sociohistorical? Both?

5. How would you characterize Du Bois's portrayal/criticism of Booker T. Washington? Is it fundamentally philosophical? Political? Educational?

6. What is Du Bois's vision of education? Where does it stem from? Is it advocacy of classical education as a path to equality for blacks in competition with whites? Or does it seem to be drawn from an appreciation of the great books for their own sake?

7. What does Du Bois mean by his use of the term *progress?* How does the concept of progress function as a theme in *Souls?*

8. In what ways is *Souls* a meditation on the distinctive historical character of black culture in America? Does the book, as a whole, argue that history made black folk in America a uniquely "spiritual" people?

9. In *Souls* as a whole, and in chapter 2 in particular, how does Du Bois write history? How does Du Bois generalize about the whole of American history?

10. What is Du Bois's particular interpretation of the meaning of emancipation and Reconstruction in African American history?

11. How is *Souls* a meditation on the meaning of racial segregation in turn-of-the-century America?

12. In what ways is *Souls* a book that illuminates its own time, and in what

ways is it a timeless book with arguments and meanings that are as relevant today as when it was written? How would you have read this book in 1903, as opposed to today?

13. How does Du Bois portray the turn-of-the-century South? In particular, how does he portray white southerners? With chapter 9, "Of the Sons of Master and Man," as a focus, discuss Du Bois's use of the concept of sympathy.

14. In the middle, sociological chapters of *Souls,* what is Du Bois's quarrel with materialism? Is he antimaterialistic? How does he criticize capitalism? To what extent does he offer an economic vision of America's "race problem"?

15. What is the significance of Du Bois's portrait of Alexander Crummell? Does Du Bois mean simply to praise Crummell, or does he also intend to criticize him?

16. What does Du Bois's elegy to his son ("Of the Passing of the First-Born") contribute to the argument of *Souls* as a whole?

17. In what ways does Du Bois's treatment of the African American experience in the essay "The Development of a People" differ from or complement his treatment of that experience in *Souls?*

18. In what ways does Du Bois's sense of *tragedy* inform *Souls?* In what passages or chapters is a vision of tragedy especially apparent?

19. How would you characterize the nature of Du Bois's prose in *Souls?* Does he write in a personal voice? A scholar's voice? A poet's voice?

20. What function does the idea of a journey serve in *Souls?*

Selected Bibliography

COLLECTIONS

Aptheker, Herbert, ed. *The Complete Published Works of W. E. B. Du Bois.* 35 vols. Millwood, N.Y.: Kraus-Thompson, 1973.
———, ed. *The Correspondence of W. E. B. Du Bois.* 3 vols. Amherst: University of Massachusetts Press, 1973–1978.
———, ed. *Against Racism: Unpublished Essays, Papers, Addresses, 1887–1961, W. E. B. Du Bois.* Amherst: University of Massachusetts Press, 1985.
Huggins, Nathan I., ed. *W. E. B. Du Bois: Writings.* New York: Library of America, 1986.
Lewis, David Levering, ed. *W. E. B. Du Bois: A Reader.* New York: Henry Holt, 1985.
Sundquist, Eric J., ed. *The Oxford W. E. B. Du Bois Reader.* New York: Oxford University Press, 1996.

AUTOBIOGRAPHY AND BIOGRAPHY

Du Bois, W. E. B. *The Autobiography of W. E. B. Du Bois: A Soliloquy on Viewing My Life from the Last Decade of Its First Century.* Edited by Herbert Aptheker. New York: International Publishers, 1968.
———. *Dusk of Dawn: An Essay toward an Autobiography of a Race Concept.* New York: Harcourt, Brace, 1940.
Broderick, Francis L. *W. E. B. Du Bois: Negro Leader in a Time of Crisis.* Stanford: Stanford University Press, 1959.
Lewis, David Levering. *W. E. B. Du Bois: The Biography of a Race, 1869–1919.* New York: Henry Holt, 1993.
Marable, Manning. *W. E. B. Du Bois: Black Radical Democrat.* Boston: Twayne, 1986.
Rudwick, Elliot. *W. E. B. Du Bois: A Study in Minority Group Leadership.* Philadelphia: University of Pennsylvania Press, 1960.
Townsend, Kim. " 'Manhood' at Harvard: W. E. B. Du Bois." *Raritan* 15 (Spring 1996): 70–82.

PHILOSOPHY

Appiah, Anthony. "The Uncompleted Argument: Du Bois and the Illusion of Race." *Critical Inquiry* 12 (Autumn 1985): 21–37.

Bell, Bernard, Emily Grosholz, and James Stewart, eds. *W. E. B. Du Bois on Race and Culture: Philosophy, Politics, and Poetics.* New York: Routledge, Chapman, and Hall, 1996.

Boxhill, Bernard R. "Du Bois's Dilemma." In *Blacks and Social Justice.* Totowa, N.J.: Rowman and Allanheld, 1984.

Gooding-Williams, Robert. "Du Bois's Counter-Sublime." *Massachusetts Review* 35 (Spring–Summer 1994): 203–24.

Kirkland, Frank. "Modernity and Intellectual Life in Black." *Philosophical Forum* 24 (Fall–Spring 1992–1993): 136–65.

Reed, Adolph. "W. E. B. Du Bois: A Perspective on the Bases of His Political Thought." *Political Theory* 13 (August 1985): 431–56.

West, Cornel. "W. E. B. Du Bois: The Jamesian Organic Intellectual." In *The American Evasion of Philosophy: A Genealogy of Pragmatism.* Madison: University of Wisconsin Press, 1989.

Zamir, Shamoon. *Dark Voices: W. E. B. Du Bois and American Thought, 1888–1903.* Chicago: University of Chicago Press, 1995.

HISTORY

Aptheker, Herbert. *The Literary Legacy of W. E. B. Du Bois.* White Plains, N.Y.: Kraus International, 1989.

Blight, David W. "W. E. B. Du Bois and the Struggle for American Historical Memory." In *History and Memory in African-American Culture,* edited by Genevieve Fabre and Robert O'Meally. New York: Oxford University Press, 1994.

Frederickson, George M. *The Black Image in the White Mind: The Debate on Afro-American Character and Destiny, 1817–1914.* New York: Harper and Row, 1971.

Meier, August. *Negro Thought in America, 1880–1915: Racial Ideologies in the Age of Booker T. Washington.* Ann Arbor: University of Michigan Press, 1963.

Moses, Wilson J. *The Golden Age of Black Nationalism, 1850–1925.* Hamden, Conn.: Archon Books, 1978.

Williamson, Joel. *The Crucible of Race: Black-White Relations in the American South since Emancipation.* New York: Oxford University Press, 1984.

LITERARY AND CULTURAL CRITICISM

Andrews, William L. *Critical Essays on W. E. B. Du Bois.* Boston: G. K. Hall, 1985.

Baker, Houston A. Jr. "The Black Man of Culture: W. E. B. Du Bois and *The*

Souls of Black Folk." In *Long Black Song.* Charlottesville: University of Virginia Press, 1972.

Byerman, Keith. *Seizing the Word: History, Art, and the Self in the Work of W. E. B. Du Bois.* Athens: University of Georgia Press, 1994.

Early, Gerald, ed. *Lure and Loathing: Essays on Race, Identity, and the Ambivalence of Assimilation.* New York: Allen Lane, 1993.

Peterson, Dale. "Notes from the Underworld: Dostoyevsky, Du Bois, and the Discovery of Ethnic Soul." *Massachusetts Review* 35 (Summer 1994): 225–47.

Rampersad, Arnold. *The Art and Imagination of W. E. B. Du Bois.* Cambridge: Harvard University Press, 1976.

Stepto, Robert B. "The Quest of the Weary Traveler: W. E. B. Du Bois's *The Souls of Black Folk."* In *From Behind the Veil: A Study of Afro-American Narrative.* Urbana: University of Illinois Press, 1979.

Sundquist, Eric J. "Swing Low: *The Souls of Black Folk."* In *To Wake the Nations: Race in the Making of American Literature.* Cambridge: Harvard University Press, 1993.

Index